RESURGENCE AND RECONCILIATION

Indigenous–Settler Relations and Earth Teachings

The two major schools of thought in Indigenous–settler relations on the ground, in the courts, in public policy, and in research are resurgence and reconciliation. Resurgence refers to practices of Indigenous self-determination and cultural renewal. Reconciliation refers to practices of reconciliation between Indigenous and settler nations as well as efforts to strengthen the relationship between Indigenous and settler peoples with the living earth and making that relationship the basis for both resurgence and Indigenous–settler reconciliation.

Critically and constructively analysing these two schools from a variety of perspectives and lived experiences, this volume connects both discourses to the ecosystem dynamics that animate the living earth. *Resurgence and Reconciliation* is a truly multidisciplinary work, blending law, political science, political economy, women's studies, history, anthropology, ecology, sustainability, and climate change. Its dialogic approach strives to put these fields in conversation and draw out the connections and tensions between them.

By using "earth teachings" to inform social practices, the editors and contributors offer a rich, innovative, and holistic way forward in response to the world's most profound natural and social challenges. This timely volume shows how the complexities and interconnections of resurgence and reconciliation and the living earth are often overlooked in contemporary discourse and debate.

MICHAEL ASCH is a professor emeritus in the Department of Anthropology at the University of Alberta and a professor (limited term) in the Department of Anthropology and adjunct professor in the Department of Political Science at the University of Victoria.

JOHN BORROWS is the Canada Research Chair in Indigenous Law in the Faculty of Law at the University of Victoria.

JAMES TULLY is emeritus distinguished professor of Political Science, Law, Indigenous Governance, and Philosophy at the University of Victoria.

Resurgence and Reconciliation

Indigenous–Settler Relations and Earth Teachings

EDITED BY MICHAEL ASCH,
JOHN BORROWS, AND JAMES TULLY

UNIVERSITY OF TORONTO PRESS
Toronto   Buffalo   London

ISBN 978-1-4875-0433-5 (cloth)   ISBN 978-1-4875-2327-5 (paper)

Library and Archives Canada Cataloguing in Publication

Resurgence and reconciliation : indigenous–settler relations and earth teachings / edited by Michael Asch, John Borrows, and James Tully.

Includes bibliographical references and index.
ISBN 978-1-4875-0433-5 (cloth).   ISBN 978-1-4875-2327-5 (paper)

1. Reconciliation – Social aspects – Canada. 2. Reconciliation – Political
aspects – Canada. 3. Reconciliation – Philosophy. 4. Indians of North
America – Canada – Ethnic identity. 5. Canada – Ethnic relations. I. Asch,
Michael, editor II. Borrows, John, 1963–, editor III. Tully, James, 1946–, editor

E78.C2R47 2018   971.004'97   C2018-903665-6

This book has been published with the help of a grant from the Federation
for the Humanities and Social Sciences, through the Awards to Scholarly
Publications Program, using funds provided by the Social Sciences and
Humanities Research Council of Canada.

University of Toronto Press acknowledges the financial assistance to its
publishing program of the Canada Council for the Arts and the Ontario Arts
Council, an agency of the Government of Ontario.

Canada Council   Conseil des Arts
for the Arts   du Canada

ONTARIO ARTS COUNCIL
CONSEIL DES ARTS DE L'ONTARIO
an Ontario government agency
un organisme du gouvernement de l'Ontario

Funded by the   Financé par le
Government   gouvernement
of Canada   du Canada   Canada

Contents

Acknowledgments

We would like to acknowledge the generous support and participation of all the institutions and individuals who made this project possible, supported the organization and running of the events, participated in the ongoing discussions, and then helped with the writing and publication phases.

Institutions at Dalhousie University: MacKay Lecture Series 2012–13 "Reconciliation: The Responsibility for Shared Futures," Faculty of Arts and Social Sciences, Dalhousie University College of Sustainability, Office of the Vice President, Research, University of King's College, Schulich School of Law, Department of Sociology and Social Anthropology, Department of Political Science, Royal Society of Canada, Open Academy Grants program, and Pierre Elliott Trudeau Foundation.

People at or supportive of events at Dalhousie University: Elder Kerry Prosper, Paqtnkek First Nation, Dr Sherry Pictou, L'stkuk First Nation, Professor Naomi Metallic, Listuguj First Nation, the many individual graduate and honours students who supported and participated in the events, and in particular, Amy Donovan, Eric Smith, Julia Howell, Chloe Westlake, Roberta Watt, Katie McLeod, Rachelle McKay, Shannon Ramsay, Janelle Young, Paul Hilborn, Caitlin Krause, Dru Morrison, Shawn Martin, students of SOSA 4005/5005 "Issues in Social Justice & Inequality," led by Dr Brian Noble, Fall 2012, and all the support staff and volunteers who made the events such a success.

Institutions at the University of Victoria: Department of Political Science, Political Science Indigenous Speaker Series, Faculty of Law, Office of the Dean of Social Science, Office of the Dean of Graduate Studies, Centre for Aboriginal Health Research (now called Centre for Indigenous Research and Community-led Engagement), Office of Indigenous

Affairs, Department of Women's Studies, Department of Environmental Studies, Department of Anthropology, Department of History, John Lutz, James H. Tully Fellowship, First Peoples House, and Pierre Elliott Trudeau Foundation.

People at or supportive of events at the University of Victoria and after: Elders May Sam and Kip Sam, Tsartlip First Nation, Richard Atleo Senior (Umeek), Joy Austin, Rosemary Barlow, Lindsay Borrows, Keith Cherry, Joanne Denton, Avigail Eisenberg, Ginger Gibson, Rob Hancock, Debra Higgins, Basil Johnston, Dennis Jones, Deanne LeBlanc, Constance MacIntosh, Johnny Mack, Warren Magnusson, Aaron Mills, Tamaya Moreton, Gina Starblanket, Heidi Stark, Carl Urion, Jeremy Webber, all the undergraduate and graduate students, faculty members, and visitors who participated in the events, and the support staff and volunteers who made the events such a success.

We editors also would like to thank all the contributors for their initial presentations, their collective and cooperative engagement in designing the edited volume, and for writing, and often rewriting, their outstanding chapters.

We would also like to acknowledge Douglas Hildebrand, Daniel Quinlan, and Wayne Herrington, at the University of Toronto Press, for all their support and assistance in moving the edited volume from its draft form through to its publication, and to the anonymous reviewers for their constructive comments. Our gratitude goes to Keith Cherry for his efficient and tireless work of editing and bringing together all the chapters into successive versions of the manuscript. Our wholehearted thanks goes to Judy Dunlop for creating an outstanding index.

A special debt of gratitude from all of us to Arthur Manuel (1951–2017) for his support and inspiration for this project and over many years of exemplary work for resurgence and transformative reconciliation.

About the cover

In the cover to this book, painted by Anishinaabekwe artist Estrella Whetung from the Alderville First Nation, Anishinaabe reconciliation and resurgence are represented by sky and water beings in creative relationship and tension. In Anishinaabe stories, adizookaanag, the encounters between reconciliation and resurgence are part of the world's continual recreation. These characters and colours represent the earth's teachings. They represent the land waking up. These characters encourage relationships, and their interactions and tensions help us understand ourselves as human beings in deeper ways. Thunder-bird, animikii, is a dream visitor who brings gifts. The underwater being, mishibizhew, is a protector of the natural world and a mediator between the water, land, and sky beings. As guardians of resources, animikii and mishibizhew are immortal and watch over the balance of eco-social relations, including climate change. The sun behind the thunderbird is also a nod to the "phoenix" story which is a reconciliation/resurgence figure in some parts of the world.

RESURGENCE AND RECONCILIATION

Indigenous–Settler Relations and Earth Teachings

Introduction

JOHN BORROWS AND JAMES TULLY

Reconciliation and Resurgence in Practice and in Question

Reconciliation and *resurgence* have become ways of describing the field of activities, relationships, and possible futures between Indigenous and settler people. Over the last two decades these terms have been widely used in practice: in community building, relating to the environment, Indigenous and settler governance and legal institutions, business, media, entertainment, commissions, alliances, negotiations, prison reform, and protests. They are also broadly deployed in academic circles. They are the focus of research, teaching, reflection, and activism in university settings and beyond. Movements like Idle No More and Standing with Standing Rock relay these ideas. They are variously used by leaders like Chief Spence of the Attawapiskat First Nation, Chief Stewart Philip and the Union of BC Indian Chiefs, and numerous chiefs and officials in the Assembly of First Nations. The language of resurgence and reconciliation also finds its way into broader political discourse. Federal, provincial, and municipal governments, as well as the media and wider public, invoke these ideas when considering the appalling living conditions of many Indigenous peoples. In particular, the designation of 2017 as the year of reconciliation gave these terms heightened prominence and urgency.

As a result of their widespread acceptance and usage, and because so much is at stake, reconciliation and resurgence are used in a wide variety of ways. These terms are continuously contested and reformulated in practice, policy, and academic research. Thus practice-based struggles over reconciliation and resurgence are also struggles over the meanings of the terms themselves. Reconciliation and resurgence have become contestable and contested concepts within the semantic field and human activities in which they are used.

For example, some say reconciliation between settlers and Indigenous peoples is an end state of some kind: a contract, agreement, legal recognition, return of stolen land, reparations, compensation, closing the gap, or self-determination. Others argue that it is more akin to an ongoing activity. Some say reconciliation embodies a relationship stretching back 12,000 years, an existential mode of being with one another and the living earth. It has also been associated with treaty relationships since early contact. For some it is the path to decolonization, for others a new form of recolonization. Some insist reconciliation must be resisted, while others see it as an essential process for ongoing relationality.

Resurgence is often used to refer to Indigenous peoples exercising powers of self-determination outside of state structures and paradigms. It is deployed by communities as a force for reclaiming and reconnecting with traditional territories by means of Indigenous ways of knowing and being. These individual and collective powers include the resurgence of governance, Indigenous legal systems and languages, economic and social self-reliance, and sustainable relationships with the ecosystems that co-sustain all life and well-being. Resurgence also refers to analogous Indigenous practices in rural and urban centres, universities, prisons, other institutions, and global networks. Some see these as new activities. Others see them as ancient life ways that stretch back through the centuries. Settlers also use the term. It can refer to decolonizing activities, enacted in alliance with Indigenous people or independently, yet in solidarity with them.

Some practitioners of resurgence refuse and reject reconciliation-based relationships between settler and Indigenous peoples, claiming they are assimilative or colonizing.[1] Others, including many Indigenous people, feel a more nuanced approach is required.[2] They strive to live more holistically and navigate the tensions they experience in creative ways. They are uncomfortable with dramatically turning away from their neighbours. While they strenuously resist oppression, they understand their deeper values require more constructively provocative approaches. Isolationism can lead to self-absorption and become marginalizing and disempowering. Dense relationships of interdependency are thus cultivated by many practitioners of resurgence, with many different sites of action, inaction, resistance, and cooperation. Robust practices of resurgence often (though not always) need to be coordinated and nested within robust, non-violent, contentious relationships of transformative reconciliation with supportive settlers, just as practices of resurgence require the same kind of empowering contestation, coordination, and reconciliation within and among Indigenous communities.[3]

At times the difference between "separate resurgence" and resurgence *and* reconciliation (or "resurgence-reconciliation") has been polarized. Disagreements among practitioners can be divisive in both theory and practice. This volume identifies diverse paths that attempt to move beyond this polarization and the disempowering divisions it generates. We accept critiques and refusals of so-called reconciliation models that threaten to reconcile Indigenous peoples to the unjust status quo. We also acknowledge and accept critiques and refusals of certain types of "recognition" that place the state or its imperial networks at the centre of social, political, and economic affairs. Recognition can be a Trojan horse–like gift; state action often operates to overpower or deflect Indigenous resurgence. Indeed, the contributors to this volume have co-developed these critiques and refusals with others. In turning from critique to construction, we distinguish between two forms and meanings of reconciliation and resurgence. The first are those that perpetuate unjust relationships of dispossession, domination, exploitation, and patriarchy. These reconcile Indigenous people and settlers to the status quo, and we strongly reject them. The second are those that have the potential to transform these unjust relationships; these are the kinds of ideas we seek to advance in this book. These are relationships of "transformative" reconciliation. To be transformative they must be empowered by robust practices of resurgence. Robust resurgence infuses reciprocal practices of reconciliation in self-determining, self-sustaining, and inter-generational ways. These unique forms of reconciliation *and* resurgence coexist in a relationship of gift-reciprocity, as many contributors argue. For example, the creation of resurgent Indigenous Studies programs often (though not invariably) grew from reconciliation efforts with settler partners in university settings. These programs, run by Indigenous scholars, have transformed curricula and teaching in their disciplines over the last twenty years – not only for their resurgent units but also for their partners whose reconciliation efforts were vital to their development. Unfortunately, despite the significant growth of resurgence-reconciliation networks and frameworks, all is not well in the field. Polarizing debates have developed through misunderstandings and/or misuses of the different meanings of resurgence and reconciliation. This volume seeks to clarify this entangled semantic field. Contributors in this book seek to move beyond the polarizing dichotomy of rejectionist resurgence and non-transformative reconciliation to renew the collaborative search for practices of robust resurgence and transformative reconciliation in their work.

From a resurgence-reconciliation perspective, a major cause of recent divisions arose through the adoption of a dialectic drawn from another colonial context. The binary of Third World decolonization and master-slave dialectics of the 1950s and 1960s was pulled into some Indigenous studies circles in ways that reject reconciliation in broad terms. While great value was derived from much of this decolonization literature, in our view, some of the claims made in its name were over-broad and thus were applied in inappropriate ways. Dichotomies and binaries were advanced in a manner that did not always distinguish between contemporary North America, and those of colonial Africa, Asia, and Latin America in the 1960s. Differences in temporal, spatial, and socio-economic circumstances were flattened and universalized. Ideas were essentialized, and deficiencies in Third World decolonization were often overlooked. Thus, positions rejecting all forms of reconciliation entered the field. This flowed from a binary framing that insisted the decolonizing resurgence of the colonized had to take place in separation from the colonizer. Some followers of this field argued that no good relationship or dialogue with the colonizer was possible, because such encounters were simply thinly disguised struggles over power between hegemons and subalterns. Those who thought otherwise were dismissed as being misguided, even colonized, by "the system." This criticism spread to critiquing the majority of Indigenous people as being co-opted. Some held that even the participation in workshops of Indigenous and settler participants, such as ours, was to be colonized.[4] Entanglement was rejected, and interdependence was discarded by those who took this position. The colonizer/colonized binary grew in different places and was cloaked in many different guises. It was used to justify the "rejection and separatist resurgence" strategy. This generated divisions among Indigenous people (between those accused of being colonized and those who claim to see through the co-optation), among settlers (between those who accept and reject separationist resurgence), and between Indigenous people and settlers, at almost every site of potentially coordinate action in which it is invoked.

The defenders of this colonization/decolonization and friend-enemy vision argue that it provides a deeper critique of the global and local system than the language of resurgence and reconciliation can provide.

Thus, they say it has to be embraced by Indigenous people to effect revolutionary resurgence. However, in our view these claims lack nuance. Simple binaries such as these can fatally conceal and obscure a complex intersectional field. Approaches to "reconciliation *and* resurgence" advanced by the authors in this book largely avoid the essentializing, a priori, absolutist, universalizing terms of separatist resurgence. They recognize that separation may sometimes be needed but that this is only one option among many in the practice of resurgent, transformative reconciliation. Separation, while powerful and sometimes necessary, must be applied with care to the context in which it is inserted. While measured separation may be very appropriate in some settings, it cannot be regarded as a comprehensive strategy that is healthy in all circumstances.

The idea we are advancing of "reconciliation *and* resurgence" acknowledges our situatedness in overlapping regimes of knowledge, power, and subjectification. It is attentive to situated freedom. This approach claims that we are all differently situated and governed, in both constraining and enabling ways, in relationships of division, patriarchy, imperialism, racism, capitalism, ecological devastation, and poverty. In our view, the failure to illuminate broader and more complex intersectional fields of power was one reason why the colonization/decolonization binary did not lead the way to Third World liberation. It might even be said that such dichotomies led to deeper forms of neocolonialism, dependency, inequality, and patriarchy in Third World settings. Global neoliberalism has thrived in such settings.[5] It is for these and other reasons, which will be explained throughout this book, that there has been a turn to new and renewed ways of conceiving and enacting resurgence and reconciliation in the twenty-first-century world.[6]

As will be developed in these pages, Indigenous people do not generally accede to the binary world view that spawns separation resurgence.[7] This approach does not coincide with many traditional ways of knowing and being. For example, Indigenous contributors to this volume cautiously argue that reconciliation and resurgence are more appropriate English terms for the unique, place-based, kin-centric, and relational ways Indigenous people conceive and enact transformative change, at least in comparison to Western theories of colonization/decolonization. Their view of transformative resurgence and reconciliation is grounded in Indigenous traditions of regenerating healthy and sustainable, gift-reciprocity relationships. These cycles of interdependent thought and action acknowledge that our connections are both fragile and resilient. They require careful attention to cultivate the positive and root out the negative in the totality of our relationships, with each other, Mother Earth, and our settler neighbours. From within these world views the problem with the simplifying and separating framework of rejection insurgency is that it constrains its adherents. It obscures the interdependent relationships in which they are already situated and from which they derive support. Again, we must stress that not all relationships should be sustained and that there is significant room in our approach for refusing, rejecting, challenging, breaking, or transforming particular connections. We strongly support action that rejects oppressive state and imperial ideas, practices, and frameworks. Yet, seen through the eyes of this book's authors, it is clear that many of our relationships can be enhanced through robust resurgence and transformative reconciliation frameworks.

The authors in this book envision the combination of robust resurgence and transformative reconciliation as a continuation and renewal of what many of their ancestors have pursued for centuries. The Two Row Wampum Treaty relationship (*Kaswentha*) combines both self-rule and shared rule; the Royal Proclamation of 1763 (when understood in light of the Treaty of Niagara in 1764) further recognizes independence and interdependence in Indigenous–settler relationships. Many Indigenous understandings of self-determination are often internally related to declarations of interdependence, in contrast to Third World declarations of self-determination as disconnection and independence.[8] As we see throughout this volume, this complementary vision of independence and interdependence also includes the interdependence of human partners on the ecological, gift-reciprocity relationships of the living earth that sustain all life.[9] With this long and continuous history in mind, we argue that "separate resurgents" must be careful not to misrepresent recent and current protests as exclusive examples of their project. Resurgence has often been combined with demands for transformative reconciliation in contemporary political life through nation-to-nation negotiations, Idle No More activities, anti-pipeline protests, environmental activism, alliances such as Standing with Standing Rock, and so on.

In practice, independence and interdependence have characterized Indigenous–settler relationships for centuries, for good and ill.[10] The attempt to improve these relationships by pursuing "resurgence and reconciliation" is not a linear process. Mistakes are often made, and setbacks are legion. Trial and error accompanies any process that recognizes the messiness of political life. When universal answers and approaches are taken off the table, we are left to muddle our way through with less than perfect information and frameworks. In these circumstances we must variously rely upon and resist one another since God, philosopher kings, and grand theories cannot be counted on to deliver us from ourselves. Contestation, agreement, rejection, and reformulation are constantly before us. These are best deployed when they draw upon robust resurgence and transformative reconciliatory practices.

Since we cannot depend upon a fusion of horizons, we are left to engage in endless forms of talking, non-violent contention, and working with good and bad neighbours *en passant*, as difficult and challenging as this has always been. Since this volume is assembled on the northwest coast, it is worth noting that this is precisely what a formidable coalition of First Nations and allied settlers, assembled in Kamloops on 25 August 1910, recommended in their submission to Prime Minister Laurier in what is now known as "The Laurier Memorial."[11] This advice has been followed and forgotten through the years, yet we argue that it must once again be resurrected to help guide practices of resurgent reconciliation outlined in this book.[12] The questions that follow from this analysis are: What are genuinely self-determining practices of resurgence and transformative forms of reconciliation today, and how are they distinguished from non-robust and non-transformative practices and relationships? This is not only a theoretical question, but a practical one that can be answered only through intergenerational trial-and-error and apprenticeship: that is, through practice and examples. The contributors to this volume respond to this general question through various examples and from various perspectives.

As we mentioned above, the first task is to clarify the various meanings of resurgence and reconciliation in the contexts in which they are being used. As should be clear, we do not pose simple solutions. This is a complex field, and we do not identify a single way of robust resurgence and transformative reconciliation. Nor do we identify a single definition of these terms. Rather, we see an intricate field of overlapping practices and corresponding meanings of reconciliation and resurgence; some are good, and some are harmful. Others are recent, and some are ancient, woven together in complex ways in language, thought, and practice.

Accordingly, the skill required to understand our way around this field is akin to the complex intricacies of cedar basket-weaving and braiding sweetgrass. It requires attentiveness and attunement and must move beyond the simplistic models and metaphors standardly used to mis-describe and dominate the field from one perspective or another (even the metaphors of weaving and braiding have their limits). Yet the kinship we are describing should not be surprising or discouraging. Weaving and braiding are always more than physical activities. Good apprenticeships must focus on both art and craft. Good teachers and wise students see their engagements as moving beyond the materials that lie before them. Relationships are horizontal, vertical, twisted, and three-dimensional. Layers of meaning and ambiguity reside in any system of instruction and practice, and they embrace the social as well as the physical activity of construction. For ancient braiders and weavers, this predominately female apprenticeship relationship took practitioners deep into the entanglements of community life. It engaged the various meanings, organizations, and structures at play in the material and social world. Working with roots, branches, fibres, and filaments was always a creative enterprise, requiring improvisation and a deep knowledge of patterns, impressions, prototypes, and conventions – in the human and natural world. Applying these skills to baskets and to life was a constant work in progress. Knowing how to best construct vessels to effectively transport water, seeds, soil, or life is ultimately a human activity. This requires that we acknowledge both the conservatism and innovativeness that mark our species.[13]

How, then, do we, as participants within this complex field, come to understand the practical meanings of reconciliation and resurgence as they are used in various practices, relationships, ways, and contexts? The answer of the contributors to this volume involves abandoning the illusion that it is possible to stand above the field and, from this transcendental view from nowhere, define the essence of these terms – the necessary and sufficient conditions of their application in every case. Rather, like learning any complex vocabulary, it is a matter of finding one's way in the dense forest of uses and the activities into which they are woven. This consists in listening carefully, asking questions, using the terms oneself, always listening and speaking truthfully, making mistakes, and learning from them. Then, through practice, gradually learning to use the terms as others use them, but also to enter into contests over different uses with others in a self-critical way, and to advance proposals for their refinement, revision, or transformation that are understandable and responsive to others.

In this way of learning one's way around life's labyrinth, participants listen carefully to what others are saying. They then ask questions such as, Who is speaking, and from what standpoint and perspective in the field of power and knowledge? For whom do they claim to speak, and on what grounds? What aspects of the field does their use of these terms reveal, and what aspects of the field does it conceal? What is the context in which this speaker's usage makes sense, and what are its strength and weakness? What do others say in response? Are these responses respected by the speaker, and does she or he take them into account in revising their own usage? The talking stick is then passed to another participant and others tell their story of reconciliation and resurgence in their way and from their standpoint and world view. Questions are raised and responded to. The talking stick is passed to the next participant, and so on and on.[14]

By listening carefully and asking and answering questions truthfully in turn, participants learn or are reminded that it is illusory to presume that their views are *the* comprehensive view of the field. They are moved around to see the complex field they inhabit from the diverse perspectives of fellow inhabitants. Then, by means of exchanges of comparisons and contrasts, they begin to see the strengths and limits of the different meanings, as well as the extent to which various meanings share features. Engagement in these exchanges also exposes the limits of one's own view and makes possible the self-critical task of accepting the epistemically humbling insight that we need each other's perspectives in order to understand the complex world we co-inhabit. This difficult reciprocal transformation of how we understand ourselves and others enables participants to understand the meanings of reconciliation and resurgence. And this dawning reciprocal, mutual understanding of the forest of overlapping meanings enables participants to begin to propose, discuss, and negotiate what reconciliation and resurgence might mean in working and living together in peace and friendship.

When concrete situations are critically examined in this dialogical way within the complex field of unequal power and scales, the best strategy in specific circumstances often can be refusal. However, the question then arises as to the most appropriate ways and means of refusing, for the *ways* always deeply influence the end. Is it to refuse with anger, hatred, and violence, or with the courage of the peaceful warrior and her way of non-violent contention, embodying goodwill and oriented to peace and friendship?[15] So this whole *way* of being resurgent and reconciliatory in thought and action is carried on as the participants move forward and pass it on to the next generation.

Learning how to use the words reconciliation and resurgence in this intersubjective and interdependent dialogical way is akin to Indigenous storytelling. It is also said to be the way good treaty negotiations were begun in the early contact period. It was acknowledged in the Royal Proclamation of 1763 and exemplified in the Treaty of Niagara in 1764. Through lengthy exchanges of stories of where each other was coming from, how each partner saw the difference at issue, and how each saw the way of reconciliation, they came to be of one mind. "One mind" did not seem to refer to complete agreement, but to understanding each other, holding all views in tension. Then reconciliation negotiations began. So this form of dialogue can be seen as a pathway of and to reconciliation. As Asch characterizes it from a settler perspective in chapter 1, it consists in coming to enough of an understanding to take small steps forward in building relationships with those already here.

This collection of stories is an example of such a preparatory dialogue. It is limited because it is a discussion of some examples of uses of these two terms by a small group of participants. However, these uses are widespread, important, and contentious; they are compared and contrasted with others; and the participants have considerable experience discussing them in practice and in academic contexts. The hope is that the dialogue helps to clarify these uses and aid readers in their self-critical participation in other contexts, or in response to this one. In so doing, it aims to clear away misunderstandings and contribute to moving the discussion and practice of reconciliation and resurgence forward.

A Guide to the Chapters

Our dialogue began in Mi'kmaq traditional territory at Dalhousie University in 2012. Brian Noble invited Michael Asch and John Borrows to give lectures in annual MacKay Lecture Series sponsored by the Dalhousie Institute on Society and Culture, entitled "Reconciliation: The Responsibility for Shared Futures." Asch's lecture was entitled "Back to the Future: The Confederation Treaties and Reconciliation." Borrows's lecture was "Aki-noomaagewin (Earth Teachings): Winter Stories, Indigenous Law, and Reconciliation." In March 2014 Asch and Borrows returned to Dalhousie along with James Tully to continue the dialogue. This event was sponsored by the MacKay Lecture Series, the College of Sustainability, King's College, the Royal Society of Canada, and the Trudeau Foundation. Tully's lecture was "Reconciliation Here on Earth: Shared Responsibilities." Mi'kmaq scholar Sherry Pictou, Asch, Borrows, and Tully participated in seminar discussions, public round tables, and sharing circles over the following days.

When Asch, Borrows, and Tully returned to the University of Victoria, they decided to hold a second dialogue the following year. This took place on the traditional territory of Coast Salish peoples and under the protocols of the oral understanding of the pre-Confederation Douglas treaties at First Peoples House, University of Victoria, on 18–19 September 2015. We acknowledged with respect the Lekwungen People on whose traditional territory the university stands and the Songhees, Esquimalt, and WSÁNEĆ peoples whose historical relationships with the land continue to this day. It was organized by Gina Starblanket and many helpful volunteers. Nine academic units sponsored the event. The presenters were Tsartlip Elder May Sam, Asch, Borrows, Tully, Brian Noble, Kent McNeil, Regna Darnell, Kiera Ladner, Aaron Mills, Heidi Stark, Gina Starblanket, Ted Chamberlin, Nancy Turner, and Pamela Spalding. Jeremy Webber and Avigail Eisenberg gave opening remarks. Valerie Napoleon and Dale Turner planned to present but were unable to do so. Starblanket and Tully co-moderated.

Approximately 150 people from across Canada attended and participated in the discussions. On the first day Tsartlip Elder May Sam gave a traditional welcome in her Hul'qumi'num language. She reminded us that reconciliation for her people is a relationship of mutual respect and sharing with Mother Earth and all our kin – human and more than human – that we have responsibilities to acknowledge and enact in every breath and step we take. Asch, Borrows, and Tully expressed their gratitude for her words and gave brief synopses of their revised Dalhousie lectures. The following day the presenters commented on the lectures and shared their views of reconciliation and resurgence. Critical and constructive discussion followed in First Peoples House, at meetings with various guests and over the following days.

True to the dialogue model of critical understanding, the presenters decided they would reflect on the presentations and critical discussions before reviewing and rewriting their contributions for publication. All of us were involved in different struggles around reconciliation and resurgence during the period of revision in 2016. This experience deepened our appreciation of the misunderstandings around reconciliation and resurgence. Furthermore, the Truth and Reconciliation Commission released its final report with its vision of reconciliation and calls to action. It was immediately picked up and interpreted in different and contested ways. We approached Paulette Regan, senior researcher at the commission and doctoral graduate of the Indigenous Governance Graduate Programs, and she kindly agreed to write a chapter on the commission's vision of reconciliation.

All the practical and semantic changes from 2012 to 2017 substantiate our view of the reciprocal relationships between struggles over reconciliation and resurgence in practice and contestations over their meanings. They also furnish the reasons for our method of situating actors and researchers within this changing field in motion and with all the epistemic interdependency and humility this requires. Yet it also makes manifest the pressing need for collections of this kind. The reason is not that they can produce definitive answers that are self-executing and self-guaranteeing. Quite the contrary. No such guarantees exist. Rather, this collection seeks to enact an exemplary way of critically understanding what is going on from various perspectives here and now. It aspires to be a way that enables readers to enter into the exchange and understand the present moment from a range of views, and, more importantly, to acquire the abilities to carry on self-critically themselves in dialogues with others in diverse contests as things change.

As we have seen, these dialogues prepare the participants for the next phase of reconciliation by learning what has happened, what is going on here and now, reflecting critically on these perspectives, and presenting proposals for discussion in going forward to the next phase. This is only one small step in these great cycles of practice, reflection, and practice again, of ongoing experiments in truth. Yet it is not insignificant. Reconciliation and resurgence are autotelic. To be successful, the way must enact and actualize the end. Just as the only guarantee of freedom is the practice of freedom, so too with reconciliation and resurgence. Our form of dialogue strives fallibly to bring into being and carry on this autotelic animacy by enacting and actualizing a preparatory way of and to reconciliation and resurgence among participants, auditors, and readers. The collection is organized in accordance with the First Peoples House dialogue. In Part One Asch, Borrows, and Tully present their explications of three major ways of thinking about and enacting reconciliation and resurgence and compare and contrast them with others. In Part Two the contributors respond by considering these three ways in relation to their own experiences of and reflections on other ways of reconciliation and resurgence. Here is a very brief synopsis of the chapters.

Chapter 1

Every participant in this volume is thinking about ways forward. Asch begins by asking us to reflect on what has been negotiated in the past and then on how it can be implemented today. Asch discusses the treaty relationship between Indigenous peoples and settler peoples as the fundamental form of reconciliation. This is the oldest mode of relationship between the Indigenous peoples who have been here, living in their diverse ways on their traditional territories for over 12,000 years, and the settler peoples who arrived a few centuries ago. In the oral traditions of Indigenous peoples, it is exemplified in the Two Row Wampum Treaty, *Kaswentha*, the early Peace and Friendship treaties, the Royal Proclamation of 1763, and the Treaty of Niagara in 1764, and some of the nineteenth-century treaties. It is the 255-year-old constitution of Canada that was overridden and forgotten by section 91.24 of the 1867 Constitution (see McNeil). This fundamental nation-to-nation relationship was recovered and recognized in section 25 of the 1981 Charter of Rights and Freedoms and re-articulated and endorsed by the Royal Commission on Aboriginal Peoples in 1995. It is this relationship that needs to be recollected, re-proclaimed, and renewed if there is to be genuine reconciliation.[16] The great question is, Is it possible historically and in the contemporary period for Canadians to come to understand and work on their relationship to this land and Indigenous peoples in this reconciliatory way? Asch has devoted his adult life to this question, and he draws on his wealth of knowledge to show us how it can be answered in the affirmative.

Chapter 2

Borrows takes us deeper into the roots of good relations of reconciliation and resurgence from his Anishinaabe perspective and his knowledge of Western legal traditions. He shows that the treaty relationship of reconciliation is one type of a much larger and more variegated family of relationships that reconcile and sustain all the forms of life that compose the biosphere (Mother Earth). Indeed, as Borrows explains, relationships of reconciliation and Indigenous legal systems are derived from studying, learning from, and living in accord with this global family of relationships among plants, animals, ecosystems, and seasons for millennia (*Aki-noomaagewin*). The English phrase for this large family of life-sustaining relationships is "gift-reciprocity" (see Mills, Turner, and Spalding). This is the meaning of the famous expression "all our relations," used by Anishinaabe, Lakota (*MItakuye Oyasin*), and many other Indigenous peoples. We are all related and interdependent. At the same time Borrows recognizes that such interdependence can be either liberating or oppressive, depending on how we act towards one another and the earth. Without respectful attentiveness to the various strands of life on the earth, and in our communities, we run the risk of replicating our worst excesses and fears. In particular, he argues that Anishinaabe people themselves and Indigenous peoples more generally can perpetuate abuse towards one another and the earth in many subtle and not-so-subtle ways. By examining Anishinaabe and Indigenous legal insights related to poverty, mobility, inherent limits, and seasonal teachings, Borrows identifies approaches and standards for measuring our activities in ways that are more attentive to our own and others' needs, including the earth on which we live. In so doing he hopes to highlight the necessity of earth-based governance practices in advancing the sort of resurgence *and* reconciliation discussed in this book.

Chapter 3

Tully argues that if he is understanding Asch and Borrows correctly, then it would seem to follow that reconciliation would have to be reconciliation with all our relations at the same time: that is, with each other (Asch) and the living earth (Borrows). Moreover, resurgence would have to be reconceived as activities involved in regenerating and renewing these life-sustaining ecological and social relationships of reconciliation. Hence, the question for him from his limited, northwest coast settler perspective is, What resources are available in settler traditions to help us understand and work on these two interwoven types of resurgence-reconciliation? He argues that some of the life, human, and social sciences provide ways of understanding and addressing these two projects in ways that complement traditional Indigenous knowledges and wisdom, such as the ones Borrows and Mills discuss. He presents a cyclical way of understanding how gift-reciprocity social and ecological relationships work: how they sustain their interdependent relatives (virtuous relationships); how they can and do become non-reciprocal (gift-taking) and unsustainable relationships (the vicious relationships of the ecological and social crises we face today); and how it is possible to repair, regenerate, and reconcile them into virtuous relationships once again through transformative practices of resurgence and reconciliation. He also suggests this way of understanding and responding to the crises we are in is analogous to the way it is understood in northwest coast Raven cycle stories as interpreted by two northwest coast elders: Umeek (Richard Atleo Senior), Nuu Chah Nulth, and Robert Davidson, Haida.

Chapter 4

Mills begins his chapter with an analysis of how settler presumptions of supremacy find expression in three types of relationships of violence over Indigenous peoples and the living earth, thereby rendering reconciliation impossible. He argues that a number of decolonizing, reconciliation, and resurgent approaches fail to address this basic problem. He then turns to his tradition of Anishinaabe rooted constitutionalism to show how this approach to reconciliation and resurgence points to a way forward. It preserves the best features of both approaches, but it integrates them into the broader webs and cycles of life-sustaining relationships (earth ways) that Borrows introduces in his chapter. This older, time-tested eco-social or earth ways constitutionalism provides the animating sources of transformative regeneration and reconciliation. He presents a way into this understanding by sharing an experience he had on Rainy Lake with a sturgeon and by considering what an Anishinaabe medicine man had to say about roots.

Chapter 5

In their chapter, Indigenous feminists Starblanket and Stark elucidate how Indigenous modes of relating provide important guidance on how disparate individuals and groups of people can interact with one another and with creation in generative and sustainable ways. Western intellectual and philosophical traditions have not always recognized the living legal and political significance of Indigenous ways of knowing and being, yet, as this volume illustrates, Indigenous philosophies of relationality are increasingly being sought to inform strategies of resurgence and reconciliation with one another and with the environment. Alongside the opportunities it presents, this shift towards a relational paradigm also carries challenges and complexities. Accordingly, they critically examine the possibilities and limits of interpreting and applying Indigenous traditions of relating in contemporary contexts, with specific focus on questions and considerations that arise from their subjective, land-based, gendered, and temporal dimensions. They demonstrate that conceptualizations of relationship can be used to empower but also disempower Indigenous people in general and Indigenous women in particular, depending on the process through which they are defined and the context in which they are applied. Further, they argue that Indigenous traditions of relationality should not be uncritically deferred to but, rather, that they are contingent and have to be taken up critically and contextually to ensure that they are not being employed in ways that reproduce the colonial tendency to essentialize pre-colonial Indigenous life.

Chapter 6

Regan examines reconciliation and resurgence through the lens of the Reconciliation volume of the Truth and Reconciliation Commission of Canada's Final Report. She begins with a personal reflection on her gratitude to residential school survivors for the lifelong gift of bearing witness to their testimonies. Collectively, these life stories hold teachings for all of us; they are both a cautionary tale about the devastating impacts of colonial violence that continue to victimize Indigenous peoples, and a powerful testament to their courage, strength, and resilience as they continue to speak truth to power, reclaim identities, cultures, and histories, and regenerate Indigenous land-based ways of life. Using excerpts from the commission's report and calls to action, Regan argues that the TRC contributes to the emerging dialogue on reconciliation and resurgence; the commission's vision of reconciliation is contingent on the land-based revitalization, regeneration, and resurgence of Indigenous cultures, languages, knowledge systems, oral histories, laws, and governance structures. At the same time, the commission's vision makes clear that resurgence does not hinge on reconciliation with the settler colonial state. Rather, the UN Declaration on the Rights of Indigenous Peoples is identified as the appropriate framework for reconciliation to ensure that the fundamental principle of Indigenous self-determination is upheld. While the work of community-driven resurgence quite rightly rests with self-determining Indigenous peoples and is undertaken outside of the formal structures of the state, implementing the TRC calls to action can support the goals and aspirations of resurgence and provide much-needed practical resources.

Chapter 7

One central theme of the volume is how people communicate with each other, come to some kind of mutual understanding, gradually generate trust and solidarity, and cooperate across all the intersectional differences and misunderstandings that so easily divide us. Darnell addresses this question from her perspective as an anthropologist, ethnographer, and qualitative researcher. In working on this topic in practice over many decades she has become a student of cross-cultural miscommunication. It is not only a matter of following protocols, but of how one acts and interacts ethically in accordance with protocols in situated discourses that are often fragile, fluid, and subject to unexpected changes. She draws on her qualitative research with the Walpole First Nation and her anthropological practices of deep listening and "sitting with friends" to discuss several features of cross-cultural communication and miscommunication. The similarities and dissimilarities of what traditional ecological knowledge and Western science teach on this topic are discussed through a number of examples, such as qualitative research on residential school trauma and environmental contamination. The role of stories and other devices are discussed in helping to understand common expressions in these conversations, such as resurgence and reconciliation, imagined communities, all our relations, seven generations both ways, and the world is sharp as a knife. She argues that the qualitative methods that practice-based researchers have developed should be recognized as "science" with their own distinctive forms of objectivity. Complementary to Asch in chapter 1, she concludes that an effective mode of communication that is both participatory and transformative has the capacity to generate an "evolving possibility of consensus, taking a different form in the mind and experience of each listener."[17]

Chapter 8

In her critical and constructive reflections on the variegated meanings of resurgence and reconciliation, Ladner stresses the importance of proceeding with caution and humility if we are to begin to understand the rich meanings of these terms in Indigenous languages and life ways. Reconciliation implies a whole "ecologically grounded ethical and political philosophy about how it is that we live together in the best way possible or how it is we live best together." She draws from Nehiyaw

philosophy and stories of reconciliation to deepen and broaden the ecological, legal and social dimensions of reconciliation offered by Asch,
Borrows, and Tully. She emphasizes the roles that belonging to and
being with the land in sustainable ways, revitalization, and personal
agency and responsibility, as well as forgiveness for irresponsibility, all
play in Indigenous stories of reconciliation. At the heart of these stories is the profoundly creative power of transformation that is involved
in ecological and social practices of reconciliation. It not only involves
redistribution of power and resources, but also Indigenous and settler
peoples coming to terms with "what it means to have multiple nations
occupying the same space," and of finding new ways "of working and
living together without convergence."

Chapter 9

Ethnoecology is the study of people's knowledge of ecosystems and
ecological relationships. Turner and Spalding explore the ecological
knowledge of First Nations' peoples and examine how their relationships to their lands and resources, so important to their food security
and cultural identities, have been restricted and in some cases severed,
by the actions and regulations imposed by newcomer settler groups.
Newcomers' impacts on First Nations' homelands, resources, and cultures have been relentless and cumulative. Not only has First Nations'
access to healthy traditional food been restricted, but also their ability to harvest key materials and medicines, and access to important
spiritual areas have been affected. In turn, the same restrictions have
affected intergenerational knowledge transmission, resulting in even
further damage to the health and well-being of First Nations. Reconciliation has been and can be achieved, in part, through recognition,
affirmation, and resurgence of Indigenous traditional foods, medicines,
and materials, as well as language and cultural revitalization. They
suggest that collaborative ethno-ecological research that historicizes
Indigenous relationships to plants and plant habitats can help support
this revitalization.

Chapter 10

No collection on reconciliation would be complete without mentioning
how the Crown and the Supreme Court understand this term across

many cases. Yet there is a vast literature on this complex topic. We see no value in duplicating a case-by-case overview here. It is sufficient to note that the Supreme Court has written that "aboriginal rights recognized and affirmed by s. 35(1) must be directed towards the reconciliation of the pre-existence of aboriginal societies with the sovereignty of the Crown."[18] It has written that "a morally and politically defensible conception of aboriginal rights" requires taking account of both Aboriginal and common law perspectives in interpreting the country's highest law.[19] On this account, Indigenous peoples' own laws should figure much more prominently in setting the rules and procedures for how we should live together in this land.[20] Unfortunately, as we mentioned in the synopsis to chapter 1, section 91.24 of the 1867 Constitution has been interpreted by the Crown and Supreme Court as asserting sovereignty over Indians and lands reserved for Indians without their consent. This assertion of power-over overrides and tends to marginalize the nation to nation treaty relationship of ongoing reconciliation between equal partners recognized in the 255-year-old Constitution of Canada of 1763.[21] It renders reconciliation impossible because reconciliation, in all its different ways, is based on the premise that reconciling partners suspend power-over relations and engage in dialogue and negotiation as equals. These negotiations give rise to partnerships based on mutual consent. This view is also in accord with a basic principle of constitutional democracy: government rests on the consent of the governed. So until this unilateral assertion of sovereignty is rectified, the present understanding of reconciliation under Crown sovereignty cannot provide a fair basis for reconciliation.

In his chapter, McNeil describes how the unilateral assertion of Crown sovereignty came to be presented as self-justifying and beyond question, effacing the older treaty relationship that Asch surveys in chapter 1. In so doing, he distinguishes between de facto and de jure sovereignty. De facto sovereignty requires actual exercise of authority in a territory, whereas de jure sovereignty is an abstract concept that depends on the application of a specific legal system. De jure sovereignty is relative because, while it may be valid in one legal system, it is not necessarily valid in other legal systems. A choice of law question is therefore involved that raises an issue of legitimacy. The chapter concludes that, although Canada has de facto sovereignty over its territory today, its claim to de jure sovereignty lacks legitimacy as long as it is not acknowledged by Indigenous legal systems.

Given this perspective, it is the role of the Supreme Court to show how Canada can move from de facto to de jure sovereignty with the consent of Indigenous peoples acting in accord with their legal systems. From the vision articulated by Asch and Borrows, this would involve nation-to-nation treaty negotiations in accord with the 255-year-old Constitution. The present federal government has said it is committed to this way of reconciliation. The Court has moved in this direction in a number of cases, and legal scholars have suggested how they can continue so Indigenous peoples can become equal partners in a renewed federation.[22] This would also bring the way of reconciliation in line with principles of rule of law, federalism, and democracy enunciated by the Court.

This outstanding issue of de facto sovereignty is an important component of most calls for reconciliation over the last two decades. However, it is important to remember that we, the democratic people and peoples of this land, can all carry on discussing and enacting practices of reconciliation and/or resurgence in every area of Indigenous and Settler life ways and earth ways without waiting for the Crown to join in. Indeed, the perspectives discussed in this collection suggest that changes do not derive from a single source above the demos, but from a multiplicity of reconciliatory and/or resurgent engagements in our everyday earth ways and life ways here and now. Then, perhaps, in a few decades we might be able to celebrate an anniversary of the resurgence and reconciliation of a much older, de jure, Indigenous and Canadian confederation. Who knows?

Chapter 11

Since Brian Noble initiated this whole cycle of workshops, dialogue, correspondence, writing, and rewriting, it is only fitting that we should end with his concluding remarks. In his chapter on treaty ecologies, Noble offers to show the complementary relation of the ideas and practices presented for discussion in the chapters by Asch, Borrows, and Tully. He characterizes this relation as an effective "treaty ecology," by recounting stories shared with him by Piikani and Ktunaxa people – stories of Following Deer, which demonstrate their peoples' treaty ecologies within their territories. These are explicit stories of movement and encounter, treaties between humans and animals, and peoples and peoples. They are wholly non-colonial – indeed they are demonstrations of what is opposite to coloniality, which he also sees as necessary to unpack if we are to find paths to shared futures. In fine, the stories are based on restoring the continuity of "living-with" and "living-together" relational practices, which together constitute "treaty ecologies." His approach aligns with those of Asch (more on inter-political ecologies), Borrows, and Tully (more on interpersonal ecologies) in shared decolonial commitment – which is to say that we must first acknowledge conditions of ongoing coloniality, so as to then seek to act in ways that interrupt, replace, and dissolve those conditions – and to do so by enacting their pragmatic opposite.

Thus, we displace the anti-ecologies of coloniality by enacting the pro-ecologies of treaty, which requires humans, animals, all things working and living well together, interpersonally and inter-politically. Drawing on the work of Leanne Betasamosoke Simpson, Noble provides a final account of how treaty ecologies entail at once personal and the political engagements akin to those described and enacted in the Following Deer stories of the Piikani and Ktunaxa. He draws this together with propositions on the kinds of actions that promote, advance, and reconnect us with liveable, decolonial, treaty ecologies of Indigenous, settler, and all peoples, as well as our more-than-human neighbours, in our current moment.

NOTES

1 The classic texts for resurgence *contra* reconciliation are taken to be Glen Sean Coulthard, *Red Skin White Masks: Rejecting the Colonial Politics of Recognition* (Minneapolis: University of Minnesota Press, 2014); and Audra Simpson, *Mohawk Interruptus: Political Life across the Borders of Settler States* (Durham: Duke University Press, 2014). Whether Coulthard or Simpson rejects all forms of reconciliation or simply the forms of non-transformative reconciliation that perpetuate the status quo that we also reject is a question for another time.

2 For the argument that the majority of Indigenous people do not accept the rejectionist resurgence thesis and the binary world view on which it depends, see Greg Poelzer and Ken S. Coates, *From Treaty People to Treaty Nation: A Roadmap for All Canadians* (Vancouver: UBC Press, 2015), 34–45. He cites Taiaiake Alfred's claim that only 5 per cent of Indigenous people embrace it (45).

3 This robust resurgence and transformative reconciliation view is associated with and developed by Valerie Napoleon, Hadley Friedland,

John Borrows, Aaron Mills, and Taiaiake Alfred in different ways. It is also the general vision that the contributors to this volume develop in their own distinctive ways. For Taiaiake Alfred, see *Wasase: Indigenous Pathways of Action and Freedom* (Peterborough: Broadview, 2005), 45–66, 204–9. He associates it with Gandhi's similar form of organization to transform British imperialism and free India and refers to it as non-violent contention. Taiaiake is sometimes associated with rejectionist insurgency, but this overlooks his commitment to non-violent contention and relationships of peace and friendship with settlers worked out through Two Row Wampum Treaty negotiations (*Kaswentha*). On this, see Asch, this volume.

4 An Indigenous participant presented this view at the Victoria workshop.

5 It might be said that the adoption of a separatist resurgence by the Black Power movement in North America had similar results. See the searching analysis of this in Martin Luther King Junior, *Where Do We Go from Here: Chaos or Community?* (Boston: Beacon, 1968).

6 The chapters in this book do not whole-heartedly adopt the decolonization dichotomies of Third World politics, which we generally regard as a historical failure. This transition from decolonization to the contemporary world of informal imperialism and practices for and of transformative freedom within it is described in James Tully, *Public Philosophy in a New Key. Vol. 2, Imperialism and Civic Freedom* (Cambridge: Cambridge University Press, 1988), 243–311; and Robert Nichols and Jakeet Singh, eds, *Freedom and Democracy in an Imperial Context: James Tully in Dialogue* (London: Routledge, 2014).

7 Poelzer and Coates, *From Treaty People to Treaty Nation.*

8 For a synopsis of how these complementary visions of independence and interdependence were presented to and discussed at the Canadian Royal Commission on Aboriginal Peoples, 1991–5, see James Tully, "The Negotiation of Reconciliation," in *Democracy and Civic Freedom*, 223–56 (Cambridge: Cambridge University Press, 2008).

9 For an earlier articulation of independent resurgence and interdependent reconciliation grounded in earth interdependency, see John Borrows, "Landed Citizenship: An Indigenous Declaration of Indigenous Interdependency," in *Recovering Canada: The Resurgence of Indigenous Law*, 138–58 (Toronto: University of Toronto Press, 2002).

10 For one type of historical analysis of independence (resurgence) and interdependence (reconciliation) working successfully and unsuccessfully in different contexts, see James Tully, "Consent, Hegemony, and Dissent in Treaty Negotiations," in *Between Consenting Peoples: Political Community and*

the Meaning of Consent, ed. Jeremy Webber and Colin M. Macleod, 233–56 (Vanvouver: UBC Press, 2010).

11 The Laurier Memorial, http://shuswapnation.org/to-sir-wilfrid-laurier/.

12 The Secwepemc (Shuswap), Nlaka'pamux (Couteau or Thompson) and Okanagan tribes, *The Memorial to Prime Minister Sir Wilfrid Laurier* (Kamloops: 1910). For the continuation of this vision of robust resurgence and transformative reconciliation, see Arthur Manuel, *Unsettling Canada: A National Wake-up Call* (Toronto: Between the Lines, 2015).

13 See Robin Wall Kimmerer, *Braiding Sweetgrass: Indigenous Wisdom, Scientific Knowledge, and the Teaching of Plants* (Minneapolis: Milkweed Editions, 2013), 205–302; Hilary Stewart and Bill Reid, *Cedar: Tree of Life to the Northwest Coast Indians* (Vancouver: Douglas & McIntyre, 1995).

14 While the volume as a whole illustrates this approach, chapter 6 by Starblanket and Stark focuses directly on how such questions bring intersectional relations of power, knowledge, subjectification, and situated freedom to light.

15 Alfred, *Wasase,* 39–100; John Borrows, *Freedom and Indigenous Constitutionalism* (Toronto: University of Toronto Press, 2016), 50–102.

16 See Joshua Nichols, "Reconciliation without Recollectio" (PhD diss., University of Victoria, 2017).

17 For further research, see two important contributions to this field of engaged study: Paulette Regan, *Unsettling the Settler Within: Indian Residential Schools, Truth Telling and Reconciliation in Canada* (Vancouver: UBC Press, 2010); and Sarah Marie Wiebe, *Everyday Exposure: Indigenous Mobilization and Environmental Justice in Canada's Chemical Valley* (Vancouver: UBC Press, 2016).

18 *R v Van der Peet,* [1996] 2 SCR 507 para 31.

19 Ibid. at para 42.

20 For further discussion, see John Borrows, *Canada's Indigenous Constitution* (Toronto: University of Toronto Press, 2010).

21 See John Borrows, "Canada's Colonial Constitution," in *The Right Relationship: Reimaging the Implementation of Historical Treaties,* ed. John Borrows and Michael Coyle, 17–38 (Toronto: University of Toronto Press, 2017).

22 See Nichols, *Reconciliation without Recollection.*

PART ONE

1 Confederation Treaties and Reconciliation: Stepping Back into the Future[1]

MICHAEL ASCH

Many of us now acknowledge in public discourse that we are living on unceded Indigenous lands. And in those parts of this country where we have negotiated treaties to give us permission to settle, routinely included are words that draw attention to that fact as well. One version, which I found because this chapter was originally presented in Halifax, comes from a Dalhousie Student Council's resolution. It reads: "The Mi'kmaq people historically granted permission through treaties with the British crown to allow settler peoples to occupy this unceded territory and therefore Dalhousie and the Students Union Building exist on Mi'kmaq territory by their permission."[2]

With one minor textual change (I would have substituted "settle in" for "occupy") this statement encapsulates what I understand as a foundation upon which to build reconciliation. Unpacking its meaning for Canada is the subject of this chapter.

Reconciliation

Let me begin with a few words on what I take reconciliation to be about. Most of us are sensitive to the notion that there is something profoundly wrong in our relationship with Indigenous peoples. By "us," I mean explicitly people like myself who are unequivocally members of the Settler community that originates with Europeans who began coming here with colonization and found when they arrived that there were peoples already here living in political societies; a group I am collectively calling Indigenous peoples. And I am suggesting that one central reason there is something wrong in our relationship is that, from the outset, Settlers and our governments have predominately acted as though Indigenous peoples did not live in societies that required our recognition or respect. That is, as a general trend we treated these lands as ours for the taking and Indigenous peoples as though they were our inferiors. So the point of reconciliation in this dimension is to reconcile our practices today with the certain knowledge that we have acted wrongly (even in our own ethical terms), accept responsibility for the harms our actions have caused, and work to ensure that our actions and values in future come into accord. That, then, is how I interpret the phrase, "Reconciliation: The Responsibility for Shared Futures," which was the title of the lecture series at Dalhousie that started the dialogue.

This chapter is aimed particularly at those who feel as I do and are looking for ideas as to how to move along this path. I also realize, after decades of teaching, that there will be those who will read my words who believe there is no issue to address. While I am not specifically addressing these people, I hope what I have to say will influence them to rethink their position.

My chapter, then, will focus on the significance of the treaties we made, around the time of Confederation, and particularly on the possibilities for instituting a rightful relationship on the terms these treaties offer. However, to get to that point, let me begin with the proposition that treaties are not important, for, after all, in the experience of most settlers, the relationships we established through treaties seems to make little difference to how we live our lives.

Canadian History

The proposition that treaties are insignificant is reinforced in many ways. One of these is how we tell the story of Canadian history. As recounted in leading English-language university-level Canadian texts,[3] the history of Canada as a civic nation is written as a "coming of age" story, with Canada and the United Kingdom as the two principal protagonists, and the path to our full maturity as a state, the central theme.

In it, there is a major transition point that is demarcated by the passage of the British North America Act in 1867, which provided us with our present institutional form – federalism – and a moment of transition we call "Confederation." From this we derive the two major periods of Canadian civic history. The first is "Pre-Confederation." Here, the key events include the fall of Quebec in 1759 and the consequent Treaty of

Paris in 1763 by means of which Britain gained authority over what is now Canada; the quest for "responsible government,"[4] its establishment in principle with Lord Durham's report of 1839, and in practice (depending on the reading) no later than 1859. It concludes with the struggle for Confederation, which is seen as a solution to the dysfunction of the existing form of legislative association.

The second, which is called "Post-Confederation," begins with Confederation itself in 1867. It is immediately followed by a period of consolidation and expansion, especially to the West so that, with the purchase of Rupert's Land in 1869 (and Manitoba's joining of Confederation one year later) and the incorporation of British Columbia in 1871, in just four years, Canada is virtually the same size as it is today. What follows is a period in which Canada incrementally gains recognition as an equal to the United Kingdom in political status, and thus permission to take our place as a state equal in standing to all others. However, the moment of transition comes only some 115 years after Confederation with the passage of the Constitution Act of 1982 by the British Parliament.

Relations with Indigenous peoples, including treaty-making, play a minor role in this account, taking a part beyond mere mention only in conjunction with the period of Western expansion in the immediate aftermath of Confederation. Here, the Riel Rebellion, negotiating the numbered treaties on the Plains, and the North-West Rebellion of 1885, along with the completion of the Canadian Pacific Railway that same year are recognized as the noteworthy events. However, in this context, treaties are represented as a convenient way in which we could realize control over the land,[5] a point explained by Granatstein: "Before the new social order could be created, the old had to be displaced. Arrangements were made to extinguish Indian title to most of the fertile lands of the southern Prairies."[6] That is, the principal role of the treaties is to provide evidence to support the importance of certain events at the time of Confederation that indicate Canada's progress to full maturity.

In short, this narrative creates the impression that treaty-making of any importance is an event that happened as a moment in our history and as one small step in the story we tell of our development as a civic nation. Treaties, then, are of little significance and certainly cannot be seen as central in reconciliation.

But that is an artefact of the way we tell our story. Here is what I mean.

On Temporal Priority

Temporal priority (by which I mean the sequence of things) is a central tenet in our culture, one that we use to order relationships in matters that range from scientific explanations (cause and effect) to priorities in serving groups of people (those who come later are served later). Therefore, temporal priority ought to apply here. That is, as newcomers, we ought to respect that we just can't barge onto lands of those who were here when we arrived. But in fact we do not. Instead, our dominant narrative relies on a belief that temporal priority does not apply, and to get there we have invented stories that have become the rationalizations we use to justify this proposition.

Among these, the one that dominates public discourse today, as it has for a century and more, suggests that those who were here when we first arrived had a "defect," which legitimately made us first in line. The most prominent of these is that they were "less advanced." Political scientist Thomas Flanagan puts it this way:

> Let me put this line of argument in the simplest terms. Initially, all people, whether hunters or farmers, have an equal right to support themselves from the bounty of the earth. But the hunting mode of life takes up a lot of land, while agriculture, being more productive, causes population to grow and leads to civilization. As their numbers increase, civilized peoples have a right to cultivate the additional land necessary for their support. If the hunters deny them that opportunity by keeping their hunting grounds as a game preserve, they impede the equal access of the farmers to the bounty of the earth. It is wrong for the hunters to insist on maintaining their way of life; rather they should adopt agriculture and civilization, which would actually make them better off while allowing more people to live. *The farmers are justified in taking land from the hunters and defending it as long as they make the arts of civilization available to the hunters.*[7]

But then, it is not just Thomas Flanagan. The Supreme Court of Canada has written, "While British policy towards the native population was based on respect for their right to occupy their traditional lands, a proposition to which the Royal Proclamation of 1763 bears witness, there was from the outset never any doubt that sovereignty and legislative power, and indeed the underlying title, to such lands vested in the Crown."[8] How can there be no doubt that we had sovereignty "from the outset," unless the principle of temporal priority does not apply!

On this basis, then, treaties do not count for much, for the fact that Indigenous peoples were here when we first arrived is discounted. And in one sense, it is this disjunction between the fact that there were people already living here in political society with the representation of these lands as vacant that requires reconciliation.

The Treaty Paradigm

But that is not the whole story. There has also been from the outset those among us who have held firmly that the principle of temporal priority applies here and thus insisted that settlers needed permission to settle on these lands. Treaty-making derives from this perspective, and in that respect at least Chief Justice Dickson is wrong: the royal proclamation asserts that, regardless of who claims sovereignty and jurisdiction, settlers have no authority to move onto the lands of Indigenous peoples without their consent: "It is just and reasonable, and essential to our Interest, and the Security of our Colonies, that the several Nations or Tribes of Indians with whom We are connected, and who live under our Protection, should not be molested or disturbed in the Possession of such Parts of Our Dominions and Territories as, not having been ceded to or purchased by Us, are reserved to them or any of them, as their Hunting Grounds."[9] Furthermore, it introduces a specific set of rules to ensure that these agreements were legitimate. That is:

> We do, with the Advice of our Privy Council strictly enjoin and require, that no private Person do presume to make any purchase from the said Indians of any Lands reserved to the said Indians, within those parts of our Colonies where, We have thought proper to allow Settlement: but that, if at any Time any of the Said Indians should be inclined to dispose of the said Lands, the same shall be Purchased only for Us, in our Name, at some public Meeting or Assembly of the said Indians, to be held for that Purpose by the Governor or Commander in Chief of our Colony respectively within which they shall lie.[10]

Treaties, then, represent a possible path to reconciliation, for, if we are here by agreement, then our settlement is legitimate. But, of course, this requires that two conditions are fulfilled: that the terms of the treaty are fair, and that consent is informed and freely given. The question is whether these conditions apply.

The dominant narrative suggests that neither does. For example, as you will likely recall, when it comes to the numbered treaties, the texts generally specify that, in return for a blanket cession of all rights in all lands, the Indigenous signatories received goods of relatively little value. Typical is the entry in Finkel and Conrad: "Like the six subsequent treaties, Treaty One established reserves where Aboriginal peoples would have their farms, and promised implements, seed and training to launch them in agricultural careers. It also promised that traditional hunting and fishing rights would be recognized."[11]

To underscore the unfairness of the treaties, the texts also report that we failed to fulfil even these promises. To put it explicitly, it reads that the Indigenous party agreed to give up everything – that is, "cede, release, surrender and yield up to the Government of the Dominion of Canada, for Her Majesty the Queen, and Her successors forever, all their rights, titles and privileges whatsoever, to the lands included within the following limits."[12] And in return received (among other things):

> two hoes, one spade, one scythe and one axe for every family so actually cultivating, and enough seed wheat, barley, oats and potatoes to plant such land as they have broken up; also one plough and two harrows for every ten families so cultivating as aforesaid, and also to each Chief for the use of his band as aforesaid, one yoke of oxen, one bull, four cows, a chest of ordinary carpenter's tools, five hand saws, five augers, one cross-cut saw, one pit-saw, the necessary files and one grindstone, all the aforesaid articles to be given, once for all, for the encouragement of the practice of agriculture among the Indians.[13]

Were this the case, I would not pursue this path to reconciliation, for it is impossible to believe that any group of people would freely agree to such one-sided terms. And this is what is frequently represented to have transpired – a position often seen as consequent to a significant power differential between the parties.[14]

But there is another understanding of what transpired. Often expressed by the Indigenous parties, it is that regardless of the presumed power differential in at least some cases, treaties were negotiated honourably on both sides. These resulted in the establishment of open-ended agreement that transformed the relationship between the parties that existed before into a partnership based on mutual sharing that was to last in perpetuity. The late leader Harold Cardinal put it this way: "To the Indians of Canada, the treaties represent an Indian Magna Carta. The treaties are important to us, because we entered into these negotiations with faith, with hope for a better life with honour."[15]

How can there be such a disconnect? The answer is that we have misread our own history. And that brings me to the heart of what we wish to convey here.

On the Shared Understanding of Treaties

Let me focus on two central issues: the conditions on the basis of which we were authorized to settle; and the obligations we made in return. As I say, in the dominant narrative, the former is none, for all political authority was transferred to us; and the latter is some insignificant things offered on a one-time basis. What do our partners say?

With regard to the first, to my knowledge, there is not one Indigenous political community that agrees that political authority was transferred in whole or in part in the treaties. Instead, the term used is "sharing the land" in the sense of "To participate in (an action, activity, opinion, feeling, or condition); to perform, enjoy, or suffer in common with others";[16] and not to "have a share" or, as the OED puts it, "to cut into parts."[17] Chief George Desjarlais of Treaty 8 put it this way in his testimony to the Royal Commission on Aboriginal Peoples: "We are treaty people. Our nations entered into a treaty relationship with your Crown, with your sovereign. We agreed to share our lands and territories with the Crown. We did not sell or give up our rights to the land and territories. We agreed to share our custodial responsibility for the land with the Crown. We did not abdicate it to the Crown. We agreed to maintain peace and friendship among ourselves and with the Crown."[18]

Elder Kay Thompson, of Treaty 4, explains it this way: her forebears "didn't give the land, they didn't say, we give you this land. They gave them permission to use the land."[19] And Elder Musqua of the same treaty explains the rationale as follows: "Because, if any man owns a piece of the Earth, then he no more respects Mother Earth. He no more respects the Earth, because he believes he can do what wants with that Earth and he can destroy it, he can do whatever he wants. That's the reason we don't own the Earth: because it belongs to all the people. For the purposes of that we cannot own the Earth. We were willing to share it."[20] And, as I have come to understand, this means that the intent is to establish a nation-to-nation relationship, notwithstanding that settlers do not have sovereignty or jurisdiction over any lands – treaty or not. But I will not go into that in any detail, for how that might be realized is a vast subject that requires address on its own.

As regards the second, our partners make it clear that we made the commitment to build a relationship with them based on our seeking to ensure that their well-being would be enhanced by our settlement. Thus, the specific commitments contained in the treaties represented a first step in that process. Elder Danny Musqua put it this way: "We agreed to the relationship, a perpetual land-use agreement between us [First Nations] and them [the Crown] in Treaty 4, that [settlers] would harvest the land for the purposes of agriculture, sow crops and we, along with that [would learn agricultural skills]; they would give us the technology to also do that ourselves."[21] Putting it another way, our partners understand that:

1) Regardless of the economic activities the signatories chose to pursue, their standard of living would be equivalent to that of the settlers;[22]
2) They would never go hungry;[23]
3) They would have assistance in times of need;[24]
4) They would not be required to make any changes in their way of living in order to affect that guarantee; that is, as the familiar phrase depicts it, the offer is "on top of what you already have."[25]

As Ray, Miller, and Tough put it, these provisions were intended "to ensure that First Nations continued to have the means of livelihood, in return for agreeing to share the use of their territory with Euro-Canadian newcomers."[26]

Where do they get these ideas? The answer: from the words of Chief Commissioner Alexander Morris, who negotiated many of the post-Confederation treaties. And we know this because he published transcriptions of what was said during negotiations in his 1880 book, *The Treaties of Canada with the Indians of Manitoba and the North-West Territories*. Here are some of the things he said.

Regarding the assertion that the purpose of the treaties was to gain permission to share the land, not take it over, here is what he said at Treaty 4 negotiations:

We have two nations here. We have the Crees, who were here first, and we have the Ojibbeways (Saulteaux), who came from our country not many suns ago. We find them here; we won't say they stole the land, and the stones and the trees; no, but we will say this, that we believe their brothers, the Crees, said to them when they came in here: "The land is wide, it is wide, it is big enough for us both; let us live here like brothers," and that is what you say; and that is what you say, as you told us on Saturday, as to the Half-Breeds I see around. You say you are one with them; now we all want to be one.[27]

Regarding the purpose of the commitments we made,

> What the Queen and her Councillors would like is this, she would like you to learn something of the cunning of the white man. When fish are scarce and the buffalo are not plentiful she would like to help you to put something in the land; she would like that you should have some money every year to buy things that you need. If any of you would settle down, she would give you cattle to help you; she would give you some seed to plant. She would like to give you every year, for twenty years, some powder, shot, and twine to make nets of. I see you here before me today. I will pass away and you will pass away. I will go where my fathers have gone and you also, but after me and after you will come our children. The Queen cares for you and for your children, and she cares for the children that are yet to be born. She would like to take you by the hand.[28]

And, as he explained at Treaty 6 negotiations, nothing was to be imposed: "Understand me, I do not want to interfere with your hunting and fishing. I want you to pursue it through the country, as you have heretofore done; but I would like your children to be able to find food for themselves and their children that come after them. Sometimes when you go to hunt you can leave your wives and children at home to take care of your gardens."[29] And, "What I have offered does not take away your living, you will have it then as you have now, and what I offer now is put on top of it. This I can tell you, the Queen's Government will always take a deep interest in your living."[30]

There is also a specific commitment in that treaty to ensure that our partners never go hungry. It is the so-called famine clause, and here is what it says: "That in the event hereafter of the Indians comprised within this treaty being overtaken by any pestilence, or by a general famine, the Queen, on being satisfied and certified thereof by Her Indian Agent or Agents, will grant to the Indians assistance of such character and to such extent as Her Chief Superintendent of Indian Affairs shall deem necessary and sufficient to relieve the Indians from the calamity that shall have befallen them."[31]

The commissioner explained this clause, which was inserted at the request of our partners, to them in these words: "In a national famine or general sickness, not what happens in everyday life, but if a great blow comes on the Indians they would not be allowed to die like dogs."[32]

But then there is the cede-and-surrender clause. To "cede, release, surrender and yield up to the Government of the Dominion of Canada, for Her Majesty the Queen, and Her successors forever, all their rights, titles and privileges whatsoever" to land seems pretty definitive. They "agreed" to come under the sovereignty and jurisdiction of the dominion government. But that interpretation is faulty. When read in the political context of that time, a better interpretation is that it was intended to protect our partners from the authority of the dominion government by establishing a direct relationship with the Crown. As Elder Musqua says, the intent is that "[the Queen] will protect you from encroachment of taxpayers, and land speculators ... she will protect you from certain encroachment on your personal lives and your culture ... and from the settlers that will come."[33] And the method: "The Queen has adopted (First Nations) as children ... a joint relationship will come out of that. And so we have a joint relationship with the Crown because the Queen is now our mother."[34]

While I do not have time here to dwell on this point, given its centrality, let me give you key evidence that leads me to this conclusion. As to equality of status, Commissioner Morris never refers to Indigenous peoples as coming under the authority of the dominion government, either before or after negotiations. Rather, he is careful to use kin terms to indicate that their members are equal in standing to settlers (i.e., friends and brothers). Furthermore, while he does refer to the Queen as Mother, he again refers to the two parties as equals, referring to her as the "Great Mother of us all" and saying that "she cares for you as much as she cares for her white children."[35] That is, brothers to each other and children of the Queen, and therefore not under the jurisdiction of the government of the other child. But perhaps the clearest example in support of this interpretation comes from his statement on Day 2 of Treaty 4 negotiations: "What I want is for you to take the Queen's hand, through mine, and shake hands with her forever."[36]

To this I need to add a remark by Lord Dufferin, who was governor-general at the time that Morris negotiated these treaties, making it clear that the intent is to ensure that Indigenous peoples do not come under the final authority of the dominion government: "You must remember that the Indian population is not represented in Parliament, and, consequently, that the Governor General is bound to watch over their welfare and especial solicitude."[37]

And finally, there is Morris's intervention during the parliamentary debate in 1865 on Confederation and the annexation of the North West. In it, he explains that his support for them derives in part because Canada needs the protection of the sovereign to avoid absorption by the United States, but that this does not mean that the Queen has the right to interfere in our governance. Here is how he puts it: "We have either to rise into strength and wealth and power by means of this union, under the sheltering protection of Britain, or we must be absorbed by the great power beside us. We will have the pride to belong to a great country still attached to the Crown of Great Britain, in which, notwithstanding, we shall have entire freedom of action and the blessing of responsible self government."[38] Thus, at that time, it is clear that one could retain jurisdiction over one's political affairs while transferring sovereignty to the Queen, which, of course, is the situation (symbolically at least – the legal story is more complex) within the Commonwealth today.

But as Canada needed the Crown to protect it from the United States, it was understood by many at that time (as, for example, in the quote by Lord Dufferin cited above) that our partners might need the intervention of the Crown to shield them from legislation of the dominion government. This approach to Indigenous relations follows the position first articulated by an influential political group in Britain that formed the Aborigines Protection Society; which in 1837 commented (in response to *The Report of the Parliamentary Select Committee on Aboriginal Tribes* which they published):

> The protection of the Aborigines should be considered as a duty peculiarly belonging and appropriate to the executive government, as administered either in this country or by the governors of the respective colonies. This is not a trust which could conveniently be confided to the local legislatures. In proportion as those bodies are qualified for the right discharge of their proper functions, they will be unfit for the performance of this office. For a local legislature, if properly constituted, should partake largely in the interests, and represent the feelings or the settled opinions of the great mass of the people for whom they act. But the settlers in almost every colony, having either disputes to adjust with the native tribes, or claims to urge against them, the representative body is virtually a party, and therefore ought not to be the judge in such controversies.[39]

That, then, was to be the arrangement: we would live together, sharing the land, and they would be protected from our excesses by the fact that they would have a direct relationship with the Queen (through the governor-general). In return, we would do our best to ensure that our presence on these lands was of benefit to them. Following from this, I am suggesting that the agreements we struck at that time offer us a path for reconciliation between Indigenous peoples and settlers today.

Hence the title of this contribution: "Confederation Treaties and Reconciliation: Stepping Back into the Future."

Recounting History

I believe that there was a reasonable expectation that the dominion government would live up to its commitments at the time these treaties were negotiated, for that is what it agreed to do in return for gaining permission from the Queen to acquire Rupert's Land from the Hudson's Bay Company. Here is what we said in a letter to the Queen in the year of Confederation:

> We, your Majesty's most dutiful and loyal subjects, the Senate and Commons of the Dominion of Canada, in Parliament assembled, humbly approach your Majesty for the purpose of representing ... *that, upon the transference of the territories in question to the Canadian Government, the claims of the Indian tribes to compensation for lands required for purposes of settlement will be considered and settled in conformity with the equitable principles which have uniformly governed the British Crown in its dealings with the aborigines.*[40]

But, of course, it did not do that. And as you may well know, our government's bad faith led to massive starvation due to the failure of the government to provide what was promised to those who chose to take up farming due to the rapid demise of buffalo. Let me give you one statistic: during the winter of 1883–4 three Treaty 6 reserves, the Mosquito, Grizzly Bear Head, and Lean Man together lost over 25 per cent of their population (seventy-seven deaths in a population of 300), of which fifty (or nearly 17 per cent) were children.[41] The causes of these deaths "can be directly linked to economic conditions."[42] Then there are the residential schools, and of course, we know well of the horrors that took place over the years. And it still continues, as can be attested to by our treatment of the Lubicon, the situation at Attawapiskat, and myriad other cases. Yet our partners by and large still speak of the respect they have for the treaties, and, as with Chief Spence of Attawapiskat, appeal to us to "respect our treaty and follow our treaty, as we did."

But that is easier said than done. What the Aborigines Protection Society said in 1837 holds today: "A local legislature, if properly constituted, should partake largely in the interests, and represent the feelings or the settled opinions of the great mass of the people for whom they act."[43] But the difference is that today there is no "executive" that stands outside of the government, for while the Crown can speak, it only can speak with the voice the government gives it. And governments are driven by expediency, not honour. As Miller aptly puts it,

> Once treaty-making was concluded in the 1870s, the self-interested and at times insensitive nature of federal treaty-making was revealed. There were numerous problems with treaty implementation because a distant government had little interest in the welfare of western peoples. Even when the collapse of the bison economy by 1879 created conditions of extreme hardship, Ottawa showed little concern. In fact, that collapse made it easier to ignore First Nations' protests ... Some later commentators – especially undergraduates, who tend toward cynicism – suggest that this heartlessness "proves" that Canada never intended to honour its treaty promises. There is no evidence from the treaty negotiations themselves to sustain such an interpretation. Rather, once setbacks in the West weakened the peoples there, it became all too easy in a parliamentary democracy in which votes – something First Nations did not have, of course – were what counted for politicians to drop treaty obligations down the priority list when it came to allocating resources.[44]

And this means that, at the end of the day, the surest way forward is to change the political calculus so that the benefit to the government of fulfilling our obligations outweighs the cost. And that is where Harold Cardinal's reference to the treaties as a "Magna Carta" comes in.

What I understand he is saying is that all peoples have principles so core that to violate them is virtually unthinkable. For settlers, one of the most basic of these, the origin of the rule of law, is embodied in the Magna Carta. As least for us, it is, as Lord Denning of the Law Lords of the Privy Council said, "the greatest constitution document of all times – the foundation of the freedom of the individual against the arbitrary authority of the despot."[45] To respect the rule of law is a fundamental principle of our governance system. It is assumed governments will adhere to it, regardless of cost.

Right now, settlers do not see treaties in the same way. They are considered to be relatively insignificant in the story of our country, an event to be mentioned in the context of what is core to our story: the establishment of Confederation, and the passage of the British North America Act of 1867 that gave it political life. As is reflected in our monuments on Parliament Hill, it is those, like George Brown and Sir John A. Macdonald, who propelled us in that direction at that time, who are counted as "Fathers of Confederation."

But that story makes no sense, for one cannot have Confederation until there is a home on which to build it, and without treaties we have no home here. That is what Commissioner Morris, Lord Dufferin, and so many others did when they chose to ground this country on the idea that our legitimacy arises from the agreements we made with those who were already here when we first arrived. This means that the treaties are as much a Magna Carta for us as they are for those with whom he negotiated, for the legitimacy of everything else, Confederation included, follows from it. And once we become aware that to violate the promises we made to bring Confederation into being is to violate the authority we have to build a home on these lands, I am convinced that our governments will never fail to find the political will to honour them.

Before concluding, let me raise one further question. The passage in which Harold Cardinal identifies Treaty 6 as a Magna Carta continues, "The treaties are important to us, because we entered into these negotiations with faith, with hope for a better life with honour. We have survived over a century on little but that hope. Did the white men enter into them with something less in mind? Or have the heirs of the men who signed in honour somehow disavowed the obligation passed down to them? The Indians entered into the treaty negotiations as honourable men who came to deal as equals with the queen's representatives. Our leaders of that time thought they were dealing with an equally honourable people."[46]

Well, we know the answer to the second question: the heirs have not acted honourably. The question is whether their leaders at that time were right in believing that they were "dealing with equally honourable people." That is, to be specific, was Commissioner Morris speaking truthfully? Today, the most frequent representation is that he was not. But on this point I demur. Rather I agree with Jim Miller that "there is no evidence from the treaty negotiations themselves to sustain such an interpretation."[47] But to this let me add the following affirmation. According to historian Robert Talbot, who recently completed a biography of the man, during his tenure lieutenant-governor of Manitoba, Morris "advocated tirelessly for the faithful implementation of the *spirit* of the treaties, arguing that oral promises, from specific agricultural implements to general principles of reciprocity and mutual assistance, should be honoured."[48]

The problem is that government was not receptive to his position. As a result, Talbot continues, "His approach [to implementation] was increasingly at odds with Ottawa."[49] By 1876 the department took steps to decrease his involvement in treaty implementation, and by 1877 his authority in that area was taken from him.[50] But he did not leave without a struggle. In that period, as Talbot says, "Morris increasingly protested against what he perceived to be a breaking of the treaties and the violation of the treaty relationship, especially the direct link between the First Nations and the Crown embodied in the office of the Lieutenant-Governor."[51]

That our partners did not hold him responsible for the privations they suffered at that time is indicated by the fact that, on his death in 1889, a number of chiefs from Manitoba and the North West made the long journey to Ontario to attend his funeral. Among them was Chief John Prince of Clandeboyne, Manitoba, who explained that he had come because "the Great Spirit called me here to be by the side of my friend."[52]

Furthermore, Morris had the status to make the representations he did on behalf of the Crown (and thus undertakings that the government of Canada was committed to fulfilling). At the time he negotiated these treaties he was also lieutenant-governor of Manitoba (and at one point its de facto premier) as well as the former chief justice in that province. In his first capacity, his authority derived from the governor-general, Lord Dufferin, and therefore he was a representative of the Crown and could in that capacity assert that by taking his hand, they were taking that of the Queen. And then there is his status in Canada. Alexander Morris had already been a long-standing member of Parliament, and indeed, had served as a minister in Canada's first post-Confederation government. Furthermore, he was a confidant of our first prime minister and an ardent supporter of Confederation, who, as a good friend of both George Brown and Sir John A. Macdonald, brokered a key deal, the "Great Coalition," that led to its establishment.[53] In short, his authority at the end of the day derives not only from the fact that he represented the Queen, but from his status as a founding figure in Confederation to take the initiative to shape its relationship with Indigenous peoples – a status that was never challenged by the government, even when he wrote into the text of Treaty 6 obligations, such as the famine clause, that were not in the version of the treaty with which he was provided. In that regard, we can take as authoritative that in speaking of his intent, he was speaking on behalf of Canada; and this is what he said it was: "One of the gravest of the questions presented for solution by the Dominion of Canada, when the enormous region of the country formerly known as the North-West Territories and Rupert's Land, was entrusted by the Empire of Great Britain and Ireland to her rule, *was the securing of the alliance of the Indian tribes, and maintaining friendly relations with them.*"[54]

Conclusion

The challenge then is ours, the current generation of legatees of those, like Morris, who signed in honour, to return us to the path down which they intended us to follow. To do this, then, requires first that we quickly remedy the harms caused (and continue to cause) as we follow a path that disavows the obligations passed down to us, and that means to begin with honouring the commitments made on our behalf by our forebears.

But I would urge this course even if you are still not convinced by this evidence that any of our forebears acted in good faith. After all, these are the conditions that those with whom we negotiated accepted as necessary to legitimate our presence on these lands. And should our partners be still willing to trust us to fulfil these faithfully, then that seems to be a good basis upon which to begin rebuilding that relationship.

In this regard, let me offer these closing thoughts. Reconciliation will require words of apology and of commitment on our part. But it requires much more than that. We need do nothing less than radically change our behaviour so that our practices come into line with our values. And here I am making two suggestions as to how to move quickly in this direction. The first is to demand that our governments' interactions with Indigenous peoples always conform to Morris's promise as explained in the famine provision that "if a great blow comes on the Indians they would not be allowed to die like dogs." While the original intent of this provision was to ensure the well-being of our partners in the face of natural disasters, we are responsible for many of the great blows, such as the residential schools, that have befallen our partners. Therefore, to keep the promise that we made to not "allow them to die [or live] like dogs" requires that we act quickly to remedy as best we can the effects of those harms and promise never to act that way again in the future. And fundamentally (especially given our past record) this means that we must commit never again to take any actions without first gaining the assent of our partners.

Second, in my view to get there requires that the we imagine our history as focused on the relationships we have built with those already living here in what was to us a New World rather than imagining it through the lens of our departure from those among whom we will never dwell again. By taking this path, we will by necessity come to see the centrality of relations with Indigenous peoples to our story, and through it the importance in our story of the solemn promises we made such as in Treaties 4 and 6 that legitimated our authority to live here in perpetuity. And from this it would follow that keeping those promises is inviolate, for to violate these promises is to invalidate our right to be here. And in that sense, following the lead of Harold Cardinal, we will come to understand that for us too treaties are our Magna Carta.

And that is the context within which I interpret what it means to recognize that "the Mi'kmaq people historically granted permission through treaties with the British crown to allow settler peoples to occupy this unceded territory and therefore Dalhousie and the Students Union Building exist on Mi'kmaq territory by their permission."

NOTES

1 In 2012 in Halifax I presented an earlier version of this chapter under the title "Back to the Future: Confederation Treaties and Reconciliation." However, given that Felix Hoehn recently published an article with the title "Back to the Future: Reconciliation and Indigenous Sovereignty after Tsilhqot'in," *University of New Brunswick Law Journal* 67 (2016): 109–45, to avoid confusion, I changed my title to the current one.

2 Dalhousie Student Union Minutes, 6 July 2012.

3 For example, Raymond Blake, Jeffrey Keshen, Norman Knowles, and Barbara Messamore, *Narrating a Nation: Canadian History Post-Confederation* (Toronto: McGraw-Hill Ryerson, 2011); Alvin Finkel and Margaret Conrad, *History of the Canadian Peoples. Vol. 2, 1867 to the Present*, 3rd ed. (Toronto: Addison Wesley Longman, 2002); Douglas R. Francis, Richard Jones, and Donald B. Smith, *Destinies: Canadian History since Confederation*, 5th ed. (Scarborough, ON: Thomson Nelson, 2004); J.L. Granatstein, Irving M. Abella, T.W. Acheson, David J. Bercuson, R. Craig Brown, and H. Blair Neatby, *Nation: Canada since Confederation* (Toronto: McGraw-Hill Ryerson, 1990).

4 "A government responsible to the representatives of the people, i.e., an executive or Cabinet collectively dependent on the votes of a majority in the elected legislature." James Careless, "Responsible Government," in *The Canadian Encyclopedia* (Toronto: Historica Canada, 2013), http://www.thecanadianencyclopedia.ca/en/article/responsible-government/.

5 Douglas R. Francis, Richard Jones, and Donald B. Smith, *Destinies: Canadian History since Confederation*, 5th ed. (Scarborough, ON: Thomson Nelson, 2004), 36; Blake et al., *Narrating a Nation*, 37.

6 Tom Flanagan, *First Nations? Second Thoughts* (Montreal and Kingston: McGill-Queen's University Press, 2000), 42.

7 Ibid., 42. Emphasis mine.

8 *R v Sparrow* [1990] 1 SCR 1075, 30.

9 The Royal Proclamation of 1763 (UK), reprinted in RSC 1985, App II, No 2, http://avalon.law.yale.edu/18th_century/proc1763.asp.

10 Ibid.

11 Finkel and Conrad, *History of the Canadian Peoples*, 31.

12 *Treaty No. 4 between Her Majesty the Queen and the Cree and Saulteaux Tribes of Indians at Qu'Appelle and Fort Elice* (Ottawa: Queen's Printer and Controller of Stationery, 1966), http://www.aadnc-aandc.gc.ca/eng/1100100028689/1100100028690.

13 Ibid.

14 Jean Friesen, "Magnificent Gifts: The Treaties of Canada with the Indians of the Northwest, 1869–76," in *The Spirit of the Alberta Treaties*, ed. Richard Price (Edmonton: University of Alberta Press, 1986), 212.

15 Harold Cardinal, *The Unjust Society: The Tragedy of Canada's Indians* (Edmonton: Hurtig, 1969), 24.

16 "share, verb, 2." OED Online (Oxford: Oxford University Press, 2016).

17 "share, verb, 1." OED Online (Oxford: Oxford University Press, 2016).

18 Chief George Desjarlais in *Report of the Royal Commission on Aboriginal Peoples* (Ottawa: Indian and Northern Affairs Canada, 1996), 2: chap. 4, s. 3.1.

19 Treaty 4 Elders Gordon Oakes and Danny Musqua put it this way: "Our land is plentiful" and "we were willing to share." Harold Cardinal and Walter Hildebrandt, *Treaty Elders of Saskatchewan: Our Dream Is That Our Peoples Will One Day Be Clearly Recognized as Nations* (Calgary: University of Calgary Press, 2000), 36, 62.

20 Elder Kay Thompson in Cardinal and Hildebrandt, *Treaty Elders of Saskatchewan*, 62.

21 Cardinal and Hildebrandt, *Treaty Elders of Saskatchewan*, 66.

22 Ibid., 47.

23 Treaty 4 elders, "Elder's Document on Treaty #4 by the Saulteaux, Cree and Assiniboine Nations," Regina: University of Regina, 1983, http://ourspace.uregina.ca/handle/10294/1723 at 2.

24 Ibid., 3.

25 Ibid., 2. Commissioner Morris uses this phrase in Treaty 6: "I cannot promise you that the Government will feed and support all of the

Indians … What I have offered you does not take away from your way of living, you will have it then as you have it now, and what I offer now is put on top of it. This I can tell you, the Queen's Government will always take a deep interest in your living." Alexander Morris, *The Treaties of Canada with the Indians of Manitoba and the North-West Territories (1880)* (Toronto: Belfords, Clarke, 1991), 211.

26 Arthur J. Ray, Jim Miller, and Frank Tough, *Bounty and Benevolence: A Documentary History of Saskatchewan Treaties* (Montreal and Kingston: McGill-Queen's University Press, 2002), 188.

27 Morris, *Treaties of Canada*, 108.

28 Ibid., 92.

29 Ibid., 204.

30 Ibid., 211.

31 *1876 Treaty No 6 between Her Majesty the Queen and the Plain and Wood Cree Indians and Other Tribes of Indians at Fort Carlton, Fort Pitt and Battle Rive with Adhesions* (Ottawa: Queen's Printer and Controller of Stationery, 1966), https://www.aadnc-aandc.gc.ca/eng/1100100028710/1100100028783, 4.

32 Ibid.

33 Cardinal and Hildebrandt, *Treaty Elders of Saskatchewan*, 47.

34 Ibid., 34.

35 Morris, *Treaties of Canada*, 92, 96, 107.

36 Ibid., 15.

37 Earl of Dufferin, *Speeches and Addresses of the Right Honourable Frederick Temple Hamilton, Earl of Dufferin*. Edited by Henry Milton (London: John Murray, 1882), 209.

38 Morris's intervention during the parliamentary debate in 1865 on Confederation and the annexation of the North West, quoted in Robert J. Talbot, *Negotiating the Numbered Treaties: An Intellectual and Political Biography of Alexander Morris* (Saskatoon: Purich, 2009), 47.

39 Parliamentary Select Committee, *Report of the Parliamentary Select Committee on Aboriginal Tribes (British Settlements) Reprinted, with Comments, by the "Aborigines Protection Society"* (London: William Ball, 1837), 117.

40 Joe Cauchon and James Cockburn, "1867 Address to Her Majesty the Queen from the Senate and House of Commons of the Dominion of Canada," in *British and Foreign State Papers 1869–1870* (London: William Ridgway, 1870), 412. Emphasis mine.

41 Maureen K. Lux, *Medicine That Walks: Disease, Medicine, and Canadian Plains Native People, 1880–1940* (Toronto: University of Toronto Press, 2001), 51.

42 Ibid., 4.

43 Parliamentary Select Committee, *Report of the Parliamentary Select Committee*, 117.

44 J.R. Miller, *Compact, Contract, Covenant: Aboriginal Treaty-Making in Canada* (Toronto: University of Toronto Press, 2009), 296.

45 Lord Denning, quoted in Anna Pallister, *Magna Carta: The Heritage of Liberty* (Oxford: Clarendon, 1971), 1.

46 Cardinal, *Unjust Society*, 28.

47 Miller, *Compact, Contract, Covenant*, 296.

48 Talbot, *Negotiating the Numbered Treaties*, 121.

49 Ibid.

50 Ibid.

51 Ibid., 149.

52 Ibid., 165.

53 Ibid., 47.

54 It seems clear that, at least at the time of this writing, Morris was of the view that the Dominion of Canada had acquired governing authority in the Northwest and Rupert's Land – at least in communication with the Canadian public at large. However, it is also clear from the transcriptions of the negotiations that he had a much more nuanced view of political relations when negotiating Treaties 4 and 6. However, be that as it may, whether or not he was of the view expressed in this passage, he nonetheless maintained the view that, whatever the legal regime he imagined, the objective was to forge an alliance based on peace and friendship rather than one based on domination. Morris, *Treaties of Canada*, 9.

2 Earth-Bound: Indigenous Resurgence and Environmental Reconciliation

JOHN BORROWS

Introduction: Indigenous Societies Are Complex

Reconciliation between Indigenous peoples and the Crown requires our collective reconciliation with the earth.[1] One source of rapprochement can be facilitated by the resurgence of Indigenous peoples' own laws and life ways.[2] Indigenous legal traditions contain broad strands of authority that are generally attentive to the environment.[3] They embody rich and vibrant insights and include deep intellectual and social resources that can help us care for the natural world.[4]

I do not claim Indigenous peoples are natural environmentalists. In fact, this can be a damaging stereotype.[5] Indigenous peoples can be as destructive as other societies on earth – we are part of humanity, not outside of it.[6] Caring for the earth is hard work; it does not always come naturally. Humans must consume to survive.[7] Accordingly we must strive to attenuate our impacts.[8] It is not easy to respect all forms of life. Even in small numbers, humans can place great stress on ecosystems.[9] For instance, numerous Indian reserves in Canada are environmentally degraded, even where populations are small.[10] Pollution flows into these lands from surrounding developments. Furthermore, our yards are too often filled with our own garbage. Ditches, ponds, and watercourses are fouled with waste that could have been easily placed in less damaging places. Our land's broader carrying capacity is over-extended. Of course, much of degradation's root causes often lie outside our borders.[11] We must not lose sight of this fact; broader structural forces have a crushing impact on Indigenous peoples' environmental degradation.[12]

At the same time, we must acknowledge that Indigenous peoples are not necessarily environmentally sound by the mere virtue of their existence.[13] As Indigenous peoples, we are not blameless. Our lands and waters can also be spoiled even where we have small degrees of stewardship and control.[14] It is not enough to be Indigenous and inherit an ethic of care. These teachings must be acted on by each generation.[15] They must be continuously reproduced for Indigenous peoples to live harmoniously with the earth.[16]

Fortunately, Indigenous peoples possess norms and practices that flow from experience that can be activated to accomplish this goal.[17] We must reject "dirty Indian" images, even as we discard stereotypical romantic "ecological Indian" views.[18] Contemporary Indigenous life is complex. For example, in contrast to the aforementioned problems, many Indigenous communities effectively apply their own laws and values to sustain and protect their homelands.[19] Their lands and lives are generally healthy, sustainable, and productive. Consequently, they enjoy clean water, fertile lands, and abundant wildlife.

This chapter discusses how Indigenous peoples' own legal systems and life ways can more fully facilitate reconciliation with the earth. Reconciliation with the earth is the kind of resurgence I value most. In my view, resurgent relations with the natural world are key to the revitalization of Indigenous peoples' relationships with the rocks, waters, insects, plants, birds, animals, and other forms of life around us.[20] They are also key to our reconciliation with other peoples. This chapter discusses the need for understanding and working within our environment's inherent limits, in ways that implement our linguistic and legal insights. The concept of "inherent limits" is part of many Indigenous peoples' world views. Inherent limits are Indigenous. They are found in our creation stories, trickster cycles, language structures, ceremonial practices, and hallowed teachings. Inherent limits are also found in Canadian law as articulated in Aboriginal title cases,[21] but the idea has a much older and broader reach, stretching back to earlier treaty relationships.[22] It is also important to remember that inherent limits are part of Canadian law more generally.[23] To repeat: inherent limits are found in treaties.[24] They apply to the legal concept known as the honour of the Crown.[25] Inherent limits are also found within wider constitutional law[26] and international law spheres.[27] Understanding Indigenous peoples own laws and life ways as sources of environmental resurgence and reconciliation deserves emphasis. But I do not want readers to think this result will materialize without intentionality and hard work. Indigenous peoples, like all other peoples, are both narrow-minded and magnanimous; they can stall in their own efforts or act in a lightning-fast fashion. Likewise, colonialism continues to be a significant force and obstacle for Indigenous peoples.[28] Turning towards Indigenous law does not automatically solve our environmental and relational crises. There must be a revitalization of Indigenous law based on seasonal relationships and structural reform to generate reconciliation. To illustrate how one Indigenous legal tradition entrenches this ethic, this chapter discusses a structural component of Anishinaabe law that tangibly embeds Anishinaabe communities in place-based cycles of life.[29]

Earth Bound: Indigenous Language, Legal Traditions, and the Environment

When I first learned Anishinaabe law from Dr Basil Johnston, an elder from my reserve, he told me that legal practice starts with understanding our language and drawing analogies from the earth. The word he used to describe this process was *akinoomaagewin*. This means we learn how to live well by giving our attention to the earth and taking direction from her. Thus, Basil emphasized that standards for making judgments can be found in the natural world as described in Anishinaabemowin, our language. He said that authority, precedent, and rules are triggered by observing the winds, waters, rocks, plants, and animals, and describing what we see in this light. Anishinaabe morphemes and words in these observations are drawn from the ecologies that sustain us. As has been said, Anishinaabe speakers inhabit a "langscape," a place where physical space interacts with human observation to give meaning to the natural and human worlds. As Professor Sakej Henderson wrote about a cognate Algonkian language, "Out of the sounds of life forces in the ecology … [a] cognitive recognition and acceptance of the interrelations of the shared space inform … languages, thus creating a shared worldview, a cognitive solidarity, and a tradition of responsible action."[30] In other words, resources for better relating to our environment are all around us, in our language and ecologies. As will be described, even in urban spaces, our law can be seen as literally being written on the earth.

When one speaks Anishinaabemowin the world is understood as being in constant motion. In fact, 70–80 per cent of the language is

verb-based. Anishinaabemowin does not rest on noun-based charac-
terizations of persons, places, or things. Anishinaabe language and law
is oriented to conjoining and organizing stable yet dynamic states of
being in their ever-shifting processes. Furthermore, when nouns are
used they are marked as animate and inanimate. As biologist Robin
Wall Kimmerer has written, about the very closely related Potowatomi
language, "Rocks are animate, as are mountains and water and fire and
places. Beings that are imbued with spirit, our sacred medicines, our
songs, drums, and even stories, are all animate. The list of the inanimate
seems to be smaller, filled with objects that are made by people. Of an
inanimate being, like a table, we say, 'What is it?' And we answer Dop-
wen yewe. Table it is. But of apple, we must say, 'Who is that being?'
And reply Mshimin yawe. Apple that being is."[31]

A language of animacy builds on the insight that the world is alive
and has an agency of its own. It must therefore be respected. If trees,
mushrooms, otters, and mosquitos are all endowed with agency, then
the scope of our relationships take on different meanings. When we
add the sun, moon, and stars to this list we may start to see and hear
the world in a different way. Each of these forces possesses powers of
communication, which humans can discern if they pay attention to
their larger natural environment and are immersed in this linguistic
and legal tradition for sufficient periods of time. The implications for
resurgence and reconciliation in this context are always present, as long
as ecologically based languages are being spoken, and we take guidance from the earth's functions around us. This methodology provides
access to living resources for reasoning and acting in contemporary circumstances.[32] It reveals further possibilities for reconciliation with one
another and the earth.

Let me illustrate. When my ancestors signed treaties, agreeing to
share millions of acres of land in what is now Ontario,[33] it was to be
"for as long as the sun shines, the rivers flow, and the grass grows."[34] As
treaty terms, as noted, they are constitutionally protected and form part
of Canada's highest laws. Moreover, as discussed, they also flow from
Anishinaabe law, which is rooted in the land itself. In this sense, these
laws bind us all. Indigenous peoples are beneficiaries of the Crown's
promises, and all other Canadians living on treaty lands are beneficiaries of Indigenous peoples' promises. More importantly, both groups
are beneficiaries of the earth's life forces, because we cannot live independently of our ecological relationships. Let me briefly explain these
mutual, ongoing promises, as they relate both to Indigenous resurgence
and our deeper reconciliation with the earth.

Sun – As Long as the Sun Shines – Revitalize Others

"As Long as the Sun Shines": Anishinaabe people call the sun *giizis*. The sun represents light, warmth, heat, and sight: *inaasagewin, waaseyaawin, gizhaatewin, waabamaawin*. The sun stimulates growth. When it shines, it falls on everyone, without discrimination. Its path through the sky represents steadiness and predictability. Its fire kindles life that might otherwise be extinguished. Plants, insects, birds, animals, and humans would not exist without this fire. There are metaphors for life in how the Anishinaabe describe the sun; these descriptions also contain information about how we might analogize the sun's activities to our own.[35] Here was one promise about how we should love together, as explained by the Crown in our treaties: "When your gaze turns towards the rising sun, you shall see that sun rising red – similar to the colour of the coat that I wear. When it rises higher, that same sun shall be very bright with light; [in this] there is the image of the life of your children. After that sun has been up a little longer, you'll see in different places, the flowers bloom. There is the image of the life of your children."[36]

As treaty beneficiaries, we are obligated to apply these legal insights.[37] They are relevant to how we treat others.[38] Like the sun, we are expected to help others grow. We are obligated to practise and apply these laws without discrimination (the sun shines equally on us all). We are taught how to be steady and dependable, as the sun travels through the sky every day. These standards encourage us to revive those who lack vitality, as the sun does through its strength; significantly, they teach us about sustainability.[39] In these promises we are encouraged to imagine ourselves making law and policies by drawing analogies from the sun. If we followed these principles, we would find ourselves implementing Indigenous law as embedded in treaties. In the process we would discover that the resurgence of Indigenous law would help reconcile us to one another and bind ourselves in healthier in relationships with the earth.

Water – As Long as the Rivers Flow – Nourish Those around You

As long as the rivers flow: in Anishinaabemowin, water is *nibi*. Danika Littlechild, a former student of mine taught me: *ni* derives from *niya*, meaning "I" or "I am." *Piy* derives from the word *pimatisiwin*, meaning "life." *Nipiy* is thus properly understood as meaning "I am life."[40] Water is life; it is living. It has an agency and life force of its own. Other countries have found this to be so. New Zealand and India have recently recognized rivers as possessing legal personality. For example, in New Zealand law the Whanganui River through the Te Awa Tupua has all the rights, powers, duties, and liabilities of a legal person,[41] with Te Pou Tupua (the human face of the river), consisting of one Crown representative and one Whanganui iwi representative,[42] responsible for the care and well-being of Te Awa Tupua, in addition to the relationships with Maori iwi and hapū with interests in Te Awa Tupua.[43] These same ideas could be recognized in a Canadian context.

Let me give you an example of how rivers are legal persons and how law can be drawn from water in a Canadian context.[44] In western Toronto lies the place of an ancient council fire, the mouth of the Credit River. Mississauga takes its name from this site: *micha*, meaning "large," and *zaagiin* meaning "river mouth." Mississauga is literally the large river mouth. But *zaagi'* has another meaning – it means "love."[45] *Micha-zaagi* is the place of great love. If you learn about a river mouth through the eyes of Anishinaabe law, you see analogies to a living being who teaches us about love. As such, the personality of rivers can be studied to identify analogies that provide standards about how we should extend our love to others.

In my interactions with Dr Basil Johnston he taught me that love, like a river, should carry sustenance. It should continually flow to sustain those around us. Its currents should be strong and lay down layers of nourishment, as the forces of life course through us and strengthen others. He said that love is about the free flow of support to others, which should be strongest where it meets others. It allows us to fortify those who gather around us. It creates a rich, varied, diverse, and abundant life. He also helped me understand that a river collects nutrients from the surrounding land. It delivers this energy through defined channels at the lake. As a result, river mouths are places of abundance. Plants, medicines, insects, birds, animals, and people thrive in these spaces. Variety and richness mark these places.

In line with Dr Johnston's counsel we could reason by way of analogy from a river's function. In line with these insights we could learn about more love as a binding legal obligation when we analogize human action to a river mouth. Love aims to deliver nourishment and energy through defined channels. Love attempts to create conditions for others to gather and thrive in the social ecosystems that surround us. Love is a flow, with organic consequences for human ecosystems. In these laws love is an aspect of our treaty relationship and is thus necessary to both our resurgence and reconciliation. It is needed now more than ever, and love can be used to strengthen how we act towards one another in ways that bind ourselves more tightly to respecting the earth.

Plants – As Long as the Grass Grows – Live for Our Children's Future

As long as the grass grows: the question that flows from this phrase is, How can we learn law from the grass? One word for grass in Anishinaabemowin is *meyashkooshag*. For the Anishinaabe, grass is medicine. It is *mashkiikii* – the strength of the earth. The earth delivers power to other beings through a plant's veins, roots, stems, branches, and leaves. Emergence allows a plant to draw further life from the sun and water. Anishinaabe lawyer Kekek has told me that *zaagi'bagaa* references energy flows found in budding, emergent leaves.[46] He says, "As a flower begins to bud, the love and beauty inside emerges or casts its self out."[47] This kind of power illustrates the earthbound nature of Anishinaabe law. It is important to recognize the budding and growing of grass as treaty principles that were embedded in the treaty relationship from an Indigenous perspective.

When Anishinaabe observe grass, and they reason together about what it represents, we again find standards for judgment. We need to draw strength from one another and think of law as medicine. Among our other duties to one another is one to act in healing and life-affirming terms. Like the plants, we must find ways to appropriately give ourselves so that others may grow. We must draw others to the sources of healing found in the earth and Indigenous laws around us, and we must do this sustainably. An Anishinaabe chief put it this way, during a treaty council: "You see that sun above us who daily shines to light and warm us, you see those green leaves which open out beneath his rays. You see that grass which clothes the earth, those waters which flow from the high lands towards the sea. Well! Whilst these things live your presents shall live. Can it be that this is forgotten?"[48]

It is now well beyond Canada's 150th year. We have not remembered our promises to learn from the earth and help one another, as we should. We have failed to offer gifts of reciprocity and respect in our relationships. This short explanation of the power of the sun, water, and grass is a reminder to support Indigenous resurgence as a means of reconciling ourselves with one another and the earth. We have not adequately recalled our promises to apply Indigenous law in the place

now called Canada. We must do a better job of remembering and practising the first laws of this country, as embedded in our treaties. A treaty
is about respecting our country and supporting one another.

Indigenous Law, Life Ways, and Cities

So far, we have discussed how Indigenous systems of law could imbue
the natural world with forms of legal personhood.[49] In the process I
have argued that Indigenous laws are best revitalized when they are
rooted in a peoples' longer-term relationship with the earth,[50] and
that the application of Indigenous law is drawn from these enduring
connections.[51]

At the same time, it is important to highlight that it is not always easy
to identify and implement Indigenous law, particularly in a contemporary context. Many of us now live in cities and do not speak Indigenous languages. Cycles of scarcity can also impose themselves in very
intense ways, which can cause us to lose sight of the bigger picture. Seasonal variations in rural and remote settings create uneven conditions
in securing food. Shelter can be precarious when weather is extreme,
and these circumstances mean that many people cannot always eat,
sleep, and play in healthy ways.

Within cities, where Indigenous peoples are overwhelmingly poor,
cycles of scarcity are never far away.[52] When food and shelter are insecure, survival can become a group experience. In these instances, city
life can separate us from the sources of earth-derived law, or – as I will
argue – it can bring some of us closer to its reality. People who live
in insecure ways often develop a heightened awareness of the natural
world, even in urban settings. They realize that humans are not the
measure of all things. They recognize that humans are dependent on
other people, plants, animals, and places to meet their needs and help
others.

City life thus contains another perspective related to environmental
health and safety for those who are more directly subject to the seasons
and their variations, as a result of inadequate shelter and food. Law
could be more fully rooted in these experiences. An enhanced awareness of dispossession could promote another kind of attentiveness
towards the need for reconciliation with one another and the earth. It
could illustrate another kind of interdependence. The need for a healthier relationship with the environment is plain when the ever-shifting
elements lead almost directly to pain, pleasure, waste, or renewal for
many urban Indigenous people.

Indigenous people share at least two general experiences in urban settings that could be drawn upon to highlight the need for environmental and social reconciliation: (1) high rates of social and physical marginalization,[53] and (2) high rates of mobility between the cities and their traditional territories.[54] These experiences can reinforce a sense environmental connection related to the earth. Both accentuate humankind's more tenuous hold on life. Therefore, they can refocus people's attention on our ecological limits.

Poverty and Indigenous Environmental Law

First of all, Indigenous poverty creates a particular kind of political dynamic that shapes a recognizable community in Canada. Poverty generates a unique relationship to the environment. Less than half of off-reserve people are employed, a figure that is almost 15 per cent higher than the unemployment rate of non-Aboriginal people.[55] Income for all Indigenous people is 36 per cent lower than Canadians as a group.[56] High school and university completion rates off-reserve are 15 per cent less than the general population,[57] and Indigenous peoples' city housing is overcrowded and in need of repair.[58] Moreover, health measures are poor and discrimination is a raw fact of life. Racism is also a significant problem for Indigenous people. As a result of their marginalization, Indigenous people do not generally feel invested in systems that create jobs and exploit the earth.[59] They must therefore depend more upon one another and pay more attention to the environmental circumstances that surround them.

These factors combine to forge a collective experience (even though Indigenous peoples have vastly different home cultures). They generate a shared identity, at least on some fronts. While often fraught with tension (as is the case in all human communities), one sees the solidarity Indigenous peoples attempt to forge in Vancouver's Downtown Eastside, and other urban Indigenous settings in western Canada. The Idle No More movement also exemplified the phenomenon of shared Indigenous community in many urban spaces, such as universities, shopping malls, offices, and streets. Indigenous peoples protested anti-environmental actions proposed by the federal government during the winter of 2013. Idle No More was the tip of the iceberg in terms of Indigenous political consciousness.[60] Living on the margins of society fosters unique environmental perspectives and experiences. It can generate deep critiques of consumptive actions that further degrade Indigenous peoples' lives.

In particular, when considering the environment, a homeless person feels the sun, rain, and snow in very direct ways. Food insecurity forces people to be attentive to broader constraints on their food supply. Inadequate shelter creates a keen awareness the elements. The extreme violence fostered by these conditions cause people to live on the edge. First-hand knowledge of cyclical downturns and seasonal changes prepares people to see the world's inherent limits. Poverty generates powerful ecological conditioning factors. It reproduces intimate ecological experiences for many Indigenous people, many of which are unpleasant or worse. Those who are materially poor cannot shield themselves from environmental insecurity and degradation in the same way as those who have greater purchasing power.

At the same time, it must be acknowledged that poverty can lead to cut-throat competition. It can cause people to further degrade their environments in order to survive. Indigenous gangs may be the prime example of this phenomenon, though other forms of social organization in the face of scarcity also present significant challenges. In making this point I hope I am clear that I reject deterministic thinking.[61] So much depends on particular contexts and on how people choose to act and respond within them. Poverty does *not* automatically lead to environmental awareness and the resurgence of Indigenous law. More is needed to accomplish this end. Reconciliation with the earth requires focused work. It must be pursued by and with those who experience environmental alienation, through their impoverished circumstances. Indigenous laws' revitalization requires resources and political/social/economic networks focused on the alleviation of poverty, not for purely consumptive ends, but for peoples' reconnection with the earth.

Mobility and Indigenous Environmental Law

Indigenous life in the city also produces a second set of unique relationships that have implications for the revitalization of Indigenous law.[62] This occurs when Indigenous people connect regularly with their ancestral homelands in large numbers. While parts of Canadian cities might seem like intergenerational Indigenous spaces, the fact is that many people continually cycle back to their homelands.[63] They do this throughout their lives. They might reside on a reserve or rural settlement for months, years, or decades. They may move from the city to be with their families, share the costs of living, and be close to the people and lands they love. As a result of this back-and-forth movement there are very few "ghettos" in Canada; Indian, Metis, and Inuit people do not generally reside in the same "project" where their grandparents and great-grandparents lived.[64] While there are definitely Indigenous areas within Canadian cities (which have existed for decades), the population within these areas is highly mobile. The environmental implication of this movement is significant. It keeps people in touch with families, lands, and life's broader seasonal rounds.

Furthermore, Indigenous nations who are dispossessed from their lands regularly count the cost of their dispossession – including ecological costs borne by their people and territories.[65] They are hypersensitive to negative impacts on their traditional lands, even when they live in the cities. Connections between urban areas and reserves constantly fuel a political dynamic that heightens this environmental awareness. It rekindles their kinship with their wider homelands. When a traditional territory is occupied by other people, Indigenous peoples still feel the land is theirs too.[66] When a river, lake, or aquifer is polluted, this fact is mourned by the traditional owners. The clearing of land for farms and forestry is experienced as the loss of traditional habitat. Opening the earth for mines, oil wells, and other development is usually felt as a desecration of their home by the effected land's original inhabitants.

Thus, Indigenous peoples do not generally feel separated from their traditional territories. As noted, this is true even if they live in a city. This is true even if the Crown secured a so-called surrender of these lands and resources by treaty, and they relocated Indians to reserves or a city. This is because Indigenous languages, economies, and world views are rooted in their homelands, and therefore reject the very idea of surrender. The English treaty language of "cede, surrender, and release" does not extinguish the idea that we will always draw our life from the sun, waters, and plants that shine, flow, and grow on our traditional territories. These environmental relationships are perpetuated through continued mobile occupation of these lands (not only as hunters and fishers, but as they range across their territories' rural/urban divide). Indigenous peoples' personal identification with specific homeland environments has not been erased. Reconnection through rural/urban mobility continually revitalizes these older Indigenous relationships.

This is why Indigenous people regularly count the cost of environment degradation in special ways. When Canadian environments are degraded, somewhere in Canada an Indigenous nation experiences this as destruction of their own homelands. Indigenous peoples have emotional, personal, social, and economic investments in their traditional lands, even though they may have been alienated to other parities. Indigenous lands fuel Indigenous identities. This is why the degradation of Indigenous land can be experienced as a degradation of Indigenous identity. This is why Indigenous peoples often fight pipelines, dams, and mines that threaten to degrade the earth. The continual reoccupation and resettlement of Indigenous reserves, communities, and hamlets heightens this phenomenon and partially explains the rising tides of resurgence.

Indigenous peoples bind themselves to the earth through their mobility. This involves them in local affairs on a national scale. In these instances, they speak about and for their environments at many scales. Unfortunately, they are often thwarted in the process, and the earth often suffers when this occurs. Indigenous peoples are politically marginalized in and by Parliament, legislatures, and municipal councils.[67] However, when they successfully intervene, this leads to laws and policies that are partially shaped by Indigenous peoples themselves, in conflict or cooperation with their neighbours.[68] When Indigenous language, culture, history, and traditional knowledge are respected, standards for judgment are created that protect Indigenous environments. In the process, national or provincial regulations adapt to local circumstances to allow Indigenous legal insights to shine through.

When the cultures, customs, symbols, and traditions of Indigenous peoples form part of Canadian law, this helps to facilitate two kinds of reconciliation: with the earth, and between humans who occupy particular places on that earth. This why reconciliation with the earth is a vital part of Indigenous peoples' reconciliation with other peoples.

I must again stress these very real human processes are not automatic. Indigenous peoples must act consciously towards these ends. They must build on the foregoing realities to continually rediscover that reciprocity, redistribution, hospitality, and hard work are necessary to sustain life. When this occurs, cooperation can be systematized to effectively manage community common goods.[69] But we must always be attentive to how these positive developments are tenuous. Cyclical conditions of abundance and scarcity can also lead to suspicion and harmful competition among Indigenous nations and with the Crown. The environment can be destroyed in the process. At the same time, while conflict and political warfare are facts of life throughout Canada, we must recognize that at some level they are all ultimately facilitated or constrained by the earth.

Life lived at the mercy of the earth can be soul-destroying. A life carefully embedded in nature can also sustain joy. It can foster meaningful connections between people and other environmental forces. Nothing is automatic when humans and nature are intertwined (which is all the time). Indigenous or other peoples display no natural propensity to either nobility or depravity when they are dependent on the earth. The practice of Indigenous law must be directed towards building living systems of thought and practice to reconcile with the earth. As Aaron Mills explains in this volume, rooted Indigenous life ways must flourish if we are to better address the mess in which we find ourselves. Poverty and homeland reconnections can generate knowledge and conditions that incentivize the revitalization of Indigenous laws rooted in specific places throughout Canada, but we have choices about how we act in relation to them.

The point is that living well in the world requires a great deal of work. And it is work of a particular type. Fortunately, Indigenous peoples have long developed practices and principles that inculcate mindfulness and purpose beyond their immediate struggle with their surroundings. These earth-based relationships reveal environment-based laws over which humans have little control. They show us our limits. They help humans see they are not the jurisprudential centre of the universe. Indigenous practices, languages, histories, cultures, and place-based philosophies that recognize and build on these views are keys to reconciliation. When embedded in the law they frequently accentuate an abiding love for the earth.

Indigenous Law and Inherent Limits

As discussed in a previous section, in addition to establishing limits, law must also find ways to embody affection for the earth and our fellow beings.[70] Laws that allow us to develop deeper feelings and mutual aid are needed to appreciate and safeguard our world. Love is a part of our vocabularies. Reciprocity and gift-giving economies are required to address poverty and reserve peoples' alienation from the earth.[71] This interdependence must emphasize intergenerational justice and interpersonal equity. Specifically, it must focus on protecting the vulnerable and those with special needs. Rocks, water, plants, insect, birds, animals, and humans with little social, economic, or political power must be part of this circle of care. Freedom for these ones often requires that we restrain ourselves rather than exploit them as resources for our own selfish purposes. Indigenous peoples' law built on these principles suggests there are inherent limits to our activities. We must find further ways to recognize these limits and to live well within them.

Canadian law has a role to play in this resurgence. In the case of *Tsilhqot'in Nation v British Columbia* the Supreme Court of Canada took a step in this direction. It wrote that Aboriginal title rights were subject to inherent limits with Canada's Constitution. While the idea of inherent limits in Aboriginal land use could be troubling if its sole purpose is to subject Indigenous peoples to the state's paternalistic control, this concept can also be developed to work consistently with Indigenous law. The Supreme Court of Canada wrote that Aboriginal title exists to reconcile current land use with the needs of future generations:

> Aboriginal title, however, comes with an important restriction – it is collective title held not only for the present generation but for all succeeding generations. This means it cannot be alienated except to the Crown or encumbered in ways that would prevent future generations of the group from using and enjoying it. Nor can the land be developed or misused in a way that would substantially deprive future generations of the benefit of the land. Some changes – even permanent changes – to the land may be possible. Whether a particular use is irreconcilable with the ability of succeeding generations to benefit from the land will be a matter to be determined when the issue arises.[72]

The inherent limit in Aboriginal title law exists to protect present and future generations. This limit correlates with self-imposed constraints on certain types of land use found within many Indigenous legal traditions. One prominent limit measures current land use against its impact on the seventh generation.[73] Seventh-generation laws limit land uses that would deny a healthy environment to our great, great, great, great, great, great, great grandchildren. Living within our limits demonstrates affection for our children. It also shows our respect and love for the earth. It is a significant principle of Indigenous law.

The *Tsilhqot'in* decision also holds that activities that harm the present generation's environment are also irreconcilable with Aboriginal title. This limits development in the present generation if it would substantially deprive Indigenous peoples from benefiting from their lands. Since Aboriginal title is constitutionalized, the Crown's activities are limited by Aboriginal title's existence.

As discussed earlier, the principle of inherent limits can also be found within Indigenous treaties.[74] Interdependence and mutuality must be a part of this area of law too.[75] Both Indigenous peoples and the Crown are constrained by them.[76] Treaties must be seen as rooted in particular environments, with the goal of sustainably using ecosystems in ways that preserve Indigenous land-based life.[77] Treaties are also meant to secure healthy, sustainable living for non-Indigenous peoples who subsequently settle on Indigenous lands.[78] Both parties can find environmental benefits flowing from treaty relationships. To enjoy these benefits each party must properly understand how treaties were created.

Treaties are a grant of rights from Indians to the Crown.[79] The Crown is the recipient of land in these arrangements.[80] Land is perpetually vested in the Indians, as first inhabitants, until they give it to other people.[81] The Crown cannot own or govern land in Canada until it receives a grant of such rights from the Indians.[82] Treaties grant the Crown rights to use lands and resources and to set up governing powers.[83] The Crown's rights are limited, because any silence in treaty agreements should be construed as leaving intact all original Indigenous entitlements. This includes the environmentally based ways of relating to the earth embedded in their own practices, customs, and traditions. When interpreted broadly, treaties should be seen as reserving for Indigenous peoples every power of governance, and every resource not explicitly given to the government through these agreements.[84] They should also be regarded as reserving the right and freedom to act in accordance with their environmental stewardships.

Understanding treaties in this light creates two kinds of inherent limits in Canadian law. First, the reserved-rights nature of treaties obviously limits the Crown's ability to claim land or governance without securing Indigenous peoples' consent to exercise these powers. The Supreme Court has written that Aboriginal peoples were not conquered by the Crown.[85] They have also rejected the doctrine of *terra nullius* – the false theory that no one owned the land prior to European arrival.[86] The implication of these views is that the Crown is under an inherent limit not to use or govern Indigenous land until it secures Indigenous agreement. If Indigenous peoples did not explicitly, clearly, and plainly surrender to the Crown their right to live sustainably with the earth, then this right continues to vest in them today.

Second, when treaties were signed, another kind of inherent limit was activated for both Indigenous peoples and the Crown. As the Court wrote in the *Mikisew Cree* case, "The fundamental objective of the modern law of aboriginal and treaty rights is the reconciliation of aboriginal peoples and non-aboriginal peoples and their respective claims, interests and ambitions."[87] For Indigenous peoples the limit is twofold. They promise to the Crown that they will continue to abide by their covenants to live in accordance with their "earth-bound" laws. Further-more, Indigenous peoples limit themselves by agreement to follow the treaty covenants they make with the Crown to live in peace, friendship, and respect. Treaty agreements allow settlers to exercise the powers given to the Crown under treaties in all ways that are consistent with the specific powers assigned to the Crown within these agreements.[88]

If the Crown promised that it would recognize Indians right to "hunt and fish as formerly," then the Crown cannot undertake activities that interfere with their promise – unless they meet a high justificatory standard.[89] Furthermore, if the Crown promised to provide education, health care, or infrastructure to the Indians, this constrains the Crown's discretion in these policy fields – it must forever act to implement these promises "as long as the grass grows, the river flows and the sun shines."[90] As I have argued elsewhere, mutual aid and interdependence underlies these agreements.[91] It is apparent that treaties create mutu-ally binding obligations, which do more than explicitly limit the parties to act in accordance with their particular promises. Treaties are also a mechanism of reconciliation binding each party to act for the benefit of future generations.

In addition, the Crown itself has independent inherent limits on its activities related to Indigenous peoples and the environment. The Supreme Court of Canada has found the Crown's own honour to be an independent source of an inherent limit.[92] Moreover, the Court has found further limits within section 35(1) of Canada's Constitution that require the Crown to justify any infringement of treaty rights.[93] This is because such activities are contrary to the agreements they made with the Indians.[94] These inherent limits to Crown action when dealing with Indigenous environments can help people reconcile with the earth and one another.

The "inherent limit" principle can be reconciled with Indigenous law and could be beneficially extended to other legal traditions. Constitu-tional law, common law, and civil law systems could embrace the idea that inherent limits related to the environment are a basic principle of the rule of law.[95] Law exists to constrain unjust and arbitrary behav-iour.[96] It subjects Parliaments, legislatures, municipal councils, and other elected bodies, not just to the will of the majority, but also to fun-damental organizing principles.[97] Could anything be more fundamen-tal than the environment around which the country is built? Without sustainable environments laws, peace, order, and government could be fatally compromised. In making these points I am arguing here for the resurgence of Canadian law, not just Indigenous law. Canadian law could do a much better job of reconciling us with the earth. The common law and civil law likewise need to undergo a vigorous reorientation in line with constitutional obligations identified in this chapter.

It is even possible to argue that the principle of inherent limits would be appropriate in a corporate context. Accountability to shareholders through shareholder profit is a guiding economic goal of most corporations. A company that "lives beyond its means" and cannot meet limits imposed by creditors will eventually lose market share. In extreme cases it will be declared bankrupt. Corporations operate within the limits.

Indigenous peoples' laws could provide analogies for other institutions, individuals, and legal systems working within limits. As noted, authority, precedent, standards, criteria, and measurements for making such judgments can be found within Indigenous law. While analogies must always compare "like" situations, Indigenous peoples' law was not developed on another planet. While contexts continue to change, these laws are rooted in the ecosystems of places we all occupy within Canada. They can maintain their commitment to environmental protection yet be adapted to contemporary circumstances. There is great wisdom to be found in local laws related to ecosystem health.

International guidance could also be drawn from Indigenous laws' function in certain spheres. The United Nations Declaration on the Rights of Indigenous Peoples contains provisions that emphasize the protection of the environment and the resurgence of Indigenous environmental laws. The Preamble to the declaration recognizes "that respect for indigenous knowledge, cultures and traditional practices contributes to sustainable and equitable development and proper management of the environment."[98] Article 34 states that Indigenous peoples' own laws should be promoted, developed, and maintained in this process. Furthermore, Articles 25–32 contain numerous clauses that highlight the importance of Indigenous peoples' "free and informed consent"[99] if states propose actions that could harm traditional territories and environments.

All this suggests that Indigenous laws' revitalization could help both Indigenous peoples and the neighbours to more productively reconcile themselves with the earth. Law should help us recognize appropriate limits for our activities. It should assist us in finding ways to develop greater affection for one another and the earth. While humans will never fully realize these goals (because life is complex), setting these priorities and working towards them would be an important step in reconciling Indigenous–Crown relationships.

Anishinaabe Law and Reconciliation with the Earth

When I claim that Indigenous law can facilitate Indigenous and Crown reconciliation with the earth (and thus with one another) I have not generally focused on Indian Act bylaws, contemporary self-government agreements, Metis settlements legislation, or Inuit hamlet regulations. While evidence of Indigenous laws' earth-care can be found in these instruments, they are not inherent therein. It takes more than community-based decision-making to revitalize Indigenous legal traditions. State-driven processes, while potentially an aid to better living (because of the measure of accountability and standard setting they may identify), can never create or replace the importance of resurgence and reconciliation in the hearts, minds, and actions of people living in more local contexts. Law is at its strongest when it is internalized and becomes a part of our everyday thinking and practice.

This section of the chapter returns to its earth-bound focus by discussing Anishinaabe principles of reconciliation and revitalization as it relates to our seasonal teachings. In the process it demonstrates that Anishinaabe law deals with inherent limits while also seeking to enhance love for one another and the earth. I will now share one of these teachings.

The Anishinaabe word for spring is *ziigwan*, which comes from the word "to flow." When we are born our blood starts to run on its own. When we leave our mother's womb our lives slip into the stream of time and begin their flow. Many stories within Anishinaabe legal traditions seek to encourage this flow to sustain a young person's healthy growth and development. Anishinaabe people learn these important legal lessons from the environment.

This is a reminder that the Anishinaabe have a word for teaching and learning that expresses this notion – *akinoomaagewin*. It is made of two roots: *aki* and *noomaage*. *Aki* means "earth." *Noomaage* means "to point towards and take direction from." Thus, teaching and learning literally means the lessons we learn from looking to the earth. As we draw analogies from our surroundings and appropriately apply or distinguish what we see, we learn about how we should live in our surroundings. The earth has a culture and we can learn from it. We must be reconciled to it.

There is a time in the early Ontario spring when cold and warm air masses intermingle, causing fine mists to rise over the earth. The word used to describe this phenomenon is *aabawaa,* which means "warm and mild."[100] At these moments winter starts to loosen her grip on the land. The snows melt, and waters start to flow. Sap can begin running through the trees as nature prepares to nurture new life. Interestingly, the Anishinaabe word for forgiveness is related to this moment; the word for forgiveness is *aabawaawendam.* Thus, forgiveness can be analogized to loosening one's thoughts towards others; to letting relationships flow more easily, with fewer restrictions. Forgiveness is a state of being warmer and milder towards another; it signifies a warming trend in a relationship. Notice that forgiveness, like the clearing of early spring mists, does not occur in an instant. Heat and the warmth need to be applied through a sustained period of time for mists to clear. Clarity of vision takes a while to develop; time is often needed to "clear the air" and bring fairer views.

There are other examples, from other seasons, about how to live well in the world. I love these seasonal teachings. For example, our word for summer is *niibin,* which is from the word *niibina* and means "plenty." This conveys expectations about how we should live as teenagers and young adults; we are encouraged to grow and draw from the richness around us.

The Ojibway word for fall is *tikwaagi* and derives from the word *tikayaa,* meaning "cool." As we reach late adulthood, the autumn of our lives, we are encouraged to draw less from the world. Growth slows, and we are encouraged to prepare for a period of sustained reflection and observation. If we live by this guidance we can become elders, or those who know and live the laws with sufficient depth that they are regarded as authoritative.

Finally, the Ojibway word for winter is *biiboon* and comes from the words *abi,* which means "here," and *boon,* which means "where growth is suspended." Thus, winter describes what happens as we die, physically our growth is suspended for a season. But this relates only to our physical bodies; our souls travel onward.

These laws could be taken to apply to an entire lifetime, but they could also relate to how we should pattern our lives each and every single day:

1) As we wake and experience a flowing of energy (*ziigwan*), we are almost like young children in these moments, as our eyes open to the new day around us.

2) During most of our day we partake of and develop practices that build on nature's plenty; we are in a period of sustained and rapid growth (*niibin*). We are like youth and adults in this long, sustained period of our day.

3) Then, it is evening. As we retire for the day, we slow down as the twilight lingers (*tikwaagi*). At this time of day, we are somewhat like those who have already raised their children but still have much to learn, as we reflect on what has happened during the long growing days. Now, at the end of the day, we are at the evening of our life.

4) Finally, a certain kind of suspension occurs as we sleep every night (*biiboon*). Before we sleep, we may find ourselves being like the elders, who leave behind what they learned for the next generation – these "bedtime" stories from elders are the ones I treasure the most.

In this way, we live a year in each day. Our years are days, and our days are years. No matter when we leave this earth, we can say we have lived an entire life, an entire change of the seasons.

We can learn how to see and read the stars – *kikoonoomo-waabandakwewin*. The rocks, waters, and lands are our companions and teachers on this journey, as they swirl through the seasons; they are inscribed with the lessons of the ages.

Life is built upon the rocks. They serve as hosts to moss, lichen, mushrooms, ivies, ferns, grasses, orchids, birches, beeches, pines, cedars, maples, and the occasional oak. Beetles, aphids, spiders, slugs, mosquitos, and hundreds of small insects live on the small organic organisms pressed into this niche. These small ones, called *manidooshensuk* (or "little spirits") nourish other lives around them. Herring, crayfish, leeches, perch, bass, pick, whitefish, trout, and sturgeon feast on airborne and aquatic insects. They also help feed their larger winged relatives, such as the sparrows, wrens, finches, vultures, hawks, eagles, and thunderbirds that fill the air around our home. Of course, they are also connected to their terrestrial relatives – the mice, weasels, otters, raccoons, porcupines, deer, bears, etc. The plants, birds, and animals are also the clans of the Anishinaabe. They are our relatives. I especially pay attention to the *otterm-nindoodem;* they are my kin and have special things to teach me. These are the relationships that make up our homelands. They help me begin to glimpse aspects of our shared responsibilities on this earth.

Conclusion

Reconciliation between Indigenous peoples and the Crown requires our collective reconciliation with the earth. Practices and partnerships of resurgence and reconciliation must sustain the living earth and our more-than-human relatives for future generations. This will not occur without the simultaneous resurgence of Indigenous laws, governments, economies, education, relations to the living earth, ways of knowing and being, and treaty relationships. Such an "approach always becomes a social approach; it must integrate questions of justice in debates on the environment, so as to hear both the cry of the earth and the cry of the poor."[101] A Pope Francis has observed, "We cannot presume to heal our relationship with nature and the environment without healing all fundamental human relationships."[102] This brief chapter has attempted to show how these relationships can be better cultivated to create stronger bonds with one another and the earth. We are earthbound, and our laws and practices must be revitalized to recognize and respond to this vital fact.

NOTES

1 Jim Tully, this volume; Truth and Reconciliation Commission of Canada, *Honouring the Truth, Reconciling for the Future: Summary of the Final Report of the Truth and Reconciliation Commission of Canada* (Winnipeg: Truth and Reconciliation Commission of Canada, 2015), 18.

2 John Borrows, *Recovering Canada: The Resurgence of Indigenous Law* (Toronto: University of Toronto Press, 2002); Kiera L. Ladner, "Governing within an Ecological Context: Creating an AlterNative Understanding of Blackfoot Governance," *Studies in Political Economy* 70 (2003): 125; Gregory Cajete, *Native Science: Natural Laws of Interdependence* (Santa Fe, NM: Clear Light Publishers, 2000).

3 Jeff Hewitt, "Reconsidering Reconciliation: The Long Game," *Supreme Court Law Review* 67 (2014): 259–87.

4 Susanna Quail, "Yah'guudang: The Principle of Respect in the Haida Legal Tradition," *UBC Law Review* 47 (2014): 673; Winona LaDuke, "Traditional Ecological Knowledge and Environmental Futures," *Colorado Journal of International Environmental Law and Policy* 5 (1994): 127; Julie Cruikshank, *Do Glaciers Listen? Local Knowledge, Colonial Encounters, and*

Social Imagination (Vancouver: University of British Columbia Press, 2005); William Robinson, as told by Walter Wright, *Men of Medeek*, 2nd ed. (Kitimat, BC: Northern Sentinel, 1962); Jo-Anne Fiske and Betty Patrick, *Cis Dideen Kat (When the Plumes Rise): The Way of the Lake Babine Nation* (Vancouver: University of British Columbia Press, 2000).

5 An excellent discussion of stereotypes in relation to Indigenous peoples is found in Wayne Warry, *Ending Denial: Understanding Aboriginal Issues* (Toronto: University of Toronto Press, 2008). For views about Aboriginal environmental images more generally, see Benjamin Richardson, "The Ties That Bind: Indigenous Peoples and Environmental Governance," in *Indigenous Peoples and the Law: Comparative and Critical Perspectives*, ed. Benjamin J. Richardson, Shin Imai, and Kent McNeil, 3–20 (Oxford, UK: Hart Publishing, 2009).

6 For a discussion of environmental challenges created by Indigenous peoples, see Robert Edgerton, *Sick Societies: Challenging the Myth of Primitive Harmony* (Toronto: Maxwell Macmillan Canada, 1992); Jared Diamond, *Germs, Guns and Steel: The Fate of Human Societies* (New York: W.W. Norton, 1997); Jared Diamond, *Collapse: How Societies Choose to Fail or Succeed* (New York: Viking, 2006), 77–177.

7 G.H. Brundtland and World Commission on Environment and Development, *Our Common Future* (Oxford: World Commission on Environment and Development, 1987), chapter 1.

8 Ways Indigenous peoples have worked to attenuate their impact on the earth are discussed in Donald Hughes, *American Indian Ecology* (El Paso: Texas Western Press, 1983); Hugh Brody, *Maps and Dreams* (Toronto: Douglas & McIntyre, 1992); Janis Alcorn, *Huastec Mayan Ethnobotany* (Austin: University of Texas Press, 1984); Robin Riddington, *Little Bit Know Something* (Vancouver: Douglas & McIntyre, 1990); Chris Vescey and Robert Venables, eds, *American Indian Environments: Ecological Issues in Native American History* (Syracuse, NY: Syracuse University Press, 1980).

9 Mathis Wackernagel and William Rees, *Our Ecological Footprint: Reducing Human Impact on the Earth* (Gabriola Island, BC: New Society Publishers, 1996).

10 Sheila Fraser, *Fall Report of the Auditor General of Canada* (Ottawa: Office of the Auditor General, 2009), chapter 6: "Land Management and Environmental Protection on Reserves," http://www.oag-bvg.gc.ca/internet/English/parl_oag_200911_06_e_33207.html; Julian Agyeman, Peter Cole, Randolph Haluza-DeLay, and Pat O'Riley, eds, *Speaking for Ourselves: Environmental Justice in Canada* (Vancouver: UBC Press, 2009).

   For a particular example, see Dayna Nadine Scott, "The Quest for Environmental Justice on a Canadian Aboriginal Reserve," in *Environment,*

Law and Poverty, ed. Yves Le Bouthillier, Miriam Alfie Cohen, Jose Juan Gonzalez, Albert Mumma, and Susan Smith (Cheltenham, UK: Edward Elgar, 2012).

11 David Boyd, *Unnatural Law: Rethinking Canadian Environmental Law and Policy* (Vancouver: UBC Press, 2003), 211–90.

12 Isabel Altamirano-Jiménez, *Indigenous Encounters with Neoliberalism: Place, Women and the Environment in Canada and Mexico* (Vancouver: UBC Press, 2013).

13 Shepard Kresh III, *The Ecological Indian: Myth and History* (New York: W.W. Norton, 1999); Calvin Martin, *Keepers of the Game: Indian–Animal Relationships and the Fur Trade* (Los Angeles: University of Los Angeles Press, 1982).

14 Some of these issues are canvassed in David Rich Lewis, "Native Americans and the Environment: A Survey of 20th Century Issues," *American Indian Quarterly* 19 (1995): 423; Traci Brynne Voyles, *Wastelanding: Legacies of Uranium Mining in Navajo Country* (Minneapolis: University of Minnesota Press, 2015); Martin Nie, "Governing the Tongass: National Forest Conflict and Decision Making," *Environmental Law* 36 (2006): 398–9; Noriko Ishiyama and Kimberly Tallbear, "Changing Notions of Environmental Justice in the Decision to Host a Nuclear Fuel Storage Facility on the Skull Valley Goshute Reservation," Waste Management 2001 Symposium, Session 51: Equity and Environmental Justice, http://www.iiirm.org/publications/Articles%20Reports%20Papers/Environmental%20Justice/ChangingNot.pdf.

15 Examples of the passage of Indigenous environmental knowledge are found in Colin Scott, "Ontology and Ethics in Cree Hunting: Animism, Totemism and Practical Knowledge," in *The Handbook of Contemporary Animism*, ed. Graham Harvey, 159–66 (Durham, UK: Acumen, 2013); Fikret Berkes, *Sacred Ecology: Traditional Ecological Knowledge and Resource Management* (Philadelphia, PA: Taylor & Francis, 1999); Robert Brighton, *Grateful Prey: Rock Cree Human-Animal Relations* (Berkeley: University of California Press, 1993); Antonia Mills, *Eagle Down Is Our Law: Witsuwit'en Feasts and Land Claims* (Vancouver: UBC Press, 1994), 122; Mariano Aupilaarjuk, Marie Tulimaaq, Emile Imaruittuq, Lucassie Nutaraaluk, and Akisu Joamie, *Interviewing Inuit Elders*. Vol. 2, *Perspectives on Traditional Law*, edited by Jarich Oosten, Frédéric Laugrand, and Wim Rasing (Iqaluit: Nunavut Arctic College, 1999).

16 An example is provided in Nancy Turner, Marianne Ignace, and Ronald Ignace, "Traditional Ecological Knowledge and Wisdom of Aboriginal Peoples in British Columbia," *Ecological Applications* 5 (2000): 1275.

17 Wendy Geniusz, *Our Knowledge Is Not Primitive: Decolonizing Botanical Anishinaabe Teachings* (New York: Syracuse University Press, 2009); Nancy Turner, *Ancient Pathways, Ancestral Knowledge: Ethnobotany and Ecological Wisdom of Indigenous People of Northwestern North America* (Montreal and Kingston: McGill-Queen's University Press, 2014); Robin Wall Kimmerer, *Braiding Sweetgrass: Indigenous Wisdom, Scientific Knowledge, and the Teachings of Plants* (Minneapolis: Milkweed Editions, 2013); Winona LaDuke, *All Our Relations: Native Struggles for Land and Life* (Cambridge, MA: South End, 1999).

18 See, generally, Michael Harkin and David Rich Lewis, *Native Americans and the Environment: Perspectives on the Ecological Indian* (Lincoln: University of Nebraska Press, 2007).

19 See the activities of the Coastal Stewardship Network at coastalguardianwatchmen.ca. The Haida efforts are discussed in Ian Gill, *All That We Say Is Ours: Guujaaw and the Reawakening of the Haida Nation* (Toronto: Douglas & McIntyre, 2009); and see Louise Takeda, *Islands' Spirit Rising: Reclaiming the Forests of Haida Gwaii* (Vancouver: UBC Press, 2015). The use of Anishinaabe laws and values is discussed in Clinton Beckford, Clint Jacobs, Naomi Williams, and Russell Nahdee, "Aboriginal Environmental Wisdom, Stewardship and Sustainability: Lessons from the Walpole Island First Nations, Ontario, Canada," *Journal of Environmental Education* 41 (2010): 239.

20 For discussions of these methodologies more generally, see Keith Basso, *Wisdom Sits in Places: Landscape and Language among the Western Apache* (Albuquerque: University of New Mexico Press, 1996); Gregory Cajete, *Look to the Mountain: An Ecology of Indigenous Education* (Durango, CO: Kivaki, 1994).

21 *Delgamuukw v British Columbia*, [1997] 3 SCR 1010 at paras 125–32.

22 Robert Williams Jr, *Linking Arms Together: American Indian Treaty Visions of Law and Peace 1600–1800* (Oxford: Oxford University Press, 1997).

23 Privately owned land can be subject to mortgages, leases, liens, easements, zoning regulations, expropriation orders, taxation, treaty rights, contractual obligations, and other statutory, common law, and equitable limitations. See Bruce Ziff, *Principles of Property Law*, 6th ed. (Toronto: Carswell, 2014). Limitations in Canadian property law more generally are discussed in John Borrows, "Aboriginal Title and Private Property," *Supreme Court Law Review* 68 (2015): 91.

24 *R v Badger*, [1996] 1 SCR 771 paras 40–1; *R v Marshall*, [1999] 3 SCR 456 paras 57–61; *R v Marshall; R v Bernard*, [2005] 2 SCR 220 paras 15–16; *R v Morris*, [2006] 2 SCR 915 paras 35–40.

25 *Haida Nation v British Columbia* [2004] 3 SCR 511 at para 48.

26 *R v Sparrow*, [1990] SCJ No 49, 70 DLR (4th) 385 at 409:

> Federal legislative powers continue, including, of course, the
> right to legislate with respect to Indians pursuant to s 91(24) of
> the *Constitution Act, 1867*. These powers must, however, now be
> read together with s. 35(1). In other words, federal power must
> be reconciled with federal duty and the best way to achieve that
> reconciliation is to demand the justification of any governmental
> regulation that infringes upon or denies aboriginal rights. Such
> scrutiny is in keeping with the liberal interpretive principles
> enunciated in *Nowegijick* and the concept of holding the Crown to a
> high standard of honourable dealing with respect to the aboriginal
> peoples of Canada as suggested by *Guerin*.

27 Article 46 of the United Nations Declaration on the Rights of Indigenous
Peoples reads:

> 1. Nothing in this Declaration may be interpreted as implying for any
> State, people, group or person any right to engage in any activity or
> to perform any act contrary to the Charter of the United Nations or
> construed as authorizing or encouraging any action which would
> dismember or impair, totally or in part, the territorial integrity or
> political unity of sovereign and independent States.
>   2. In the exercise of the rights enunciated in the present Declaration,
> human rights and fundamental freedoms of all shall be respected. The
> exercise of the rights set forth in this Declaration shall be subject only
> to such limitations as are determined by law and in accordance with
> international human rights obligations. Any such limitations shall be
> non-discriminatory and strictly necessary solely for the purpose of
> securing due recognition and respect for the rights and freedoms of
> others and for meeting the just and most compelling requirements of a
> democratic society.
>   3. The provisions set forth in this Declaration shall be interpreted in
> accordance with the principles of justice, democracy, respect for human
> rights, equality, non-discrimination, good governance and good faith.

28 Alfred Taiaiake and Jeff Corntassel, "Being Indigenous: Resurgences
against Contemporary Colonialism," *Government & Opposition* 40 (2005):
597–614; Joshua Nichols, "A Reconciliation without Recollection: An

Investigation of the Foundations of the Indian Act" (PhD diss., University of Victoria, 2017).

29 Anishinaabe people are the fourth-largest tribal group in North America, after the Navajo, Cherokee, and Lakota nations. They live within the Great Lakes watershed, surrounding, in large part, Lakes Superior, Huron, and Michigan and occupying the farmlands and woodlands north of Lake Ontario and Lake Erie. They also have reservations in the forests and prairies of Manitoba, northern Minnesota, and North Dakota; see Helen Hornbeck Tanner, *Atlas of Great Lakes Indian History* (Norman, OK: University of Oklahoma Press, 1982), 58–9; Diamond Jenness, *The Indians of Canada* (Ottawa: Queen's Printer, 1967), 277.

30 Sakej Henderson, "Mikmaw Tenure in Atlantic Canada," *Dalhousie Law Journal* 18 (1995): 220–1.

31 Robin Wall Kimmerer, "Learning the Grammar of Animacy," *Anthropology of Consciousness* 28 (2017): 128–34.

32 I am not a fluent speaker of Anishinaabemowin, though I can teach beginners how to start their learning journey. Despite my limitations, decades of study have taught me that a linguistic focus on verbs and animacy, connected to the living world, make a tremendous difference to working with law.

33 For greater detail, see John Borrows, "A Genealogy of Law: Inherent Sovereignty and First Nations Self-Government" (1992) 30 *Osgoode Hall Law Journal* 30 (1992): 291.

34 For a discussion of this concept in law, see Charles Wilkinson and John Volkman, "Judicial Review of Indian Treaty Abrogation: As Long as Water Flows, or Grass Grows upon the Earth – How Long a Time Is That?," *California Law Review* 63 (1975): 601. An early use of a similar phrase is found in a treaty made by William Penn with the Conestoga in 1701; see Kevin Kenny, *Peaceable Kingdom Lost: The Paxton Boys and the Destruction of William Penn's Holy Experiment* (New York: Oxford University Press, 2009), 15: "as long as the Sun and Moon shall endure." Benjamin Franklin reported this treaty as saying, "as long as the sun shall shine, or the waters run in the rivers," in Jared Sparks, ed., *The Works of Benjamin Franklin: Autobiography*, pt. 2 (T. MacCoun, 1882). Other associations between treaties and the phrase are found in Harold Cardinal and Walter Hildebrandt, *Treaty Elders of Saskatchewan: Our Dream Is That Our Peoples Will One Day Be Clearly Recognized as Nations* (Calgary: University of Calgary Press, 2000), 20; Treaty 7 elders and Tribal Council with Walter Hildebrandt, Sarah Carter, and Dorothy First Rider, *The True Spirit and Original Intent of Treaty 7* (Montreal and Kingston: McGill-Queen's

University Press, 1996), 133; Rene Fumoleau, *As Long as This Land Shall Last: A History of Treaty 8 and 11* (Toronto: McClelland and Stewart, 1976), 74, 133, 240, 257, 314, 340, 502; Arthur Ray, J.R. Miller, and Frank Tough, *Bounty and Benevolence: A History of Saskatchewan Treaties* (Montreal and Kingston: McGill-Queen's University Press, 2000), 116–17.

35 For example, when Alexander Morris proposed Treaty 6 he said, "What I trust and hope we will do is not for today or tomorrow only; what I promise and what I believe and hope you will take, is to last as long as that sun shines and yonder river flows." Alexander Morris, *The Treaties of Canada with the Indians of Manitoba and the North-West Territories, Including the Negotiations on Which They Were Based, and Other Information Relating Thereto* (Saskatoon: Fifth House Publishers, 1991), 202; see similar words in relation to Treaty 3 on 51. This phrase was also used in an 1818 treaty with the Ojibway; see J.R. Miller, *Compact, Contract, Covenant: Aboriginal Treaty-Making in Canada* (Toronto: University of Toronto Press, 2009), 101.

36 Manitoulin Island Chiefs, 27 June 1862: LAC, RG 10, vol. 292, reel C-12 669, file 195683–7; LAC, RG 10, vol. 292, 195678–82.

37 For example, see Deanna Christensen, *Atahkakoop: The Epic Account of a Plains Cree Head Chief, His People, and Their Struggle for Survival, 1816–1896* (Shell Lake, SK: Ahtahkakoop Publishing, 2000), 5–14, for a brief discussion of laws related to the sun, waters, and earth.

38 For an extended discussion of these principles, see chapter 1 of John Borrows, *Law's Indigenous Ethics* (Toronto: University of Toronto Press, forthcoming).

39 "Look towards the rising sun, my Nation is as brilliant as it and its word cannot be violated," Minutes of a council held at Drummond Island, 7 July 1818, LAC, RG 10, vol. 35, C-11011, 20381–8.

40 Danika Billie Littlechild, "Transformation and Re-Formation: First Nations and Water in Canada" (LLM thesis: University of Victoria, 2014), 19, 20, 24.

41 *Te Awa Tupua (Whanganui River Claims Settlement) Bill.*

42 "Whanganui iwi" is defined in clause 8 of the bill as every individual who has exercised customary rights and responsibilities in respect to Whanganui River and is descended from Ruatipua, Paerangi, or Haunui-ā-Pāpārangi. It also includes the hapū and tūpuna rohe groups of Whanganui iwi.

43 *Te Awa Tupua (Whanganui River Claims Settlement) Bill,* ss. 18 and 19.

44 Information is this paragraph is also found in Arthur Schfar and Steven Lecce, eds, *Indigenous Love, Law and Land in Canada's Constitution* (London: Oxford University Press, 2016).

45 Anishinaabe language professor and linguist Brenda Fairbanks explained
   the technical meaning of these words as follows (person correspondence
   17 January 2014):

   Zaagiing and *zaagi'idiwin* are based upon two different roots and are not
   related.
      zaag- "out, stick out"
      zaagi'- "stingy"
      zaagikweni "sticks his head out," for example, for root *zaag-*.
   Zaagi' has replaced the old word *dabaan* for "love" for many Ojibwe
   dialects but remains in some and in other related languages like
   Kickapoo and meskwaki. But *zaagi'* and *zaagitoon* are words for "be
   stingy with him" and "be stingy with it" and are unrelated to *zaagiing*.
      Though these two roots look alike, they are not the same and not
   usually considered to be related. In Ojibwe, similarity in look does not
   indicate degree of relatedness.

46 My special thanks to Jason Stark, Kekek, for reminding me of some of these
   teachings and bringing others to my attention for the first time. Miigwech.
47 Jason Stark.
48 In the 1850s Chief Shingwaukonse said, "Father – We heard your words +
   we believed when you said, 'You see that sun above us who daily shines
   to light and warm us, you see those green leaves which open out beneath
   his rays. You see that grass which clothes the earth, those waters which
   flow from the high lands towards the sea. Well! Whilst these things
   live your presents shall live.' Can it be that this is forgotten?," in The
   Speeches of Mo.ko.ma.nish, Wa.ka.ow.se, Chinguakonse, 7 August 1852,
   Manitowaning. LAC, RG 10, vol. 621a, 107.
49 See John Borrows, "Living between Water and Rocks: First Nations,
   Environmental Planning and Democracy," *University of Toronto Law Journal*
   47, no. 4 (1997): 417.
50 Examples of these relationships are found in Jace Weaver, ed., *Defending
   Mother Earth: Native American Perspectives on Environmental Justice* (New
   York: Orbis Books, 1996); Ron Trosper, *Resilience, Reciprocity and
   Ecological-Economics: Northwest Coast Sustainability* (London: Routledge,
   2011); Nancy Turner, *The Earth's Blanket: Traditional Teachings for Sustainable
   Living* (Vancouver: Douglas & MacIntyre, 2005).
51 An excellent example is found on the west coast of Vancouver Island
   in Canada; see Richard Atleo, *Tsawalk: A Nuu-chah-nulth Worldview*
   (Vancouver: UBC Press, 2004); Richard Atleo, *Principles of Tsawalk: An
   Indigenous Approach to Global Crisis* (Vancouver: UBC Press, 2011).

52 Peter Dinsdale, Jerry White, and Calvin Hanselmann, eds, *Urban Aboriginal Communities in Canada: Complexities, Challenges, Opportunities* (Toronto: Thompson, 2011).

53 National Aboriginal Economic Development Board, *Aboriginal Economic Progress Report, 2015* (Gatineau: National Aboriginal Economic Development Board, 2015), http://www.naedb-cndea.com/reports/NAEDB-progress-report-june-2015.pdf.

54 John Borrows, *Freedom and Indigenous Constitutionalism* (Toronto: University of Toronto Press, 2016), chap. 1.

55 National Aboriginal Economic Development Board, *Aboriginal Economic Progress Report 2015*, 15.

56 Ibid., 19.

57 Ibid., 26–9.

58 Ibid., 41–2.

59 Again, I am not arguing that Indigenous peoples would not engage in development that has severe environmental impacts, just because they are native to a place. By and large Indigenous people do not have access to capital for these purposes. Nevertheless, while there are notable exceptions in this regard (Navajo, Hopi, Tsimshian, Tlingit, etc.), Indigenous peoples do not generally create the conditions to develop large-scale development projects that pollute, degrade, and contaminate the environment.

60 Kino-nda-niimi Collective, *The Winter We Danced: Voices from the Past, the Future, and the Idle No More Movement* (Winnipeg: Arb, 2014).

61 This is the thesis of my book *Freedom and Indigenous Constitutionalism* (Toronto: University of Toronto Press, 2016).

62 The unique circumstances of Indigenous peoples in Canada is discussed in Evelyn Peters and Chris Andersen, eds, *Indigenous in the City: Contemporary Identities and Cultural Innovation* (Vancouver: UBC Press, 2013).

63 Evelyn J. Peters, *Urban Aboriginal Policy Making in Canadian Municipalities* (Montreal and Kingston: McGill-Queen's University Press, 2012).

64 Evelyn Peters, "Three Myths about Aboriginals in Cities," Breakfast on the Hill Seminar Series, Canadian Federation for the Humanities and Social Sciences, Ottawa, 25 March 2004 (Ottawa: Canadian Federation for the Humanities and Social Sciences, 2004).

65 Yale Belanger and P. Whitney Lackenbauer, eds, *Blockades of Breakthroughs: Aboriginal Peoples Confront the Canadian State* (Montreal and Kingston: McGill-Queen's University Press, 2015).

66 Nicholas Blomley, "Shut the Province Down: First Nations Blockades in British Columbia, 1984–1995," *BC Studies* 111 (1996): 5–35; Laura Devries, *Conflict in Caledonia: Aboriginal Rights and the Rule of Law* (Vancouver: UBC Press, 2012); Leanne Simpson and Kiera Ladner, eds, *This Is an Honour*

Song: Twenty Years since the Blockades (Winnipeg: Arbeiter Ring, 2010); Harry Swain, *Oka: A Political Crisis and Its Legacy* (Toronto: Douglas & McIntyre, 2010).

67 Harold Cardinal, *The Unjust Society: The Tragedy of Canada's Indians* (Edmonton: Hurtig, 1969); Boyce Richardson, ed., *Drum Beat: Anger and Renewal in Indian Country* (Ottawa: Summerhill, 1989); Glen Coulthard, *Red Skin, White Masks: Rejecting the Colonial Politics of Recognition* (Minneapolis: University of Minnesota Press, 2014).

68 John Borrows, *Canada's Indigenous Constitution* (Toronto: University of Toronto Press, 2010).

69 Elinor Ostrom, *Governing the Commons: The Evolution of Institutions for Collective Action* (New York: Cambridge University Press, 1990).

70 John Borrows, "Indigenous Love, Law and Land in Canada's Constitution," in *Fragile Freedoms: Human Rights in Global Context*, ed. Arthur Schfar and Steven Lecce, 123–66 (London: Oxford University Press, 2017).

71 Dara Kelly, "An Ethic of Reciprocity: Illuminating Stó:lō Gift Economy," in *Indigenous Spiritualities at Work: Transforming the Spirit of Business Enterprise*, ed. C. Spiller and R. Wolfgramm (Charlotte, NC: Information Age Publishing, 2015).

72 *Tsilhqot'in Nation v British Columbia*, 2014 SCC 44, [2014] 2 SCR 256 at para 74.

73 Barry S. Gower, "What Do We Owe Future Generations?," in *The Environment in Question: Ethics and Global Issues*, ed. David Cooper and Joy Palmer (New York: Routledge, 1992). I have discussed the issue of seven generations more fully in John Borrows, "Seven Generations, Seven Teachings: Ending the Indian Act," research paper for the National Centre for First Nations Governance, 2008, http://fngovernance.org/resources_docs/7_Generations_7_Teachings.pdf.

74 Sakej Henderson, "Empowering Treaty Federalism," *Saskatchewan Law Review* 58 (1994): 241.

75 Michael Asch, *On Being Here to Stay: Treaties and Aboriginal Rights in Canada* (Toronto: University of Toronto Press, 2014).

76 *Beckman v Little Salmon/Carmacks First Nation*, 2010 SCC 53 at para 10:

The reconciliation of Aboriginal and non-Aboriginal Canadians in a mutually respectful long-term relationship is the grand purpose of s 35 of the *Constitution Act, 1982*. The modern treaties, including those at issue here, attempt to further the objective of reconciliation not only by addressing grievances over the land claims but by creating the legal basis to foster a positive long-term relationship between Aboriginal and non-Aboriginal communities. Thoughtful administration of the treaty will help manage, even if it fails to eliminate, some of the misunderstandings and grievances that have characterized the past. Still, as the facts of this case show, the treaty will not accomplish its purpose if it is interpreted by territorial officials in an ungenerous manner or as if it were an everyday commercial contract. The treaty is as much about building relationships as it is about the settlement of ancient grievances. The future is more important than the past. A canoeist who hopes to make progress faces forwards, not backwards.

77 This was the conclusion in *Saanichton Marina Ltd v Claxton*, [1989] CanLII 2721 (BCCA).
78 Office of the Treaty Commissioner, *Treaty Implementation: Fulfilling the Covenant* (Saskatoon: OTC, 2007).
79 *United States v Winans* 198 US 371 (1905).
80 John Borrows, "Ground Rules: Indigenous Treaties in Canada and New Zealand," *New Zealand Universities Law Journal* 22 (2006): 188.
81 This is one of the meanings of *reserve* in Canadian law; see *Delgamuukw v British Columbia*, [1997] 3 SCR 1010 at para 120.
82 John Borrows, "Wampum at Niagara: The Royal Proclamation, Canadian Legal History, and Self-Government," in *Aboriginal and Treaty Rights in Canada*, ed. Michael Asch (Vancouver: UBC Press, 1997), 155.
83 Aimee Craft, *Breathing Life into the Stone Fort Treaty: An Anishinaabe Understanding of Treaty One* (Saskatoon: Purich Publishing, 2013).
84 The canons of treaty construction in Canadian law dictate that the treaties must be given a large, liberal, and generous perspective, and be interpreted as Indians would naturally understand them; see *R v White and Bob*, (1964) 50 DLR (2d) 613 (BCCA); aff'd (1965) 52 DLR (2d) 481n; *R v Taylor and Williams* (1981) 34 OR (2d) 360 (Ont CA); *R v Simon* (1985) 24 DLR (4th) 390; *R v Horseman*, [1990] 1 SCR 901 at 907; *R v Badger*, [1996] 1 SCR 771 at paras 4 and 41; *R v Sundown*, [1999] 1 SCR 393 (SCC) at paras 24–5; *R v Marshall*, [1999] 3 SCR 456 at paras 9–14, 19; *R v Marshall, R v Bernard*, [2005] 2 SCR 220 at para 26; *R. v Morris*, [2006] 2 SCR 915 at paras 18–19.
85 *Haida Nation v British Columbia (Minister of Forests)*, [2004] 3 SCR 511 at para 25: "Put simply, Canada's Aboriginal peoples were here when Europeans came, and were never conquered."

86 *Tsilhqot'in Nation v British Columbia*, [2014] SCC 44 at para 69: "The doctrine of terra nullius (that no one owned the land prior to European assertion of sovereignty) never applied in Canada."

87 *Mikisew Cree First Nation v Canada (Minister of Canadian Heritage)*, [2005] 3 SCR 388 at para 1.

88 Crown limits are found in what they pledged to do for the Indians and in relation to their lands within the treaties.

89 *R v Sparrow*, 1 SCR 1075 at 1109.

90 Wilkinson and Volkman, "Judicial Review of Indian Treaty Abrogation," 601; Cardinal and Hildebrandt, *Treaty Elders of Saskatchewan*, 20; Treaty 7 elders and Tribal Council et al., *True Spirit and Original Intent of Treaty 7*, 133; Fumoleau, *As Long as This Land Shall Last*, 74, 133, 240, 257, 314, 340, 502; Ray, Miller, and Tough, *Bounty and Benevolence*, 116–17. For a contrary view about questioning this relationship of this phrase to treaties see Sharon Venne, "Understanding Treaty Six: An Indigenous Perspective," in *Aboriginal and Treaty Rights in Canada: Essays on Law, Equality, and Respect for Difference*, ed. Michael Asch (Vancouver: UBC Press, 1997), 194.

91 John Borrows, "Let Obligations Be Done," in *The Calder Case*, ed. J. Webber, H. Foster, and H. Raven (Vancouver: University of British Columbia Press, 2007).

92 *Haida Nation v British Columbia* 2004 SCC 73, at para 27.

93 L.I. Rotman, "Defining Parameters: Aboriginal Rights, Treaty Rights, and the *Sparrow* Justificatory Test," *Alberta Law Review* 36 (1997): 149.

94 *Mikisew Cree First Nation v Canada (Minister of Canadian Heritage)*, [2005] 3 SCR 388 at para 54.

95 Failure to embrace the rule of law in relation to Indigenous peoples is discussed in Andrew Orkin, "When the Law Breaks Down: Aboriginal Peoples in Canada and Governmental Defiance of the Rule of Law," *Osgoode Hall Law Journal* 41 (2003): 445.

96 See *Reference re Language Rights under s 23 of the Manitoba Act, 1870 and s 133 of Constitution Act, 1867*, [1985] 1 SCR 721 at 748–9.

97 *Reference re Secession of Quebec*, [1998] 2 SCR 217 at 240.

98 United Nations, Declaration on the Rights of Indigenous Peoples, Resolution adopted by the General Assembly, 107th plenary meeting, 13 September 2007 (New York: United Nations, 2008). http://www.un.org/esa/socdev/unpfii/documents/DRIPS_en.pdf.

99 Ibid. Part one, chapter II, section A.

100 John Borrows, "Canadian Law Schools and Indigenous Legal Traditions," in *Indian Subjects: Hemispheric Perspectives on the History of Indigenous Education*, ed. Brenda Child and Brian Klopotek (Santa Fe: SAR, 2014), 204.

101 Pope Francis, *Encyclical on Climate Change and Inequality: On Care of Our Common Home* (London: Melville House, 2015), para 85, http://w2.vatican.va/content/francesco/en/encyclicals/documents/papa-francesco_20150524_enciclica-laudato-si.pdf.

102 Ibid., para 119.

3 Reconciliation Here on Earth

JAMES TULLY

I Overview

I would like to discuss two interconnected projects of reconciliation. The first is the reconciliation of Indigenous and non-Indigenous people (Natives and newcomers) *with* each other in all our diversity. The second is the reconciliation of Indigenous and non-Indigenous people (human beings) with the living earth: that is, reconciliation *with* more-than-human living beings (plants, animals, ecosystems, and the living earth as a whole). I will not discuss formal reconciliation procedures carried on by governments, courts, and commissions. Rather I focus on more basic, informal, and transformative practices of reconciliation and the shared responsibilities we all have to engage in these two projects of reconciliation.[1] The first section sets out the general argument, and the following three sections explore aspects of it.

I.1 Two Connected Projects of Reconciliation

My suggestion is that these two projects of reconciliation have to be brought into being and carried on together if they are to be successful. Our relationships with each other and our relationships with the living earth are far too interdependent and entangled to treat their reconciliation separately, as if they were independent. They have been woven together since first contact in countless ways; sometimes in good ways, but also in multiple forms of intergenerational social and ecological suffering; understanding and misunderstanding; working together and domination, dispossession, colonization, cultural genocide, subordination, impoverishment, residential school, and starvation; and through treaty negotiations, violations, blockades, armed and unarmed conflicts, constitutional change, court cases, modern treaties, successful and failed consultations, and the complex web of relationships in every area of contemporary life that has evolved over the last thirty years.

Just think for a moment of trying to separate these two types of reconciliation: with each other in our diversity and the living earth in its diversity.[2] If we try to reconcile Indigenous and non-Indigenous people with each other without reconciling our way of life with the living earth, we will fail, because the unsustainable and crisis-ridden relationship between Indigenous and non-Indigenous people that we are trying to reconcile has its deepest roots in the unsustainable and crisis-ridden relationship between human beings and the living earth.[3] To put it more strongly, as long as our unsustainable relationship to the living earth is not challenged, it will constantly undermine and subvert even the most well-meaning, free-standing efforts to reconcile the unsustainable relationship between Indigenous and non-Indigenous peoples through modern treaties and consultations, as we have seen over the last thirty years. These two crises form an interconnected "dual crisis," as I call it.

If, conversely, we try to reconcile the unsustainable relationship with the living earth without addressing the unsustainable relationship with Indigenous and non-Indigenous people, we will struggle to discern and realize a good, sustainable relationship, because such a relationship is discovered and learned through practice. We come to see the contours of this sustainable way of life here on earth through enacting it. Indigenous people have been living in sustainable ways with the living earth on Turtle Island for 10,000–14,000 years. Many Indigenous peoples have preserved their ecological knowledges of sustainable practices in the eco-regions and living traditions in which this practical knowledge has been acquired by trial and error and passed on each generation. Indigenous peoples and their practical knowledge systems have co-evolved with the ecosystems in which they have co-inhabited, learned from, shaped, and been shaped by. These place-based traditions of embedded practical knowledge are how we make the transition to sustainable relationships with the ecosystems of the living earth.[4] Bypassing Indigenous peoples and Indigenous sciences would be epistemic folly. It would continue the social and epistemic injustice of dispossession and colonization, and the consequence would be continued ecological injustice.[5]

Of course, we need to draw on Western natural and human sciences as well. However, several of these sciences developed along with the underlying unsustainable relationship with the living earth during the last four hundred years of European global imperialism. As a result, they presuppose and overlook the unsustainable extraction relationship to the living earth that is the cause of the ecological crisis, including climate change and its social and economic consequences. Many of their responses to the ecological crisis thus tend to reproduce, rather than question, this underlying feature and thereby amplify its destructive effects. Moreover, Western sciences often dismiss Indigenous knowledges and life ways as primitive, superstitious, soon to die off, lower, or less-developed relative to the superior knowledge and processes of civilization, modernization, and globalization spread around the globe by Western peoples. And these two imperious attitudes to the living earth and Indigenous peoples are closely related historically and conceptually.[6]

Although these attitudes persist in several quarters, fortunately for life on earth, a very different way of thinking about the living earth and our *interdependent* relationships within and with it has developed and gained support in the life and earth systems sciences over the last fifty years.[7] During the same period, a different way of recognizing and relating with Indigenous and non-Indigenous people and peoples, as different yet equal and interdependent, has developed slowly in the human sciences and in practice.[8] Building on this double revolution, groups such as the Indigenous Peoples Working Group on Climate Change argue that Indigenous and non-Indigenous people are now able to join hands and work together, sharing Indigenous and Western knowledges on equal footing, to get at the roots of the dual crisis and work out reconciliatory and sustainable futures together.[9] I agree. This double revolution and convergence can provide the common ground for a profound, transformative reconciliation with each other and the living earth, if it is understood and enacted slowly and carefully in mutually respectful, responsible and diversity-aware ways.

I.2 The Educational Gift-Reciprocity Cycle of Reconciliation Practices

Once we begin to see the two relationships with each other and the living earth as systemically interdependent (as the result of the two epistemic revolutions above), we can also see the reciprocal educational relationship between the two types of reconciliation. We learn how to reconcile differences between Indigenous and non-Indigenous people and live together, not only by learning the arts of conciliation, or peace-making, but also the arts and sciences of learning to live sustainably with the living earth. There are important lessons from a sustainable human-with-nature relationship for a sustainable human-with-human relationship because all human-with-human relationships (social systems) are embedded in and dependent on human-with-nature relationships. Second, there are even more fundamental lessons to be learned from the ways that non-human living systems have sustained themselves and co-evolved over 3.8 billion years for working up sustainable human-with-nature relationships, and then from there to Indigenous-with-non-Indigenous relationships.

The ways that "life sustains life" in the webs of life that comprise the ecosphere are our primary teacher in both cases of reconciliation. Indeed, this multidisciplinary education – of the ecological and life sciences, the social sciences and humanities, and the Indigenous arts and sciences – is the most important pedagogical task of the twenty-first century if we are to have a sustainable shared future.[10] It is our task as educators and students working together to bring about this reunion of the natural and human sciences and traditional ecological knowledge and wisdom. This is how one of the pioneers, Fritz Capra, puts the educational challenge:

> The key to an operational definition of ecological sustainability is the realization that we do not need to invent sustainable human communities from scratch but can model them after nature's ecosystems, which are sustainable communities of plants, animals and micro-organisms. Since the outstanding characteristic of the Earth household is its inherent ability to sustain life, a sustainable human community is one designed in such a manner that its ways of life, businesses, economies, federations, physical structures, and technologies do not interfere with nature's inherent ability to sustain life. Sustainable communities and networks evolve their patterns of living over time in continual interaction with other living systems, both human and non-human.[11]

However, this great project of our time cannot be done justly or intelligently without the ongoing consent and cooperation of Indigenous people who have co-evolved with and learned from their ecosystems: the very ecosystems from which non-Indigenous people now want to learn how life sustains life in order to save themselves from the anthropogenic crisis they have created by ignoring both teachers.[12]

This cooperative, interactive, and dynamic view of eco-social education is not new. First, ever since settlers arrived on Turtle Island, Indigenous peoples have said that the proper way to reconcile our differences and live sustainably together is to enter into conciliatory treaty negotiations, and these will bring into being peaceful and friendly relationships among us. These conciliatory negotiations are never perfect. They are activities in which the participants learn by trial and error how to conciliate each other. Future generations always have to return to treaty talks and renew them as new circumstances arise.[13]

Second, Indigenous people also have insisted that sustainable coexistence by means of treaty negotiations and the peaceful and friendly relationships they create is not a social system they invented ex nihilo. Rather, they say that they learn lessons of how to conciliate and live with the settlers from their interactions and negotiations with their other living relatives and kin: that is, sustainable relationships with plants, animals, streams, rivers, mountains, seasons, ecosystems, and Mother Earth as a whole. They often speak of these relationships with their more-than-human relatives as treaty relationships. Third, even these pedagogical relationships are not the primary ground of their knowledge of how to live in conciliatory and sustainable ways. They say they have learned how to live sustainably *with* the living earth by learning from how the webs of non-human forms of life live together symbiotically; that is, how life sustains life. This is the basic life-world in which the other two sustainable ways of life emerge and in which they have their interdependent being. For example, in chapter 2 of this volume, Borrows explains the Anishinaabe concept of education (*akinoomaage*) in the following way: *akinoomaage* "is made of two roots: *aki* and *noomage*. *Aki* means 'earth.' *Noomage* means 'to point towards and take direction from.' Thus, teaching and learning literally means the lessons we learn from looking to the earth."[14]

But this is not all. Indigenous people have an important way of trying to bring settlers around to see that the conciliatory and sustainability skills one is supposed to learn in treaty negotiations are derived from the two broader types of living relationships in which treaty negotiations take place. They exchange gifts. The cyclical exchange of gifts is the exemplar and reminder of the ways life sustains life symbiotically: that is, by gift-reciprocity networks and cycles.[15]

Every second of the day the living earth gives countless gifts of goods and services needed to sustain all the interdependent forms of life, beginning with the air you are breathing here and now. Each interdependent form of life not only sustains itself, but also, in so doing, produces goods and services that help to sustain others; and vice versa. Accordingly, the *way* life sustains life by reproducing the conditions of life is portrayed as the mutual exchange of gifts among interdependent partners.

Gift exchange at treaty talks reminds the partners that they too should see themselves as both embedded in these cyclical gift-reciprocity relationships and bringing into being new ones in the negotiations. Just as the living earth consists of gift-reciprocity relationships that sustain the living members, so humans should relate to the living earth and each other in their eco-social relationships in the same general way. That is: a gift is given, the recipient expresses gratitude, and the giver perceives this. Gratitude moves the recipient to reciprocate by giving a gift to the giver and/or to others in reciprocity. In so doing, participants bring into being and continue gift-gratitude-reciprocity networks and cycles that co-sustain all participants: treaty and social networks that mimic self-sustaining ecological networks. If, conversely, they fail to reciprocate with Mother Earth or their treaty partners, take and exploit gifts with ingratitude and greed, they break the cycles that sustain life in both cases, destroy the cyclical networks that are the conditions of life for their neighbours and themselves, and eventually destroy themselves.[16]

Accordingly, the exchange of gifts before and after treaty talks reminds the participants that they have shared responsibilities to connect or reconnect with the gift-gratitude-reciprocity cycles that sustain all forms of life. As Taiaiake Alfred reminds us, the Haudenosaunee acknowledge the responsibilities humans have to live in accordance with these life-sustaining relationships before entering into treaty negotiations:

> We gather together and see that the cycle of life continues. As human beings we have been given the responsibility to live in balance and harmony with each other and with all creation. So now, we bring our minds together as one as we give greetings and thanks to each other as People. Now our minds are one. We are thankful for our mother, mother earth, for she gives us all that we need for life. She sustains and supports us as our feet move upon her. We are joyful in knowing that she continues to care for us as she has from the beginning of time. To our Mother, we send greetings and thanks. Now our minds are one.[17]

The living networks and cycles of gift-gratitude-reciprocity are the model not only for educational and treaty relationships, but for social and economic relationships more generally. On the Northwest Coast, for example, the central term for systems of law, governance, and civic education is *potlatch*. Potlatch derives from the Nootka term *pa-chitle*, which means "to give and to give in reciprocity."[18] Nancy Turner refers to this gift-reciprocity understanding of the networks and cycles that sustain life a "kin-centric" world view.[19]

I.3 The Independence View

Accordingly, these views of interdependency and shared responsibilities are not new or unusual. Quite the contrary. The new and unusual view is the one that has become predominant in the Anthropocene: the independence of human relationships from ecological relationships and from each other, and so the separation of the two activities of reconciliation.[20]

It is astonishing that anyone ever thought that Indigenous and non-Indigenous peoples could reconcile themselves without simultaneously reconciling our relationship with the living earth, as if they were independent causally and educationally. It shows how deeply we have been shaped and formed by an alienated relationship to the living earth and each other in the modern period. It is as if we are negotiating treaty relationships with one another and not realizing that we are also walking on this living earth, breathing its clean air, and receiving all the gifts it provides to keep us alive. As deep ecologists say, we independent and autonomous moderns overlook our interdependent "ecological footprint" and "ecological self."[21]

I am not referring to the relationships that are negotiated in formal reconciliation processes: sovereignty, jurisdiction, land claims, and so on. These are not overlooked – quite the opposite. I am referring to the primary underlying relationship of *Homo sapiens* with the living earth that is articulated in terms of gift-reciprocity relationships and cycles by Indigenous people. This is a basic mode of being-in-the-life-world with other living beings; a reciprocal and interactive relationship of ongoing sensuous attunement, disturbance, and re-attunement by means of our pre-reflective, embodied, and reflective senses, perception, and cognition.[22] Following Aldo Leopold I call this primary relationship an "ethical" relationship. Our shared responsibilities to reconcile unsustainable relationships derive from, and are the expression of, this basic ethical relationship. These are shared responsibilities we have as "plain members and citizens" of the commonwealth of biotic communities of all forms of life on earth.[23]

The irresponsible attitude of overlooking this ethical relationship of interdependency has come along with the rise of the underlying unsustainable relationship to the living earth over the last four hundred years. From within this way of life, it appears as if we are independent of the living earth and of each other. Not only are the two projects of reconciliation seen as separate. We have no shared responsibilities to address them, because we do not see ourselves as interdependent citizens of a commonwealth of all forms of life. This ground of being-with is overlooked. As I argue below, this alienated view of our social and ecological relationships and responsibilities is self-defeating – unable to see clearly or address effectively the ecological crisis or the indigenous-settler crisis.

I.4 Conciliation, Crisis, Reconciliation Cycles

If the two projects of reconciliation are *interdependent* systemically and educationally, then what is the appropriate form of reconciliation to carry them out successfully? This is the question I wish to explore. I will set out five defining criteria of the transformative concept of reconciliation (reconciliation-with) I use. It is not to be confused with the predominant concept of reconciliation (reconciliation-to) in use today. This less-demanding concept of reconciliation (reconciliation-to) rests on the assumption that processes of reconciliation of Indigenous and non-Indigenous people are independent of their current unsustainable relationship with the living earth. In German there are two separate terms: *Versöhnung* (transformative reconciliation-with) and *Vertragen* (reconciliation-to some independent, background system of knowledge and power). In English, there is only one word for both, and this has caused immense confusion.[24]

Nuu-chah-nulth people have an expression for reconciliation-with and within the complex webs of interdependency that sustain life. As Umeek (Richard Atleo Senior) explains, when things are out of balance and in crisis, such as the global crisis, and require reconciliation, they usually begin by reminding themselves that everything is connected with and dependent on everything else. The Nuu-chah-nulth phrase is *heshook-ish tsawalk*.[25] Being is "being-with" (*mitsein*). Once we perceive ourselves to be always already in life-sustaining relationships of mutual dependence and assistance, the appropriate concept of both conciliation and reconciliation then appears to be: reconciliation-with all living beings, rather than reconciliation-to a presumptively unproblematic relationship to the living earth; reconciliation as ongoing, shared practices with all our relatives, rather than reconciliation as segmented processes oriented to independence; and the way of reconciliation as the enactment of the conciliatory and sustainable mode of being we are trying to bring about, rather than reconciliation as instrumental means different from the ends. That is, transformative reconciliation is the enactment and continuation of the primary ethical relationship mentioned above.

For our purposes, there are five main features of reconciliation as reconciliation-with. First, it is a form of activity that comes on the scene in response to a crisis in the sustainable and conciliatory way of life of the people involved, whether this crisis irrupts in family relationships, relationships among communities and peoples, or among humans and non-human forms of life. The relationships among them become crisis-ridden and unsustainable. In the conciliatory phase, the members work and live together in mutually sustainable ways among themselves and with all other interdependent social and ecological communities on which they co-depend. When disagreements, problems, and conflicts arise, as they always do, they normally can conciliate them by the means available to them within their way of life, or within *ways* of life if it is a dispute with neighbouring communities, human or non-human.

A crisis of sustainability and conciliation irrupts when conciliation fails.[26] The people involved become ungrateful, greedy, distrustful, conflictual, and aggressive rather than peaceful and conciliatory – alienated from each other and estranged from the living earth. If they continue to reproduce these behaviours, they will destroy themselves and interrelated forms of life (their relatives or neighbours). When they try to respond to the crisis, the result is often to amplify rather than attenuate the destructive effects of their crisis-ridden way of life. Their way of life becomes unsustainable and self-destructive (vicious) rather than self-sustaining and mutually beneficial (virtuous). From within the crisis phase, their relationships appear to be irreconcilable. This is the crisis we are in today in relations between Indigenous and non-Indigenous peoples and the living earth.[27]

The crisis of Indigenous peoples has been exhaustively reported, studied, and documented from the 1960s, through the Royal Commission on Aboriginal People in the 1990s, the attempts to address it in the 2000s, and the Truth and Reconciliation Commission, and National

Inquiry into Missing and Murdered Indigenous Women and Girls today.[28] As Borrows puts it, "Aboriginal peoples' lives are drastically shorter than other Canadians and marked by more suffering as measured by considerably higher rates of poverty, injury, and incarceration, and significantly lower levels of education, income and health. This did not occur in an instant; we have long passed the 'tipping point' in the relationship between Aboriginal peoples and others. We are in crisis mode, and there is no politically driven prospect of salvaging the relationship; it is already broken and lies in ruins all around us."[29]

The ecological crisis of the very conditions of life on earth is also beyond reasonable doubt. Since the early reports on climate change, global warming, pollution, and the limits to growth in the 1970s to endless studies and reports of the leading earth scientists in the world and the Intergovernmental Panel on Climate Change, we have known that our dominant way of life is overshooting the carrying capacity of the earth and destroying the conditions that sustain life. Climate change, non-renewable and renewable resource depletion, species and ecosystems extinction, the melting of glaciers and the polar ice cap, the acidification of the oceans and desertification of former agricultural and forest lands are not only past the tipping point to unsustainable warming and a possible sixth mass extinction. They are already bringing about horrendous social effects: mass starvation and migration, social divisions and a planet of slums and gated communities, wars over resources and water, and failed states. The ruthless race among states and corporations for the resources that are left is accelerating climate change and other factors in a vicious, cascading, and runaway spiral. The intensified race to control the world's remaining resources has increased intervention and exploitation of the territories and resources of Indigenous peoples, drawing them into the spiralling social and economic consequences.[30] The interdependent relationships, systems, and cycles that sustain life on earth are "on the edge."[31]

Second, reconciliation is a mode of ethical practice with others here and now, in the unsustainable and crisis-ridden relationships Indigenous and non-Indigenous people inhabit. Reconciliation consists in the exercise of our shared responsibilities to care for ourselves and for all the interdependent others on whom our own well-being depends. That is, the practice of reconciliation is simply the attempt to bring into being or to regenerate, enact, and carry on the basic ethical relationship of mutual responsiveness, care, conciliation, and sustainability with all forms of life that is being overlooked and destroyed by the dominant self-destructive relationships that are causing the crisis.

The extreme difficulty of reconciliation in this profound sense is that we are ourselves located within the self-destructive relationships: subject to them and their legitimating ideologies, governed and swept along by them in our everyday producing and consuming.[32] Yet this feature is not unique to this present crisis. "Transformative reconciliation" always has to come into being when human relationships of conciliation spiral out of control, and it has to be exercised within them, whether within intimate family relations or in global peace movements in the context of war and conflict. It rejects the alternate idea of an independent process outside the crisis in which elites can do the reconciliation for us.

Third, the role of practices of reconciliation at this phase is to transform the crisis-ridden relationships in which we are entangled and the social and ecological suffering they cause. The aim is to work together to transform unsustainable relationships into conciliatory and sustainable ones: that is, to transform the vicious system into a virtuous one that sustains the ways of life of all affected. This cooperative work of transformation is carried out by exercising the shared responsibilities of the members involved.

These responsibilities are "shared" in a special sense. We cannot see that we have shared responsibilities from within the practices and world view of the unsustainable relationship to the earth. They are overlooked. From this dominant perspective, we see ourselves as independent of the living earth and our neighbours, with individual responsibilities to look after ourselves and those with whom we choose to contract. We have to free ourselves from these everyday practices and begin to interact with others as our interdependent kin for these more basic shared responsibilities of interdependent relationships to come into view. When we do this, we bring to self-awareness the common good of interdependent conciliation and sustainability and our corresponding responsibilities. We become aware of our interdependency and the co-sustaining responsibilities it entails.[33]

The fourth feature of transformative reconciliation is that means and ends are the same, as acorn to oak tree. The only way to bring about reconciliation is by conciliatory means, because means prefigure and constitute ends. Reconciliation is really a radical regeneration and reconciliation of the partners by acting and interacting in non-violent, conciliatory, and sustainable ways in our everyday relations with each other and the living earth – by "being the change." These ways can be constructive, obstructive, and contestatory. In so doing, these members regenerate sustainable ways of life within the interstices of the hegemonic unsustainable system, gradually expanding the circles of participants until it reaches a critical mass of networked practices that transform vicious systems into virtuous ones.

This constitutive view of means and ends is at the heart of the alternative dispute-resolution tradition in the West, made famous by Gandhi and his many followers: transformative reconciliation and peace by peaceful and non-violent means.[34] Not surprisingly, there are complementary peacemaking traditions in Indigenous civilizations. Here, the people in a crisis exercise their "shared responsibilities" by "burying the hatchet," forgoing violence and turning to the path of peacemaking by peaceful preparation, obstruction, non-cooperation, and negotiations. They begin to enter into practices of reconciliation by "becoming of one mind," beginning to become conciliatory in their own interactions. They enter into tough treaty negotiations in conciliatory and friendly ways oriented to transforming the crisis-ridden relationships between them. By negotiating in this contentious, yet conciliatory and friendly way, they bring into being peaceful and friendly relationships that sustain them until another crisis irrupts and they return to treaty negotiations and reconcile themselves once again.[35]

Hence the term "peace and friendship treaties" as the name for both the early-modern treaty negotiations and the relationships they brought into being between Indigenous peoples and settlers. The way of reconciliation – of tough and lengthy peaceful and friendly negotiations – is thus non-violent, but not non-contentious. Drawing in part on Gandhi, Taiaiake describes the practical philosophy of the peace and friendship way of reconciling crises in contrast to the ways of either armed resistance or resignation (reconciliation-to): "With the vision of nonviolent contention, Onkwehonwe [Indigenous people] face the untenable politics and unacceptable conditions in their communities and confront the situation with determined yet restrained action, coherent and creative contention supplemented with a positive political vision based on re-establishing respect for the original covenants and ancient treaties that reflect the founding principles of Onkwehonwe–settler relationships ... with the hope of recreating the conditions of co-existence."[36]

Fifth, reconciliation in this transformative sense literally means to "conciliate *again*." Practices of reconciliation transform the conduct of the partners from the conflict-ridden and unsustainable relationships into the kind of conciliatory and sustainable way of life out of which the crisis emerged.

In summary, the three phases or ways of life can be seen to comprise a meta-cycle of life. First is the basic conciliatory or virtuous way of

life that sustains all life on earth and in which disturbances and dis-
putes are resolved by normal practices of conciliation. The second is the
unpredictable transformation of this stage into a vicious, unsustainable,
and seeming irreconcilable cycle that tends towards the destruction of
the contending parties. The third phase is the response of extraordinary practices of reconciliation that, if successful, reconnect the partners to conciliatory and sustainable relationships with each other and
the living earth. If reconciliation fails, the crisis-ridden system crosses a
tipping-point and collapses in whole or part, taking many of the forms
of life with it.

When practices of reconciliation reconnect people to conciliatory and
sustainable webs of life together, they are not the same as before the
crisis. They have gone through a "learning cycle" by trial and error concerning the conditions that sustain life together on this planet. They
acquire new skills of reconciliation and re-sustainability. They are edu-
cated and thus more precautionary and better prepared to respond to
and cope with the next outbreak of aggressive and unsustainable interaction. They also know each other better. They become friends who
have suffered and overcome enormous challenges together. They have
overcome alienation and are at home with each other and the living
earth ("biophilia"). And so the conciliatory and sustainable cycles of
life become paramount once again.[37]

There are many representations of this meta-cycle of life across the
civilizations of Turtle Island. The Two Row Wampum nation-to-nation
relationship of the Haudenosaunee confederacy, the Peace and Friendship treaties of the Mi'kmaq people, the Royal Proclamation of 1763
and the Treaty of Niagara of 1764, the great treaty traditions of the
Plains Cree, and the Raven cycle stories of the peoples of the Northwest
Coast are some of the better-known exemplars.[38] For my generation of
guests on Coast and Straits Salish territories, an iconic representation
of this transformative reconciliation cycle is the monumental work of
art by Haida artist Bill Reid: the black canoe, called *The Spirit of Haida
Gwaii*. This work of art was crafted by a team of Indigenous and non-
Indigenous artists under Reid's supervision during the reconciliation
struggles of the Haida to exercise jurisdiction over Haida Gwaii, protect the old growth forests, and work with non-Indigenous allies, and,
with Raven at the helm, as a Haida representation of transformative
reconciliation-with.[39]

The co-evolution of life on earth has experienced many successful
and unsuccessful cycles of conciliation, crisis, and reconciliation, and
we are in the sixth now.[40] The Royal Commission on Aboriginal Peoples

suggested that the history of relationships between Indigenous peoples and settlers also can be seen in terms of cycles of conciliation, conflict and crisis, and reconciliation – successful and unsuccessful. The sustainable and conciliatory inter-societal "middle ground" of the early peace and friendship treaties gave way to periods of treaty violation, marginalization, and genocide; then the courageous resilience and resurgence of Indigenous peoples in the twentieth century; further encroachment on their territories and resources; and the contemporary attempts to address the Indigenous crisis separately by reconciliation through modern treaties and other means.[41] The contemporary attempts at reconciliation have brought about positive change in several cases, but they have not been transformative.[42] Hence the continuing dual crisis. My argument is that the dual crisis continues because it has not been tackled by the kind of coordinated, reconciliation-with practices outlined in this section.

In the following sections I examine what the life and human sciences teach us about sustainable and conciliatory ways of living together (section II); how this knowledge enables us to see how an unsustainable and self-destructive relationship to the living earth and each other, consisting of four global processes, brings about the dual crisis (section III); and how the regeneration and resurgence of practices of reconciliation-with can transform the unsustainable relationship (section IV). That is, I explore the three phases of the meta-cycle of life I have sketched in this section.

II Conciliatory and Sustainable Ways of Life: The Life Systems and Human Sciences View

So far we have seen how to understand transformative reconciliation in terms of a meta-cycle of relationships of conciliation, crisis, and reconciliation by drawing on resources in the Hegelian and Gandhian traditions.[43] We have also seen the way several Indigenous traditions understand reconciliation in terms of a meta-cycle of conciliatory gift-reciprocity relationships, ingratitude and greed, crisis, and reconciliation as regenerating gift-reciprocity relationships anew. There are similar teachings about transformative reconciliation of the social and ecological crises in Buddhist and Christian traditions.[44] This section is a brief summary of similar explanations of how life sustains life in the life and human sciences. These similarities provide common ground for cooperating in practices of reconciliation.

II.1 The Gaia Hypothesis

In the early 1960s Sir James Lovelock, an earth systems scientist, formulated the Gaia hypothesis. This is the hypothesis that despite the vast changes in the solar energy coming to the earth over the last 3.8 billion years, the profound transformations in the forms of life on earth over the same long period, and all the changes in earth, ocean, and atmospheric conditions over the same period, the atmospheric conditions and the temperature of the earth have somehow remained in the range that sustains life on earth. The Gaia hypothesis is that the ecosphere and all the systems of life that compose it somehow regulate the atmosphere and temperate so as to sustain life. That is, the biotic and abiotic ecosphere as a whole is "self-organizing" and "self-sustaining," often referred to as "autopoiesis."

The reason James Lovelock called it the Gaia hypothesis is that William Golding pointed out to him that the Greeks also believed that the earth is alive. They called the spirit of the living earth *anima mundi* (the soul, *pneuma*, "breath"; spirit, energy, or *animacy* of the living earth). And they took the living earth to be a goddess – Gaia. This hypothesis has survived a number of tests since the 1960s and is now considered not only a hypothesis, but a theory – the Gaia theory. It has been endorsed by a majority of scientists on the Intergovernmental Panel on Climate Change.[45]

This discovery led to attempts to explain how the systems that compose the ecosphere actually regulate the content and temperature of the atmosphere within a fairly broad range of cycles that sustain most forms of life – from ice ages to warm periods, such as the Holocene in which we live. This led to the revolutionary development of life systems theories, complexity theory, and nonlinear causality.[46] For the purposes of those of us who wish to know how we should live within this complex system of systems in ways that sustain rather than damage it, the crucially important insight came from Lovelock's colleague, the life scientist Lyn Margulis. She argued that the Gaia hypothesis is not based on the assumption that the system of systems that compose the ecosphere is itself a purposeful living being that regulates the climate and temperature to sustain life. Rather, the self-sustaining quality of Gaia is an "emergent property" of the life-systems or ecosystems that compose the ecosphere. She argues that the Gaia hypothesis is symbiosis on a planetary scale.[47]

There is nothing strange or speculative being smuggled in here. The emergence of new properties in the course of the complex interaction of life systems is the way that life itself has developed in increasingly complex ways – that is, through life systems living-with each other in complex interdependent ways (symbiosis) and giving rise to new life systems (symbiogenesis). Spatially, symbiosis refers to the immensely complex webs or networks that link all forms of life in relationships of reciprocal interdependence. Temporally, these networks are cyclical. They form cycles in which the "waste" of one interdependent member is always used in some sustaining way by another member, so that nothing is "wasted" (zero emissions), and at a temporality that enables species and ecosystems renewal. Photosynthesis and the oxygen and carbon dioxide cycles between plants and animals constitute the paradigm of this spatio-temporal quality of symbiosis – of reciprocal interdependency and cyclical renewability. It is the basis of the way life sustains life – the animacy of Gaia.[48]

II.2   Symbiosis as the Animacy of Life

We can describe and study these endlessly complex and fascinating networks and cycles of symbiosis in terms of the negative and positive feedback loops, tipping points, virtuous and vicious systems, and so on, of systems theory and complexity theory. However, the key feature of the way life sustains life for Margulis is not that the system regulates the conditions of life for its members. Rather, it is the other way around. The plain members and citizens of Gaia sustain it through their symbiotic participation in it. And *Homo sapiens*, as one minor and recent species among millions, is a member and citizen just like all others, with ecological responsibilities to participate in ways that reciprocally sustain the networks that sustain us. That is, ecosystems and their members sustain themselves by living in ways of life (life ways and earth ways) that co-sustain the forms of life with which they are interdependent.[49]

Accordingly, *symbiosis* and *symbiogenesis* are technical terms in the life sciences for how forms of life live together in mutually supportive ways and, in so doing, give rise from time to time to new symbiotic forms of life (symbiogenesis). These virtuous feedback relationships of mutual sustainability are now seen as the major factor in the evolution of life on earth. Life systems that sustain life symbiotically, in mutually supportive ways, are called "virtuous life systems." Sustainable life systems are not harmonious. They are often far from equilibrium: patchy, full of cheaters or free riders, and subject to perturbations that can cause a life system to tip over into a vicious system. Yet, for all that indeterminacy, their remarkable qualities of resilience enable them to sustain themselves over vast stretches of time. Conversely, life systems that destroy rather than sustain their interdependent neighbours, or destroy the life systems on which they depend, and thus destroy themselves, are called "vicious life systems."[50]

If vicious life systems were the major factor in evolution, as Western scientists tended to suggest not so long ago, then life on earth would have ceased to exist long ago. But the opposite is the case. Life has become more complex: that is, symbiosis and symbiogenesis have prevailed most of the time, even recovering from five mass extinctions and periodic ice ages approximately every 100,000 years. Moreover, vicious systems, like virtuous systems, are also far from equilibrium and subject to change. They too are subject to tipping points that transform them into virtuous systems. That is, life has resilient powers of "regeneration" (or reconciliation). Life systems recover by regenerating networks of symbiosis and symbiogenesis within vicious systems, or within the ruins of vicious systems. The third phase of the meta-cycle of life (transformative reconciliation) works within vicious or damaged systems by being the change. Forms of life interact and network symbiotically and symbiogenetically within vicious systems, gradually repairing and transforming them into virtuous systems if they have time to regenerate.[51] Hence, regeneration is similar to reconciliation by means of conciliation in section I.4. It is autotelic. Michael Simpson provides an example of the recovery of a forest from clear cutting:

> Living systems do not only reproduce themselves. Their very life processes nourish their habitat and strengthen the conditions of life around them. They thereby create an organism that is larger than themselves or their individual species. When a forest is growing back from a disturbance, herbaceous (non-woody) plants are the first to move in. These plants exude sugars that attract bacteria around their roots. The bacteria in turn exude an alkaline "bioslime" that creates a favorable habitat for themselves as well as for the pioneer plant species. The alkaline condition of the bioslime also allows the bacteria to break down ammonia in the soil into nitrates that are taken up by plants, allowing them to grow vegetatively. This cycle of life creating the conditions for more life continues as the forest gradually grows into a rich, biodiverse ecosystem (ecological succession). Living systems are not only self-regulating but they are relational in so far as they build the conditions of life around them.[52]

The similarity between the systems view of life in the life and earth sciences and the gift-reciprocity view of many Indigenous traditions is striking. The Potawanimi biologist Robin Wall Kimmerer draws the connection for us: "Reciprocity – returning the gift – is not just good manners; it is how the biophysical world works. Balance in ecological systems arises from negative feedback loops, from cycles of giving and taking. Reciprocity among parts of the living earth produces [dynamic] equilibrium, in which life as we know it can flourish."[53]

Indigenous peoples also have ways of describing the "far from equilibrium" feature of living systems. As Nuu chah nulth legal scholar Johnny Mack explains, a familiar example of cascading positive feedback loops is when a canoe begins to tip in response to a disturbance, and further responses amplify the tipping until the canoe overturns: *hoquotisht*. He uses this to describe the disastrous consequences of colonization and neo-colonization of his people.[54]

Similarly, the Haida have a mantra to remind themselves of to the tipping-point feature inherent in all living systems. They say, "The world is as sharp as the edge of a knife." Haida artist Robert Davidson explains:

> Naanii told me that wherever we walk, we're walking on the knife's edge.
> The world is as sharp as the edge of a knife is a Haida expression. The
> knife's edge is just on the ground, and if we are not careful, we will fall off:
> that's how Naanii said it. It guides you on how to live your life. I see the
> knife's edge as the present moment.[55]

That is, it is always possible that the multiplicity of conciliatory and sustainable relationships in which we live may tip over into unsustainable relationships if selfish, non-reciprocal interaction outweighs gift-reciprocity interaction. The Raven cycle stories of the Northwest coast remind humans how unexpectedly these transformations often occur in everyday life. However, Raven stories also teach humans to be aware of this feature and to learn from the inherited stories of how their ancestors learned – by trial and error – to avoid them or recover from them: to be precautionary. If we are not careful – if we do not take care of each other – we will fall off.

II.3 Symbiosis in Ecological and Social Systems: Towards a New Synthesis

The human sciences have entered into a dialogue with these earth systems and life sciences over the last thirty years. One central thesis of this movement is "integral ecology."[56] The common ground on which a dialogue of mutual learning has begun is provided by the shared terms *symbiosis* and *symbiogenesis*. These concepts do not originate in the non-human life sciences but rather have a long history in the human sciences. They refer initially to how human beings have lived together in interdependent relationships of mutual aid and sustainability, and how various communities have learned to live beside each other in peace and mutual support. Moreover, the "communities of practice" research has taught us that such informal virtuous, symbiotic social relationships of mutual aid exist within and across every social system, even within the most vicious and damaging social systems. So the vicious social systems that are embedded within and damaging the ecosystems that sustain life are also embedded within and damaging informal symbiotic social systems that sustain the communities in which we live.[57]

Next, scholars in the humanities and social sciences have begun to realize that we are not dealing with two parallel paths of symbiotic evolution, one for non-human life and the other for human life. Rather, non-human symbiotic ecosystems and human symbiotic social systems are now seen as evolving interdependently and reciprocally. They are now seen as interdependent, "coupled," or "co-evolving." As a result, humans are now seen and studied as co-evolving and co-sustaining apprentices within their social and ecological systems, or what are now called eco-social systems.

This realization is a revolution of the twentieth century. For the previous 500 years, most Western scholars and scientists saw themselves and their social system as separate from and independent of nature. We now realize that when we are citizens of various social systems, such as states, corporations, and markets, we are also Gaia citizens of the ecosystems in which these social systems are embedded and on which they depend. If follows that human beings not only have to think of ourselves as participants in the interdependent ecological relationships that support us. We also have to think of our social systems in the same way – as interdependent – and as coupled to the co-evolution of ecosystems in either mutually sustaining or non-sustaining ways. Hence the term *eco-social systems*. As William Rees states, "We can no longer understand the dynamics of either the natural system or the human subsystem in isolation without understanding the dynamics of the other component."[58]

Furthermore, thinking about living systems in this symbiotic and cyclical way brings to awareness the interdependent ecological self, in contrast to the independent ego-self of our dominant way of life.[59] From this participatory perspective, we come to realize that if we wish to live well, we should live so that our way of life supports the ways of life of those with whom we are related, and they should do the same in reciprocity. We also realize that if we are suffering, it is probably because we are not living in ways that support such mutually support-ive networks. This way of life is neither altruistic nor egoistic, for that debilitating distinction rests on the presupposition that organisms are independent and self-sufficient to begin with.

Despite the individualistic and competitive relationships of the dominant formal economy, we are participants in multiple informal social systems of this symbiotic kind. Relationships within families, neighbourhoods, communities of practice with fellow workers, and an array of social networks are often symbiotic. Many psychologists and sociologists argue that informal symbiotic relationships are the basis of the health and well-being of all communities and their members, yet remain unnoticed by the dominant competitive ethos. They even describe them as gift-gratitude-reciprocity networks.[60]

Finally, this realization has brought about a revolution in the field of ethics. Rather than seeing the realm of ethics consisting of the ways of being with and within the complex communities of relationships that humans inhabit with other humans – past, present, and future – and with the spiritual realm, it is now seen by many to encompass the human relationships with all the non-human fellow members of their biotic communities and Gaia as a whole.[61] Here again, Leopold is a pioneer:

> All ethics so far evolved rest upon a single premise: that the individual is a member of a community of interdependent parts. His instincts prompt him to compete for his place in the community, but his ethics prompt him also to cooperate (perhaps in order that there may be a place to compete for). The land ethic simply enlarges the boundaries of the community to include soils, water, plants, and animals, or collectively: the land.
>
> An ethic, ecologically, is a limitation on freedom of action in the struggle for existence. An ethic, philosophically, is a differentiation of social from anti-social conduct. These are two definitions of the same thing. The thing has it origin in the tendency of interdependent individuals or groups to evolve modes of cooperation. The ecologist calls these symbioses.[62]

The next step for the life sciences and human sciences working together in community-based research networks is the practical, transformative step of designing and implementing new eco-social systems and transforming existing unsustainable eco-social systems so they sustain rather than destroy themselves and the ecological life systems on which they depend. This is the task announced by Fritz Capra in section I.2. However, as we have seen, if this task is to be successful it has to bring together the two projects of reconciliation to address the ecological and the Indigenous-non-Indigenous crises. This is the topic of the section IV. Before it can be addressed, we need to understand the unsustainable relationship to the living earth at the root of both crises.

III The Unsustainable System

III.1 Belonging-to versus Mastery-over

Given the convergence in understanding how life sustains life on earth, it is not surprising that traditional Indigenous knowledge and Western life systems knowledge also converge on the underlying non-linear causes of the dual crisis in our relations with each other and the living earth. For many Indigenous people, the major factor is captured in the mantra "The earth does not belong to us. We belong to the earth, Mother Earth." As we have seen in section I, to say that we belong to the earth is to say that humans and their eco-social systems are plain, interdependent members and citizens of the living earth with responsibilities of taking care of the gift-reciprocity ecological and social relationships that take care of us. On this *heshook-ish tsawalk* view, Indigenous peoples see and experience themselves as participatory apprentices within and with the living earth who have co-evolved by trial and error along with the regional ecosystems they inhabit and learn from. They have complex "property systems," but these consist of responsibilities of caretaking and reciprocity. This is how *Homo sapiens* has co-evolved for roughly 95 per cent of its brief time on earth.[63] In contrast, to forget this relationship and its responsibilities and to treat the earth as belonging to us as our property is irresponsible and vicious. Ojibway Elder Basil Johnston says this is like claiming property in your own mother – Mother Earth.[64]

Accordingly, the dual crisis is brought about by the contrasting property system that was brought to Turtle Island by the settlers. This specific and unique property system is based on the presupposition that the earth belongs to humans as their commodifiable private property, for sale on the market like any other commodity.[65] It began in England with the Enclosure movement and was spread around the world by Western imperialism and colonization. It was celebrated by Adam Smith and Karl Marx, and their many followers, as bringing civilization to uncivilized peoples through stages of development. Since the earth is the property of the members of this system, it appears to them as if they are separate from or independent of it, and in a relationship of mastery, control, and often conquest. It also brings with it an attitude of towering and unquestionable superiority over Indigenous peoples and of the so-called civilizing duty to impose the system over them and their lands.[66] No non-Indigenous person diagnosed and began to call into question this dual attitude of mastery over nature and Indigenous peoples better or more systematically than Franz Boas in *The Mind of Primitive Man* in 1911.[67] In the 1940s Aldo Leopold was among the first generation in North America to argue that this property system and presumption of mastery was both false and destructive of the ecological and social basis of life. He developed his participatory land ethic in response.[68] At the same time (1944), Karl Polanyi began to analyse this unique property system as a global system and to compare it with other property systems, including Indigenous systems (economic anthropology). This gave him a comparative and critical distance that was unavailable to earlier critics and opened a pathway to the social, ecological, and Indigenous criticisms of the global system today. He called the development of this system the great dis-embedding and transformation.[69]

III.2 The Great Transformation

Polanyi argued that during this great transformation humans have been dis-embedded from participation in the symbiotic ecological and social relationships that sustain life and re-embedded in abstract and competitive economic, political, and legal relationships that depend on yet destroy the underlying interdependent ecological and social relationships. This great dis-embedding from basically virtuous and conciliatory systems and re-embedding in vicious and unsustainable systems takes place in four major processes over the last 300–400 years called, successively, civilization, modernization and globalization.

First, the peoples who are embedded in symbiotic ecological and social relationships are dispossessed of this way of life and the territories in which it is carried on – first by the enclosure of the commons in England and then by the forceful dispossession of Indigenous peoples throughout the non-European world, often referred to as the second (global) enclosure. In Canada, despite almost a century of nation-to-nation treaty federalism among roughly equal partners, the Indian Act, a vast administrative dictatorship that governs every detail of Indigenous life, was imposed over Indigenous people and their lands without their consent, in 1876, as the expression of jurisdiction given in section 91(24) of the British North America Act, passed by the Imperial Parliament in 1867 (now referred to as the Constitution Act, 1867). This colonial system was and continues to be warranted by the fictitious assertion of Crown sovereignty and underlying title over Indigenous peoples and their lands.[70] Under this genocidal system, Indigenous peoples' traditional ecological and social knowledges and complex eco-social systems have been discredited and criminalized as "uncivilized." Indigenous peoples have been removed to tiny reserves and residential schools and subjected to endless policies of assimilation to "civilization" or face marginalization. Despite near extinction, many Indigenous peoples have continued to practise and sustain their ways of life, and, with the aid of well-meaning settlers, contested and modified the system.[71]

The second process is to impose an ownership relation to the land by the spread of Western legal systems of commodifiable property, thereby transforming earth into property. Polanyi describes the privatization of land as a "fictitious commodity," because land is not an extractable commodity produced for sale on the market. What we now treat as extractable, commodifiable, and exchangeable "natural resources" are, as we have seen, interdependent co-participants in the symbiotic webs and cycles of life that sustain life on earth.

Relating to the living earth as a storehouse of commodifiable resources dis-embeds them from these interdependent ecological relationships and re-embeds them in the abstract and competitive relations of the global market system. The natural world is radically transformed by continuous extraction and commodification. The result of "development" under this system is the destruction of the webs of interdependent ecological relationships that sustain the natural and human world, giving rise to the environmental crisis and climate change.[72] Yet the damage that this complex set of processes causes to the ecosphere all along the chains of dispossession-extraction-finance-commodification-production-consumption-and-waste-disposal is treated as "external" to the systemic relationship that is responsible for it.

Once the means of the reproduction of human life are placed under the ownership of corporations within systems of competition, the third process is to treat the productive capabilities of human beings as commodities for sale on the labour market by the spread of Western contract, labour, and corporate law. This kind of commodification dis-embeds human producing and consuming capabilities and activities from the surrounding social and ecological relationships in which they take place and re-embeds them in abstract, competitive, and non-democratic global market relationships. Polanyi describes the com-modification of the productive capabilities of individual humans as the second fictitious commodity.

It is fictitious because abilities to work together and sustain our-selves are not commodities made for the market. These capabilities are, as we have seen in the previous section, the cooperative response-abilities and sustain-abilities through which we humans participate in the social and ecological systems that conciliate and sustain life on earth. They are the capabilities through which we belong to the land and are grounded in it. Yet they are now treated as abstract capabilities that we as separate individuals "own" (self-ownership); and, by selling the use of these abilities to a corporation, they become the means by which we insert ourselves in the global market system. The underlying informal social systems that producers and consumers live in and that sustain them – such as families, communities, First Nations, networks, and so on – are treated as "external" to the market system. The result of "development" under this system is the destruction of the webs of interdependent social relations of mutual aid that sustain human com-munities, giving rise to the well-known forms of social suffering of modern life: alienation and anomie, the horrendous inequalities in life-chances, and the planet of slums and gated communities in which we find ourselves.[73]

Fourth, during the same processes, the intersubjective, every-day human powers and responsibilities of local self-government are extracted from their local practices and alienated to centralized, rep-resentative governments through competitive electoral systems in which political parties compete for individual votes in the electoral marketplace. This fictitious transfer of powers of self-government atomizes citizens into independent voters on the one hand and ren-ders representative governments dependent on powerful actors in the production system for taxes, jobs, funding, and thus re-election on the other. In these systems of "economic democracy," subjects expect rep-resentatives to govern for them. The damage this does to learning and exercising reciprocal responsibilities of participatory democratic self-government with fellow citizens in their social and eco-regions is yet another externality.[74]

Polanyi predicted that the long-term result of this great transformation would be the demolition of society and the destruction of the environment.[75] Despite Polanyi's warning and hundreds of others, this competitive system, or, more accurately, assemblage of four main processes, continues to expand. As systems theorists explain, it has become the major non-linear cause of the ecological and social crises.[76]

Briefly, corporations are caught up in a competitive system in which they must continuously extract and exploit natural and human resources at the lowest possible price and at maximum speed in order to make a profit or go under. Any damage to the environment and communities in which they operate is treated as external and off-loaded to governments. Individuals, communities, and governments are constrained to compete for these corporations, because they fund their campaigns, bring jobs to the electorate, and provide the taxes that enable governments to provide basic services and repair the damage they do to social and ecological systems. If governments try to internalize the externalities and regulate and charge the corporations, corporations are legally protected from "interference," and they can move to more compliant countries or they take the government to international courts under the system of global law that now overrides national governments. Transnational corporations, institutions of global governance, compliant states, and the formation of networks expand the property system and a massive global military network of wars and war preparation that protects it from the resistance it encounters. As non-renewable resources become scarce, it becomes more expensive and destructive to extract and exploit them, and it becomes more difficult to regulate the race for what's left. Even renewable resources are depleted or destroyed, because the temporality of market competition and development is faster than the natural cycles that renew aquifers, fish, forests, and oceans.[77]

III.3 Understanding the Vicious System

Over the last century there have been struggles over the first process (struggles of Indigenous peoples), second process (decolonization and ownership of the means of production), third process (global inequality, antagonism, and destruction of self-sustaining communities), and fourth process (for local participatory democracy). These diverse struggles have brought about important reforms and modifications, and they have made the processes they contested more interactive, contestatory, uneven, and unpredictable, rather than unilateral, developmental, and inevitable (as earlier theorists portrayed them and some still do). Except for the first, Indigenous struggles, these struggles have been oriented towards gaining power within and modifying the processes of modernization, by reform or revolution, not towards transformation and reconciliation-with.

We can now see that the error and injustice of the first process is of fundamental importance. This is the ongoing dispossession and alienation of human communities from their participatory ways of being in the living earth as plain members and responsible citizens, and the discrediting of the participatory ways of knowing that go along with them. This process provides fictitious misrepresentations of the Indigenous civilizations it destroys and of the civilization that repossesses the living earth. Indigenous cyclical ways of being and knowing are not only discredited as primitive errors from which moderns have nothing to learn. They are also assimilated into the new fictitious narrative and re-described as the lowest and poorest stage of human, linear development, which is presented as universal progress. The idea of alternative, gift-reciprocity civilizations, oriented to the sustainability and well-being of their human and more-than-human members, is treated as an anthropological curiosity. Dispossession from the living earth is thus not only a monumental ongoing social injustice to Indigenous peoples. It is also a monumental ongoing ecological, epistemological, and social injustice to one and all.[78]

However, since the 1950s we have seen the networking of struggles for Indigenous, social, and ecological justice in a multiplicity of sites and ways as the escalating destructive effects of the dual crisis become more manifest and better researched and understood (as in sections I and II). At the core of these movements is the dawning realization that the first process of dispossession, dis-embedding and discrediting of the participatory-reciprocity view of life, is the precondition of the rise of the unsustainable system and the dual crisis, not one of the other three processes, as earlier critics presumed.[79] For example, the sustainability of communities and the well-being of their members depend upon underlying gift-reciprocity social relationships of mutual aid, and these on similar ecological relationships. When these are destroyed, inequality and violent antagonisms increase. There is no solution to global inequality and violent conflict without addressing these underlying conditions.[80] These new networks have not yet been oriented towards transformative reconciliation-with each other and the living

earth. They have been constrained to reconciliation-to the more powerful vicious global system they question and contest. Yet, as I will argue
in section IV, they provide the regenerative permaculture of practices of
transformative reconciliation-with.

For example, the struggles, reforms, and modifications over reconciliation of Indigenous and non-Indigenous people and peoples have
certainly modified the first process, including the way Crown sovereignty and underlying title are exercised through Parliament, the
courts, and the Indian Act – from direct rule to indirect, consultative,
contestatory, and interactive hegemon-subaltern rule. However, these
great changes have modified but not transformed the four processes
of the great transformation, as the right to infringe Aboriginal title for
the sake of development and the pre-set conditions and economic certainty of treaty negotiations illustrate.[81] Indeed, in several cases the
result of lengthy litigation or negotiation has been indebtedness and
thus deeper dependency on the vicious system (similar to the debt trap
that the Third World faced after decolonization). Also, the majority of
struggles, modifications, and reforms over pollution, global warming,
and ecological justice over the same period have had a minor effect on
global warming and the larger ecological crisis so far.

If the rise of the four processes of dis-embedding and re-embedding
is examined in the light of the conditions of sustainability and well-
being of social systems and ecosystems presented by the life, earth,
and human sciences (symbiotic networks and cycles) and by traditional Indigenous sciences (gift-reciprocity networks and cycles), as I
have already foreshadowed in my description of the four processes,
the precise nexus of conditions that sustain the vicious system and its
dual crisis and how to transform them come into clear view. As Polanyi
pointed out, in contrast to all examples of sustainable market civilizations in the past, the modern economic, political, legal, technological,
and military system became dis-embedded from within the virtuous
background Indigenous and non-Indigenous eco-social systems of the
world (processes 1, 2, and 4) and the background ecological systems
(process 2) on which it and all life depend. The four fictions hide this
dis-embedding by misrepresenting the participatory members of these
symbiotic systems as if they were separable, independent commodities (natural and human resources), like any other commodity made for
the market. The system then acts in and on the living earth and living
communities in accordance with this misrepresentation, economically,
politically, legally, and technologically (the "autonomous" public and

private spheres of modernization). The legitimation of this estranged form of life is reinforced by the secondary explanations of it in terms of linear progress, development, and so on.

Thus, the fictions conceal the great transformations that have taken place. Unsustainable, non-reciprocal extraction, rather than sustainable, reciprocal regeneration, has become the dominant relationship to living earth and social systems. Externalization and independence are seen as prior to internalization and interdependence. Unsustainable linear economics, based on unlimited growth, waste disposal, and external regulation, has become dominant over sustainable, cyclical economics. In interdependent, cyclical, and regenerative ecological and social systems everything is connected, so nothing is external and there is no waste. The emissions of members are always used by other members in all their activities. Everything recycles. Thus, they are "cradle to cradle" systems like trees in forests from seed to nurse log. In contrast, our present system of unlimited extraction out of and waste disposal into somewhere external is a "cradle to grave" system.[82]

As we can see, the result is a "super-predatory" system. It depends on, and is nested within, the informal social and ecological relationships that sustain life on earth. Yet, at the same time, it preys on them in an extractive, linear, and non-reciprocal way. It treats the damage it does to them as external and independent. Like all super-predatory systems, human or non-human, it destroys the life systems that sustain it faster than they can regenerate. If "business as usual" continues, the system will destroy the social and ecological conditions that sustain life for most human beings and for hundreds of thousands of other species and ecosystems (the sixth mass extinction) – a set of processes that is well underway. When humans respond simply by trying to regulate the system by technical means of the political and legal institutions of the system, they have been unsuccessful, primarily because these institutions depend on the system's growth. If humans responded by recognizing the damage and trying to internalize the full costs to repair all the damage it was causing, the system would be shown to be unprofitable and it would collapse. That is, it is economically irrational, as well as socially and ecologically irrational.[83]

Despite the mounting scientific evidence of unsustainability and self-destructiveness, the global system persists for several reasons. The four fictions that legitimate the processes continue to be taken for granted for the most part. The secondary explanations of progress as linear development, unlimited growth, freedom as free trade, and so on continue to hold sway, despite many refutations. But the main reason is simply that the majority of the world's population are subjects of, dependents on, and in financial debt to the global system for their livelihood and well-being, including those who are working hard to question, contest, and change it. That is, we reproduce it through most of our everyday work and play, even when we try to act otherwise. It is our paramount way of life – our way of acting – that reproduces the system. We are conscripts of the vicious system whether we accept or critique the scripts that legitimate it ("domination without consent").[84] As a result of acting accordingly we cannot help but acquire the corresponding background form of subjection and subjectivity – of disclosing and perceiving the world around us. Despite our eco-social and ecological interdependency, we perceive ourselves from within the dis-embedded global system, as independent of the life-sustaining eco-social and ecological webs of life that appear to be external from within the vicious system. The fictional misrepresentation of the four processes becomes our pre-reflective perception of the world in which we live as conscripts.[85]

Therefore, the way to change the system is not only to think differently, as we have been doing so far. It is also necessary to act differently. This involves freeing ourselves from the ways of acting that reproduce the unsustainable system and its way of perceiving the world, and then beginning to act as plain, participatory members and citizens in the damaged and endangered symbiotic ecosystems and informal social systems we inhabit. As people act in participatory, interdependent, and mutually sustainable ways in more and more relationships, the way that the world is perceived and disclosed to them begins to change accordingly. In so doing, they begin to experience and be moved by the gift-reciprocity animacy of life itself. This regenerative movement of potentially transformative reconciliation-with is called the great "reconnection."

IV Reconnection and Transformative Reconciliation

IV.1 Raven Brings the Light

Given the previous section, how can Indigenous and non-Indigenous people begin to perceive our eco-social systems in interdependent and cyclical ways and begin to become plain members and citizens of them with reciprocal dispositional responsibilities to sustain them and the well-being of their members? Robert Davidson provides an exemplary

Indigenous way of bringing about this transformation. He tells a contemporary story of how Raven, the transformer, tries to bring to light the damage that a vicious way of life is causing to the people who are caught up in it, yet who misperceive it and so continue to reproduce it. Raven removes one eye from the villagers as they are sleeping so they will see with only one eye when they awake. In so doing, "Raven creates an imbalance with his voraciousness, because if you take away one eye, you take away the depth of vision. Right now on Haida Gwaii, there is logging in very sensitive areas where the marbled murrelets live. We are so ravenous, so voracious. There is no thinking of the next generation – and even then, we are not fulfilled."[86]

To view the world from the perspective of the dominant extractive system is to be one-eyed, to lose our depth of vision, our ability to see the extractive system as a recent transformation of a much older and deeper conciliatory and sustainable system that endures and underlies this unsustainable system. When villagers re-awake and see with two eyes, they are able see the interdependency between the forests and the marbled murrelets that sustains life. The one-eyed view also fails to think ahead to the conditions that sustain future generations. It is self-centric rather than kin-centric. Moreover, this egocentric way of life is never satisfied: "We are not fulfilled."

One way that Indigenous people on the Northwest Coast regain their depth of vision in the middle of a crisis is to gather together, wear the masks of the life-forms affected, dance and sing like them, and tell stories of how they have recovered from damaging animals, plants, and ecosystems before. In so doing, they remind themselves what it is like to think and act like the animals that their masks represent and see their interdependent world from their perspectives, thus seeing in contrast the damage their one-eyed way of life does to the interconnected world. As Lévi-Strauss realized, "The essential function of the mask is to be the transformation of the individual wearer into another being."[87] This practice of deep empathy, of inhabiting the ways of being of one's human and non-human relatives in order to see what one is doing wrong, especially seeing non-reciprocation (such as over-harvesting) or non-reciprocation, is one of the oldest sustainability practices of *Homo sapiens*.[88]

However, one can perform the mask dances and stories only if she or he already has the experience of living with animals and ecosystems, learning their interdependent life ways, and how to live with them. For example, Aldo Leopold could "see like a mountain," rather than like an extractor, developer, consumer, or disposer, only after years of living as a forest ranger.[89] Yet our extractive and species-centric way of life severs its members from this living interconnection with all forms of life. So the way to depth of vision for those of us who have been disconnected is through practices of "reconnection."[90] Reconnection is a task for both Indigenous and non-Indigenous people, yet in different ways. This is how Davidson sees reconnection with Haida ways of knowing, learning from and then regenerating Mother Earth, and doing so in partnership with non-Haida citizens of Haida Gwaii:

> We are now coming full circle, we are the fourth generation in which the white people have instilled their ideas and values, and denied our way of life, without any knowledge or concern of who we were and where we were coming from. It is our generation that is making the attempt to bridge the gap, to reclaim our identity, our cultural values, the philosophies developed by our ancestors for generations and generations. We are also making a great effort to reconnect with the land. The land is the very foundation of our culture. It is our homeland. We were born into it. We are the stewards: it is our right and responsibility to maintain, nurture and preserve it for the future.[91]

It is important to remember that the Indigenous peoples of the Northwest Coast have been through a similar dual crisis before. During the period of dispossession and dislocation from 1800 to 1880, 90 per cent of their populations died from smallpox brought by the settlers. Then as now, they turned to their stories and teachings of cyclical regeneration to survive and recover.[92]

IV.2 Reconnection through Practices of Resurgent Reconciliation

Humans have not been completely disconnected from social and ecological relationships of interdependency. Rather, we have become conscripts of a vicious social system that operates as if it were disconnected. Accordingly, reconnection, if it is to be transformative, means becoming self-aware of our discursive and non-discursive subjection to this system; freeing ourselves from its hold on our perception and behaviour by moving around so we can begin to experience our eco-social interconnection and interdependency; seeing the social and ecological suffering that our vicious system causes; and taking up our eco-social responsibilities of earth-learning, repair, and regeneration that we have as plain members and citizens of the commonwealth of all forms of life on earth. These four steps constitute non-violent practices of transformative reconciliation-with each other and the living earth. They "realize" transformative reconciliation in the double sense of becoming aware of what it involves and bringing it into being by changing one's way of life, as the quotation from Davidson illustrates. This is also the way reconnection and reconciliation are conceptualized in other traditions.[93]

There are many ways in which these transformative steps can be enacted. However, they all share the five features of transformative reconciliation set out in section I.4. Like Raven in the Davidson example, the massive empirical evidence, scientific reports, and academic and non-academic writing bring the crisis to awareness (feature one). The central feature that then animates transformative reconciliation is feature four: being the change by acting and interacting in conciliatory, symbiotic, and co-sustainable ways in our everyday activities with each and the living earth. This is the earth teaching that we have learned from Indigenous traditions in section I and the life and human sciences in section II.

The reason why the means of transformation of the vicious system have to be reconnective practices of conciliatory and sustainable cooperation is that the means sow the seeds of the end. This is the way that life systems recover from crises in the three meta-cycles of life (sections I.4, II.2). The practical reason for this constitutive relationship between means (practices of reconciliation) and ends (transformation) is that we cannot possibly bring to light and know what counts as responsible reciprocation (repair and regeneration) unless and until we begin to interact-with and within eco-social systems as cooperative and co-evolving participants and learn our way around. This participatory way of being in the world discloses the world as a living interdependent world, whereas, in contrast, our extractive and mastery-over way of being discloses the world as an external storehouse of proto-commodities.[94]

As we have seen, the participatory way of being in the world brings to light the way that life sustains life, and thus the way of transformative reconciliation. This is expressed in the view that co-sustaining symbiosis is the major factor in the co-evolution of life on earth. Living beings sustain themselves by living in ways that co-sustain the interdependent ecosystems and eco-social systems that co-sustain them. The way people come to know what ways of life co-sustain their interdependent neighbours, human and more-than-human, is to enter into dialogues of mutual learning with them. The members learn from each other, cooperate, and thus conciliate and reconciliate the mutually supportive relationships between them.[95] If such cooperative practices of reconciliation are to be transformative and overcome the injustices of dispossession in section III.2, non-Indigenous peoples have to enter into cooperative relationships of mutual learning and cooperation with Indigenous peoples, in accordance with their laws and ways of learning and cooperating, when they are living, working on, or affecting their traditional territories. The convergence of Indigenous and Western knowledge now makes this form of cooperation possible and mutually enlightening (section II).[96]

Everyone can engage in practices of reconciliation here and now. There is no privileged position or class. Everyone can become aware of and work on the three types of eco-social relationships in which all find themselves in their everyday lives: the relationships they have with their selves (practices of the self), with other human beings (communities of practice), and with the living earth (earth practices). Like the recovery of an ecosystem after clear-cutting, this begins by becoming aware of and connecting with the symbiotic ecosystems and informal social systems that continue to exist and sustain life, despite superpredation by the vicious global system.[97] Moreover, it involves becoming aware of and connecting with the eco-social ecology generated by practices of reconciliation over the last decades and learning from their successes and failures.[98]

Valerie Napoleon and Hadley Friedland have developed one exemplary way of doing this.[99] They invite members of a community to get together and map the relationships they find themselves in: both the vicious relationships of the dominant system and the virtuous relationships they inhabit. They then discuss how they can work to change vicious and unsustainable relationships and to regenerate and scale out the virtuous relationships into expanding networks. These activities involve ethical practices of the self (self-change); ways of reforming the vicious relationships they inhabit from within the practices and institutions available to them (reform); as well as the more confrontational ways of non-violent protest, contestation, civil disobedience, boycotts, and so on (contestation). They also involve innovative practices of disengaging from the dominant system as much as possible, reappropriating and exercising the human capacities of self-organization and self-government in their producing and consuming activities in local, co-sustaining networks and cycles (constructive programs). These are neither exclusively reconciliation practices from above nor below, but, as they succinctly put it, "everywhere and every day."[100] In these four types of gift-reciprocity practices and networks of reconciliation-with, Indigenous and non-Indigenous partners engage in mutual learning, reforming the dominant institutions from within, tradespeople and inventors developing green technologies, cyclical economic organizations, local food revolutions, bio-mimicry, cradle-to-cradle technology, architecture and town planning, post-carbon fuels, cooperatives rather than private corporations, fair trade rather than free trade, commoning rather than privatizing the living earth, engaging in shared, land-based and community-based education and research, establishing Indigenous peoples working groups on climate change, and countless other examples.[101]

Some Indigenous people engaging in these activities prefer to work with their own community and not with non-Indigenous partners as much as possible. This is often referred to as resurgence.[102] Yet "resurgence" in this sense consists in reconnecting with and regenerating the living earth and relationship with members of their Indigenous community. That is, while the practitioners are often critical of processes of reconciliation-to, their practice consists in community-based practices of transformative reconciliation-with. Respect for these resurgence practices is an important part of the ethics of reconciliation-with.[103] Others, such as the Haida and the Great Bear Rainforest Alliance, prefer to work with their non-Indigenous neighbours, building these relationships of mutual aid as they go along.[104] There are many kinds of conciliatory and sustainable partnerships between Indigenous and non-Indigenous peoples, and they are possible even in the most polluted and difficult circumstances today.[105] However, what makes them transformative is that they are based on the gift-reciprocity relationship of interdependency and mutual aid learned from Mother Earth. The early modern peace and friendship treaties and the Two Row Wampum treaty relationship are often used as the model for these partnerships. The reason is that the way the partners treat each other in the treaty negotiations manifests the kind of relationship they aim to bring into being among their respective peoples as a result of the negotiations.[106] Moreover, the revitalization of Indigenous legal orders empowers Indigenous people to relate to each other, their non-Indigenous neighbours, and Mother Earth through their legal and governmental traditions.[107]

The repair, regeneration, creation, and scaling-out of these gift-reciprocity practices, networks, and cycles of reconciliation-with can be transformative, both locally in the short term and globally in the long term. They grow on the basis of the gifts that have been given to us by the living earth and those who came before us, and they will continue to grow on the basis of what our generations have given in reciprocity. The biggest challenge today is not to design or invent practices of trans-formative reconciliation. Appropriate sustainable and cyclical ways of knowing and of acting already exist in practice for many areas of human activity. The challenge is to find ways to connect and coordinate these four different kinds of reconciliation practices in larger webs of gift-reciprocity relationships of mutual learning and mutual support, for none of these kinds of practice is sufficient in independence from the other three. Educational institutions can play an important role in this coor-dination with the appropriate kind of teaching, learning, and research.

No one doubts the enormity of the task of the two projects of rec-onciliation and the seeming insignificance of the non-violent, human-scale means I am suggesting. However, as we have seen, the alternative means of either violence or mega-projects by elites are part of the dual crisis. As the small, local, symbiotically coordinated webs of steps and practices of reconciliation grow, they first reach tipping points and bring about transformations of vicious relationships locally. These small changes have significant ripple effects, especially on the younger generations who see and hear about them. If these continue to multiply and accumulate here, there, and everywhere, they have the potential gradually to reach a point where the global vicious system as a whole is transformed into an assemblage of virtuous ones. Then, once again, conciliatory and sustainable relationships and cycles become domi-nant, and humans and their relatives begin another meta-cycle, hope-fully having learned how to avoid another massive crisis like the one we are in today. This is how damaged ecosystems incrementally trans-form themselves and how human civilizations have survived collapse in the past.[108]

The most important feature of this ethical view of reconciliation is that it enables everyone to act responsibly and reciprocally here and now, to realize reconciliation here on earth and with each other to some small extent in every step we take. If this view of life is correct, then some of our interdependent relatives, human and more-than-human, will be moved to reciprocate in response. Then we will be reconnected to and empowered by the cyclical and regenerative animacy of life itself – the greatest power on earth.

NOTES

1 The two kinds of reconciliation, formal and informal, overlap. However, I suggest that specific policies and practices of formal recognition, such as the recommendations of The Truth and Reconciliation Commission, need to be grounded in a broader and more basic kind of informal, cyclical reconciliation, which I call reconciliation-with, if they are to become effective in the long term. Informal reconciliation-with is the living ethos and ecology that sustains formal and specific policies of reconciliation. For a concise synopsis of the Truth and Reconciliation Commission's view of reconciliation, which shows its complementarity, see Paulette Regan, this volume.

2 Reconciliation with each other "in all our diversity" refers to practices of reconciliation that are aware of the criss-crossing and overlapping identity-related differences and similarities within and across indigenous and non-indigenous peoples, such as class, race, gender, sexual orientation, place, age, education, and health, as well as the diversity of meanings of indigenous and non-indigenous. I call this intersectional approach "diversity awareness." See James Tully, *Democracy and Civic Freedom* (Cambridge: Cambridge University Press, 2008), 291–316. The phrases "indigenous and non-indigenous" and "with each other" always refer to this complex life-world, even though I am not able to analyse the complex diversity of instances of reconciliation in this brief exposition. This approach contrasts with approaches that abstract an "indigenous and non-indigenous" binary from the diverse field of lived experience in which it exists. For an excellent introduction to diversity-aware approaches, see Gina Starblanket and Heidi Stark, this volume.

3 For an introduction to the ecological crisis, including climate change, see the Intergovernmental Panel on Climate Change (IPCC), *Climate Change 2014: IPCC Fifth Assessment Synthesis Report* (Geneva: IPCC, 2014), www. ipcc.ch/pdf/assessment-report/ar5/syr/SYR_AR5_FINAL_full.pdf; James Lovelock, *A Rough Guide to the Future* (New York: Penguin, 2014); Craig Dilworth, *Too Smart for Our Own Good: The Ecological Predicament of Humankind* (Cambridge: Cambridge University Press, 2010); Peter Sale, *Our Dying Planet: An Ecologist's View of the Crisis We Face* (Berkeley: University of California Press, 2012); Richard Heinberg and Daniel Lerch, eds, *The Post-Carbon Reader: Managing the 21st Century's Sustainability Crises* (Healdsburg: Watershed Media, 2010). See section III.

4 See Kim Sterelny, *The Evolved Apprentice: How Evolution Made Humans Unique* (Cambridge: MIT Press, 2012); Nancy Turner, *Ancient Pathways, Ancestral Knowledge: Ethnobotany and Ecological Wisdom of Indigenous People of Northwestern North America* (Montreal and Kingston: McGill-Queen's University Press, 2014); Craig Dilworth, *Too Smart for Our Own Good: The Ecological Predicament of Humankind* (Cambridge: Cambridge University Press, 2010), 52–75; Robin Wall Kimmerer, *Braiding Sweetgrass: Indigenous Wisdom, Scientific Knowledge, and the Teachings of Plants* (Minneapolis: Milkweed Editions, 2013).

5 See sections III.3, IV.2.

6 The first person to expose this double injustice systematically was Franz Boas, *The Mind of Primitive Man* (New York: Macmillan, 1922 [1911]). See James Tully, "Rediscovering the World of Franz Boas: Anthropology, Equality/Diversity, and World Peace," in *Indigenous Visions: Rediscovering the World of Franz Boas*, ed. Ned Blackhawk and Isaiah Wilner, 111–46 (New Haven, CT: Yale University Press, 2018).

7 For a synthesis, see Fritjof Capra and Pier Luigi Luisi, *The Systems View of Life* (Cambridge: Cambridge University Press, 2014).

8 This is associated with the recognition of Indigenous peoples' ways of knowing (and being), often referred to as traditional ecological knowledge and wisdom (TEKW), as equal in epistemic status to Western scientific knowledges, and the recognition of Indigenous peoples as peoples with the right of self-determination in international law, in accordance with their ways of knowing and being, in the United Nations Declaration on the Rights of Indigenous Peoples.

9 Zoltan Grossman and Alan Parker, eds, *Asserting Native Resilience: Pacific Rim Indigenous Nations Face the Climate Crisis* (Corvalis: Oregon State University Press, 2012).

10 For an introduction to this vision of education, see Sean Esbjorn-Hargens and Michael E. Zimmerman, eds, *Integral Ecology: Uniting Multiple Perspectives on the Natural World* (Boston: Integral Books, 2009); Capra and Luisi, *Systems View*.

11 Fritjof Capra, *The Hidden Connections: A Science for Sustainable Living* (New York: Anchor Books, 2004), 230.

12 See sections I.4, III.3, IV.2.

13 Robert Williams Jr, *Linking Arms Together: American Indian Treaty Visions of Law and Peace 1600–1800* (Oxford: Oxford University Press, 1997); Michael Asch, *On Being Here to Stay: Treaties and Aboriginal Rights in Canada* (Toronto: University of Toronto Press, 2014); Michael Asch, this volume.

14 John Borrows, *Freedom and Indigenous Constitutionalism* (Toronto: University of Toronto Press, 2016), 221. See John Borrows, this volume;

Aaron Mills, "The Lifeworlds of Law: On Revitalizing Indigenous Legal Orders Today," *McGill Law Journal* 61, no. 4 (2016): 847–84; Mills, this volume; Winona LaDuke, *All Our Relations: Native Struggles for Land and Life* (Cambridge: South End, 1999).

15 Cary Miller, "Gifts as Treaties," *American Indian Quarterly* 26, no. 2 (2002): 221–45. Kimmerer, *Braiding Sweetgrass*, is an exploration of earth teachings of gift-reciprocity and their roles in establishing sustainable, gift-reciprocity social relationships.

16 Kimmerer, *Braiding Sweetgrass*, 303–10, 380–4. For similar gift-reciprocity cycle stories on the Northwest coast, see Ron Trosper, *Resilience, Reciprocity and Ecological-Economics: Northwest Coast Sustainability* (London: Routledge, 2011); Isaiah Lorado Wilner, "A Global Potlatch: Identifying the Indigenous Influence on Western Thought," *American Indian Culture and Research Journal* 37, no. 2 (2013): 87. For a recent analysis of the gift-reciprocity relationship and the literature on it in the Western tradition, see Marc Hénaff, *The Price of Truth: Gift, Money, and Philosophy*, trans. Jean-Louise Morhange (Stanford: Stanford University Press, 2010), 101–290.

17 Taiaiake Alfred, *Wasase: Indigenous Pathways of Action and Freedom* (Toronto: University of Toronto Press, 2009), 13–17. This is his adaptation of the Rotinoshonni Thanksgiving Address in the Haudenosaunee Environmental Task Force's "Greetings to the Natural World," in *Haudenosaunee Environmental Restoration: An Indigenous Strategy for Sustainability* (Cambridge: Indigenous Development International, 1995).

18 George Clutesi, *Potlatch* (Sidney: Grey Publishing, 1969), 3.

19 Nancy Turner, *The Earth's Blanket: Traditional Teachings for Sustainable Living* (Vancouver: Douglas & MacIntyre, 2005), 69–95.

20 "Independence" in this section refers to the family of views that derive from the premise that independence is ontologically prior to relationships of interdependence and a moral and political ideal. It does not refer to the kind of "contextual independence" agents have or acquire in awareness of and respect for life-sustaining relationships of interdependence.

21 See, respectively, Mathis Wackernagel and William Rees, *Our Ecological Footprint: Reducing Human Impact on the Earth* (Gabriola Island, BC: New Society Publishers, 1996); Alan Drengson and Bill Devall, eds, *The Ecology of Wisdom: Writings of Arne Naess* (Berkeley: Counterpoint, 2008), 99–144.

22 David Abram, *The Spell of the Sensuous* (New York: Vintage Books, 1996).

23 Aldo Leopold, "The Land Ethic," in *A Sand County Almanac: With Essays on Conservation from Round River*, 237–95 (New York: Ballantine Books, 1966). The cyclical view of life sustaining life is at 137–41, 188–202.

24 For this distinction, see Michael O. Hardimon, *Hegel's Social Philosophy: The Project of Reconciliation* (Cambridge: Cambridge University Press,

1994), 84–126. This is a helpful guide to the distinction between the two senses of "reconciliation": reconciliation-to and reconciliation-with. However, the five criteria of transformative reconciliation-with that I employ are not identical to Hegel's, but have been crafted in light of other traditions of transformative reconciliation of unjust relationships, especially the Gandhian tradition and the Indigenous traditions of the Northwest Coast. There have been many criticisms of the formal processes of reconciliation-to in Canada, but most have remained within the background assumptions of reconciliation-to, and thus their alternatives remain within the unsustainable relationship to the living earth and each other (see section III). For a definitive critical analysis of the persisting colonial foundations of processes and policies of reconciliation-to from the nineteenth century to today to which I am indebted, see Joshua Nichols, "A Reconciliation without Recollection: An Investigation of the Foundations of the Indian Act" (PhD diss., University of Victoria, forthcoming).

25 Umeek, E. Richard Atleo, *Tsawalk: A Nuu-chah-nulth Worldview* (Vancouver: UBC Press, 2004), 117–32; Umeek, Atleo, *Principles of Tsawalk: An Indigenous Approach to Global Crisis* (Vancouver: UBC Press, 2011), 9–78.

26 These disruptions are often unpredictable and can irrupt and transform any conciliatory relationship. In Indigenous traditions it is often the trickster who initiates such a disruption in order to teach a lesson about sharing, gratitude, responsibility and so on. The Raven cycle stories on the Northwest Coast are exemplary (Atleo, *Tsawalk*, 1–22). For a careful analysis of how such disruptions break out in human relationships and how they can be transformed by practices of reconciliation in the Buddhist tradition, see Pema Chodron, *Practicing Peace in Times of War* (Boston: Shambhala, 2007). For an introduction to contemporary Anishinaabe trickster (Nanaboozhoo) stories, see John Borrows (Kegedonce), *Drawing Out Law: A Spirit's Guide* (Toronto: University of Toronto Press, 2010).

27 The terms "virtuous" and "vicious" systems are drawn from systems theory and its application to the ecological crisis. See Stephan Harding, *Animate Earth: Science, Intuition and Gaia*, 2nd ed. (Cambridge: Green Books, 2013), 68–91. See section II.1. It is similar to virtuous and vicious in Indigenous gift-reciprocity (and non-reciprocity) stories.

28 See Paulette Regan and Kiera Ladner, this volume; Marin Cogan, "The Vanishing of Canada's First Nations Women," *Financial Post*, 6 July 2016, https://foreignpolicy.com/2016/07/06/the-vanishing-of-canadas-first-nations-women-harper-trudeau-violence-highway-of-tears-indigenous/.

29 John Borrows, "Interview on Idle No More," CBC Radio, 28 December 2012.

30 Michael Klare, *The Race for What's Left: The Global Scramble for the World's Last Resources* (New York: Picador, 2012).

31 Lester R. Brown, *World on the Edge: How to Prevent Environmental and Economic Collapse* (New York: W.W. Norton, 2011); and references in note 3 above.

32 See sections III.2, III.3.

33 See sections IV.1, IV.2.

34 Dennis Dalton, *Mahatma Gandhi: Nonviolent Power in Action* (New York: Columbia University Press, 2012); Richard Gregg, *The Power of Nonviolence* (New York: Schocken Books, 1966).

35 See, for example, Jeanette Armstrong and the En'owkin Centre, Penticton Indian Band, BC, https://www.enowkincentre.ca; Alfred, *Wasase*, 45–97; Borrows, *Freedom and Indigenous Constitutionalism*, 50–102.

36 Alfred, *Wasase*, 21; compare 229–30.

37 Eric Fromm coined the term *biophilia* in the 1950s to describe this participatory, gift-reciprocity ways of being in the world with other living beings.

38 See, respectively, Michael Mitchell, "An Unbroken Assertion of Sovereignty," in *Drumbeat, Anger and Renewal in Indian Country*, ed. Boyce Richardson (Toronto: Assembly of First Nations: Summerhill, 1989), 105–36; Alfred, *Wasase*, 266; Borrows, *Canada's Indigenous Constitution*; John Borrows, "Wampum at Niagara: The Royal Proclamation, Canadian Legal History, and Self-Government," in *Aboriginal and Treaty Rights in Canada: Essays on Law, Equity and Respect for Difference*, ed. Michael Asch (Vancouver: UBC Press, 1997), 155–73; Aaron Mills, "The Treaty of Niagara 1764, Political Community and Non-Domination: A Perspective from Anishinaabe Constitutionalism on Being Well Together" (public lecture at "The Treaty of Niagara 1764 and Canadian Constitutionalism Today: Crown/First Nations Relations 250 Years In," sponsored by the Centre for Human Rights and Legal Pluralism and the Aboriginal Law Students' Association, McGill University Faculty of Law, Montreal, 15 September 2014); Asch, *On Being Here to Stay*; Kimmerer, *Braiding Sweetgrass*, 3–11; and K'san book builders, *We-gyet* [Raven] *Wanders On: Legends of the Northwest* (Saanichton, BC: Hancock House Publishing, 1977); and Xsiwis (Jane Smith), "Placing Gitxsan Stories in Text: Returning the Feathers. Guuxs Mak'am Mik'aax" (PhD diss. University of British Columbia, 2004); Vernon Wilson, "A Post-Delgamuukw Philosophical Feast: Feeding the Ancestral Desire for Peaceful Coexistence" (MA diss., Trinity Western University, 2016).

39 Ulli Steltzer and Robert Bringhurst, *The Black Canoe: Bill Reid and the Spirit of Haida Gwaii* (Vancouver: Douglas & MacIntyre, 1992). The canoe is full

of diverse myth creatures with all their crisscrossing and overlapping stories, yet conciliating their differences through non-violent dialogues. Bill Reid was involved in the Haida assertion of jurisdiction over Haida Gwaii and the protection of the old growth forests while the canoe was being constructed. See Leslie Dawn, "RE: Reading Reid and the 'Revival,'" in *Bill Reid and Beyond: Expanding on Modern Native Art*, ed. Karen Duffek and Charlotte Townsend-Gault, 251–80 (Vancouver: Douglas & MacIntyre, 2004). For Reid's view of the Raven stories, as the bringer of enlightenment by means of transformation, see Bill Reid and Robert Bringhurst, *The Raven Steals the Light* (Vancouver: Douglas & MacIntyre, 1984), esp. 11–18. For Reid's view of reconciliation with the living earth, after centuries of subduing and plunder, and with Indigenous and non-Indigenous people, see Bill Reid, "These Shining Islands" and "Becoming Haida" in *The Essential Writings of Bill Reid*, 2nd ed., ed. Robert Bringhurst, 222–8 and 229–34 (Vancouver: Douglas & MacIntyre, 2009): "As for what constitutes a Haida – well, Haida only means human being, and as far as I'm concerned, a human being is anyone who respects the needs of his fellow man, and the earth which nurtures and shelters us all" ("Becoming Haida," 233). See also Haida artist Robert Davidson, who learned to carve under Reid's mentorship, at Sections III.3 and IV.1

40 Elizabeth Kolbert, *The Sixth Extinction: An Unnatural History* (New York: Henry Holt, 2014).

41 *Report of the Royal Commission on Aboriginal Peoples*. Vol. 1, *Looking Forward, Looking Back* (Ottawa: Canadian Communication Group, 1995), 43–244.

42 James Tully, "Consent, Hegemony, and Dissent in Treaty Negotiations," in *Between Consenting Peoples: Political Community and the Meaning of Consent*, ed. Jeremy Webber and Colin M. MacLeod, 233–56 (Vancouver: UBC Press, 2010); John Borrows, "Nanabush Goes West: Treaties, and the Trickster in British Columbia," in *Recovering Canada: The Resurgence of Indigenous Law*, 77–110 (Toronto: University of Toronto Press, 2002).

43 It is important to realize that Gandhi criticized the two traditions of reform and violent revolution during Third World decolonization, as both reconciliation-to unsustainable social and ecological relationships, and developed his practices of *satyagraha* – nonviolent transformative decolonization and reconciliation-with – in response. See Mahatma Gandhi, *Hind Swaraj and Other Writings* (Cambridge: Cambridge University Press, 1996). See also Dennis Dalton, *Mahatma Gandhi: Nonviolent Power in Action* (New York: Columbia University Press, 2012); Gregg, *Power of Nonviolence*; and Alfred, *Wasase*, 55–8, 204–6 on Gandhian *satyagraha* and Indigenous non-violent strategies of decolonization.

44 See Joanna Macy and Chris Johnstone, *Active Hope: How to Face the Mess We're in without Going Crazy* (Novato: New World Library, 2012); Pope Francis, *Encyclical on Climate Change and Inequality: On Care of Our Common Home* (London: Melville House, 2015); Gregg, *Power of Nonviolence*.

45 See James Lovelock, *Gaia and the Theory of the Living Planet* (London: Gaia Books, 2005); John Gribbin and Mary Gribbin, *He Knew He Was Right: The Irrepressible Life of James Lovelock* (London: Penguin, 2009); and Harding, *Animate Earth* for the most relevant introductions to the Gaia theory for our purposes.

46 Capra and Luisi, *Systems View of Life*.

47 Lynn Margulis, *Symbiotic Planet* (London: Weidenfeld & Nicholson, 1998); Gribbin and Gribbin, *He Knew He Was Right*, 3.

48 Peter Kropotkin was the first life and social scientist to advance this hypothesis in the modern period in his 1901 classic, *Mutual Aid: A Factor of Evolution* (1901; Mineola, NY: Dover, 2006). It was re-articulated by Barry Commoner, the founder of ecology in the United States, in *The Closing Circle: Nature, Man and Technology* (New York: Alfred A. Knopf, 1971).

49 Harding, *Animate Earth*, 46–68.

50 Ibid., 68–91.

51 Ibid., 92–112, 190–207.

52 Michael Simpson, PhD student in geography, University of British Columbia, personal correspondence. Compare Alan Rike Drengson and Duncan MacDonald Taylor, *Ecoforestry: The Art and Science of Sustainable Forest Use* (Gabriola Island, BC: New Society, 1997); David Suzuki and Wayne Grady, *Tree: A Life Story* (Vancouver: Greystone Books, 2004).

53 Robin Wall Kimmerer, "Returning the Gift," *Minding Nature* 7, no. 2 (2014): 4.

54 Johnny Camille Mack, "Thickening Totems and Thinning Imperialism" (LLM diss., University of Victoria, 2009); Mack, "*Hoquotisht*: Returning to Our Canoes through Stories," in *Storied Communities: Narratives of Contact and Arrival*, ed. Rebecca Johnson, Hester Lessard, and Jeremy Webber, 287–307 (Vancouver: UBC Press, 2010).

55 Robert Davidson, *The Abstract Edge*, ed. Karen Duffek (Vancouver: Museum of Anthropology, 2004), 26. This is his commentary on his artwork entitled *The World Is as Sharp as a Knife*. For the Raven stories on which Davidson draws, see Robert Bringhurst, *A Story as Sharp as a Knife: The Classical Haida Mythtellers and Their World* (Vancouver: Douglas & McIntyre, 1999).

56 Sean Esbjorn-Hargens and Michael E. Zimmerman, eds, *Integral Ecology: Uniting Multiple Perspectives on the Natural World* (Boston: Integral Books, 2009).

57 Capra, *Hidden Connections*, 98–128.

58 William Rees, "Thinking Resilience," in *The Post-Carbon Reader: Managing the 21st Century's Sustainability Crises*, ed. Richard Heinberg and Daniel Lerch, 25–42 (Healdsburg, CA: Watershed Media, 2010).

59 Alan Drengson and Bill Devall, eds, *The Ecology of Wisdom: Writings of Arne Naess* (Berkeley: Counterpoint, 2008), 99–144; Stephanie Kaza, *Mindfully Green: A Personal and Spiritual Guide to Whole Earth Thinking* (Boston: Shambhala, 2008).

60 See Macy and Johnstone, *Active Hope*, 43–56, 85–139; Asoka Bandarage, *Sustainability and Well-Being: The Middle Path to Environment, Society, and the Economy* (London: Palgrave Macmillan, 2013).

61 Patrick Curry, *Ecological Ethics: An Introduction*, 2nd ed. (Cambridge: Polity, 2011).

62 Aldo Leopold, "The Land Ethic," in *A Sand County Almanac: With Essays on Conservation from Round River* (New York: Ballantine Books, 1966), 238–9.

63 Kim Sterelny, *The Evolved Apprentice: How Evolution Made Humans Unique* (Cambridge, MA: MIT Press, 2012).

64 Basil Johnston, *Ojibway Heritage* (Toronto: McClelland & Stewart, 1987), 41.

65 Anthony J. Hall, *Earth into Property: Colonization, Decolonization, and Capitalism* (Montreal and Kingston: McGill-Queen's University Press, 2010).

66 James Tully, *Imperialism and Civic Freedom* (Cambridge: Cambridge University Press, 2008), 195–222, 243–67.

67 Boas, *Mind of Primitive Man*, 2–4. See also Tully, "Rediscovering the World of Franz Boas." It is significant that Boas came to question Western superiority as the result of extensive discussion with George Hunt and the Kwakwaka'wakaw people of the Northwest Coast. See Isaiah Lorado Wilner, "A Global Potlatch: Identifying the Indigenous Influence on Western Thought," *American Indian Culture and Research Journal* 37, no. 2 (2013): 87.

68 Leopold, "Land Ethic," 240: "In short, a land ethic changes the role of Homo sapiens from conqueror of the land-community to plain member and citizen of it. It implies respect for his fellow-members, and also respect for the community as such."

69 Karl Polanyi, *Great Transformation: The Political and Economic Origins of Our Time*, foreword by Joseph E. Stiglitz, introduction by Fred Block (1944; Boston: Beacon, 2001). I added the first and fourth processes to Polanyi's second and third. I omitted Polanyi's third fictitious commodity, the commodification of money.

70 John Borrows, "Sovereignty's Alchemy: An Analysis of Delgamuukw v British Columbia," *Osgoode Hall Law Journal* 37 (1999): 537; Nichols, "Reconciliation without Recollection"; Kent McNeil, this volume.

71 *Report of the Royal Commission on Aboriginal Peoples,* vol. 1 (Ottawa: Indian and Northern Affairs Canada, 1996). See John Borrows, "Domesticating Doctrines: Aboriginal Peoples after the Royal Commission," *McGill Law Journal* 46 (2001): 615–61.

72 See sections I.1, I.4, references at notes 3, 29, 30; and Harding, *Animate Earth*; 208–49.

73 Naomi Klein, *This Changes Everything: Capitalism versus the Climate* (New York: Simon & Schuster, 2014); Irene Khan, *The Unheard Truth: Poverty and Human Rights* (New York: W.W. Norton, 2009).

74 For this transformation to representative democracy in the nineteenth century, see Francis Dupuis-Déri, *Démocratie: Histoire Politique d'un mot* (Montreal: Lux Éditeur, 2013). For the globalization of this module, see Tully, *Imperialism and Civic Freedom,* 243–67.

75 Polanyi, *Great Transformation,* 181: "To allow the market mechanism to be sole director of the fate of human beings and their natural environment … would result in the demolition of society. Robbed of the protective covering of cultural institutions, human beings would perish from the effects of social exposure; they would die as the victims of acute social dislocation through vice, perversion, crime and starvation. Nature would be reduced to its elements, neighbourhoods and landscapes defiled, rivers polluted, military safety jeopardized, the power to produce food and raw materials destroyed."

76 See Dilworth, *Too Smart for Our Own Good;* Capra, *Hidden Connections,* 129–57.

77 Klare, *Race for What's Left;* Brown, *World on the Edge.*

78 Compare Robert Nichols, "Disaggregating Primitive Accumulation: The Dialectic of Labor and Land," *Radical Philosophy* 94 (2015): 18–28; Kamran Nayeri, "'Capitalism in the Web of Life': A Critique," *Climate and Capitalism,* 19 July 2016, 1–2, 8–13, http://climateandcapitalism.com/2016/07/19/capitalism-in-the-web-of-life-a-critique. I am indebted to conversations with Robert Nichols on how best to characterize this first process of "dispossession."

79 Paul Hawken, *Blessed Unrest: How the Largest Movement in the World Came into Being and Why No One Saw It Coming* (New York: Viking, 2007); Boaventura de Sousa Santos, *Epistemologies of the South: Justice against Epistemicide* (Boulder, CO: Paradigm Publishers, 2014). Hawken argues that Indigenous people are the leading edge of these social networks.

80 Asoka Bandarage, *Sustainability and Well-being: The Middle Path to Environment, Society, and the Economy* (London: Palgrave Macmillan, 2013).

81 John Borrows, "The Durability of Terra Nullius: Tsilhqot'in Nation v British Columbia," *UBC Law Review* 48, no. 3 (2015): 701; and see note 67.

82 William McDonough and Michael Braungart, *Cradle to Cradle: Remaking the Way We Make Things* (New York: North Point, 2002).

83 This was the finding of the first Limits to Growth model in 1972. Donella H. Meadows, Dennis L. Meadows, Jørgen Randers, and William W. Behrens III, *The Limits to Growth: A Report for the Club of Rome's Project on the Predicament of Mankind* (New York: Universe Books, 1971). It was defended and updated in 2012; see Ugo Bardi, *The Limits to Growth Revisited* (New York, Springer, 2012). Lester Brown refers to this as the "fatal flaw" of the global economy; see Brown, *World on the Edge*, 15, 8.

84 This is the first feature of a crisis of reconciliation in section I.4.

85 This is the "independent" mode of self-perception at section I.3. For the first analysis of the ecological crisis as this kind of perceptual/praxis misrepresentation, see Commoner, *Closing Circle*, 14. For a striking example of the disastrous effects of this misperception in settlement patterns, see Nancy Turner and Pamela Spalding, this volume.

86 Davidson, *Abstract Edge*, 36. This is his commentary on his artwork entitled *Ravenous*.

87 Claude Lévi-Strauss, in conversation with Wilson Duff in 1974, cited in Wayne Suttles, "The World Is as Sharp as a Knife: A Review Article [of Donald N. Abbott, ed., *The World is as Sharp as a Knife: An Anthology in Honour of Wilson Duff* (Victoria: Provincial Museum, 1981)] (1983) 56 *BC Studies* at 90.

88 See Kim Sterelny, *The Evolved Apprentice: How Evolution Made Humans Unique* (Cambridge, MA: MIT Press, 2012); David Abram, *Becoming Animal: An Earthly Cosmology* (New York: Vintage Books, 2010).

89 Leopold, "Land Ethic," 137–41.

90 For an introduction to the ways of "transformative reconnection" with the living earth and with Indigenous peoples, see Macy and Johnstone, *Active Hope*, 13–84; Hawken, *Blessed Unrest*; Harding, *Animate Earth*, 36–67.

91 Robert Davidson, "Untitled Document," included in the catalogue for "Robert Davidson Exhibition: A Voice from Inside" (Vancouver: Derek Simpson Gallery, 1992), 1–3, 3. For the whole movement of transformative reconnection on Haida Gwaii to which Davidson refers, see Louise Takeda, *Islands' Spirit Rising: Reclaiming the Forests of Haida Gwaii* (Vancouver: UBC Press, 2015).

92 See Isaiah Lorado Wilner, "Raven Cried for Me: Narratives of Transformation on the Northwest Coast of America" (PhD diss., Yale University, 2016); Alan Hoover, "Charles Edenshaw and the Development of Narrative Structure in Nineteenth-Century Haida Art," in *Charles Edenshaw*, ed. Robin K. Wright and Daina Augaitis, 67–73 (London: Black Dog Publishing, 2015).

93   See references at note 41; Thich Nhat Hanh, *Love Letter to the Earth* (Berkeley: Parallax, 2014), Kaza, *Mindfully Green.*

94   This internal relationships between being, disclosing, and knowing is now called the Santiago theory of cognition, but, as we have seen, it is as old as traditional Indigenous knowledge and stories. For the Santiago theory, see Capra and Luisi, *Systems View of Life*, 255–7, 262.

95   This is the revolution in education called for by Fritjof Capra in section I.2 and explained in the life and human sciences in section II, sometimes referred to as biomimicry and holistic science. For an introduction, see references at note 10; and Harding, *Animate Earth*, 35–45.

96   See, for example, Grossman and Parker, *Asserting Native Resilience.* For a leading example in the area of law, see the programs in the Faculty of Law at the University of Victoria for the teaching of Indigenous and Common law: www.uvic.ca/law/assets/docs/jid/JIDBrochureWeb2.pdf.

97   This is the central theme of Vandana Shiva, *Earth Democracy: Justice, Sustainability and Peace* (Cambridge, MA: South End, 2005).

98   See section III.3. For a recent survey of the field, see Greg Poeltzer and Ken S. Coates, *From Treaty Peoples to Treaty Nation: A Road Map for All Canadians* (Vancouver: UBC Press, 2015).

99   Valerie Napoleon and Hadley Friedland are law professors at the University of Victoria. The teaching method they have developed is used in the classroom and in Indigenous communities throughout British Columbia. It is called the "TullyWheel" because they draw creatively on the types of engaged and landed citizen practices I discuss in James Tully, *Public Philosophy in a New Key* (Cambridge: Cambridge University Press 2008), 2:243–311. See Val Napoleon and Hadley Friedland, "Accessing Tully: Political Philosophy for the Everyday and the Everyone," *Freedom and Democracy in an Imperial Context: Dialogues with James Tully*, ed. Robert Nichols and Jakeet Singh, 202–22 (London: Routledge, 2014).

100 These four types of transformative practices of reconciliation-with are similar to the four main types of practices of Gandhi's *satyagraha*: his way of transforming oppressive relationships and reconciling the partners. See references at notes 33, 34, and 40 to convergence among several Indigenous and non-Indigenous scholars on the centrality of these four types of gift-reciprocity practices in response to the dual crisis.

101 The list of examples in this paragraph is drawn from the literature referred to in the notes to this chapter. For "cyclical" or ecological economics, see Peter G. Brown and Peter Timmerman, eds, *Ecological*

Economics for the Anthropocene (New York: Columbia University Press, 2015). For a survey of research on sustainable systems, see Gar Alperovitz, James Gustave Speth, and Joe Guinan, *The Next System Project: New Political-Economic Possibilities for the 21st Century,* (2016), https://www.thenextsystem.org. The world of transformative practice is outgrowing by far the academic research and surveys of it. I discuss some examples and respond to criticisms of them in James Tully, *On Global Citizenship: James Tully in Dialogue* (London: Bloomsbury, 2014); and Robert Nichols and Jakeet Singh, eds, *Freedom and Democracy in an Imperial Context: Dialogues with James Tully* (London: Routledge, 2014); but this is barely the tip of the regenerative world of conciliatory and sustainable practices and networks.

102   For example, Taiaiake Alfred, "On Reconciliation and Resurgence," in *Civic Freedom in an Age of Diversity: The Public Philosophy of James Tully,* ed. Dimitrios Karmis and Jocelyn Maclure (forthcoming, chapter 11).

103   The Two Row Wampum treaty relationship (*Tekani Teioha:te*) manifests both self-government and shared-government.

104   For the Indigenous and non-Indigenous partnerships on Haida Gwaii, see Takeda, *Islands' Spirit Rising.*

105   See, for example, Sarah Marie Wiebe, *Everyday Exposure: Indigenous Mobilization and Environmental Justice in Canada's Chemical Valley* (Vancouver: UBC Press, 2016).

106   See section I.2; and Asch, *On Being Here to Stay;* Michael Asch, this volume.

107   See Borrows, *Canada's Indigenous Constitution;* Borrows, this volume; Aaron Mills, this volume.

108   See sections I.4, II.

PART TWO

4 Rooted Constitutionalism: Growing Political Community

AARON MILLS

The Breach

I live on Koojijing Zaaga'igan, Rainy Lake. Through the red pines and across the bay is Giineshingwak'kag, the point of pines that locals call the Reef Point. Before settler[1] damming raised the water level, the old Anishinaabeg used to make birchbark canoes on its prominent, sandy beaches. The weight of the sand was used to shape and set the curve of the bark.[2]

I moved here two months ago, after having spent the first two years of my doctoral program in Victoria, learning my rapidly developing field and reflecting on my place within it. A large part of that effort was spent watching and listening to others, and then reflecting on the spirit that I'd like my scholarship and, more importantly, my spoken words to echo.[3] For this I turned to my doctoral committee,[4] my friends, my peers, and so many others I admire in the unique University of Victoria environment.[5] I've attended five universities, but UVic is unique among them. The thoughtfulness, rigour, and tremendous generosity of spirit of the gifts shared with me there inspired my best.

I returned to Koojijing Zaaga'igan to ground my doctoral work and to ground myself in the land, elders,[6] and stories of my being. I want my dissertation to be in and through Anishinaabe constitutionalism, not merely of it. For many years now I've carried the gift and responsibility of living in the kind of relationship with two *gete-anishinaabeg* that empowers them to share our traditional law. It's an honour to receive their teachings, and it was that feeling more than anything else that called me home. I want to be near those old ones who judge me worth teaching.

The night I arrived from my cross-Canada drive it was late and dark. My house sits on a rise twenty metres back from the lake. Access is through a wide but steep pathway through spruce and pine, so I didn't go down to the water until the next morning. When I did, something happened.

I stood at the water's edge for no more than twenty seconds before I had a visitor. Giizis (the sun) was high, the sky was clear, and the water was calm. A gentle breeze marked the morning. Name (pronounced "nuh-may"), the sturgeon, emerged from the depths and slowly swam towards me. I do mean s l o w l y. His measured undulation was an underwater saunter. An occasional sway of that muscular tail propelled his two-foot body forward, but mostly he glided over the lake bottom. It was amazing to have him visit. Name is one of our oldest brothers. They say he was around when dinosaurs roamed the earth. Seeing him, I recalled the *aadizookaan*[7] of Great Name trying to avoid Nanabozho's insistent fishing line, and when at last sufficiently pestered, engulfing the line and Nanabozho entirely.[8] I recalled the picture I have from 1979 of Francis Kavanaugh holding a 249-pound sturgeon nearly two feet longer than he is high,[9] and how important our relationship with Name was for the traditional economy and wellness of my ancestors. I thought also of how Name helped to mediate our relationship with the newcomers.[10] I remembered sharing a story with John Borrows about a particular kind of *namewag* from Lac La Croix traditional territory, not far from here.[11] It's a fasting story, and I shared it one night during my *gii'igoshimo* (vision quest) on Georgian Bay, in a remote area of Neyaashiinigmiing (Cape Croker, Borrows's community). As Name reached the shoreline I realized I was recalling ways I'm rooted in *Anishinaabe akiing* (Anishinaabe traditional territory). That was a remarkable thing to realize just then, given what he proceeded to do.

Name had stopped six inches from the shoreline. I was perched four feet the other side of the divide on a slick mossy rock. Name casually chewed the roots of a small section of bog that had been knocked free in a storm two nights earlier, drifted east, and become tangled around my water intake line. Name hovered at the pipe, leisurely munching on the exposed bog roots, one fishy eye turned my way. He was so close to shore, his belly rubbed the stony bottom, and the top two inches of his cartilaginous notochord (*namewag* don't technically have spines) poked through lake surface into air.

That was an incredible moment to hold! As Name sustained himself through those roots, he held his gaze on me, drawing me into that vital water-air-land connection and disclosing something magnificent. I saw how he breached what I had thought were his impassable aquatic boundaries, and in so doing bound three cosmological orders of Earth together (the water, land and sky worlds) in the gift of a simple shore-line hello, a hello that but for our mutual immanent rootedness would have been a world apart.

And then, comfortably as he came, he ambled away.

Accepting his gift, I too stepped into the breach, and I've never left. Yes, this is a fine place to call home, I thought, as I climbed the hill, chuckling with spruce and pine.

Violence, Identity, and the Languages of Decolonized Relationship

Two years later I can say that home, my house on Koojijing Zaaga'igan, has indeed proven a beautiful place to live and to grow. I've gained a partner, and we're now growing here together. Part of that adventure includes raising a son, now eight weeks old. We're doing our best to grow him within Name's teaching: our gift of a boy may have been planted on Earth, but he will grow rooted within the whole of creation. I feel joy when I consider what this means for his potential. Yet every time we make the fifteen-minute trip into Fort Frances, we drive along Colonization Road, and I often feel sad or angry. Sometimes I don't even notice, but most often I'm reminded to worry. I worry that I can find none of Name's teaching in the Canada I know, and I wonder what this will mean for my son. I suspect that from Name's perspective, Canada (I mean the liberal state) is a structure[12] of violence from which little may grow.[13] It has its origin in ethnocide, the destruction of Indigenous peoples as peoples, and this has never changed. To be sure, the modes of its operation have shifted,[14] but always the relation of settler–Indigenous domination – colonialism – survives.[15]

Colonialism isn't merely a process of newcomer settlement and Indigenous displacement; it's a mode of relationship between settler peoples, Indigenous peoples, and land in which all are harmed (albeit certainly not equally). Settler peoples, I argue below, harm them-selves in founding their political community upon violence, which slowly destroys it from within. So long as they maintain their earth-alienated constitutional order, which treats non-humans as resources to be exploited, there is no escape from this fate, although settlers are always welcome to abandon their current constitutional project and, through treaty, root their political communities in earth.[16] Indig-enous peoples experience much more direct violence to their bodies, minds, and spirits, and the theft and redistribution of their territories

and knowledges. I understand that colonialism, as the praxis of settler supremacy, performs three kinds of violence to Indigenous peoples. The first is to Indigenous persons. It's individual-centred violence
that hurts our bodies, minds, and spirits. This kind of violence is the
least abstract and thus the easiest to identify and understand. It's often
discussed empirically. The second kind of violence is to Indigenous
peoples. It's group-centred violence that attacks our languages, ceremonies, child-rearing practices, medicinal and wellness practices, and
systems of law, just to list a few of its objects: all the knowledge forms
and practices of being that, albeit provisionally, help persons to identify collectively as a people. It seeks to undo our collective sense of self
such that there is no longer an identifiable Indigenous group in which
a recovering individual might seek membership.

The third form of violence, to Indigenous life ways and thus to indigenous constitutional orders, is more abstract. It's structural violence
that denies us our ability to speak and, over enough time, even to imagine our lives lived within our own understandings of what a person is,
what a community is, and what freedom looks like. Life ways aren't
about specific shared practices or qualities, but rather about how the
world appears to us: the ontological, epistemological, and cosmological system within which a people consistently becomes itself, within
which forms and substance continually change. This third, *structural*
violence demands that any changes Indigenous peoples make to their
lives occur within the settler concept of persons, freedom, and political
community, and in short, within the settler constitutional framework.
Eventually we come to see our own life ways as anachronistic; we internalize the Western progress epic and become capable of seeing ways
we lived and acted otherwise only as a kind of "going back." If we
still experience the first two forms of violence, we're only capable of
imaging our freedom from them within the range of settler visions of
freedom, applied to our unique contexts.[17] Lost is the sense of our own
notions of persons, freedom, and belonging – and critically, the constitutional order that organized them as political community.

The injustice of colonialism's third form of violence is clear, but a
second problem arising from it is even more pressing. The Indigenous
constitutionalisms imposed upon and supplanted by settler liberal
constitutional orders are disclosures of the earth way: the order inherent in earth, of which Name sought to share just a glimmer with me.
Instead of deriving from land, liberal constitutionalism – mapped over
the very same land as pre-existing Indigenous constitutional orders – is

predicated on its alienation, as though land were simply a substrate upon which humans acted. The social contract constitutional tradition[18] suggests a reaction in which humans add themselves together, in the presence of land, to yield up political community. I suspect if I could hear Name talk, she'd find nothing just about the resulting society – which not only excludes her but considers the prospect of her belonging incoherent. It is thus in colonialism's third form of violence – in the attempted erasure and supplanting of Indigenous constitutionalisms – that colonial violence to Indigenous peoples and to lands is connected.

Colonialism is a relationship requiring violence to Indigenous peoples and to the earth, and we're living it in Canada today. Like so many before and alongside me, my work strives to change our relationship. While our options need not be so limited, today we have two dominant languages through which to bring a decolonized relationship into being: resurgence and reconciliation. They haven't had an easy relationship.

In the starkest examples, decolonization as an imagined future state of transformed relationship simply means different things to speakers of either language. Yet even where we may have the same rough picture in mind, resurgent and reconciliatory paradigms of decolonization take strikingly different views on at least two matters of central importance to that goal.

Probably the most obvious is how each understands power to organize the field of possible movement for getting from here to there. Much has been written about this first difference.[19] In broad strokes the resurgence paradigm holds that decolonization can be brought about only by acting outside of the formal mechanisms that liberal constitutionalism provides for the expression of dissent ("change from without"). Those means should be avoided, as they merely reinforce the status quo: they allow for contestation within, but never over the colonial state's imposed liberal constitutional order, and thus its structural commitment to violence against Indigenous peoples, lands, and life ways.

In sharp contrast, the reconciliation paradigm centres on the enormity of the decolonial enterprise and, in what it sees as a pragmatic commitment, determines that only those efforts that seek reformation from within the given (liberal) structures and institutions – albeit insisting that they be reformed – are practical ("change from within"). It just isn't helpful, and it may even be irresponsible to seek transformative change directly. A smaller, stepwise approach is what prudence demands, and the condition of its possibility is, at least initially, active (if only strategic) participation in mechanisms of the imposed constitutional order.

People are suffering now; decolonization can't wait on the ideal conditions for a new world order to get started.

A second core difference between these paradigms has received far less attention and it's what I want to focus on. This second difference regards what resurgence and reconciliation have to say about the relationship between identity and decolonization. It seems to me that in the (what below I argue is a false) contest between resurgence and reconciliation, one's stakes turn on what role one thinks identity has to play.

The resurgence paradigm often emphasizes an inward orientation, in which Indigenous peoples give priority to the understanding that, in Taiaiake Alfred's words, "There is great danger in attempting to negotiate structural changes to our relationships before our minds and hearts are cleansed of the stains of colonialism. In the absence of mental and spiritual decolonization, any effort to theorize or to implement a 'new' Onkwehonwe–settler relationship is counter-productive to the objectives of justice and the achievement of a long-term relationship of peaceful coexistence between our peoples."[20]

Leanne Simpson describes this impulse as one that seeks to transform our labour and core ethical commitments "from trying to transform the colonial outside into a flourishment of the *Indigenous* inside."[21] She adds that we are to accomplish this by attending to our own Indigenous processes, and, to resolve all doubt, "we need to do this on our own terms, without the sanction, permission or engagement of the state, western theory or the opinions of Canadians."[22] Resurgence says that before we can stand in a decolonized relationship, we need to do the inner work of knowing who we are. If we lack a strong sense of Indigenous identity, we lack both the means of transforming our colonial relationship and a clear sense of the ends towards which our transformation aspires. This inward orientation is sometimes referred to as "the turn away," a phrase coined by Taiaiake Alfred but has since become a kind of shorthand for the resurgent orientation.[23]

Identity also appears to matter for reconciliation folk, but not in the same way. For the most part they also insist that colonialism is violence and that decolonization means that Indigenous individuals, families, and communities must be made whole again. They see that identity regeneration is part of that process. However they don't seem to hold with resurgent folk that a strong sense of Indigenous identity is a precondition for decolonization *across* the Indigenous–settler divide. Where that tension arises, the reconciliation paradigm is outwardly oriented. Its adherents often take the view that meaningful steps can (many would say must) be taken to transform settler–Indigenous relationships even as Indigenous persons, families, and communities remain broken, sometimes with little sense of themselves as Indigenous. Some would go further still and collapse this colonial impact into an instance of the general condition of identity, being imperfect, dynamic, forever becoming.

Unpacking Resurgence and Reconciliation

I've tried briefly to characterize differing foundational commitments in resurgent and reconciliatory paradigms of decolonization. Before reflecting critically on each and thus preparing the way for a third framework for thinking about Indigenous–settler relationships, I want to pause to comment on how I proceed.

In this section I've tried to follow my mentors' and supervisors' advice that the best scholarship shares what needs to be said without tearing anybody down. A large part of this is simply *how* one speaks. But also important is a sensitivity to those about whom one speaks. Thus while I still use the occasional quotation in this section or identify folks who've openly claimed a language for themselves, instead of a close textual analysis that proceeds by attributing particular positions to particular authors / orators / activists / community members and then interrogating them thereon, I take a step back and offer my own reflections. These are based on the large body of literature I absorbed and the many challenging conversations I had on the identity component of the resurgence-reconciliation tension during my three years at the University of Victoria and the countless conversations I've had with Indigenous folks across Turtle Island. I'd be foolish not to note that this is also an effort at the academic practice of the third paradigm of settler–Indigenous relationship I go on to argue for below: the gifts of those I engage with are among the many that allow for mine. I'll try to honour them as such.

There are also practical reasons for proceeding in this way. I suspect for the most part we don't share understandings of what exactly terms like *reconciliation* and *resurgence* mean and that we could waste a good deal of time mis-attributing and speaking over one another. As Mark Walters has observed, even though the Supreme Court of Canada offers the appearance of a stable definition of reconciliation in its Aboriginal rights jurisprudence, through an often-referenced sequence of words,[24] it invokes that definition in different ways when it wishes to produce different meanings.[25] Finally, I suspect that most of us would say these languages of decolonization represent two poles, not a strict binary. Some of us just tilt slightly in one direction, while others want to plant a flag on one end. Some of us would insist on how complicated it all is and want to claim partial allegiance to both and neither paradigm. Finally, all of us have views that shift over time.

I realize that these dynamics are always in play. My point isn't to suggest that we ought to refuse to engage critically with one another. It's rather that thoughtfulness is as important as rigour here. Given the scope of what I'm trying to achieve with this chapter, I don't have the space necessary to critically but charitably engage with the ideas and positions of the many distinct authors associated with resurgence and reconciliation. Others might be able to; I'm talking about myself, discussing this tension, in this format. That said, I want to explore what's at stake in each paradigm, what sorts of things each may have to say about the other, and what understandings I can take from this. Let's start with resurgence.

Resurgence

As a foundational commitment, the resurgence view of decolonization calls for a turn away from the settler state and a turn towards a revitalized sense of Indigenous identity. Both sides of the turn seem to me to be absolutely necessary and absolutely impossible. Consider Taiaiake Alfred's thunderous statement of where he stands:

> What it comes down to in confronting our imperial reality is that some of us want to reform colonial law and policy, to dull that monster's teeth so that we can't be ripped apart so easily. Some of us believe in reconciliation, forgetting that the monster has a genocidal appetite, a taste for our blood, and would sooner tear us apart than lick our hands. I think that the only thing that has changed since our ancestors first declared war on the invaders is that some of us have lost heart. Against history and against those who would submit to it, I am with the warriors who want to beat the beast into bloody submission and teach it to behave.[26]

I have long admired this passage for the conviction its words can hardly contain, for the artful fusion of heart and mind Alfred renders so powerfully. His hand seems to jump from the page and, meeting my face, slap all complacency away. I've read it many times and it always strikes me as the expression of a sense of resolute purpose I've often lacked. Despite my best efforts, my way forward has often been less clear. How do I turn away? What does it mean to stand against history? I'm all for pushing back on colonial imposition, but how to go about that isn't so straightforward to me. Consider this message from *gete-Anishinaabe* Fred Kelly:

> While international conflicts are fought between enemies on a very clear and simple proposition of win or lose, the choice here in Canada is one that must be made among friends and neighbours. We must face the underlying tensions. We must understand them and we must resolve them. Neither side believes that the other is going anywhere. This is home. So, how do we live side-by-side and build a future of prosperity together? We share space in a common land. We constitute a society that is envied by other countries. We are economically interdependent. We have many social ties. Our children are married to one another through which we share generations of grandchildren. So inextricably tied are we that our options are also very clear and simple: we can all win or we can all lose.[27]

I find Kelly's message equally powerful. I hear him saying that, despite all injustice, our profound interdependence means that any approach to improving our relationship based on a strict us-them (i.e., settler–Indigenous) divide must fail. Let's be very clear that this isn't because of a reduction to sameness. It's because distinct Indigenous-settler realities are deeply interwoven: we can no longer affect the other without also profoundly affecting ourselves.

We have here the gifts of two sweeping statements from two enormous minds, each long-committed to undoing contemporary colonial violence. I certainly don't intend to resolve the tension. My point is only that for me the idea of turning away is much more complicated than it might at first seem.

What about the turn towards? I've heard from many that the Indigenous alternatives resurging individuals are turning towards seem unclear to them. What are we pointing our aspirations towards? The first obstacle is thus quite basic: if the goal is to turn towards revitalized indigeneity, then *what does Indigenous identity look like*? Immediate and vexing follow-up questions are, How do we know? Who gets to say? With respect to community well-being (and more practically, community agreement if either resurgence is in part to be a collective enterprise or if community resources are to be used to foster individual resurgence commitments) much is at stake in these questions.

Now here I think is the critical moment. The identity question is often framed as a search strictly for content: what are the things that identify us as Indigenous persons? The candidates have been many. Recurring suggestions include language fluency, a land-based presence, local relationships, ceremonial participation, engagement in traditional knowledge acquisition (through the training and use of practical skills, ongoing engagement with the old people, etc.), location within a kinship network, and in addition to any or all of these, community acceptance (or not!). There are others; these are just some of the proposals I've often encountered – in and out of the academy.

But I fear none of these addresses the worry about authenticity policing, which seems rather to be about the predication of Indigenous identity (i.e., "an Anishinaabe, or Cree, etc. person is ...") in the first place. To the mind of some community members (and a great many academics) that live or anticipate oppression, there's no content that will exhaust the question of identity. Whatever an acceptable answer might be, they're sure it can't proceed by an attempt at exhaustive determination. A frequent worry I've heard is that once something is determined it becomes timeless, and this inspires critiques of fundamentalism, specifically cultural romanticism. It's said that any party tendering its preferred substantive criteria as determinative of Indigenous identity necessarily invokes an imagined golden age when its identified criteria were more or less homogeneously distributed throughout community membership, and thus suffers from a false belief in a time in which Indigenous cultures were pure. Identity just isn't the sort of thing one accomplishes by pointing towards any particular goal, critics say, for there will always be someone who fails to meet the conditions of that goal and who is thus done violence by arbitrary exclusion. And that moment – especially when triggered through a claim of cultural purity – discloses that what the substantive way of thinking about Indigenous identity *does* point toward is ethno-nationalism.

This is hardly surprising; a great many Indigenous folks I know – amongst folks forty and under, perhaps the majority of them – identify as members of an Indigenous *nation*. *Ethno-nationalist* (or more accurately, Anishinaabe, Kanienkehaka, Nehiyaw, Dene, etc. nationalist) seems to be a label that some resurgence folks may happily wear. But for many, the focus is rather on the turn away: naming and rejecting contemporary practices of colonialism (*dispossession* is a keyword here) and celebrating Indigenous resistance. It seems obvious that for resurgence folks centred on the turn away, the object from which they turn must not be as nebulous as colonialism. So from what exactly are resurgence folks turning away? The answers here have been rich and thoughtful. The response hasn't been to proceed only via rejection of a list of determined settler practices and behaviours. Instead of focusing narrowly on the content of settler society, they also reject its forms. They propose a turn away from liberalism as a political and spiritual form; a turn away from capitalism as an economic form; a turn away from discrete, autonomous families as a social form; a turn away from law as a normative form (in the strict sense of "law" as rules; Indigenous peoples, at least in the academy, often describe our normative forms as "legal"); a turn away from the instrumentalization of non-humans (including sustainability) as an ecological form.[28] With a rejection of both content and forms of settler society, one might be tempted to characterize the resurgence movement as turning away from settler life ways writ large.

If the answer is "settler life ways" and not merely a list of substantive criteria we take to be constructive of settler identity, then the reciprocal question – what are we turning towards? – should find a parallel reply. To be sure, some do answer in like fashion. Yet often I have instead found a significant disconnect here. Instead of answering the turn-towards question with "Indigenous life ways," we have often proceeded to offer lists we take to be sufficient to establish Indigenous identity, as if the establishment of the right list will somehow amount to an Indigenous life way.

It won't. No matter how specified the conditions for identity become, a list of substantive candidates will never amount to a life way. This would be so even if we possessed an anti-oppression machine that could magically produce a list reflecting everyone's substantive agreement. Missing are the forms that hold all of us together, and more important still, the story of who we are and how we came to be, which allows for both the content and the forms of our identities to shift through space and time and yet for us to continue to recognize identity with one another. I think this is one of the deep challenges the resurgence language of decolonization is struggling with and I'm keen to see how it develops.

I don't for a moment pretend that either side of the authenticity worry described here (whether we can turn away or towards) undoes the resurgence paradigm. Nothing I've said here is intended to have that effect. I hope my next move, exploring reconciliation, the other pole, in just the same way makes that obvious enough. We're infinitely better for the insights and tools that have and are emerging through resurgent frameworks. One of the greatest has been the creation of a generation of scholars prepared to tackle colonial power in a way no previous generation has been. Yet these gifts also come to us with ambiguity, a risk of violence, and a wide range of reasonable disagreement.

Reconciliation

First, reconciliation is also a language of decolonization. It begins with an acknowledgment of colonial violence, but it offers a starkly different account of it. John Borrows is often taken as an influential proponent of this discourse.[29] Of his many diverse works, his influential text, *Canada's Indigenous Constitution*,[30] arguably stands among those most pointed in this direction. In introducing the project of that book, he succinctly lays out a reconciliatory vision that, if my experience is any indication, many in this paradigm would accept:

> It is a mistake to write about Canada's constitutional foundations without taking account of Indigenous law. You cannot create an accurate description of the law's foundation in Canada by only dealing with one side of its colonial legal history. When you build a structure on an unstable base, you risk harming all who depend upon it for security and protection. This book is about attempting to put Canadian law on a stronger footing. Acknowledging the traditional and contemporary place of Indigenous law in this country – alongside the common law and civil law – is a necessary step in this process. It is crucial to creating a healthier and more accurate conception of Canada's broader constitutional order.[31]

Canadian constitutionalism can, should, and does include Indigenous law, Borrows argues. Yet for all its considerable and immediate appeal, I worry about the project of reconciliation, especially in respect of constitutionalism. In particular, I appreciate that reconciliation begins by acknowledging colonial violence, but I worry that in taking as its goal expanded space for Indigenous peoples "in" Canada, it often misidentifies colonialism's most vexing dynamic today as a project of sustained omission and exclusion. Let me unpack that.

Resurgence and reconciliation languages of decolonization equally reject the first two forms of colonial violence I presented (to persons and peoples) but have a dramatic parting over structural violence: violence to Indigenous life ways and constitutionalisms via imposed settler (in Canada, liberal) constitutionalism. Resurgence generally rejects the entire settler constitutional framework[32] as part of an ongoing colonial relationship. Reconciliation generally accepts the imposed settler constitutional order but not as given: they demand its *re*formation, and some adherents desire its eventual *trans*formation.[33] The structural violence these folks experience isn't *subjection to* settler life ways but rather *exclusion from* them. They want in, again with the caveat that this means a genuine accommodation of the Indigenous component of who "we" are. Through this lens, structural violence is experienced when Indigenous persons or peoples are systematically excluded from full participation in Canadian life by virtue of their indigeneity; freedom is experienced when those occlusions are disclosed and smashed. The demand for full participation always consists of at least one kind of project – a demand to break down the barriers that cause us to be treated as less than full citizens. It often includes a supplementary project, a demand that space be made for Indigenous peoplehood practices within the liberal constitutional order. Common examples are requests that space be made for Indigenous family arrangements,[34] systems of law,[35] and systems of health and well-being,[36] just to name a few.

I know more than one resurgence-embodying person for whom this vision of freedom hurts the brain. They struggle to understand how someone else's vision of freedom is any freedom at all. They suggest the seeming logical contradiction can't be resolved, and some go on to declare that if reconciliation folk aren't deafened by its dissonance, it's because they're now so colonized they can't hear the difference. Because they've effectively signed onto the liberal constitutional order, they no longer identify its imposition as a form of violence. They aren't affirming and then overcoming their experience of its violence; there's no violence left to affirm.

This is a strong version of resurgent reaction to the reconciliatory position on structural violence; not all go this far. This view, distilled, says that folks speaking the language of reconciliation have become Western at the cost of being Indigenous. That claim will, for reasons already discussed, strike many as essentialist. Yet despite the affront it may present to a reader's sense of self, I think it has real teeth. For me, it's a serious view, despite the discomfort it creates, and it demands my full engagement. In particular, I fear that anyone who thinks it can be immediately dismissed on grounds of fundamentalism is dangerously mistaken. On the contrary, the resurgence paradigm can level a fundamentalism charge squarely at the reconciliation paradigm of decolonization, just as easily and in two ways. The first regards liberal fundamentalism, the second, postmodern.

Reconciliation as the Goal of Liberal Fundamentalism

I can't lay out the case for seeing liberal constitutionalism as a kind of fundamentalism here; the field of inquiry is far too big. I can only hope to identify two central themes that are for me persuasive. I've taken further steps elsewhere.[37] First, it isn't the case that constitutional orders based in Indigenous life ways are biased while liberal constitutional orders somehow achieve neutrality. Indigenous constitutionalisms aren't neutral, let's be clear about that. No constitutional order ever is. In "Opichi: A Transformation Story, an Invitation to Anishinaabe (Ojibwe) Legal Order,"[38] I tried to explain why we so often forget this. I suggest that those now in the privileged position of being able to simply take their constitutional order as given tend to fail to identify its partiality. To claim non-neutrality is to acknowledge that every constitutional order represents a positive project: it seeks to bring into being and to sustain a particular vision of freedom for its members.[39] In so doing, it makes choices and eliminates possibilities. With sufficient time, stability, and the passing of generations, some of us forget how things might have been; the constitutional order we ended up with is naturalized, as if it has always been and as if no exercise of power is reflected within it. But trading out the self-acknowledging partiality of an Indigenous life way for the self-denying partiality of a settler one isn't an exit from the reality that every society has a political-philosophical foundation.

This first theme is thus about the ubiquity of constitutional stories. My claim isn't that liberalism is in some way uniquely vulnerable to fundamentalism, but rather that insofar as by *fundamentalism* we mean the existence of a genesis story disclosing a fixed ontological claim about what persons and freedom are, and an epistemological claim setting boundaries around what it is to know, that liberalism – like all kinds of constitutionalism – necessarily shares in the need to reflect such commitments. This is, of course, fundamentalism in a sense quite different from a fundamentalism that seeks to contain contention, specifying, for instance, that certain persons or peoples have privileged interpretation of norms or privileged access to norm-setting and that ordinary members of the community have no say in the distribution of these privileges. My sense is that many of us often assume that where the first kind of fundamentalism exists, the second must follow. But the situation is rather that fundamentalism in the sense of underlying story is a universal condition for all constitutionalisms – regardless of whether they result in the second (anti-difference, anti-contention) sense of fundamentalism. Constitutional orders that don't claim an authorizing story just aren't being transparent.

This being my view, I have a request for folks (Indigenous and non-Indigenous) to consider. A great many reconciliation folks I know, in and out of the academy, are rarely in the habit of justifying their acceptance of imposed settler life ways but are often quick to demand justification from anyone with a resurgent orientation. But surely we don't get to say there's no neutral ground when talking about Indigenous constitutional orders and then fail to make the same acknowledgment when speaking of life under Canadian constitutionalism. That's either racist or ethnocentric and often probably both. Clearly such a double standard can't be justified (although tautologically justifications are often claimed).[40] In my view it constitutes a fresh harm each time this occurs, because it reinforces the false but seeming naturalness of settler supremacy.

Second, many will see Canada's ethnocide project (the three forms of colonial violence through which Canada seeks to erase indigeneity as such) as fundamentalism. It is an ideological, programmatic, and foundational project which is a necessary condition for Canadian nationhood and nationalism. The intellectual effort and the costs involved are staggering. It was a gargantuan undertaking to build a citizenry so profoundly ignorant about its historical foundations and about the contemporary cost of sustaining its quality of life. It takes many full-time jobs to keep them misinformed, uneducated, and, once knowing, uninterested in the cost of settler supremacy for Indigenous peoples. It's a stunning feat of public education[41] and social engineering to have calibrated the sense of citizen entitlement that serves the state's interest, to have generated a national community that will consistently desire and even demand that its federal government offer support during humanitarian crises abroad, while maintaining a casual disinterest in Indigenous suffering in Canada. It's stunning how many Canadians I meet who have no idea what the Truth and Reconciliation Commission was about, or who return from Europe and explain to me "what a rich sense of history" they found there. Only fundamentalism could sustain so powerful an absence, so powerful a forgetting, in so many minds. It's a science fiction plot. It's utterly unbelievable – like Omelas – except for it being real.[42]

Reconciliation as Goal of Postmodern Fundamentalism

I want to suggest there's an equally strong case to understand at least one kind of postmodernism[43] as a species of fundamentalism.[44] I'm careful to specify the fact of its particularity at the outset, because I'm not reflecting on postmodernism generally. I realize that the first rule of postmodernism is that you do not talk about postmodernism. It's a word with only a plural form. So as not to be over-inclusive in my critique, let me clarify the narrower range of ideas I mean when I use the term *postmodernism* or sometimes *ethos-postmodernism.*

First, I don't mean those for whom postmodernism is merely a toolkit. As a categorical claim that power is always present and as a repertoire of skills to be deployed in disclosing and challenging its operation, postmodernism has been a tremendous gift. It's no small thing to have tools to explore how power appears as consistent constellations of privilege and oppression across differently situated (and always plural) identities. It has done much to help me identify bad stories (progress, dominant among them) and empowered me to embrace better ones.

However, I am often made uncomfortable around those for whom postmodernism is an ethos: where the concern with essentialism has developed from a toolkit into something that is (mistakenly) thought to approximate a life way. My anxiety hasn't developed in response to a detailed survey of postmodern thought. There's some of that from my undergrad work in literary and postcolonial theory and graduate work in law, but for the most part it's a response to my own experiences of a certain kind of intervention into what is claimable about Indigenous peoples and their normative orders. I have in mind specifically the position against positions: the view that for Indigenous identity, nothing is claimable without collapsing into essentialism. In consequence, none can ever offer a view of what it means to be, for instance, Anishinaabe. This position goes well beyond a toolkit used strategically for assessing and responding to power; it makes a strong claim about what there is (or perhaps more accurately, isn't) in the world – an ontological claim – and, most important, it's closed to contestation: there can be no basis upon which two Anishinaabe persons may agree or disagree on what it is they share in. As such, this position constitutes a kind of fundamentalism.

This view may strike some as paradoxical; after all, postmoderns claim the battle against essentialism as their core project, and that's straightforwardly an anti-fundamentalist commitment – one I'm grateful for. But much turns on how the war is waged. One battle plan seems merely to redirect the identity-based oppression postmoderns reject. For instance, I worry that postmoderns' preoccupation with the tremendous scope of substantive difference between our embodied, plural identities blinds some to a still deeper level of difference. For some of us, our identities are not *merely* different, they're different *in kind.*[45]

In particular, some markers of identity do much more than signal a relative distribution of privilege and oppression via subject position. They speak also of ways of being and knowing. Another way to put the point is that difference operates in multiple registers at once. One of these regards substantive embodiment. Postmoderns are (in my view, rightly) deeply concerned with how power works within this "thin" register of difference, which includes, for instance, race, gender, class, and many other identity markers. Yet another (I'll say "thick") register regards structural difference. It's about the ontological and epistemological frameworks that may underlie a great diversity of embodied locations (in my experience, many postmoderns respect thick difference and seek to account for power in this structural register too). I understand my Anishinaabe identity to be of this latter sort. It conditions not only my experience of the world (i.e., the first register), but also *how the world appears to me* such that I might have experiences of it at all.[46] I understand that my cis male, heterosexual, middle-class, and white identities aren't like this. They mark me between privilege and oppression (in the vast majority of circumstances, privilege) within the many shifting contexts in which I'm enmeshed. They too affect how I see the world, but only in consequence of power stacked upon itself over time. While powerful and significant, this is neither the what-there-is nor the how-we-can-know point; it speaks only of social construction.[47]

Whether I'm writing, speaking, or listening, within academia I'm constantly reminded of the thick sense of difference I inhabit. And I'm grateful that in the majority of my academic interactions I find it respected and often even appreciated. Yet there remain far too many instances where I've found my Anishinaabe identity reduced to an embodied marker of unspecified indigeneity. For some, the reality of the structural register of difference constitutes an uncomfortable state of affairs. This makes sense, because it presents a much deeper challenge to the status quo than does having to account for one another's subject position. Thus some would prefer to equivocate on the word *community* such that identities of the thick sort (like Indigenous communities) can be passed off as identities of the thin sort (like class or gender communities). If life way is overlooked or reduced to a storehouse of essentialisms, then embodied subject position emerges as the centre of analysis. But subject positions never actually convey power independent of life ways; indeed, as ontological, epistemological, and cosmological systems, there is no space outside of life ways. To allow for the lie that they can do so serves only to conceal the work that they're doing. Thus we should make express that while the resulting decentred subject allows much better prospects for social justice than does liberalism's fictitious universal subject, it also reflects a radical deepening of its individualism. For life ways that don't conceive of subjectivity in terms of individual persons, this pushes the battle for justice a level down. Here we have to fight for justice, not only in respect of our *subject position* difference (as do all other oppressed communities), but also for the non-erasure of our *subjectivity* difference. I would argue that for those Anishinaabeg (and many other Indigenous people) whose life ways conceive of subjectivity in respect of relationships, this result is perverse, for it widens the gap between present injustice and the just relations sought when it should be narrowing it.

It strikes me that ethos-postmoderns caught up in this problem offer a militant openness. Its radical individualism tolerates no boundary and it's precisely this closing off – even though well-intentioned – that discloses its hidden fundamentalism. Ironically, ethos-postmoderns essentialize the concept "change." Change in this radically individual key presents itself only ever as a binary: it is ceaseless and groundless subject to no internal limits, or it's ossified – in which case it ceases to be itself. Again, I'm not presenting this as a crisis of postmodernism generally. I'm responding to a particular perspective I've frequently encountered and that I think exercises considerable power over the question centrally at issue in this chapter: how might one best respond to the structural violence that is Canada's liberal constitutional order imposed over already-existing Indigenous constitutionalisms?

Now having said that, let me be clear that I don't know any Indigenous person who aspires to be a stereotype. Renowned Anishinaabekwe artist Daphne Odjig voiced my feelings too when she said, "We are a living people and a living culture. I believe we are bound to move forward, to experiment with new things and develop new modes of expression as all peoples do. I don't intend to stay in the past. I don't feel like no museum piece."[48] But avoiding that fate should hardly mean I have to sacrifice any sense of indigeneity I have that goes deeper than how I'm read by others – my embodied subject position as an Indigenous person. Thus I no longer celebrate Indigenous artistic productions that subvert settler narratives and then immediately stop.[49] I'm all for smashing stereotypes (Indigenous peoples have become extraordinarily effective at this) and it is important work, but I fear something vital to our well-being is lost if we don't also insist that being Indigenous means more than privilege and oppression. When we make the first point without the second, I believe we do harm.

The radical individualism of ethos-postmodernism that attends the erasure of life ways looks an awful lot like neoliberalism. If it's impossible to draw any *kind* of collective identity boundary, even in the case of a thick identity like "Anishinaabe," then I think two things follow.

First, the insistence that substantive difference is the only kind of identity-based difference with which reconciliation is concerned is imperial. It proceeds by overwriting indigeneity, as if distinct Indigenous ways of being and knowing don't exist or are of no value and require no consideration. There's one, universal way of being and knowing; *within it* difference abounds. If that can be called a kind of reconciliation, it isn't one I accept. If this stream of the reconciliation decolonization paradigm judges that the resurgence decolonization paradigm suffers from an over-determination of identity causing it to collapse into essentialism, the resurgence paradigm may reply that this postmodern road into reconciliation suffers from an under-determination of identity, causing it to collapse into hegemony.

Second, where no functional boundaries exist, community collapses into individuals assembled in aggregate, and identity markets fill the interstices.[50] Anything can be Anishinaabe, Cree, Haudenosaunee. We can shop, borrow, repurpose, and throw away from wherever we like without anyone else having anything to say about it; indigeneity becomes a celebratory melange of anything goes. Consume at will: teachings, stories, material culture, ceremony, land. I doubt whether many ethos-postmoderns would *want* to own so radical a position, but I don't see a logical stopping point that would allow them not to.

Thus while liberal and postmodern politics offer sharply differing accounts of persons, freedom, and community, they seem to share an equally religious commitment to individual autonomy. Postmoderns have decentred the self in the sense of having established that its identity is contingent and constructed; to be sure, liberals and postmoderns offer different accounts of individual autonomy (whether it is socially constitutive, etc.). Yet for many postmoderns, the individual self (and usually, the individual *human* self) remains just as much the centre of political thought. The universal subject is gone, but a universal subjectivity remains, one in which *name* cannot act. In this they're perhaps not so radical as compared to their liberal forebears as they might think. Resurgence folk decidedly against giving either normative or ontological priority to the self have good reason to be wary of postmoderns' potential contributions to decolonization. Rather than *post*-modernity, the ethos-postmoderns I'm concerned about may appear more as modernity's second coming.[51]

Finally, no community can fail to attend to internal power dynamics and maintain its integrity over time. But failure to vigilantly monitor external power dynamics is also an error. Structural violence is hard to spot if our eyes are only ever on individual bodies. When we lose sight of life ways, the impact is extraordinary: change resulting through ongoing relations of colonialism is sometimes rendered uncritically as *just* change, change simply as the relentless condition of all being. Perspectives grounded in Indigenous ontologies and epistemologies can thus be carelessly described as "going back," even if they're as relevant to and focused on the present as are perspectives tied to a liberal life way.

I haven't intended for my concern with reconciliation's erasure of structural violence or for my articulations of reconciliation's liberal or postmodern fundamentalisms to suggest that those who speak this decolonial language are lost. I hope that I've contributed something of value in demonstrating where I think the paradigm faces challenges, and that in this regard I've handled resurgence and reconciliation paradigms of decolonization fairly. I also hope I've given voice to where I've learned and taken gifts from it, because they've been significant. Yet just as it was with resurgence, reconciliation's gifts come with a risk of violence and a wide range of reasonable disagreement.

Rootedness: A New Language

With considerable help, I've found a way forward that I believe at least provisionally overcomes the vexing impasse of duelling fundamentalisms. That tension, it seems to me, too often causes speakers of resurgent and reconciliatory languages of decolonization to dismiss and speak over one another. However, from an Anishinaabe standpoint, there's no avoiding the possibility of a wide range of reasonable disagreement.[52] That being the case, hopefully someone with gifts, experience, and perspective that differ substantially from mine will soon share where my preferred vision of Indigenous–settler relationship faces challenges and can be improved.

Let's start with my encounter with Name. If that story were part of an *aadizookaan* you'd have to discern your own meanings from it.[53] Of course, you'll still do that. But given that it's one of my *dibaajimowinan*,[54] permit me to share my meaning.

Name reminded me that in a deep sense I was already rooted here even before returning to Koojijing Zaaga'igan. He then showed me – literally, root-in-mouth *showed* me – that he too is rooted in the same place. Each of us is rooted through our respective life ways to the same earth. But *the way* he chose to disclose this for me[55] opened up a second and even deeper aspect to the teaching: he waited to reveal that he too is rooted until the moment his body occupied three of Earth's cosmological spaces. It was a remarkable use of space and time to create meaning. He's a water being, but he remains connected to all land and sky beings through a shared rootedness in one creation. I'm a two-legged of the land order, but as someone who does my best to live a rooted life, I too am linked to all of creation. He showed me I'm with him, and then he showed me the vastness of what he – and therefore I – am part of. Our life ways certainly differ, but *by virtue of their rootedness, both are reconcilable to the earth way.*

His gift was the double disclosure of my connection, and the breach was his reaching across the shoreline – the boundary between water and land worlds – to relate with me so that I might receive it.[56] I walked down the hill that morning hoping to begin deepening my connection to the colloquial "red road" of Anishinaabe life way.[57] As I stepped back up the trail I was still on that path. And each step was now placed within the whole of creation.[58]

I'll spend the rest of my words explaining that, because I believe rootedness offers a new way of speaking about resurgence and reconciliation, a way that speaks of both in a single breath, dissolving their tension. Rootedness reveals how we can change and remain at the same time: we can avoid both the too-much-somethingness of ethno-nationalism and the militant nothingness of postmodern oblivion.

Constitutional Rootedness

Ron Geyshick was a medicine man from Lac La Croix First Nation (on Zhingwaako Zaaga'igan – Lake of the Pines), another Anishinaabe community in the southern end of Treaty #3 Territory. I was immediately struck by his account of his people's annual round, the traditional Anishinaabe pattern of seasonal movement:

> The land around Gawa Bay was used by the old Indians during the summer, for Spring ceremonies and Fall ceremonies, and for fishing. It wasn't a place where people lived year-round. In those days, people didn't live in any one place all year. They'd travel to one place for sturgeon in the spring, then another place for blueberries, somewhere else for wild rice. In the winter, there'd be hunting and traplines to follow. They didn't plant any vegetables because they didn't want to stick around to take care of them; they only bothered with a few vegetables that grew beneath the ground; potatoes, turnips, maybe onions. Roots they could just leave and come back for later.[59]

On the surface the passage seems to address only the (economic and spiritual) bases for our patterned mobility. But something about Geyshick's decision to voice his intentional rejection of mainstream[60] agriculture – they didn't *want* to stick around – wouldn't quite let go of me. And as I returned to the passage again and again, I started to find new meaning. Soon I began to wonder if *gete-Anishinaabe* Ron Geyshick was a genius.

Beneath his teaching on the annual round, I think Geyshick was speaking to us about Anishinaabe identity. As mobile peoples, part of the answer to the "who are we" question is "inherently dynamic." Change isn't something that periodically interrupts who we are; it's a permanent state of affairs. If all Geyshick had to say about identity was the mobility point, it would seem to suggest an almost unfettered range of individuation. It would be hard even to speak the word *Anishinaabe* before it dissolved on the tongue. But he does say more. He adds the remarkable bit towards the end that before departing their (always temporary) community site, they *did* plant a few vegetables, but only ones "that grew beneath the ground."

They planted roots. Root vegetables have a quality other vegetables lack. Roots, Geyshick's ancestors "could just leave and come back for later." Roots need us to ensure for them the basic conditions of growth. Beyond that, they care for themselves: the earth provides. If we've cared for them, no matter how far a journey takes us, our roots will remain strong. We will go to many places in a year, and each will be different from the last; the roots will remain. We will practise many different things in a year; the roots will remain. We will behave many different ways in a year; the roots will remain. We will learn, take on new understandings, and leave old ones on the path behind; the roots will remain. We will grow. We will age. We will bring forth new life. The roots will remain.

No matter what a year brings, so long as we've cared for them, the roots will remain. That means renewing our responsibility each year to fill ourselves with new life: the roots will keep us grounded, but they aren't *all* we need, and, living as if they were, weakens us. We can't point specifically to (if I may continue the food production metaphor) ricing, sugaring, berry-picking, fishing, hunting, trapping, or any future food production practice not yet imagined as essential to our identities. Each of those works well with the roots, but if any were absent, the roots would remain. Anishinaabe roots require only that we have practices that are life-sustaining for Anishinaabeg.[61]

Caring for the roots means returning to renew them, too. The roots are the place to which we always return. So long as we renew our earth link, we'll always grow. Life *is* change: there's no end to its striving. It's so easy to miss so simple a statement's meaning. Not being aimed towards an end point at which change finally stops means that, for the rooted, there is no progress. Ours is a life of recurrence. The direction of growth is a wide arc that finds its way humbly back to itself. Forward is a curve, and the best of us return throughout its turning: tobacco for medicine taken from the bush; the swollen banks of spring; the crayfish moult; the bears' hibernation; the crawlers' temporary burial; the geese flapping south; the *windigokaan* eliciting laughter and scowls; the broken prayer of an unbeliever; the day within a year within a life. The leaves falling each year before, at last, the trunk.

And what should happen then? So far I've considered what rooted-ness has to say about the identity of persons. But what does this mean for the identity of peoples? Gary Potts, then chief of the Teme-Augama Anishnabai, has offered a reply. He begins with what follows from the fallen trunk: "I remember once coming across an old white pine that had fallen in the forest. In its decayed roots a young birch and a young black spruce were growing, healthy and strong. The pine was returning to the earth, and two totally different species were growing out of the common earth that was forming. And none was offended in the least by the presence of the others because their own identities were intact."[62]

As each tree completes its hoop, it returns to the earth that birthed it and grounds the generations still to come. It supports them and, should they choose growth over progress, finally it's called into them, shaping the range of what they may become. Change is ceaseless, but never, ever groundless, which bears repeating: *change is never groundless.*

This explains how the birch and spruce stand in relation to the pine: those who've come before help root us in creation. But what about how they relate with one another? The birch and spruce are different beings inhabiting the same space. Why is it that neither tries to dominate the other? Why does neither seek to maximize its share of the scare resource, the roots of the young birch, upon which its existence depends? For many of us, this privileging of self-interest would be the expected behaviour.[63] Yet here we find a different picture: neither concerned about what the other may take; its own identity intact. Why?

The answer Potts provides is in how each calls the space common to both "earth." The condition allowing for birch's and spruce's non-violent relationship is that each accepts its genesis from the earth.[64]

Neither tells a story of autonomous existence in which earth is merely the setting. All roots bind in one earth, and it establishes that the logic of life is growth. Progress is a short story told by those who've lost sense of their roots. Growth is messy. But each of us committed to it understands that the ceaseless change we'll experience and the identity it grows is both empowered and constrained by our roots. And so the stories we tell of our own creation differ, but each is a story in which the possibility of all change is a function of our rootedness in a common earth.[65]

That's a vision of reconciliation I can follow. Our foundational commitment is to reconcile our life way (and the constitutional order it gives rise to) with the earth way. If we accept that this is the deep condition of all non-violent relationship both within political communities and across them, our tasks become relatively straightforward. Other than renewing ourselves and our roots, reconciliation means listening to the stories others tell of their creation, for this allows us to see that, despite the vast difference separating their life ways from ours, theirs, too, is a disclosure of the earth way. Ultimately that's all that matters, for once this is known, our differences become gifts to be celebrated, not problems to be solved. This never does away with conflict, of course. It isn't supposed to; conflict is a healthy and even vital part of interdependent relationships. But it means that even in the face of conflict we're grateful to leave the identity of others intact because we need them. The vision of harmony that the earth way sustains isn't one of non-conflict, but of non-disconnection. We affirm our interdependence and share our gifts to meet one another's need.[66]

Let me explain that. Picture a tree. Beneath the tree is the earth itself. Grounding the tree in the earth is a complex mass of roots that draw life from it. Emerging upwards from the roots is a broad, powerful trunk – strong enough to support the entire canopy above it. As the trunk climbs higher into the sky, branches begin to grow out of it at all different angles and of all different lengths. None grows in straight lines, and each is different from all the others. The branches produce leaves that thrive, explode into a cacophony of colour, and then fall. The fallen leaves return nutrients to the earth, and the circle continues.

The earth conditions a range of possibility for what the roots may become. The roots condition the trunk. The trunk conditions the branches. The branches condition the leaves. The roots never *determine* what the trunk will become; determination is much too strong a word for the kind of relationship existing between parts of the tree. But they constrain and empower its range of possibility.[67] As the tree expresses itself with increasing degrees of finitude, the range of possibility it has for doing so is progressively constrained and empowered: the leaves by the branches, branches by the trunk, trunk by roots, and finally, roots by earth.

I want to argue that healthy human societies are like this too. We begin with the earth – creation itself, in all its vast complexity – and recognize that we grow from, through, and in it. Of course, as carefully as we might observe earth processes and relationships in our efforts to root ourselves in creation, none of us has unmediated access to earth's rhythms. We can only ever understand them through a story. Thus our roots are not really the earth itself, but rather the stories we tell of it. Creation stories set out a people's way of being in and (if rooted) of the earth. They give us our ideas of what a person is, what freedom is, and thus what community is. The trunk is the constitutional order that manifests these understandings as political community. It's our framework for living together called into being by the story we tell. I mean constitutionalism broadly in the sense of how we constitute ourselves as peoples, which may have nothing to do with founding documents. Our branches are our legal tradition(s): the assemblage of processes and institutions we use to generate, sustain, alter, and destroy norms.[68] The leaves are our provisionally settled norms. They experience the highest degree of change within the set of relationships that constitute a normative order. Some will fall off, never to return. Others will return after renewal. All come from, all recur with, earth.

Ron Geyshick's invocation of roots as identity gets us this far. But Gary Potts reminds us that there's always more than one tree. The second image is of the forest. This wider image begins with the same scene: there is one earth beneath us all. But there are many different stories of its being, each generative of a distinct constitutional order, with a distinct legal tradition (or traditions), and finally, distinct norms. When we compare norms, we may find considerable variability in how distinct peoples coordinate various forms of social interaction and manage instances of the same kind of conflict. But for Indigenous peoples of Turtle Island, the further down the tree we go to draw our comparisons, the higher the degree of similarity. At the roots, we find that yes, we tell distinct stories of creation, but that each is a disclosure of the earth way; each is similarly rooted in the earth beneath it.[69]

Once we see the other's rootedness, we see that we can have a good relationship, no matter the degree of difference in our norms. Of course, having a good relationship can still be a great deal of hard work. But once we see that we come from and return to the same place, that we just have different ways of moving through the circle, a good relationship is, at least, always possible.

Treaty is the relation of travelling the circle in our unique, respective ways, together.[70] We recognize that through our mutual rootedness we're always already in relationship, and through treaty we choose to strengthen that relationship and thereby to honour one another. This now intentional relationship strengthens our capacity to share our gifts with one another, so that all have their needs met.[71] Treaty is the ongoing relationship that allows for all exchange, not the set of terms that establish actual exchange in a given instance (i.e., treaty is not a contract). The needs of peoples standing together in a treaty relationship change through time; it's thus the fluidity of friendship, not the certainty of contract, that makes possible the appropriate connections of gift with ever-changing need, which flow differently but symbiotically to all participants in the treaty relationship. And, like all of creation, treaty is tied into the annual round and must each year be renewed.

Roots All the Way Down

Canadians aren't circle people, and therein lies the problem. Instead of growing from the earth, they're progressing away from it. In Canada's case, dominating the northern half of Turtle Island is part of that progress story. Indigenous persons, peoples, lands, and life ways are consumable on the road to liberal constitutionalism's imagined end state. In the first part of this chapter I shared concerns I have with both resurgence and reconciliation as paradigms of response to colonial violence. I then introduced a third way of thinking about the problem of contemporary colonialism: rooted constitutionalism. Resurgence and reconciliation movements describe and hence respond to Canadian colonialism in different ways. With rooted constitutionalism I've tried to learn from and include the best of each in a distinct vision: a vision that dissolves the tension between them by demonstrating that each is necessary to realizing a world beyond settler supremacy, although perhaps not in the way that either imagined.

Within rooted constitutionalism Indigenous identity is neither determined before individual variation (i.e., essentialized) nor radically open to individual free play (i.e., imperial). Thus if someone insists to me that he can interpret an Anishinaabe story any way he likes and that giving itself totally over to interpretation is the very thing that stories are intended to do, I cannot agree. To be sure, there are countless ways of reading a story (this is actually intended with Anishinaabe *aadizoo-kaanan*), and new interpretations will always emerge as listeners and readers move across space and time. But all possible readings remain a function of the life way from which the story emerged.[72] Without this constraint, change isn't only ceaseless but also groundless: severed from its roots.[73]

Thus rooted constitutionalism rejects any reconciliatory vision calling Indigenous peoples to resign themselves to violence to their life ways.[74] First, since there exists no space beyond a life way, such calls are necessarily also calls for Indigenous peoples to reconcile themselves *to* the life ways of another: a relation of power-over. Second, from within a rooted constitutional framework, reconciliation between peoples is a coherent project only if each is first reconciled with the earth way.

This identifies a deep challenge to undoing Canadian colonialism and creating a healthy Indigenous–settler relationship. Canadian constitutionalism isn't a disclosure of the earth way; it finds its origin in a social contract story. The turn away that rooted constitutionalism supports is never from persons and peoples, for as Name showed me, we're always already connected. However, what it not only supports but requires is a turn away from any and all forms (political, legal, economic, social, spiritual, ecological) premised on alienation from the earth way. Liberalism, rule of law, and capitalism are settler forms of political, legal, and economic ordering respectively, openly hostile to interdependence. They recognize only earth, not earth way, and as such fail to treat earth as an always already connected family of beings with whom to stand in relationship.[75] They regard earth only as a set of resources to be used (or preserved) instrumentally.[76]

While I sometimes can't identify with resurgent proposals on how to confront structural violence, I recognize it as one of their core projects. In fact, some resurgence folks might see rooted constitutionalism as simply one more contribution to their cluster of ideas, rather than a distinct, third framework. I frequently find much to celebrate in the works of Leanne Simpson, Taiaiake Alfred,[77] Jeff Corntassel, and others. In many instances, however, I think there is a significant difference. Resurgent thinkers and actors have often advocated for a vision of Indigenous political autonomy that I take to be irreconcilable with the deep interdependence of the earth way. The insight that I fear has in some instances been lost is that getting out from under contemporary colonialism cannot mean standing alone! Our range of relational choice is not a narrow binary between domination and disconnection. We must steadfastly reject the imposition of foreign rule, but the rooted alternative is not self-rule. To the best of my knowledge, although Anishinaabe communities have frequently clashed with settler and other Indigenous groups, we've never been self-ruling. On the contrary, self-determination is the language of our settler colonizer. There's no sovereignty for a rooted, growing, political community: sovereignty is a peoples-level articulation of an autonomous, not a relational, conception of self. If we're always already connected in relations of deep interdependence, then the question of freedom is never about standing apart from the other and always about *how* to stand with it. Another way to put the point is that I fear some within the resurgence paradigm don't see that beneath the myriad political, legal, economic, social, spiritual, and ecological settler forms from which they turn away is an ontological settler form they turn into: disconnection. Rooted constitutionalism would say disconnection doesn't exist except artificially, and I would add that it's the first step off of the path of growth, onto the path of progress.

The fact that there's no space of disconnection within rooted constitutionalism doesn't mean that rooted persons and peoples can't take action, including direct action, against others. On the contrary, conflict is a vital means through which interdependence functions: it's one of the ways we remain connected. It means only that *how* we exercise direct action is empowered and constrained by our own, rooted, normative orders. As Robert Lovelace of Ardoch Algonquin First Nation put the point, "Direct action should take its shape and purposes from the intrinsic goodness embedded in Indigenous epistemologies."[78]

I've been careful not to describe this third way of organizing Indigenous–settler relationships as yet another language of decolonization. I don't want to privilege a politics of negation or unmaking and then, as a second step, follow up with my understanding of Anishinaabe life way. I think that would be to miss the teaching of Name's double disclosure. Nor have I ever heard any of the *gete-Anishinaabeg* I sit with talk about decolonization. *Nokomis* (my grandmother), Bessie Mainville, talks about a total way of living: how *to be* in every day.[79] For some of us, the distinction will just be semantics: we're saying the same thing in different ways. For others, however, something important is at stake: I've never heard *nokomis* talk about unmaking Canada. Rather, she continues to bring a rooted reality into being by living in her Anishinaabe life way despite Canada. And yet I think she's been railing against the structural violence of contemporary colonialism her entire life. In her I see that railing against doesn't take the form of a violent reaction, or of a general dismissal of settler peoples. In fact it's not reactionary at all. It's the reflective, steady and often quiet making irrelevant of Canadian constitutionalism.[80] She's railing against every time she practises and every time she discloses to me a little more about our Anishinaabe constitutional order: a rooted vision of law, economics, ecology, spirituality, sociality, and politics. And I'm growing.

ACKNOWLEDGMENTS

I thank Deanne LeBlanc, Keith Cherry, and Meaghan Daniel for innumerable conversations that have shaped and sharpened so many aspects of my thought herein. Their challenges have been deep and numerous; their unique gifts, remarkable. And I acknowledge Scott Webber, who's been a kind of intellectual brother for me for three fascinating years. Scott has attacked, defended, reformulated, and celebrated most of the ideas I share here, and all of this with exceptional thoughtfulness and remarkable charity. To each of you, my deepest gratitude. Finally, I thank Sarah Marie Wiebe, Ethan Krindle, Regan Burles, Nancy Turner, Keith Cherry, and James Tully for comments and rich conversation on this chapter and, in some instances, for drawing new sources to my attention.

NOTES

1 By *settler* I mean all those whose creation stories place them beyond Turtle Island but who've settled here. The number of generations passed since settlement in the narrow sense of arrival is irrelevant to one's claim of belonging, because arrival merely marks a location in the movement between creation and settlement. What matters is the necessity to account for one's presence in place. This place is Turtle Island, and it has been home to distinct Indigenous peoples since time immemorial. Thus *settler* isn't a pejorative. It identifies distinct political statuses here, correlative to the need for non-Indigenous peoples to account for their presence in Indigenous peoples' spaces. Belonging is a function of this accountability. The rooted constitutionalism paradigm I present offers one way for settler society to manifest its accountability. I thank Deanne LeBlanc for

our conversations on the politics of settler identity as she prepared her thesis on that topic: Deanne Aline Marie LeBlanc, "Identifying the Settler Denizen within Settler Colonialism" (MA diss. University of Victoria, 2014). Another exemplar is Michael Asch, *On Being Here to Stay: Treaties and Aboriginal Rights in Canada* (Toronto: University of Toronto Press, 2014). While I differ with Asch's account of treaty, I strongly recommend that anybody interested in thinking through settler accountability engage this thoughtful, rigorous, and ethically compelling work.

2 Teachings of an anonymous elder of Mitaanjigamiing First Nation, who I've been learning from for a decade. The elder shared these traditional names and his knowledge about canoe-making at Giineshingwak'kag with me on 13 and 15 June 2014 at Mitaanjigamiing.

3 I choose this word intentionally. I was profoundly moved by the five Anishinaabekweg (Anishinaabe women) from Lac Seul who perform in this song: Jenelle Manitowabi, Tayler Drew Bottle, Cassie Capay, Chelsea Bunting, Melody McIver, Joey Langlois, and David Hodges, "Echo My Soul," *The Gathering: N'we Jinan*. Vol. 2 (Toronto: SOCAN, 2015).

4 John Borrows, James Tully, Heidi Stark, and Jeremy Webber. Beyond the intellectual contribution they're each making to my dissertation, I chose each because of how fully I trust them to grow me as an academic. These are scholars I want to be more like.

5 There are too many people to mention here, but Rita Dhamoon, Michael Asch, and Jeff Corntassel really stand out.

6 Despite its nearly ubiquitous use today, I don't think the term *elder* adequately represents the role, authority, or responsibility it's intended to convey. It suggests a structural commitment to hierarchy and deference that I understand not to have been institutionalized within Anishinaabe political community before colonization began. I prefer the term *gete-anishinaabeg*. Rather than a title, it's a descriptor meaning the old or old-time people and its connotation recognizes knowledge, thoughtfulness, and a deep relational mode of being acquired through long years. I'll use that term instead.

7 The *aadizookaanan* are our stories from time immemorial. *Aadizookaanan* is frequently translated (in my view in a way that misinforms) as "legends" or "myths" in English. They speak of creation, knowledge, power, being, and what it means to be good. They're instructive for how to stand in relationship with self and others. They involve spirit beings, *aadizookaanag*, whom many of us believe are alive today.

8 Midaasooganj (Ten-Claw), "Nanabushu Swallowed by the Sturgeon," in *Ojibwa Texts, Part 1,* in William Jones, ethnographer, and Truman Michelson, ed. (Leiden: E.J. Brill Publishers and Printers, 1917) 207.

9 Grand Council, "Grand Council Treaty No. 3," *Ontario Indian* 4, no. 4 (1981): 31.

10 Tim E. Holzkamm, Victor P. Lytwyn, and Leo G. Waisberg, "Rainy River Sturgeon: An Ojibway Resource in the Fur Trade Economy," *Canadian Geographer* 32, no. 3 (1988): 194.

11 Ron Geyshick, "The Sturgeon Girl," in Ron Geyshick, with Judith Doyle, *Te Bwe Win (Truth): Stories by an Ojibway Healer* (Toronto: Summer Hill, 1989), 49; Norval Morriseau, *Legends of My People the Great Ojibway,* ed. Selwyn Dewdney (Toronto: Ryerson, 1965), 33–8. A similar story is Basil H. Johnston, "Mer-Man / Nebaunaubae," in *The Bear-Walker and Other Stories* (Toronto: Royal Ontario Museum, 1995), 21–5.

12 Turtle Island is a place. Canada is an idea, one that organizes power over peoples and place.

13 Aaron Mills, "Constitutional Stories: Pride, Violence and Citizenship in Canada," *Cairo Review of Global Affairs* 17 (2015): 115.

14 James Tully, "The Imperial Roles of Modern Constitutional Democracy," in *Public Philosophy in a New Key.* Vol. 2, *Imperialism and Civic Freedom* (Cambridge: Cambridge University Press, 2008), 195, 211–12; Taiaiake Alfred and Jeff Corntassel, "Being Indigenous: Resurgences against Contemporary Colonialism," *Government and Opposition* 9 (2005): 597; Kent McNeil, "Judicial Treatment of Indigenous Land Rights in the Common Law World," in *Indigenous Peoples and the Law: Comparative and Critical Perspectives,* ed. Benjamin J. Richardson, Shin Imai, and Kent McNeil (Oxford: Oxford University Press, 2009): 257–8.

15 Colonialism's survival has been sustained through powers of law. For a Canadian instance, see James Tully, "On Local and Global Citizenship: An Apprenticeship Manual," in *Public Philosophy in a New Key.* Vol. 2, *Imperialism and Civic Freedom* (Cambridge: Cambridge University Press, 2008), 243, 250–5 (organizing the hierarchy of four tiers of rights under liberal constitutionalism). For the role of law in sustaining colonialism internationally, see Tully's discussion of "imperial right," ibid., 210–12.

16 I expand on this claim below but I take it up in more detail in Aaron Mills, "What Is a Treaty? On Contract and Mutual Aid," in *The Right(s) Relationship: Reimagining the Implementation of Historical Treaties,* ed. John Borrows and Michael Coyle, 208–47 (Toronto: University of Toronto Press, 2017).

17 Tully, *Public Philosophy in a New Key,* 2:116.

18 I'm referring to the robust contractarian justification for political authority
   that began with pre-Enlightenment thinkers like Thomas Hobbes and
   John Locke, which was championed during the Enlightenment by such
   writers as Jean-Jacques Rousseau and Immanuel Kant, and was revived,
   refined, and reformulated in the twentieth century by John Rawls and
   his contemporaries. Although the advent of neoliberalism has greatly
   complicated the claims of contemporary states to sovereign autonomy,
   the idea of the social contract, as a justification for sovereign authority,
   continues to play a leading constitutional role in the political theory and
   practice of the liberal nation state today.

19 For me, one of the most probing is Tully, "Unfreedom of the Moderns," 91.

20 Taiaiake Alfred, *Wasáse: Indigenous Pathways of Action and Freedom* (Toronto:
   University of Toronto Press, 2009), 180.

21 Leanne Simpson, *Dancing on Our Turtle's Back: Stories of Nishnaabeg
   Re-creation, Resurgence and a New Emergence* (Winnipeg: Arbeiter Ring
   Publishing, 2011), 17. Emphasis in original.

22 Ibid.

23 Glen Coulthard helpfully discusses "the turn away" in the thought of
   Alfred and Simpson in Glen Sean Coulthard, *Red Skin White Masks:
   Rejecting the Colonial Politics of Recognition* (Minneapolis: University of
   Minnesota Press, 2014), 154–5.

24 *R v Van der Peet*, [1996] 2 SCR 507 at para 31.

25 Mark D. Walters, "The Jurisprudence of Reconciliation: Aboriginal Rights
   in Canada," in *The Politics of Reconciliation in Multicultural Societies*, ed. Will
   Kymlicka and Bashir Bashir (Oxford: Oxford University Press, 2008), 165.

26 Alfred, *Wasáse*, 37.

27 Fred Kelly, "Confession of a Born Again Pagan," in *From Truth to
   Reconciliation: Transforming the Legacy of Residential Schools*, ed. Marlene
   Brant Castellano, Linda Archibald, and Mike Degagné (2008; Ottawa:
   Aboriginal Healing Foundation, 2011), 15, 29.

28 I recognize that many settlers strive to opt out of these forms. I want to
   allow for and honour that. The contention I present here regards aspects of
   liberal constitutionalism (which expresses the problematic settler lifeway)
   and not the individual people caught up in them.

29 Although it's unlikely Borrows would accept *reconciliation* as descriptive
   of his general orientation, my reading of his body of work suggests a
   concerted effort to avoid any identification other than Anishinaabe.
   Consistent with this, while much of Borrows's work is aimed explicitly
   at the uptake of Indigenous law within Canadian law, constitutionalism,
   and legal education, he leaves space for other possibilities. This requires

a careful eye, however, for he generally chooses to present this goal only implicitly. The contrast in aims is perhaps most clearly seen in the very different orientations and communicative styles of John Borrows, *Canada's Indigenous Constitution* (Toronto: University of Toronto Press, 2010); and Kegedonce, *Drawing Out Law* (Toronto: University of Toronto Press, 2010), which were published together.

30 Borrows, *Canada's Indigenous Constitution*.

31 Ibid., 15–16 (citation omitted).

32 Implicit within any constitutional framework are ontological and epistemological commitments. Thus to speak expressly of a *constitutional* framework is not to speak "only" of political community, but also and necessarily of how the vision of political community at issue represents and manifests a view of the nature of persons, freedom, and knowing.

33 The link between reformative means and transformative ends is far from clear. Adherents of this approach must argue, not assume, that reformation creates more fertile ground for transformation. The counter-assumption is, of course, that reformation (1) further entrenches settler supremacy by providing it a firmer foundation, and, perhaps more significantly, (2) as participation within the imposed liberal constitutional order, validates settler supremacy.

34 Some examples include Awasis Agency of Nothern Manitoba, *First Nations Family Justice: Mee-noo-stah-tan Mi-ni-si-win* (1997; Thompson: Awasis Agency of Northern Manitoba, 1999); Tthow Legwelth (Lavina White) and tlakwakse (Eva Jacobs), *Liberating Our Children, Liberating Our Nations: Report of the Aboriginal Committee* (Victoria: Community Panel, Family and Children's Services Legislation Review in British Columbia, 1992) (specifically disclaiming the legitimacy of Canadian law for Indigenous nations, vii–viii).

35 Borrows, *Canada's Indigenous Constitution*; Val Napoleon, "Thinking about Indigenous Legal Orders," in *Dialogues on Human Rights and Legal Pluralism, Ius Gentium,* Comparative Perspectives on Law and Justice 17, ed. René Provost and Colleen Sheppard (New York: Springer, 2013), 229, 245; Law Commission of Canada, ed., *Indigenous Legal Traditions* (Vancouver: UBC Press, 2007); Ross Gordon Green, *Justice in Aboriginal Communities: Sentencing Alternatives* (Saskatoon: Purich Publishing, 1998).

36 Anishnawbe Health Toronto, Anishnawbe Mushkiki (Thunder Bay), and the Wabano Centre for Aboriginal Health (Ottawa) are examples of urban Indigenous institutions creating and supporting Indigenous practices of well-being within Canada's constitutional framework.

37 Mills, "Constitutional Stories," 15; Aaron Mills, "The Lifeworlds of Law: On Revitalizing Indigenous Legal Orders Today," *McGill Law Journal* 61, no. 4 (2016): 847.

38 Aaron Mills, "Opichi: A Transformation Story, an Invitation to Anishinaabe (Ojibwe) Legal Order," *For the Defence* 34, no. 3 (2013): 40.

39 This is what I endeavoured to show, through the lens of a difficult conflict between my own community and a neighbouring municipality, in Aaron Mills, "Driving the Gift Home," *Windsor Yearbook of Access to Justice* 33, no. 1 (2016): 167.

40 Paul Kahn writes of intercultural judgment that "every criticism is thought to rest on a particular community's values; there is no way to make cross-cultural comparisons of value. To condemn another's practices is simply to produce a kind of tautological affirmation of one's own values." Paul W. Kahn, *Putting Liberalism in Its Place* (Princeton: Princeton University Press, 2005), 5.

41 Verna St Denis, "Silencing Aboriginal Curricular Content and Perspectives through Multiculturalism: 'There Are Other Children Here,'" *Review of Education, Pedagogy, and Cultural Studies* 33 (2011): 306.

42 Of course, I recognize that a minority of settler Canadians have apprised themselves of what the existence of Canada costs Indigenous peoples and actively seek to change our relationship. I know many who are deeply committed to this work. In my personal experience, these folks come predominately from university (whether students or faculty) and from faith communities.

43 Given how I go on to use this term, I realize political theorists would generally be happier if I spoke instead of post-structuralism. I don't disagree with them. However, despite the benefit of that term's narrower meaning, it doesn't translate well beyond political theory, and this chapter is intended for a diverse audience. I also considered using *constructivism*, since social construction is the aspect of postmodernism that my worry takes up. It might have been clearer in communicating that I'm not talking about art or architecture, and that I'm not meaning to privilege French social construction theorists over others. At the end of numerous probing conversations on this issue, I decided it would be best to follow my initial impulse, but to explicitly set out what I mean when I use the term *postmodern*.

44 While probably none of them shares my view, I recognize Regan Burles, Michael Asch, Rob Hancock, Heidi Stark, Keith Cherry, Sarah Wiebe, and Rita Dhamoon for rich conversations as I sought to deepen my understanding of postmodern thought.

45 Here I'm speaking against a hegemonic liberal standpoint shared by a majority of Canadians, which often refuses to see itself as a product of world view at all or that takes its world view, centred on individual autonomy, as neutral – hence "different *in kind*" from Canadian liberal world view.

46 Importantly, this allows for internal differentiation. See, for instance, Simpson, *Dancing on Our Turtle's Back*, 53. My point rather is that just as subject position is inescapable, so too is world view.

47 Which is to say that subject position is not at all the same as world view. If social construction sought to reckon with differences in world view, we would necessarily speak of *kinds* of social construction (which notion is not to be confused with the broadly accepted reality of differing accounts of a single kind of social construction), because what counts as "social" discourse differs across distinct life worlds. Many Indigenous peoples, for instance, take as a discursive starting point that not only humans speak; other kinds of beings co-constitute the social.

48 Bonnie Devine, *The Drawings and Paintings of Daphne Odjig: A Retrospective Exhibition* (Ottawa: Publications Division, National Gallery of Canada, 2007), 48.

49 See, for instance, Thomas King, *I'm Not the Indian You Had in Mind* (Toronto: Big Soul Productions, 2007), http://www.nsi-canada. ca/2012/03/im-not-the-indian-you-had-in-mind/. King's short film is brilliant insofar as it goes, but after exposing what indigeneity doesn't mean (by challenging stereotypes), it declines to offer a suggestion as to what indigeneity does mean – or even that it might mean something. My worry is that in an effort to destroy the damaging, false stereotypes associated with particular subject positions – like "Indigenous" – we sometimes eliminate (or more softly, disappear) life way from identity as well.

50 Compare with Tully, "Unfreedom of the Moderns," 91, 104.

51 Compare with Gordon Christie's discussion of this point: Gordon Christie, "Law, Theory and Aboriginal Peoples," *Indigenous Law Journal* 2 (2003): 105–12.

52 Ogimaawigwanebiik [Nancy Jones], "All Teachings Are Correct," in *Dibaajimowinan*, ed. H. James St Arnold and Wesley Ballinger (Odanah: Great Lakes Indian Fish & Wildlife Commission, 2013), 11; Basil Johnston, "Is That All There Is? *Tribal Literature*," *Canadian Literature* 128 (1991): 57.

53 Within *Anishinaabe-inaadiziwin* (Anishinaabe life way) we recognize not only that the truth of a story varies with its teller, but also that stories

differ *in kind*. If one wishes to avoid the neoliberal consumption of stories, understanding and attending to their distinct logics really matters.

54 A *dibaajimowin* is a story from time memorial: a personal, family, or community narrative.

55 I owe Albert Hunter of Manidoo Bawating (Manitou Rapids) for this insight. One of the most helpful teachings I ever got was when he answered a question I posed by saying that he prefers to listen to *how gete-Anishinaabeg* speak. In this way, contradictions tend to become seeming.

56 In the Woodlands School of Algonquian art, a convention called "communication lines" exists for visually representing these connections between beings. I draw particular inspiration in my work from Norval Morriseau's *Harmony in Nature* (oil on canvas, 1980), in which they feature prominently.

57 Margo Little, "Gordon Waindubence (1955–): Giving His Gifts Away," in *Portraits of Spirit Island: The Manitoulin School of Art Comes of Age* (Timmins, ON: HighGrader Magazine, 2009), 114.

58 I realize there's a disconnect here in saying "the whole of Creation," since earlier I spoke only of three *earthly* orders of land, water, and sky. We have stories that demonstrate that these connections exist also with star-beings. See, for instance, the *Aadizookan* of the water lily: Patronella Johnston (text) and Francis Kagige (illustration), "The First Water Lily," in Patronella Johnston, *Tales of Nokomis* (Okemos: Nokomis Learning Center, 1994), 45; Kah-ge-ga-gah-bowh [George Copway], "The Star and the Lily," in *Indian Life and Indian History* (London: Charles Gilpin, 1850), 99; Basil H. Johnston, "Anung-ipeessae-bugoonee" / "White Water Lily," in *Living in Harmony: Mino-nawae-indauwaewin* (Neyaashiinigmiing: Kegedonce, 2011), 23, 29. Additionally, our *gete-anishinaabeg* (especially those who are *midewiwin*) explain how the earth way comes from the orders above it. See James Dumont, "Anishinabe Izhichigaywin," in *Sacred Water: Water for Life*, ed. Edward Benton-Banai, Lea Foushee, and Renee Gurneau, 13–94 (Lake Elmo: North American Water Office, 2010); Kelly, "Confession of a Born Again Pagan," 15, 33–5; Tobasonakwut Kinew, "'Let Them Burn the Sky': Overcoming Repression of the Sacred Use of Anishinaabe Lands," in *Sacred Lands: Aboriginal World Views, Claims, and Conflicts*, ed. Jill Oakes, Rick Riewe, and Kathi Kinew, Canadian Circumpolar Institute Occasional Publication No. 43 (Edmonton: Art Design Printing, 1998), 33; Edward Benton-Banai, *The Mishomis Book: The Voice of the Ojibway* (1988; Minneapolis: University of Minnesota Press, 2010), 16, 57.

59 Ron Geyshick, "Gawa Bay," in *Te Bwe Win (Truth)* (Toronto: Summerhill, 1989), 94.

60 I say "mainstream" agriculture because we did practise some agriculture. Of course, we were and are hugely invested in aquaculture in the form of *manoomin*, wild rice.

61 See Heidi Stark's fantastic study of Anishinaabe change and continuity in the context of treaty relationships: Heidi Kiiwetinepinesiik Stark, "Marked by Fire: Anishinaabe Articulations of Nationhood in Treaty Making with the United States and Canada," *American Indian Culture and Research Journal* 36, no. 2 (2012): 119.

62 Gary Potts, "Growing Together from the Earth," in *Nation to Nation: Aboriginal Sovereignty and the Future of Canada*, ed. Diane Engelstad and John Bird (Toronto: House of Anansi Press Limited, 1992), 199.

63 An influential account of competition as the natural relational dynamic not just for humanity but for all of nature is proposition five, in Immanuel Kant, "Idea for a Universal History with a Cosmopolitan Purpose," in *Kant: Political Writings*, ed. H.S. Reiss, trans. H.B. Nisbet, 2nd ed. (1970; Cambridge: Cambridge University Press, 2003), 45–6. Proposition three (pages 43–4) lays out Kant's vision of social progress, which contrasts with the vision of social growth that I go on to present in this section.

64 James Tully's chapter in this volume makes the same point in a different way when he argues for his two connected practices of reconciliation. His argument and mine for rooted constitutionalism share a powerful affinity. I think this is extremely important, because it shows that this way of thinking is equally available to Indigenous and non-Indigenous persons: it's a foundation for political community available to all.

65 Importantly, claiming that the roots empower and constrain the structure within which all change occurs is not the same as saying that the roots are the *cause* of all change. For instance, phloem transports sap in the opposite direction, from leaves to earth. The production of phloem sap requires sun: trees exist in relation to all manner of other beings (insects, animals, fungi, wind, rain, rivers, winter, etc.), and these beings, too, affect the tree's growth. John Borrows's chapter in this volume beautifully illustrates the many levels of relationship between different kinds of beings.

66 I explain the logic that drives this statement in detail elsewhere for those who want to push further here. See Mills, "Driving the Gift Home," 167; Aaron Mills, "Nokomis and the Law in the Gift: Living Treaty Each Day," in *Surviving Canada: Indigenous Peoples Celebrate 150 Years of Betrayal*, ed. Kiera L. Ladner and Myra J. Tait (Winnipeg: Arbeiter Ring Publishing, 2017), 17; Mills, "Lifeworlds of Law," 847; Aaron Mills, "What Is a Treaty?

On Contract and Mutual Aid," in *The Right Relationship: Reimagining the Implementation of Historical Treaties*, ed. John Borrows and Michael Coyle (Toronto: University of Toronto Press, 2017), 208.

67 Although in his work he uses trees quite differently from the way I do, Johnny Mack also makes this point in his thesis when he speaks about thickening totems/Indigenous constitutionalism. See Johnny Camille Mack, "Thickening Totems and Thinning Imperialism" (LLM diss., University of Victoria, 2009), 129. Rob Clifford also talks about trees in the context of what informs an Indigenous legal order in his work. See his brilliant article, Robert YELḰÁTŦE Clifford, "Listening to Law," *Windsor Yearbook of Access Justice* 33, no. 1 (2016): 59.

68 I greatly appreciate Jeremy Webber's tremendous contribution to legal theory. In Jeremy Webber, "Legal Pluralism and Human Agency," *Osgoode Hall Law Journal* 44, no. 1 (2006): 167, he established that little of interest will come from looking squarely at law to answer the question, What is law? Law's contingency exists against widespread normative disagreement, and this necessarily shifts the focus of legal analysis from "the" law to processes of norm generation. Three years later in Webber, "The Grammar of Customary Law," *McGill Law Journal* 54 (2009): 579, Webber pushed his analysis further still. He demonstrated that the processes of norm-generation, too, are conditioned by what he called a "language," and that each society has a legal language unique to it. With rooted constitutionalism I aim to offer a distinct articulation of this roughly shared mode of theoretical inquiry, to push it further back still and to comment on the nature of relationships across what Webber would call legal languages.

69 Possibly the strongest assertion of this reality I've encountered is Oshoshko Bineshiikwe – Blue Thunderbird Woman, Osawa Aki lkwe (Florence Paynter); Zoongi Gabowi Ozawa Kinew lkwe – Strong Standing Golden Eagle Woman (Mary Maytwayashing); Nii Gaani Aki lnini – Leading Earth Man (Dave Courchene); Giizih-lnini – (Dr Harry Bone); Zhonga-giizhing – Strong Day (Wally Swain); Naawakomigowiinin (Dennis White Bird); Kamintowe Pemohtet – Spirit Walker (D'Arcy Linklater), and Mah Pe Ya Mini (Henry Skywater), *Ogichi Tibakonigaywin, Kihche Othasowewin, Tako Wakan: The Great Binding Law* (delivered 28 November 2015 at Turtle Lodge), http://www.turtlelodge.org/wp-content/uploads/2015/11/ScrollBanner_TheGreatBindingLaw_24x36-PROOFv03.pdf. See also Thomas J. Stillday's remarks at numbered paragraph 29 in Thomas J. Stillday and Anton Treuer, "Bawatig / Sault Ste Marie," *Oshkaabewis Native Journal* 7, no. 1 (2009): 119; and Oren Lyons,

"Traditional Native Philosophies Relating to Aboriginal Rights," in *The Quest for Justice: Aboriginal Peoples and Aboriginal Rights*, ed. Menno Boldt and J. Anthony Long (Toronto: University of Toronto Press, 1985), 19.

70 Heidi Stark offers an account of this in Heidi Kiiwetinepinesiik Stark, "Respect, Responsibility, and Renewal: The Foundations of Anishinaabe Treaty Making with the United States and Canada," *American Indian Culture and Research Journal* 34, no. 2 (2010): 145, 147.

71 Although for my purposes the foundation for treaty is established when distinct peoples share rootedness in a common earth, my tree-legality analogy can be extended here to account for the deepened relationship that treaty represents. Earlier I explained that healthy roots are a necessary but not a sufficient condition for a healthy community. In at least some instances, certain fungi assist in sustaining communities of trees. They do this by connecting symbiotically to a tree's roots, underground. The resulting funghi-root union is called a mycorrhiza. We might analogize these fungi to wampum belts or *opwaaganan* (peace pipes), those beings who help us create and maintain treaty relationships, because as they enter into symbiotic relationships with the roots of more than one tree (including altogether different kinds of trees) and thereby connect them together, individual mychorrhiza become complex mycorrhizal networks. Like a treaty, these mychorrizal networks allow for gifts (in this case, vital nutrients) to be shared throughout the network and distributed to those most in need. For the ecology of this phenomenon, see Suzanne W. Simard, Melanie D. Jones, Daniel M. Durall, David A. Perry, David D. Myrold, and Randy Molina, "Reciprocal Transfer of Carbon Isotopes between Ectomycorrhizal *Betula papyrifera* and *Pseudotsuga menziesii*," *New Phytologist* 137 (1997): 529; Kevin J. Beiler, Daniel M. Durall, Suzanne W. Simard, Sheri A. Maxwell, and Annette M. Kretzer, "Architecture of the Wood-Wide Web: Rhizopogon Spp. Genets Link Multiple Douglas-Fir Cohorts," *New Phytologist* 185 (2010): 543. More accessible for non-scientists will be Dan McKinney and Julia Dordel, *Do Trees Communicate?* (New York: Black Forrest Productions, 2011), https://www.youtube.com/watch?v=iSGPNm3bFmQ – a fantastic video in which Dr Suzanne Simard explains how trees' mychorrizal networks function (i.e., how trees communicate). Sincere thanks to Nancy Turner for connecting me with these sources.

72 In the introduction to their collection of *aadizookaanan*, Sister Bernard Coleman, Ellen Frogner, and Estelle Eich state, "The narratives reflect the Ojibwa way of life, illustrating the fact that folk literature should not be separated from other aspects of a culture. Throughout the book, we have tried to make clear this vital relationship." Sister Bernard Coleman, Ellen Frogner, and Estelle Eich, eds, *Ojibwa Myths and Legends* (Minneapolis:

Ross and Haines, 1962), 9. See also Mary B. Black-Rogers, "Foreword," in *Clothed-In-Fur and Other Tales: An Introduction to an Ojibwa World View*, ed. Thomas W. Overholt and J. Baird Callicott (Lanham, MD: University Press of America, 1982), xv.

73 Because it powerfully reflects the vision of change that animates rooted constitutionalism (ceaseless but always grounded), I thought I might reference one movement within the Anishinaabe *aadizookan* of the flood, an Anishinaabe creation story. There was a time when Nanabozho, a powerful half-human, half-*manido* (spirit being) strayed from a rooted existence. He sought to satisfy not only his needs, but also his wants, without thought to the impact of his consumption on the gifts of others – acting as if autonomous – and his actions resulted in the flooding of the world. He and the lonely animal survivors found themselves on a raft on a turtle's back looking at the end of things. Nanabozho has unique powers of transformation, yet he didn't try to unmake the flood. He left the world that was beneath the waves. Nor did he try adapting the survivors to the conditions of inundation, focusing exclusively on the power surrounding them to the detriment of who they already are and the lifeways through which they knew and lived within creation. Instead he proposed to reach for earth beneath the flood, and he asked various animals to assist in the daunting task. It was *wazhashk* (the muskrat) who succeeded, floating to the surface with a clump of mud in his rigid, unmoving paw. Nanabozho breathed life back into this brave one, then called on the four winds and all his relations for help. His vision: *to grow a new world from the earth of the old*. With all orders of beings contributing their gifts, the speck of mud placed on the turtle's back grew into Mikinaakominis, Turtle Island – a new world with endless capacity for change, but all of which is literally grounded in the earth that came before.

74 Compare with Trish Monture in Patricia A. Monture-Okanee, "The Roles and Responsibilities of Aboriginal Women: Reclaiming Justice," (1992) 56 *Saskatoon Law Review* 56 (1992): 247.

75 See Oren Lyons, "Spirituality, Equality, and Natural Law," in *Pathways to Self-Determination: Canadian Indians and the Canadian State*, ed. Leroy Little Bear, Menno Boldt, and J. Anthony Long (1984; Toronto: University of Toronto Press, 1989) 5, esp. beginning at 8.

76 Many are quick to balk at the statement that liberalism, capitalism, and rule of law are inherently bad. While unfortunate, this is understandable and even predictable. It is hard to see radicalism in the familiar, status quo, in which many of us find if not safety, certainty – and that is often enough. We understand that "radical" identifies a dramatic degree of

difference, but we confuse the point of reference from which difference is marked, replacing "earth" with "that which we know." In consequence, we dismiss profoundly different, earth-centred constitutional alternatives as too radical and thus not worthy of serious consideration. Powerful replies to this critique include Tully, "On Local and Global Citizenship," 243; and Nancy J. Turner, Carla Burton, and André Vallillee, "Developing Ecocultural Symbiosis: Caretaking Relationships in Land and Resource Management" (paper prepared for workshop "Moving beyond the Critiques of Co-Management: Theory and Practice of Adaptive Co-Management," Wilfrid Laurier University, 4–5 February 2005).

77 In a distinct but related use, Taiaiake Alfred invokes the notion of rootedness ("Old Roots into the Earth") in Alfred, *Wasáse*, 236. His discussion ultimately privileges languages above other aspects of Indigenous identity, but he's careful to say that this is because on his account Indigenous languages most effectively disclose the cultures (I would say life ways) beneath them. Similarly, in a recent talk, he offers rootedness as the first of three core resurgence principles: Taiaiake Alfred, "A Talk by Taiaiake Alfred: Research as Indigenous Resurgence" (12 November 2015, Fenn Lounge, Residence Commons, Carleton University). Again, we aren't using the term in quite the same way, but the connection in our respective uses is obvious.

78 Robert Lovelace, "Prologue. Notes from Prison: Protecting Algonquin Lands from Uranium Mining," in *Speaking for Ourselves: Environmental Justice in Canada*, ed. Julian Agyeman, Peter Cole, Randolph Haluz-Delay,and Pat O'Riley (Vancouver: UBC Press, 2009), ix, xvii.

79 Nokomis gives me teachings on this general theme almost every time she shares teachings with me. She has shared some of this perspective in print in Bessie Mainville, "Traditional Native Culture and Spirituality: A Way of Life That Governs Us," *Indigenous Law Journal* 8, no. 1 (2010): 1.

80 I'm grateful to Jeff Corntassel for his insight upon hearing me reflect on nokomis's teachings that my dissertation doesn't actually need the language of decolonization; that in the face of the Anishinaabe theoretical framework I was describing, "decolonization" had become redundant. I felt only a tension around this; Jeff moved that vague sensation to a conscious understanding.

5 Towards a Relational Paradigm – Four Points for Consideration: Knowledge, Gender, Land, and Modernity

GINA STARBLANKET AND
HEIDI KIIWETINEPINESIIK STARK

Resurgence, Reconciliation, and Relationality

Relationships are the pivotal theme in the recent works of John Borrows, Jim Tully, and Michael Asch. We offer to these foundational works an intervention on the risks and possibilities of a relational paradigm in considering four critical concepts: knowledge, gender, land, and modernity. We look to these four concepts to target colonizing logics that operate in both Western and Indigenous ideas and take up relationships as generative, active processes. In each of their works, Borrows, Tully, and Asch demonstrate ways in which settlers and Indigenous peoples can look to the relations we inhabit as a source of direction for environmental, social, and political change. Asch draws attention to the ways in which treaty-based modes of relating can provide frameworks for relationships that are oriented towards reconciliation; Tully argues that human-to-human reconciliation is inextricably linked to reconciliation with the living earth, and that neither project is independent from the other; and Borrows demonstrates how Indigenous knowledge and traditions exist in relation to specific contexts, and that neither is fixed or fundamental. All focus on the potential for renewed awareness of our roles and responsibilities within relationships to correct the violent ways that humans have interacted with each other and our environments in past and present contexts. Their works speak to the vast range of possibilities for Indigenous philosophies of relationality to help illuminate the limits of individualistic, hierarchical, anthropocentric, and exploitative ways of being, while offering alternative conceptions of how humans might govern and organize ourselves in relation to one another and to the living earth.

Each of these authors offers compelling visions of the transformations that can occur if we see the limits of Western conceptions of freedom and begin to understand ourselves as inhabiting relations of interdependence with one another and with the world we live in. Their proposals represent a shift away from an atomistic, human-centred world view and towards a relational way of being that is inspired by the principles of interconnectedness inherent in many Indigenous legal and political orders. These authors are not introducing novel concepts, nor do they claim to, but give due credit to the many Indigenous intellectuals and knowledge holders who have taken up the transformative potential of relationship over the years.[1] In Indigenous scholarship, relationality has often been taken up as characteristic of Indigenous ways of knowing and being within comparative analyses of Indigenous and Western epistemologies.[2] It has had a particularly prominent place within the discourse on Indigenous research methodologies, many of which are grounded upon relational paradigms.[3] Feminist scholars have also taken up the potential for women's relationship with the self, the family, or the natural world to inspire change in the ways in which we interact with others and our environments.[4] In addition, the works of Indigenous scholars such as Vine Deloria, Kiera Ladner, John Borrows, Leanne Simpson, Robert Williams, Isabel Altamirano-Jiménez, Mishuana Goeman, Audra Simpson, and others have elucidated the distinct legal and political significance of Indigenous modes of relating with the world around us.[5] These scholars have emphasized the need to re-conceptualize Indigenous visions of law and governance in ways that account for our position within reciprocal relations with all of creation and with past, present, and future generations. As Indigenous peoples from grassroots to academic realms have become more acquainted with the limits of articulating our political imperatives through state-sanctioned mechanisms of rights and recognition, there has also been heightened attention to the need for political strategies that are grounded upon the resurgence of a relational way of being.[6] As a result, more and more Indigenous peoples are engaging in forms of political action that are not mediated by the colonial state or imposed through state legislation.

Instead, many are focusing on the primary need to attend to the underlying relationships that configure and delimit Indigenous peoples' contemporary political movements. These include relations between humans, with creation, and between Indigenous governments and state institutions. This shift has been accompanied by increased scholarly attention to the possibilities that treaty relations hold for rei-magining social and political relations within Indigenous communities and between Indigenous and non-Indigenous peoples.[7] Collectively, this renewed attentiveness to relationship represents a resurgence of forms of political organizing that are grounded upon relationships to creation, one another, and future generations.

The works of Borrows, Tully, and Asch contribute to this growing body of discourse by drawing out the conciliatory potential of relation-ships when they are inhabited in a healthy and forward-looking way. They focus not only on the need to bring forth greater awareness and appreciation for our interconnectedness, but on the transformative pos-sibilities of understanding and actively embodying our responsibilities within those relationships. The idea here is that the reconnection of people with one another, and of individuals and the land isn't neces-sarily transformative in and of itself, but that it is the proliferation of relationships of care and nurturance, in which we see ourselves hav-ing concrete roles and responsibilities, that have the greatest promise. Imagine the transformations that could occur when humans begin to realize that we are not neutral in the face of crises that surround us, but instead recognize that through our choices we have the potential to actively change the world we inhabit. There is thus an important dif-ference between *understanding* our place in the world as situated within relations of interdependence with all of creation and *living* in a way that carries out our responsibilities within these relationships.

This chapter reflects upon the need to remain attentive to the way in which individual roles and responsibilities within relationships are identified and taken up on an everyday level.[8] Here we are interested in identifying considerations that can help us be mindful of the ways in which relationality can either advance or constrain political move-ments, as well as the ways they can be invoked to either confront or insulate the violation of individual and collective well-being. The dis-cussion unfolds through reference to four dimensions of relationality that elucidate its dual potential to function as either empowering or restrictive when invoked in various contexts: knowledge, gender, land, and modernity. While there are other potential sites worthy of inter-rogation, we focus on these concepts because of their centrality in the Indigenous politics literature and reflect the tensions and struggles in our efforts towards the embodiment of resurgence. In each section of this chapter, we reflect upon the possibilities for the visions of rela-tionality offered by the authors to dissolve the boundaries imposed by Western discursive, social, and political orders. At the same time, we are also mindful of the ways in which the discourse of relationship can be invoked to overlook or reproduce oppressive power dynamics within Indigenous communities and have structured our analysis to simultaneously shed light on the possibilities and consequences of such instances.

In keeping with the spirit of relationality and its inherent fluidity, dynamism, and context-dependence, this chapter raises considerations that we see as relevant in working towards the resurgence of relational modes of being rather than providing a definitive or prescriptive set of strategies for implementation. Our preferred approach is to engage in an overview of factors that we see as significant to the current discussion, while acknowledging that the applicability of these considerations may vary from person to person and that there are many additional considerations that merit exploration but that lie beyond the focus of this chapter. In our view, the emancipatory potential of proposals that prescribe specific, predetermined processes for decolonization and resurgence are inherently limited by their presumed universality and lack of consideration of context-specific variables.[9] We recognize that conciliatory practices take different shapes and forms in varying contexts and encourage readers to take or adapt what is useful and leave the rest.

Relationality and Knowledge

The first consideration we would like to raise is power, with our focus on *knowledge*. We ask how a shift towards a relational paradigm can aid us in being attentive to power and the asymmetrical relationships born out of power imbalance. The shift towards the relational requires that we not just acknowledge these imbalances but also actively work to mitigate the positions and privileges they produce. We must ensure we are not reproducing the very logics that have too often ordered our relationships in violent and destructive ways.

While attention to power can provide insight into various dimensions of relationship, we focus our attention here on how power operates through knowledge production and its classification and codification. We must contend with how we are engaging with and producing knowledge. We have to ask ourselves what knowledge counts and in what ways. In varying ways, the works of Borrows, Tully, and Asch each ask readers to critically reflect upon their own sources of knowledge. This is an important starting point, yet we call for moving beyond merely a considerate citational politic. Beyond *which* sources of knowledge we take up, we are also intently focused on *how* we take up these sources. For example, why do we classify some works as theory and others as stories? What is lost when we fail to understand *theory* as a set of *stories*? Or when we fail to consider theories produced and contained within stories. And story is not just theory. As Leanne Simpson reminds us, within Anishinaabe thought, "'Theory' is generated and regenerated continually through embodied practice and within each family, community, and generation of people."[10] Story is also a practice. It is rooted in relationality, in our relationships with one another and with creation.

Taking Indigenous knowledge seriously means not just taking up different answers but instead (or at least in addition) requires raising a different set of questions. Indigenous knowledge is too often treated as an additive to Western knowledge, eclipsing its transformative powers. For example, many Indigenous scholars have highlighted the colonial entrapments of state-driven projects such as recognition that contain Indigenous knowledge within settler colonial logics that foreclose alternatives to these initiatives. Indigenous legal traditions are often taken up in U.S. and Canadian courts only so far as they can provide insight into predetermined questions constrained within Western legal traditions. In these contexts, the scope and breadth to which Indigenous knowledge can shape conciliatory practices is already circumscribed and constrained.[11]

For example, the courts have at times turned to Indigenous knowledge, developing canons of treaty interpretation and calling for treaties to be interpreted as they were understood by the signatories.[12] While these canons, when they are adhered to, can be favourable for unearthing Indigenous interpretations of their treaties, they nonetheless take up and apply Indigenous interpretations through a Western frame of reference that is informed primarily by the need to reconcile Indigenous claims with the sovereignty of the Crown. In addition, judges are often able to recognize Indigenous rights to hunt and fish for subsistence, but they struggle in extending these rights to commercial activities that would provide Indigenous peoples with considerable economic autonomy. Similarly, judges in Canada struggle to envision treaty signatories as having reserved their sovereignty in their treaty relationships with the Crown while putting forward a vision for coexistence across a multinational terrain in which Indigenous nations and Canada are bound by their obligations and treaty commitments.

Along a similar vein, while legal scholars have, of course, been careful to position Aboriginal and treaty rights as pre-existing, the attention to section 35 of the Canadian Constitution Act, 1982, has nonetheless locked these discussions, in some ways, within a state framework instead of situating them as part of a dialogue about nation-to-nation relationships. Indeed the Canadian courts often close off and contain discussion of self-government and fail to affirm and recognize Indigenous sovereignty. They have failed to consider even more narrow questions about treaty rights that focus – for example, on taxation, small business enterprises, or Indigenous economic development efforts that fall outside of capitalist market-driven, extraction-oriented agendas.

We must be attentive to how power structures and determines which narratives, modes of understanding our world, and the web of relationships in operation are given primacy. Furthermore, we must untangle how these narratives have ordered *how* we relate to one another and to creation. Too often, conventional Western knowledge is willing to turn to the relational only insofar as this attention to relationships doesn't threaten the stability of the state. For example, foreclosing more expansive conceptions of treaty relationships eclipses the concomitant questions these understandings produce in relation to state claims to sovereignty, land title, and political authority over Indigenous lives. Asch, Borrows, and Tully each challenge the exclusion of Indigenous and Western knowledge that challenges state-centric narratives that ostensibly reproduce oppressive relationships. Asch seeks to bring forward settler narratives and understandings of treaty that adhere to these expansive views and whose exclusion has left Canadians with limited pathways for transforming their relationships with Indigenous nations.[13] Borrows critiques Canada's omission of Indigenous legal traditions as foundational to the development of Canadian law, asserting the need to shift towards a multi-juridical legal culture.[14] Tully asserts the recovery of these expansive narratives are essential for the development of just relationships.[15]

As their works demonstrate, if we are going to take Indigenous knowledge seriously, we must give careful consideration to Indigenous assertions of sovereignty and nationhood, as well as the laws and political traditions that give shape and meaning to Indigenous sovereignty and nationhood. We must ask what treaty rights exist beyond the scope of hunting and fishing. If Indigenous peoples were not ceding lands, as Indigenous knowledge posits, but instead creating a shared territory that would enable peaceful and mutually beneficial coexistence of separate nations, how must our understandings of treaty rights be transformed to account for these interpretations? We need to be attentive to how asymmetrical power relationships have enabled conventional Western knowledge to produce hierarchies of knowledge that too often mute modes of understanding the world as deeply relational and interconnected.

We see similar forms of containment operating in educational contexts – for example, with efforts towards indigenizing the academy. This rarely involves the expansion of Indigenous programming that takes Indigenous knowledge production as its base or is directed and driven by the questions and concerns of Indigenous communities (the grounded concerns of Indigenous nations and their citizens or the related intellectual inquiries coming out of the field of Indigenous studies). Instead, widespread attention and resources are dedicated to the expansion of Indigenous responses to and critiques of the central tenets and concerns within the Western disciplines. Indigenous knowledge becomes contained within these disciplinary traditions that drive both the questions deemed important to their respective field and determine the metrics for successful engagement and mobilization of knowledge.

In fact, even within Indigenous studies, much of the celebrated and well-funded scholarship is focused on works that make critical interventions in long-standing Western disciplines, dismantling the theories critical to a particular field. These works often brilliantly theorize Indigenous experiences with and responses to settler colonialism and warrant considerate engagement. Indeed, Indigenous studies scholarship recognizes we are not outside of colonialism but are actively engaging with and affected by the structures and logics that enable its continued flourishing. This is important work. But the question remains why Western academic fields will often engage Indigenous knowledge *only* when it's translated through the language of their discipline. Why does the onus continue to reside with Indigenous knowledge holders to translate Indigenous knowledge into cognizable frames? And even when Indigenous and non-Indigenous scholars do this work, as we see with the scholarship of Borrows, Tully, and Asch, Indigenous knowledge is most often given consideration or taken up by Western thinkers when there is either a *vacancy* or *bankruptcy* in Western thought, replicating a power binary between Western and Indigenous knowledge.

For example, when Western scientific knowledge fails to provide insights for how to live in a precarious world affected by devastating natural events such as earthquakes and tsunamis, attention will be given to Indigenous knowledge systems, recognizing Indigenous peoples have had to contend with these concerns since time immemorial. Yet even when Western thinkers are willing to consider the stories that detail these historic events that are absent from the Western historical record, they often fail to consider how Indigenous knowledge posits we are a part of the web of relationships that give rise to these moments. Instead, Western divisions between humans and nature are reified, even while considering the Indigenous stories that actively work against this categorization and binary by detailing the interconnectedness of Creation.[16] These tendencies minimize or contain the transformative potential of Indigenous knowledge, rendering it easier to incorporate and assimilate into the Western categories of knowledge. We argue it is not enough to make space for Indigenous knowledge. We must allow for this space to be reconfigured by Indigenous knowledge.

A shift towards a relational paradigm can also aid us in resisting the continued containment of Indigenous knowledge. Noelani Goodyear-Ka'ōpua asserts, "Such containment can manifest in geographic forms as reservations or small school spaces, in political forms as legal recognition frameworks that seek to subsume sovereignty within the settler state's domestic laws, and in ideological forms as school curricula that allow a sprinkling of Indigenous history and culture only to maintain its marginality."[17] This *logic of containment* ensures that just enough Indigenous knowledge or "culture" in engaged and incorporated, so long as the settler state and its colonial relations of power are not disturbed.[18] This logic of containment operates as an extension of the epistemological and physical violences endemic to settler colonialism.[19] We see this logic at work, for example, in land claims and title cases that utilize a temporal framework that contains Indigenous relationships with and responsibilities to Creation as historical claims of prior occupancy. As Mishuana Goeman highlights, "A consequence of colonialism has meant a translation or too easy collapsing of *land* to *property*, a move that perpetuates the logics of containment."[20] This valuation of land to jurisdictional legal value fails to account for the relationality of land as a "storied site of human interactions."[21] In the process of this power-knowledge dynamic, land becomes devoid of its agency and meaning-making potential and instead becomes objectified as a quantifiable good we live *on* rather than a living entity we live *with* and generate knowledge *through*.[22]

Attention to relationality enables us to see how colonialism is always in relationship. It is not some abstract logic that operates outside of people. It is structural, but it is also a process that is dynamic, interactive, and fluid. Attention to the power and logic at work in state narratives enables us to better identify the *productive* (read: generative) quality of settler colonialism. As Patrick Wolfe has noted and many others have taken up, nuanced, and expanded upon, "Settler colonialism is inherently eliminatory."[23] While bringing much-needed attention to the structural aspects of settler colonialism, as an analytic, it risks eliding both power relations and decolonial possibilities if too much focus is given to a Native/settler binary.[24] Furthermore, we assert this analytic also risks becoming over-determined if focus is given exclusively to the eliminatory logic that Wolfe draws out to the exclusion of the *productive nature of settler colonialism*. This productive nature of settler colonialism is rooted in relationality. Indeed, settler colonialism doesn't just try to eliminate but, in its place, seeks to produce something new. But in the process, settler states do so through relationship with Indigenous nations. Settler colonialism, then, is not so much eliminatory as it is concomitantly *reductive* and *productive*. We risk becoming further entangled within these productive and reductive tenets of settler colonial logics when we fail to account for how settler regimes regulate or circumscribe our relationships.

As Leanne Simpson reminds us, "Our sovereignty does not come from a document. Our sovereignty comes from an abundance of healthy, responsible, respectful relationships with all of our relations."[25] How do we ensure we are contending with, mitigating, and resisting colonial power that seeks to obscure Indigenous knowledge systems that shape our relationships – relationships with one another and with creation? How do we ensure we are making the space for present and future generations to dream a new way forward for our people, to learn from and with the land, to learn through our knowledge systems to derive new meaning from the long-standing knowledge that has sustained our peoples from time immemorial in order to contend with the shapeshifting forces of colonialism? Understanding ourselves as inhabiting relationships and always being in relation may produce answers to these challenging questions.

Relationality and Gender

Our next and related consideration concerns the gendered nature of discourses of relationship. While there are a variety of power relations that we could explore with respect to gender, sexuality, and relationality, we have chosen to focus specifically on the ways that relationality implicates Indigenous women. Critical dialogue about women's experiences is a particularly important part of projects that aim to explore the political significance of bringing forward more conciliatory ways of relating with one another and our environments, and this is especially important in Indigenous contexts. We therefore invoke gender as an analytical category to explore the precise ways that the rhetoric of relationship can function to simultaneously centre Indigenous womanhood and close off Indigenous women's voices. We argue that this dual potential emerges from discourses that posit Indigenous women as primarily responsible for maintaining healthy relationships within Indigenous communities,[26] minimizing and/or eclipsing Indigenous women's political agency. Our focus in this section is not to reinforce the primacy of binary notions of gender, but to understand the ways that gender emerges both within and in efforts to oppose conditions of colonialism.

The highly gendered nature of colonialism has been well recognized in contemporary feminist and Indigenous studies literature.[27] The imposition of Western gender ideals within Indigenous communities has historically aimed to distort Indigenous notions of identity to render them legible to (and easier to regulate within) colonizing orders. In the process, the internalization of gendered ideals presents a host of problems, transforming the way Indigenous peoples understand the self and the relationships we inhabit, as well as our systems of kinship, law, and governance. While women across cultures have a tendency to be associated with ideals of nature and relationship (and men with ideals of human autonomy and independence),[28] the gendered nature of the discourse of relationship also carries particular implication in Indigenous communities because of the ways in which gender is produced within contexts of colonialism, as well as the ways in which it is invoked as a remedy to the violence of colonialism.

Our intention isn't to dismiss Indigenous women's association with creation and with relationship but to highlight the need for critical awareness of the ways in which notions of care and nurturance have been associated with femininity through and in response to colonialism. This can help us reveal and remain mindful of the potential for essentialist or bounded constructions of gender to restrict men and women's involvement in reconciliation and resurgence to roles and responsibilities cast along gender-based constructions of Indigeneity. For instance, the prospect of revitalizing traditional modes of relating is often proposed as a means of addressing contemporary sexism and misogyny in Indigenous communities, placing the onus on Indigenous women to address and remedy unhealthy relationships and violence within Indigenous and settler contexts while also ensuring the maintenance of traditional practices. Often these dual mandates coalesce into arguments that urge Indigenous women to eschew strategies such as feminism that aim to analyse and address violence based on gender or sexual orientation. As putatively individual concerns that stand in contrast to the "broader" or "collective" political issues, unhealthy relationships are continually relegated to the private sphere. Theoretically, all Indigenous peoples are to be held accountable for a renewed conception of what it means to maintain good relationships, while on the ground level, women who have experienced violence frequently continue to be expected to address their conflicts with perpetrators in private, at the family or community level.[29] Not only does the notion that women are the "keepers of relationship" minimize the responsibility of men to address patriarchal gender relations and other violence that plagues our relationships, it discounts the capacity for women to engage in vicious and abusive practices and overlooks forms of violence against queer Indigenous peoples.[30]

When invoked in an essentialist fashion, Indigenous women's association with nature and creation, and men's association with science and rationality puts women in the contradictory position of being primarily responsible for the maintenance of healthy relationship while having less agency on how to address those relationships in the public sphere. Consequently, the range of strategies that we can utilize for addressing violence continue to be conditioned by gendered ideals of relationship and nature. Furthermore, when Indigenous women do invoke the discourse of relationship in the public sphere, these works are often seen as less authoritative than those of men. For instance, many Indigenous women have adopted a relational approach to reveal the limits of Western conceptions of law and politics and / or have proposed alternative frameworks that are grounded in Indigenous world views. However, these analyses have a tendency to be interpreted as "women's issues," often positioned in the domestic and private sphere, eclipsing important interventions in the political and public sphere – contributions that unfortunately remain unacknowledged more often than not.

While a comprehensive review of the works of Indigenous women on relationality is beyond the parameters of this section, even a brief overview can help elucidate the extent of Indigenous women's contributions in this area. For instance, Indigenous legal scholars Val

Napoleon and Sharon Venne explore the ways in which relationality can ground Indigenous peoples' individual and collective self-determination efforts without privileging either of these pursuits over the other.[31] Rauna Kuokkanen and Isabel Altamirano-Jimenez's analyses of women and neoliberal economies describe the possibilities for relational conceptions of Indigeneity to facilitate recognition of women's agency, resilience, and contributions to their communities, demonstrating that these are neither opposing nor contradictory.[32] Kim Anderson and Leanne Simpson have made foundational contributions in the field through their examinations of the central role of maternal and family relations within projects of decolonization and the reconstitution of traditional governance structures.[33] Makere Stewart-Harawira's work argues that a spiritually grounded and feminine-oriented political ontology of love and compassion can help address colonial commodification and exploitation of the land and its inhabitants. Dory Nason and Rachel Flowers have explored ways that relations of love and anger can reveal the violence of colonialism and propel the transformation of colonial relationships.[34]

These and many other Indigenous women look to relationships as a way to illuminate, disrupt, and provide alternatives to colonial and heteronormative systems of power and privilege. The multiplicity and vitality of their voices demonstrates the extensive length and breadth of contributions that Indigenous women have made in exploring the profoundly transformative possibilities that relationship can offer Indigenous law and politics. It is in recognition of their efforts that we aim to honour their work but also to consciously trouble the tendency for Indigenous women's scholarship to be overlooked or marginalized in these fields.

As Indigenous women in the academy, we are put in the difficult position of having to continually evidence the centrality of our work in the respective fields that we occupy, in contrast to the way in which the scholarship of men who challenge normative understandings of relationship is interpreted. Although Indigenous women comprise the central subjects in discussions of relationship, our scholarship is often discredited as autobiographical or as too personal if we ground it too heavily in those same relations. When women invoke personal experiences, our work is read as anecdotal, while men's perceived distance from the realm of relationships allows their scholarship to be read as neutral and empirically evidenced. In fact, when men enter into discussions that aim to draw out the political significance of their familial, spiritual, or communal relations, they are widely applauded for their innovative and ground-breaking contributions.

Whether it is due to the stigmas surrounding feminism in Indigenous communities or the patriarchal nature of the academy generally, Indigenous women's analyses of relationship are often read more cautiously than those of men. When we challenge power relations in either Indigenous or non-Indigenous communities, our perspectives are frequently discounted or dismissed as overly personal, hostile, feminist, or Westernized. These perceptions position our analyses as ancillary, irrelevant, or even in opposition to the issues of central importance in Indigenous politics. We are not suggesting that Indigenous women's analyses of relationships should not be engaged with in a critical fashion, but that their merits need not be gratuitously discounted while those of Indigenous men are taken for granted.

Indeed, men retain greater authoritativeness when writing on these same topics, and the relevance of their analyses of relationship to broader political projects is generally presumed. Beyond being relevant, they are often considered to be revolutionary for taking up and addressing the same colonial, anthropocentric, and patriarchal relations that Indigenous women have been disrupting at length for many years. As a result, it is ironically the voices of men that are now lending legitimacy to the political significance of relationships, something women have been arguing for since the earliest origins of feminist organizing.

We have both personally experienced our works being interpreted through reference to or through comparison with that of our male colleagues who are doing similar work in the field. The fact that there are Indigenous men who are doing consistent work seems to render ours more identifiable or legitimate. This raises what we see as an important disjuncture in the field of Indigenous politics, that is, the way that identity is politicized in Indigenous scholarship when it comes to race but not gender. Critics are eager to identify the problematic of non-Indigenous academics discussing the transformative possibilities of relationality, dictating the specific terms and guidelines that non-Indigenous allies must adhere to if they are to engage with Indigenous content. Non-Indigenous scholars must proceed cautiously, with proper care and acknowledgment of the sources of Indigenous knowledge they are engaging with, ensuring that they are not appropriating, misrepresenting, speaking for, or reproducing one of the many other paradigms that have plagued academic engagements with Indigenous knowledges and experiences.

Yet there is a notable lack of similar criteria to ensure that men engage responsibly with topics that are gendered in ways that have disproportionate impact on women. At the symposium that led to this book, John Borrows posed the important question, Who are we citing? The intent of his question seemed to be to highlight the importance of looking to the living earth, the seasons, animals, places, and elements to draw out important lessons about reconciliation and resurgence. Yet his question can also prompt further reflection on which works we see as authoritative and which ones we have a tendency to overlook in our writings.

In our view, the discourse of relationality has the potential to disrupt and complicate the ways that Indigeneity gets constructed along gender lines, both in Western representations of Indigenous culture as well as in decolonial efforts to reframe Indigeneity. A relational approach is well-suited to demonstrate that gender classifications are not biologically or spiritually determined but are social and cultural productions shaped in relation to colonial and decolonial projects. If we understand relationality as an analytical lens through which we recognize difference as socially and culturally produced rather than allowing the discourse of relationship to essentialize these differences in ways that confine our movements, we stand to cultivate a greater range of grounds for Indigenous identity and a broader spectrum of modes for engaging in acts of resurgence.

The project of re-conceptualizing systems of law and governance upon relational grounds can be profoundly empowering for many women. It can facilitate an appreciation of the political significance of our everyday relations by calling into question the public/private and individual/collective rights dichotomies and demonstrating that there are important legal and political principles that can be drawn out of our everyday interactions.[35] Furthermore, it can introduce greater awareness of women's political agency by demonstrating that Indigenous women's role within the family and community has important implications beyond the domain of cultural maintenance and transmission, and by drawing out the distinctly political nature of women's everyday relations and interactions.

Yet for the concept of relationship to truly represent a source of critical consciousness, it is also important to examine the full extent of its gendered implications. This means contemplating the different ways that the discourse of relationship implicates Indigenous men and women, depending on the how their responsibilities within relationships are invoked and the context in which they are applied. As we reflect on the possibilities for relationship to represent a source of knowledge and direction for change, it is vital that we remain mindful of the potential for both men and women to either reproduce or challenge gendered hierarchies and dynamics in our own works.

Neither Tully, Asch, nor Borrows takes credit for introducing a relational way of seeing the world or understanding our place in it. Rather, their perspectives have been informed by listening to what Indigenous peoples have been saying since first contact and reflecting on how they can honour those teachings from their own locations. Their work signals a perceivable shift towards a relational paradigm in the discourse of Indigenous law and politics, and specifically one where both Indigenous people and settlers are drawing on Indigenous notions of relationality to inform their works. Borrows has done a particularly strong job of demonstrating the need to critically evaluate rhetoric about gender, culture, and tradition that emerges in discussions of Indigenous law and relationality, demonstrating how Indigenous legal sources can be engaged in a way that either forecloses or opens up space for thinking about power and gender.[36] Yet there remains much work to be done in this area, and it is our hope that readers who are inspired by the possibilities of relationality think carefully about the politics, gendered and otherwise, underlying the process through which "traditional modes of relating" are identified and invoked. Such precautions will contribute to the important project of moving beyond treatments of Indigenous women as central subjects in the politics of relationship, towards one where we are active agents in these conversations.

Relationality and Land

The third consideration we want to take up is land. Specifically we are interested in exploring the ways relationship to land is taken up in Indigenous studies. We ask how our attempts to combat colonial framings of land risk reifying these Western containments or eliding a broader understanding of the range of relationships we have to place. In our efforts to assert our political authority in the face of state assertions of title over our territories, we ask how we have foreclosed alternative forms of resistance by centring our attentions on articulations of land that risk reifying statist notions of bounded space. We also question how this attention to land, while important, has eclipsed our focus on relationships to other aspects of Creation beyond the land, such as water and waterways. While we often use the language of land to connote all of Creation, has this framing prefigured relationships with and across land as pre-eminent to relationships with and across the ocean, lakes, rivers, and life-waters that enable our very existence? And finally, how have our attempts to assert our political authority through framing nationhood become wedded to territorial boundaries and fixed political formations that close off our rich understandings of relating to one another? In the process, do we enable the fulfilment of colonial efforts to restrict Indigenous mobility by tethering Indigeneity to land?

Vince Diaz reminds us to be attentive to this trap, noting the need to be "cognizant of how we as Native peoples sometimes unwittingly perpetuate colonial definitions of land (and self) through ways that we invoke primordial connectedness to landedness, particularly in political programs of reclaiming stolen land bases."[37] This romanticizing of pre-contact Indigenous life poses at least two significant risks for Indigenous nations: (1) it obscures the hard work that produces Indigenous knowledge and enables the flourishing of relationships with humans and non-humans,[38] and (2) in the absence of this attention to the work involved in living out our relationality, makes space for settler replacement narratives that posit Indigenous relationships and knowledge as *natural* and *innate*. Consequently, these narratives position Indigenous realities as *inauthentic* and *contaminated* by colonialism and frame the rise of settler-states as *inevitable* and thus *inculpable*.[39]

Settler colonialism aims to separate land from the rest of Creation in order to facilitate territorial expansion. Discourses of land that essentialize our relationships as fixed in some pre-contact context risk eliding the ways in which grammars of race, class, gender, sexuality, and sovereignty operate at the local, regional, and global levels to produce the settler state.[40] One way we can combat this is by being attentive to how place matters. This requires operationalizing a critical positionality and reflexivity that is about understanding ourselves in relationship to the place we are.[41] To understand how settler colonialism has (re)ordered our relationships to place requires us to take greater care in understanding our engagement with place as a series of meaning-making practices. We must bring forward our own rich stories about how we relate to Creation, which means we must expand our focus to include both the other living beings that have shaped and regulated our relationships to land as well as how our relationships with and across land are generated through our movements across these territories.

We need to actively work against colonial narratives that seek to divorce us from these relationships by configuring land as bounded territories in which only our primordial practices can permeate so long as they are understood as temporally and spatially fixed and discursively remade as "cultural rights" to ensure minimal material impacts for the state. We can resist this move, however, by ensuring we are creating space for relationships that are generative, that cultivate not just the continued *transmission* of Indigenous knowledge but also ensure the *production* of Indigenous knowledge.

In detailing land as pedagogy, Leanne Simpson relays the story of Kwezens, a young girl who learns both *from* the land and in interaction *with* the land, bringing the knowledge of how to make maple syrup to her people. It is not just Kwezens's ability to learn with and from the land that generates this knowledge. It is further cultivated through her loving relationships with her family, her mother and aunties who trust in her knowledge and support her in working through her understanding of the land and, in this context, the maple trees, when she is unable to reproduce the running sap at first attempt. Simpson asserts, in this way, "The land, aki, is both context and process."[42] It is through the activation of our relationships with the living entities that constitute this expansive space – the land, animals, spirits, and humans – that knowledge is produced and transmitted. The generative quality of our movement across Creation necessitates attention to and accountability for our positionality. This requires that we be attentive to and ground our analysis of relationships in the place we are, and where we are is always changing.[43] The containment of Indigenous lands to reserves or even the more expansive Aboriginal territory can risk our assuming that our movements through our own territories are not also always regulated and conditioned by relationships and responsibilities. In fact, it is our engagement with place and with others in these places that gives rise to our political practices, exchanges, and development of new relationships. A greater understanding of how our mobility is generative can also enable us to see how discourses that fix us spatially (as well as temporally) are reductive.

For example, the story of Kwezens nicely demonstrates the danger of failing to see what Leanne Simpson calls *land as pedagogy.* If we fail to account for how our movement across and engagement with place give rise to our knowledge production and practices, then we see the practice of making maple sugar as a primordial practice of Anishinaabeness, instead of seeing the practice of engaging creation and nurturing new knowledge production as essential. Surely this story is about how the Anishinaabe came to receive the gift of maple syrup. But more importantly, this story is a guide for how we can bring forward new gifts to aid us in this ever-changing world. The greatest tool available to Indigenous peoples is not in the revitalization of our traditional practices but instead can be found in the processes that gave rise to these ever-growing and flourishing traditions.

It is our mobility, our movement across the lands and waters that activates our relationships and responsibilities. The flattening of Indigenous space to territorial delineations of bounded spaces marking "ours" and "theirs" not only reifies settler claims to unceded lands but also presumes Indigenous spaces are unregulated, failing to account for the ordering of relationships that produce the balanced interactions with Creation that become posited as *natural* and *innate.*

Attention to how we relate to one another can combat colonial containments of Indigenous political authority. As Goeman states, "Indigenous peoples came to occupy certain physical and imaginative spaces in the colonial mindset that existed within strict gender and racial hierarchies. Indigenous subjects became and become subsumed in these differences."[44] The abstraction of this difference has served as a tool of settler creation myths to legitimate the state. She warns, "In our pursuit to differentiate ourselves from settler colonists, we have territorialized land and body." This territorialization has resulted in our focusing on Western conceptions of nationhood and citizenship that centre on rights of and responsibility to the nation rather than to our relations to one another and Creation. Indigenous assertions of our nationhood have been important mechanisms to protect and carry out our relationships to Creation and one another. But in the process, we wonder if this form of resistance has distracted us from exploring how we understand ourselves in relation to others. When we express the place we come from, we often name our reserves or treaty territories. While these are important linkages, we wonder how these assertions centre our focus on our Indigenous polities at the expense of our attention to the territory and relations we come from. Of course, we often acknowledge these as well, delineating our familial and geographic lineage. But we nonetheless wonder how we are complicit in the perpetuation of colonial containments of Indigenous political formation by centring our attention on the bounded spaces produced out of treaty relationships with the state. Indeed Robert Innes asks these questions in his study of the Cowessess First Nation,[45] and these are questions that have increasingly come to our attention through conversations with the Zagime First Nations as chief and council explore what their relationships were historically with their neighbouring bands in order to bring forward relational alternatives for Indigenous governance today.

Harvey and Thompson propose thinking about indigeneity as "belonging to a place" versus "belonging in a place."[46] This framing accounts for the responsibilities and obligations we have to those who came before, as a turn towards the relational necessitates. For the Anishinaabe, we speak of ourselves as the last of creation. It is not just some inversion of the hierarchy of creation, with ourselves as the lowest and thus the least valuable. Instead Anishinaabe attention to our order of placement on the earth reminds us of our obligations to those who came before us, who already governed the territories we came to inhabit. As our stories and the practices they give rise to denote, the animals stood up for us and brought us into an already regulated and governed territory.[47] Our clan governance is the extension of these relationships, reminding us that whether we are moving through our lands or visiting the lands of others, we must account for the web of relationships that order these spaces. We offer tobacco to the water beings before we enter our canoes, we petition the plants and animals in recognition of their agency and our relationships with these beings. We engage in political exchange and the expansion of kin relationships when moving into the territories of others. We are always in relationship and are also always aiming to nurture and expand these relationships. We contend that attention to our expansive relationships with Creation and with others in our movements across Creation enables us to unearth the generative nature of these relationships.

Relationality and Temporality

This section extends the previous discussion on physical mobility, borders, and containment to questions of epistemological confinement and exclusion. Here we explore the temporal complexities of bringing forward interdependent and reciprocal modes of relating that find their origins in a past time and applying them in a contemporary context. We argue that many of the perceived difficulties in this project emerge from the conceptual boundaries that result from the perceived dichotomy between tradition and modernity. This dichotomy emphasizes the incompatibility between Indigenous peoples' ancestral cultural practices and the conditions that shape our lives today. While we recognize the need to identify and work against the structural barriers that contain and marginalize Indigenous modes of relating in contemporary contexts, we also find it particularly important that Indigenous peoples don't unintentionally or intentionally reproduce dichotomous ways of thinking about tradition and modernity in our own resurgence efforts. In our view, a relational way of conceptualizing the world has the potential to challenge and overcome these dualistic logics while providing unique possibilities to reframe Indigeneity within modern contexts.

Indigenous ways of relating with one another, animals, and the environment, and with past and future generations form the basis for projects of decolonization as they call into question the hegemony of Western thought.[48] They provide alternatives to the Western natural and social sciences and have an important emancipatory dimension as they liberate us from the need to engage Western sources, institutions, and concepts in constituting ourselves politically. They promote strategies that help us think about law and politics in ways that are autonomous from Western philosophical foundations. Perhaps even more importantly, Indigenous modes of relating can be profoundly empowering as they provide a framework for social and political mobilization that is grounded in a world view that sees humans as interconnected with all of Creation, past, present and future. At the same time, they evidence the continuity and generative capacity of Indigenous peoples' approaches to education, governance, kinship, spirituality, and law in the face of ongoing efforts aimed at their assimilation, restriction, or reconfiguration within the confines of Western thought.

Each of the authors reviewed in this book can be taken up in ways that elucidate the temporal significance of Indigenous modes of relating. Tully argues that the vicious impacts of modern human interactions with the earth are in part an effect of losing sight of ways of interacting with the environment that have sustained life on earth for thousands of years. But they are also the result of losing sight of our relationship with the future, a consequence of focusing strictly on the present and relying on modern science, innovation, and economics in understanding the role of the living earth and our responsibilities towards it. For Tully, the project of re-conceptualizing our existence both in relationship to the past and the future can help bring forth more conciliatory modes of relating with the living earth and with other humans.

Asch demonstrates how colonial mythologies that represent treaties as a thing of the past, or as historical events that are disconnected from the present, blind contemporary generations of settlers to the ongoing significance and applicability of treaties. Such representations disregard the ongoing relevance of treaties, eclipsing their potential for inspiring alternative frameworks for coexistence. In his view, the original spirit and intent of treaties can help address many contemporary issues in the

Indigenous–settler relationship, particularly those that stem from the privileging of Western narratives of settlement and development. For instance, Indigenous visions of relationality that were expressed in treaties can help challenge and deconstruct colonial mythologies, including Indigenous acquiescence and land cessation through treaty-making. By highlighting the disjuncture between the actual terms of treaty relationships that were agreed upon and records of policy implementation over time, Asch argues that settlers can be held more accountable and take actions to legitimatize their presence and pave a better future.

Borrows explains that our contemporary preoccupation with the need for present, immediate legal and political solutions can lead us to overlook the transformative potential of long-term, incremental, and cyclical change. He demonstrates how our focus on the present obscures the natural currents of our lives and relationships, which can offer possible alternatives to regeneration, protection, healing, and coexistence. Looking to the natural processes of the living earth helps us remember that human beings are part of these cycles and that we all bear responsibilities within them. From this vantage point, we can see the limitations of linear modes of thinking and imagine alternative possibilities for human interactions. Furthermore, Borrows emphasizes the interconnection of the past and present, as his work is dedicated to bringing forward past stories, laws, practices, and ways of relating in order to examine their relevance to contemporary challenges.

Each of these authors demonstrates how neglect of the present's relationship with the past and future can drastically inhibit our ability to understand the breadth and depth of our responsibilities to one another and to imagine alternative ways of enacting them. Collectively, they elucidate the epistemological possibilities that colonial mentalities foreclose through the conceptual separation of humans and nature, but also the separation of past, present, and future. Their work demonstrates the transformative potential that the revitalization of a relational philosophy holds for both Indigenous peoples and settlers, but also brings to mind several temporal challenges and complexities that are important to account for in the process.

One of the primary challenges surrounding the resurgence of Indigenous philosophies of relationality emerges from the ever-evolving problematic of how to revitalize Indigenous ways of knowing and being without having them further marginalized, appropriated, or distorted by the Western world. This dilemma follows from legacies of colonial oppression that positioned Indigenous world views and life ways as inferior to or in opposition to the modern and purportedly more civilized ways of Western culture. Colonialism, both past and present, has relied upon the distinction between traditional and modern that underlies notions of progress, development, and civilization to provide the ideological justification for the extension of settler laws and regulations on Indigenous peoples and their lands. In practice, this distinction has manifested through the forceful imposition of Western values and ways of life alongside the simultaneously banning, stigmatizing, or assimilating of Indigenous ones. In light of these legacies, settler movements towards development, technological advancement, progress, and innovation have a strong association with the discontinuity or loss of Indigenous traditions. While Indigenous ways of knowing and being are not static and have had to change and adapt to multiple contexts and variables throughout history, these changes have seldom been of our choosing but are a result of colonial interference. As a consequence, the move to preserve, renew, or revitalize Indigenous ways of life are often conceptualized as necessitating Indigenous peoples' conscious refusal of the terms of modernity to prevent further interference from the West. Indeed, imperatives of decolonization and resurgence are centrally driven by the need not just to revitalize Indigenous cultural practices, but to do so in ways that are not reliant upon Western resources, whether ideological or material. However, as Indigenous peoples look to a pre-contact past to draw out a more robust vision of our cultural traditions as they existed before they were affected by the violence of colonialism, we must ensure that we are not creating temporal boundaries or reproducing dichotomous ways of thinking about the past and present within our own communities. As struggles over the meaning of precolonial cultural practices are deeply marked by relations of power, such dichotomous ways of thinking can have the unintended effect of reinforcing fundamentalist, exclusionary, or oppressive practices within our own communities.[49]

In our view, a relational way of being has the potential to challenge and move beyond dichotomous treatments of past/present or tradition/modernity. By adopting a relational world view, we are better positioned to see the continuity between past, present, and future while also recognizing tradition as dynamic, contingent, and context dependent. By conceptualizing Indigenous cultural knowledge and practices as constantly evolving and adapting to new contexts, a relational approach can direct our attention to the values and precepts underlying Indigenous modes of relating rather than getting caught up with defining and replicating the specific configuration of past practices. It can serve the important purpose of helping to conceptualize Indigenous customs and knowledges as an interaction of lessons and teachings with different contexts. Indeed, relational understandings of knowledge are a key feature of Indigenous intellectual traditions and can perhaps most clearly be seen in oral traditions of knowledge generation and transmission. As Saulteaux oral historian Alexander Wolfe recalls, "[The oral tradition] was used by the grandfathers to preserve a way of life through remembering the stories which make up not only the history of a family but the history of a nation. These stories are very important because they contain a philosophy of life that is adaptable to any time and any place."[50] By looking to stories or other lessons as relation of knowledge-sharing rather than static ideology or dogma, we can draw out and reinterpret the philosophies underlying them while also recognizing that interpretations of knowledge differ between and within communities. This can help us broaden the space for dialogue surrounding past values and practices, which in turn can help us imagine a broader spectrum of ways to apply them in the present and future.

For instance, previous sections of this chapter have highlighted some of the challenges that contemporary restrictions on mobility can impose on our relationships with one another and with our ability to share and transmit cultural knowledge. Indigenous peoples' capacity to live a traditional lifestyle has been inhibited in many ways by our physical disconnection from one another, from the land, and from knowledge holders in our communities. Our capacity to revitalize laws, governance practices, and educational pedagogies that are informed by our relationship with the natural world are even further jeopardized by our restricted ability to physically live in relationship with geographies and places that haven't been irreversibly affected by settlement, development, or extraction.

In light of these conditions, Indigenous people are challenged to find alternative ways to apply and share cultural knowledge within the contemporary context.[51] As we continue to strategize methods to overcome the barriers imposed through colonialism, we have had to imagine new opportunities to increase our access to and engagement with cultural knowledge and histories and to make these accessible and relevant to future generations. One strategy for doing so has been through the use of digital technologies. While remaining mindful of their limitations, Indigenous people are increasingly using new technologies to create localized digital resources and educational tools, to archive and disseminate traditional knowledge, and to mobilize collectively at a distance from one another. The possibilities for digital technology to aid in cultural renewal and education are now becoming widely recognized, specifically in remote areas and in the realm of language revitalization technologies.[52] These initiatives speak to the high level of creativity that Indigenous peoples are exercising to subvert the homogenizing forces of Western culture and instead utilize modern tools and technologies to our advantage.[53]

These uses of new technologies do not mean that we should overlook their limitations and costs but engage with them cautiously and critically. While the digital era has certainly ushered in new forms of relationship, we must also take care to weigh the quality of these relationships against their ease and accessibility. Although digital technologies have facilitated the creation of networks and streams of communication across extended geographies, these online relationships often lack a connection to shared contexts and social environments that are characteristic of our traditional modes of relating. They may also have the effect of increased individuation from the environments we live in and those we share them with. By allowing ourselves to become immersed in these virtual or constructed realities, we run the risk of becoming more disconnected from and destructive towards our physical environments. It is much more difficult to learn anything from the natural world or understand the impacts of neglect or violence towards the natural world when we insulate ourselves from it. Furthermore, in the digital realm we gain less experience cultivating human relationships in shared geographies, as we are not required to learn how to inhabit relationships in a healthy way or negotiate sustainable practices of coexistence across difference.

While there are many opportunities that digital forms of connectivity have provided Indigenous peoples to network across borders and difference, we must be careful not to lose sight of the ways in which these technologies are transforming our approach to living in-relation, nor should we forget the unique benefits of being situated physically in relationships. This might mean engaging in more concentrated efforts to build and sustain connections in shared contexts and physical environments, while ensuring that our use of modern technologies is approached critically and informed by our own philosophies of relationality. For instance, we can understand digital technologies as providing complementary tools to help grow our traditional knowledge and practices and adapt them to contemporary contexts, without supplanting or replacing them entirely. Rather, we can infuse our cultural values and imperatives into contemporary contexts if and when it is appropriate to do so. These are the sorts of possibilities that are foreclosed by a static understanding of tradition and culture, or a dichotomous vision of the past and present.

Conceptually, a relational orientation can help Indigenous people move beyond dichotomous thinking about the past/present/future in a number of ways. Cultural practices can be understood as the ways in which knowledge manifests itself in relation to particular contexts and can thus take many different shapes across space and time. Rather than seeing traditional practices as existing in opposition to or as incommensurable with modern conditions, we may be able to gain greater appreciation of possible ways to usher in new forms of relationship. Looking at the potential for traditional knowledge to interact with present contexts, rather than aiming to bring forward static or fixed versions of past practices, can help to avoid the forms of essentialism and fundamentalism that can emerge in efforts to safeguard Indigenous cultural practice against further incursion from the West. By understanding traditional knowledge and practice as existing in relation to past and present contexts and conditions, we are better positioned to conceptualize and implement strategies of resurgence that draw upon traditional knowledge while taking into account the socio-economic and demographic realities of our communities today so that they are accessible from grassroots, to institutional, to academic levels.

Such ways of seeing the world transcend bounded notions of time, demonstrating that the past and present are not mutually exclusive periods that we need to decide in between to understand our place in the world. Grounding our contemporary identities as Indigenous people upon a relational orientation can challenge the tendency to periodize Indigeneity in a historic past as a measure of authenticity. Conversely, it can confront the notion that identification with the present equates to a loss of authenticity. A relational orientation can help Indigenous peoples move beyond this dichotomy by helping imagine new possibilities for traditional and modern practices to exist in tandem.

In our view, it is most useful to understand Indigenous modes of relating as presenting a *challenge* to modernity that calls into question its hegemonic claims and highlights the destructive and oppressive nature of its inherent logic by way of contrast, while also creating specific opportunities to bring forward the values and precepts underlying our traditional laws and values within contemporary contexts. Rather than getting discouraged by the seeming futility of enacting past practices in the present, we might instead understand these practices as the embodiment of values and beliefs that were given life in the past in relation to particular contexts, that have lived on in spite of efforts explicitly aimed at their erasure or assimilation, and that can continue to be given life anew.

Conclusion

Alongside the transformative possibilities of a renewed conception of relationship, we contend it is important to remain mindful of the ways in which the discourse of relationship can be invoked to mask or legitimate oppressive practices. This distinction can draw our attention to the ways in which we might violate our responsibilities within relationships through neglect or oversight, or through explicitly destructive and abusive forms of interaction. With an eye for this dual potential, we can become more cognizant of the various ways in which we all stand to reproduce or challenge forms of violence in our day-to-day actions. For instance, many people recognize that they inhabit treaty relationships but continue to tacitly or explicitly contribute to the violation of the commitments that they entail. Or they claim a deep connection to particular geographies with little awareness of the ways in which their actions might contribute to harming those same spaces. In other words, acknowledging a relationship between self and other doesn't necessarily translate to the full range of actions that are required to inhabit those relationships properly. Furthermore, the very process of drawing out our responsibilities within relationships is itself subjective and highly politicized, with the potential to implicate others in ways that they find disempowering. While being committed to the regeneration of a relational way of being is relatively straightforward at a theoretical level, enacting this commitment in our day-to-day lives gives rise to many complex questions and contradictions. Further dialogue and work is needed to continue to complicate and advance the discourse of relationality as it continues to grow, both in regard to the considerations raised in this chapter and beyond.

NOTES

1 Borrows looks to Anishinaabe teachings, stories, and principles to draw out the sources and significance of Indigenous modes of relating and to

propose ways that Indigenous peoples can work towards implementing them in legal and political realms. Tully and Asch demonstrate how settlers can learn about more conciliatory modes of co-existence from Indigenous understandings of relationship with creation and with one another.

2 Leroy LittleBear, "Jagged Worldviews Colliding," in *Reclaiming Indigenous Voice and Vision*, ed. Marie Battiste, 77–86 (Vancouver: University of British Columbia Press, 2000); Vine Deloria Jr, *God Is Red: A Native View of Religion* (Golden, CO: Fulcrum, 1994); Gregory Cajete, *Native Science: Natural Laws of Interdependence* (Santa Fe, NM: Clear Light Publishers, 2000); Willie Ermine, "Aboriginal Epistemology," in *First Nations Education in Canada: The Circle Unfolds*, ed. Marie Battiste and Jean Barman, 101–11 (Vancouver: UBC Press, 1995).

3 Margaret Kovach, *Indigenous Methodologies: Characteristics, Conversations and Contexts* (Toronto: University of Toronto Press, 2009); Marie Battiste and James Youngblood Henderson, *Protecting Indigenous Knowledge and Heritage: A Global Challenge* (Saskatoon: Purich, 2000); Shawn Wilson, *Research Is Ceremony: Indigenous Research Methods* (Halifax: Fernwood Publishing, 2009); Linda Tuhiwai Smith, *Decolonizing Methodologies: Research and Indigenous Peoples*, 2nd ed. (London: Zed Books, 2012); Kathleen Absolon, *Kaandossiwin: How We Come to Know* (Halifax: Fernwood Publishing, 2011); Betty Bastien, *Blackfoot Ways of Knowing* (Calgary: University of Calgary Press, 2004).

4 Leanne Simpson, *Dancing on Our Turtle's Back: Stories of Nishnaabeg Re-Creation, Resurgence, and a New Emergence* (Winnipeg: Arbeiter Ring, 2011); Sarah Hunt and Cindy Holmes, "Everyday Decolonization: Living a Decolonizing Queer Politics," *Journal of Lesbian Studies* 19, no. 2 (2015): 154; Peta Bowden, *Caring: Gender-Sensitive Ethics* (London: Routledge, 2007); Jennifer Nedelsky, *Law's Relations: A Relational Theory of Self, Autonomy, and Law* (Oxford: Oxford University Press, 1990); Helen O'Grady, *Women's Relationship with Herself: Gender, Foucault and Therapy* (New York: Routledge, 2005); Rauna Kuokkanen, "The Politics of Form and Alternative Autonomies: Indigenous Women, Subsistence Economies and the Gift Paradigm," *Globalization Working Papers* 7, no. 2 (2007): 1–31; Genevieve Vaughan, *Women and the Gift Economy: A Radically Different Worldview Is Possible* (Toronto: Inanna Publications, 2007).

5 Kiera Ladner, "Governing within an Ecological Context: Creating an Alternative Understanding of Siiksikaawa Governance," *Studies in Political Economy* 70 (2003): 125; Russel Lawrence Barsh, "The Nature and Spirit of Native American Political Systems," *American Indian Quarterly* 10, no. 1 (1986): 181; Taiaiake Alfred, *Peace, Power, Righteousness: An Indigenous*

Manifesto (Oxford: Oxford University Press, 2009); John Borrows, *Recovering Canada: The Resurgence of Indigenous Law* (Toronto: University of Toronto Press, 2002); Simpson, *Dancing on Our Turtle's Back*; Deloria Jr, *God Is Red*; Robert Williams, *Linking Arms Together* (New York: Oxford University Press, 1997); Isabel Altamirano-Jiménez, *Indigenous Encounters with Neoliberalism: Place, Women and the Environment in Canada and Mexico* (Vancouver: UBC Press, 2013); Audra Simpson, *Mohawk Interruptus: Political Life across the Borders of Settler States* (Durham, NC: Duke University Press, 2014).

6 Elizabeth Povinelli, *The Cunning of Recognition: Indigenous Alterities and the Making of Australian Multiculturalism* (Durham, NC: Duke University Press, 2002); Taiaiake Alfred, *Wasáse: Indigenous Pathways of Action and Freedom* (Toronto: University of Toronto Press, 2005); Stephanie Irlbacher-Fox, *Finding Dahshaa: Self-Government, Social Suffering and Aboriginal Policy in Canada* (Vancouver: UBC Press, 2009); Glen Coulthard, *Red Skin, White Masks: Rejecting the Colonial Politics of Recognition* (Minneapolis: University of Minnesota Press, 2014); Noelani Goodyear-Ka'ōpua, Ikaika Hussey, and Erin Kahunawaika'ala Wright, eds, *A Nation Rising: Hawaiian Movements for Life, Land and Sovereignty* (Durham, NC: Duke University Press, 2014); Jeff Corntassel, "Re-envisioning Resurgence: Indigenous Pathways to Decolonization and Sustainable Self-Determination," *Decolonization: Indigeneity, Education, and Society* 1, no. 1 (2012): 86.

7 Robert Innes, *Elder Brother and the Law of the People: Contemporary Kinship and Cowessess First Nation* (Winnipeg: University of Manitoba Press, 2013); Margaret Kovach, "Treaties, Truths, and Transgressive Pedagogies: Re-Imagining Indigenous Presence in the Classroom," *Socialist Studies* 9, no. 1 (2013): 109; Heidi Stark, "Respect, Responsibility, and Renewal: The Foundations of Anishinaabe Treaty-Making with the United States and Canada," *American Indian Culture and Research Journal*, 34, no. 2 (2010): 145; Simpson, *Dancing on Our Turtle's Back*.

8 For discussions of everyday resurgence, see Jeff Corntassel, "Re-envisioning Resurgence: Indigenous Pathways to Decolonization and Sustainable Self-determination," *Decolonization: Indigeneity, Education and Society* 1, no. 1 (2012): 86. For a discussion of everyday decolonization, see Hunt and Holmes, "Everyday Decolonization."

9 For instance, in some cases practices of reconciliation and resurgence cannot begin to occur for Indigenous peoples prior to necessary healing from the violence of colonialism. In many contexts, the day-to-day crises and socio-economic issues that Indigenous communities are grappling with limits their capacity to engage in overarching changes to governance structures and political processes.

10 Leanne Betasamosake Simpson, "Land as Pedagogy: Nishnaabeg Intelligence and Rebellious Transformation," *Decolonization: Indigeneity, Education, and Society* 3, no. 3 (2014): 7.

11 Heidi Kiiwetinepinesiik Stark, "Changing the Treaty Question: Remedying the Right(s) Relationship," in *The Right Relationship: Reimagining the Implementation of Historical Treaties*, ed. John Borrows and Michael Coyle, 246–76 (Toronto: University of Toronto Press, 2017).

12 Treaties are to be given large, liberal, and generous interpretations in favour of Indigenous peoples, ambiguities in treaties are to be resolved in favour of Indigenous peoples, treaties are to be interpreted in a flexible manner, and extrinsic evidence should be used to determine the meaning and intent of treaties. The courts in the United States have even applied and upheld the "reserved rights" doctrine, which notes that any Indigenous nations' rights, not expressly ceded or extinguished, remain intact. For discussion of U.S. canons of treaty interpretation, see David E. Wilkins and K. Tsianina Lomawaima, *Uneven Ground: American Indian Sovereignty and Federal Law* (Norman: University of Oklahoma Press, 2001); Charles F. Wilkinson and John M. Volkman, "Judicial Review of Indian Treaty Abrogation: 'As Long as Water Flows, or Grass Grows upon the Earth' – How Long Is That?," *California Law Review* 63, no. 3 (1975): 601; Felix S. Cohen, *Cohen's Handbook of Federal Indian Law* (Newark, NJ: LexisNexis, 2005).

13 Michael Asch, *On Being Here to Stay: Treaties and Aboriginal Rights in Canada* (Toronto: University of Toronto Press, 2014).

14 John Borrows, *Canada's Indigenous Constitution* (Toronto: University of Toronto Press, 2010); Borrows, *Recovering Canada*.

15 James Tully, *Strange Multiplicity: Constitutionalism in an Age of Diversity* (Cambridge: Cambridge University Press, 1995); Tully, *Public Philosophy in a New Key* (Cambridge: Cambridge University Press, 2008).

16 See, for example, "The Great Quake and the Great Drowning," *Hakai Magazine*, 14 September 2015, https://www.hakaimagazine.com/features/great-quake-and-great-drowning/.

17 Noelani Goodyear-Ka'ōpua, *The Seeds We Planted: Portraits of a Native Hawaiian Charter School*, First Peoples: New Directions in Indigenous Studies (Minneapolis: University of Minnesota Press, 2013), 26.

18 Ibid.

19 Stephanie N. Teves, Andrea Smith, and Michelle H. Raheja, eds, *Native Studies Keywords* (Tucson: University of Arizona Press, 2015); Ned Blackhawk, *Violence over the Land: Indians and Empires in the Early American West* (Cambridge, MA: Harvard University Press, 2006); Smith, *Decolonizing Methodologies*.

20 Mishuana Goeman, "Land as Life: Unsettling the Logics of Containment," in Teves, Smith, and Raheja, *Native Studies Keywords*, 72.

21 Ibid.

22 Mishuana Goeman notes, "Land is foundation to people's cultural practices and if we define *culture* as meaning making rather than as differentiation and isolation in a multicultural neoliberal model, then by thinking through *land* as a meaning-making process rather than a claimed object the aspirations of Native people are apparent and clear." Ibid., 73.

23 Wolfe recognizes that "on the one hand, settler society required the practical elimination of the native in order to establish itself on their territory. On the symbolic level, however, settler society subsequently sought to recuperate indigeneity in order to express its difference – and, accordingly, its independence – from the mother country." Patrick Wolfe, "Settler Colonialism and the Elimination of the Native," *Journal of Genocide Research* 8, no. 4 (2006): 389.

24 See Manu Vimalassery, Juliana Hu Pegues, and Alyosha Goldstein, "Introduction: On Colonial Unknowing," *Theory and Event* 19, no. 4 (2016): 1.

25 Teves, Smith, and Raheja, *Native Studies Keywords*, 22.

26 As Kim Anderson writes that in the women's circle, emphasis was placed on the types of work that were imperative for the survival of the community, including activities that were essential to building and maintaining community: "Personal and family relationships were paramount, and the women held important responsibilities in these areas." She explains further that, given the interdependence of land-based communities, relationship building was "vital to the well-being of the collective, and as the keepers of relationships, women held important roles." Kim Anderson, *Life Stages and Native Women: Memory, Teachings, and Story Medicine* (Winnipeg: University of Manitoba Press, 2011), 111–12.

27 Emma LaRocque, "The Colonization of a Native Woman Scholar," in *Women of the First Nations: Power, Wisdom and Strength*, ed. Christine Miller and Patricia Churchryk, 11–18 (Winnipeg: University of Manitoba Press, 1996); Bonita Lawrence, "Gender, Race, and the Regulation of Native Identity in Canada and the United States: An Overview," *Hypatia: A Journal of Feminist Philosophy* 18, no. 2 (2003): 3; Mary-Ellen Turpel, "Patriarchy and Paternalism: The Legacy of the Canadian State for First Nations Women," *Canadian Journal of Women and the Law* 6, no. 1 (1993): 174; Anne McClintock, *Imperial Leather: Race, Gender, and Sexuality in the Colonial Contest* (New York: Routledge, 1995).

28 Sherry Ortner, "Is Female to Male as Nature Is to Culture?" in *Woman, Culture, and Society*, ed. Michelle Zimbalist Rosaldo and Louise Lamphere,

68–87 (Stanford: Stanford University Press, 1974); Marilyn Friedman, *Autonomy, Gender, Politics* (Oxford: Oxford University Press, 2003), 83.

29 Emma Larocque, "Re-examining Culturally Appropriate Models in Criminal Justice Applications," in *Aboriginal and Treaty Rights in Canada*, ed. Michael Asch, 173–208 (Vancouver: UBC Press, 2002).

30 Andrew Jolivette argues that GLBTQ2 people have been overlooked in most research studies of violence within Indigenous communities and communities of colour. Andrew Jolivette, *Indian Blood: HIV and Colonial Trauma in San Francisco's Two-Spirit Community* (Seattle: University of Washington Press, 2016), 92.

31 Val Napoleon, "Aboriginal Self-Determination: Individual Self and Collective Selves," *Atlantis* 29, no. 2 (2005): 31; Sharon Venne, "The Meaning of Sovereignty," *Indigenous Woman* 2, no. 6 (1999): 27.

32 Rauna Kuokkanen, "The Politics of Form and Alternative Autonomies: Indigenous Women, Subsistence Economies and the Gift Paradigm," *Globalization Working Papers* 7, no. 2 (2007): 1.

33 Kim Anderson, *A Recognition of Being: Reconstructing Native Womanhood*, 2nd ed. (Toronto: Women's Press, 2016); Simpson, *Dancing on Our Turtle's Back.*

34 Dory Nason, "We Hold Our Hands Up: On Indigenous Women's Love and Resistance," *Decolonization, Indigeneity, Education & Society*. Blog (2013), https://decolonization.wordpress.com/2013/02/12/we-hold-our-hands-up-on-indigenous-womens-love-and-resistance/; Rachel Flowers, "Refusal to Forgive: Indigenous Women's Love and Rage," *Decolonization, Indigeneity, Education & Society* 4, no. 2 (2015): 32.

35 As Sarah Hunt and Cindy Holmes have argued, the day-to-day forms of resurgence that take place within the relationships that we inhabit can provide some of the most important sources of strength and solidarity as we work towards decolonization and resistance to gender-based violence. Relationships are also emancipatory, as they provide alternatives to engagements with the settler state and its institutions. By looking to their own partnerships, families, and friendships, Hunt and Holmes elucidate the many strategies for addressing violence against women that emerge from practices of allyship, solidarity-building, advocacy, and political organization within their interpersonal relationships. Their work provides important insight into the everyday ways in which relationships can be transformative for Indigenous women. Hunt and Holmes, "Everyday Decolonization."

36 See Emily Snyder, Val Napoleon, and John Borrows, "Gender and Violence: Drawing on Indigenous Legal Resources," *UBC Law Review* 48, no. 2 (2015): 593; John Borrows, "Aboriginal and Treaty Rights and Violence against Women," *Osgoode Hall Law Journal* 50, no. 3 (2013): 699.

37 Diaz, 91.
38 Hokulani K. Aikau, Maile Arvin, Mishuana Goeman, and Scott Morgensen, "Indigenous Feminisms Roundtable," *Frontiers* 36, no. 3 (2015): 94.
39 Jean M. O'Brien, *Firsting and Lasting: Writing Indians out of Existence in New England*, Indigenous Americas (Minneapolis: University of Minnesota Press, 2010). For discussion of American innocence, see Boyd Cothran, *Remembering the Modoc War: Redemptive Violence and the Making of American Innocence* (Chapel Hill: University of North Carolina Press, 2014).
40 Aikau et al., "Indigenous Feminisms Roundtable." Also see Brendan Hokowhitu, "Monster: Post-Indigenous Studies," in *Critical Indigenous Studies: Engagements in First World Locations,* ed. Aileen Moreton-Robinson, 83–101 (Tucson: University of Arizona Press, 2016).
41 Aikau et al., "Indigenous Feminisms Roundtable."
42 Simpson, "Land as Pedagogy," 7.
43 Aikau et al., "Indigenous Feminisms Roundtable."
44 Mishuana Goeman, *Mark My Words: Native Women Mapping Our Nations* (Minneapolis: University of Minnesota Press, 2013), 28–9.
45 Robert Alexander Innes, *Elder Brother and the Law of the People: Contemporary Kinship and Cowessess First Nation* (Winnipeg: University of Manitoba Press, 2013).
46 Graham Harvey and Charles D. Thompson, eds., *Indigenous Diasporas and Dislocations* (2005), cited in Teves, Smith, and Raheja, *Native Studies Keywords*, 66.
47 Stark, "Changing the Treaty Question."
48 See Rolando Vázquez, "Towards a Decolonial Critique of Modernity: Buen Vivir, Relationality and the Task of Listening," in *Capital, Poverty, Development, Denktraditionen im Dialog,* ed. Raúl Fornet-Betancourt, 33:241–52 (Aachen: Wissenschaftsverlag Mainz, 2012).
49 See Joyce Green, "Exploring Identity and Citizenship: Aboriginal Women, Bill C-31 and the Sawridge Case" (PhD diss. University of Alberta, 1997); see also J. Kēhaulani Kauanui, "Native Hawaiian Decolonization and the Politics of Gender," *American Quarterly* 60, no. 2 (2008): 281.
50 Alexander Wolfe, *Earth Elder Stories: The Pinayzitt Path* (Saskatoon: Fifth House, 1988).
51 As Neil McLeod writes, "The central challenge for nehiyawak in the climate of modernity is to create, in the wake of colonialism, modern institutions which draw upon traditional beliefs." Neil McLeod, "Nehiyawiwin and Modernity," in *Plain Speaking: Essays on Aboriginal People and the Prairie,* ed. Patrick Douaud and Bruce Dawson (Regina: Canadian Plains Research Centre, 2002), 43.

52 Candace Galla, "Multimedia Technology and Indigenous Language
Revitalization: From Traditional to Contemporary Domains," in *Indigenous
Language Revitalization: Encouragement, Guidance & Lessons Learned*, ed.
Jon Reyhner and Louise Lockard, 167–83 (Flagstaff: Northern Arizona
University, 2009); Brian Beaton and Penny Carpenter, "Digital Technology
Innovations in Education in Remote First Nations," *Education: Exploring
Our Connective Educational Landscape* 22, no. 1 (2016): 42–60; Mark
Warschauer, "Technology and Indigenous Language Revitalization:
Analyzing the Experience of Hawai'i," *Canadian Modern Language Review*
55, no. 1 (1998): 140; Timothy Pasch, "Towards the Enhancement of
Arctic Digital Industries: 'Translating' Cultural Content to New Media
Platforms," *Jostrans: The Journal of Specialized Translations* 24 (2015): 187.
53 While the digital era has facilitated our interconnectedness in many ways,
we have also had to remain mindful of the limits of these new forms of
relationships while continuing to engage in efforts to build and sustain
connections in shared contexts and physical social environments.

6 Reconciliation and Resurgence: Reflections on the TRC Final Report

PAULETTE REGAN

A Personal Reflection

I'm thankful for this opportunity to share my reflections on how the Truth and Reconciliation Commission of Canada's (TRC) final report and its vision of reconciliation relate to the resurgence of Indigenous life-ways on the land. I begin by acknowledging that as a non-Indigenous woman living in Coast Salish territory who worked for the commission, I have been fortunate and so deeply honoured to bear witness – to be gifted with – the testimonies and life stories of residential school survivors, their families, and communities. With respectful gratitude, I acknowledge that without their courage, resilience, and vision, there would have been no TRC.

I've been both humbled and inspired by survivors. They have taught me so much about the power of truth-sharing in their quest for human dignity, justice, and freedom. I learned not only of the terrible abuses they suffered as children, but about how they, along with their families and communities, are actively reclaiming Indigenous histories, revitalizing their own cultures, languages, ceremonies, and traditions, and regenerating traditional governance systems and laws – those land-based ways of life that the residential school system sought to destroy. Several years ago, I explained,

> *My writing represents one way of honouring, not just in words, but through my actions, those IRS [Indian residential school] survivors who offered me the gift of their testimonies. Somehow, these testimonies cut to the heart of the matter. The people and their stories teach us ... I began the difficult process of learning how to listen differently to these stories – to engage in the act of bearing witness as an ethical undertaking ... I now realize that their gift is a life-teaching that I will always carry with me and learn from in new, unsettling ways ... This is my*

reciprocal gift to Indian residential school survivors – offered with humility, in the
spirit of acknowledging, honouring, and remembering their teachings.[1]

This earlier reflection stands equally true today. I am still learning to listen
differently. I still contemplate the many teachings this gift holds for me on my
own life journey. I humbly continue to offer my reciprocal gift. I will do so
always.

Setting the Context: The TRC's Vision of Reconciliation

In the introductory chapters of this volume, Michael Asch, John Borrows, and Jim Tully invite us to put aside binary thinking about reconciliation and resurgence to consider how these seemingly oppositional discourses might intersect in fruitful ways. Broadly speaking, four connective and overlapping themes run through their chapters. First, authentic reconciliation between Indigenous and settler peoples is possible only if we also reconcile our relationship with the land. Second, Indigenous peoples' world views, values, knowledge systems, and laws are integral to reconciliation and resurgence, and settler peoples must undertake their own decolonizing work. Third, treaty relationships are the historical foundation for sharing the land, and both treaty partners have responsibility for our shared future. Fourth, education and pedagogy have a critical role to play in learning about the legacies of our shared settler colonial history in ways that foster constructive practices of reconciliation and resurgence. These themes are consistent with the TRC's vision of reconciliation and the key findings and calls to action in the reconciliation volume of the final report.[2]

The TRC's vision of reconciliation evolved over the course of its mandate to be defined as "an ongoing process of establishing and maintaining respectful relationships."[3] From this perspective, reconciliation "is about coming to terms with the events of the past in a manner that overcomes conflict and establishes a respectful and healthy relationship among people moving forward."[4] In the commission's view, "A critical part of this process involves repairing damaged trust by making apologies, providing individual and collective reparations, and following through with concrete actions that demonstrate real societal change. Establishing respectful relationships also requires the revitalization of Indigenous law and legal traditions. It is important that all Canadians understand how traditional First Nations, Inuit, and Metis approaches to resolving conflict, repairing harm, and restoring relationships can inform the reconciliation process ... These traditions and practices are the foundation of Indigenous law; they contain wisdom and practical guidance for moving towards reconciliation across this land."[5]

For six years as the commission travelled across the country, we sought input on the multiple concepts and meanings of reconciliation. We heard from Indigenous elders and knowledge keepers whose understandings and teachings about reconciliation extend well beyond the need to remedy the significant harms of residential schools and the ongoing impacts of colonization. They told us that while there is no word for reconciliation in their languages, there are many concepts, stories, teachings, laws, ceremonies, protocols, and practices that their respective nations have used for millennia to resolve conflicts, repair harms, and restore good relations among diverse peoples and with the Earth.[6] The commission concludes, "Reconciliation between Aboriginal and non-Aboriginal Canadians, from an Aboriginal perspective, also requires reconciliation with the natural world. If human beings resolve problems between themselves but continue to destroy the natural world, then reconciliation remains incomplete. This is a perspective that we as Commissioners have repeatedly heard: that reconciliation will never occur unless we are also reconciled with the earth. Mi'kmaq and other Indigenous laws stress that humans must journey through life in conversation and negotiation with all creation. Reciprocity and mutual respect help sustain our survival."[7]

Unlike other truth and reconciliation commissions across the globe, Canada's TRC was not established unilaterally by the state. The commission was created as part of an out-of-court settlement agreement negotiated to resolve lawsuits filed against the federal government and churches by residential school survivors for the abuses they suffered in the schools.[8] Thus the TRC was accountable not only to government and the churches but to residential school survivors, the Assembly of First Nations, and Inuit organizations, who were also parties to the settlement agreement. TRCs are problematic when their work of repairing and reconciling the nation strengthens dominant culture national histories and identities while marginalizing others in the name of national unity.[9] Adopting this state-centric approach to reconciliation in the Canadian context would have put premature closure to the past in ways that simply replicate rather than transform settler colonial relations. The commission resists this imperative in two key ways: by making Indigenous knowledge, perspectives, and practices central to its work, and by expanding the scope of reconciliation beyond residential schools to encompass the whole settler colonial project.

Critics point out that the limitations of the TRC's mandate precluded achieving genuine reconciliation based on the recognition and exercise of Indigenous peoples' self-determination and political rights.[10] Indeed, to expect otherwise from a temporary quasi-judicial body is unrealistic and raises expectations that cannot be met.[11] While a TRC cannot advance political rights or compel legislative or policy reform, its recommendations can nevertheless be a powerful voice for societal change.[12] Canada's TRC established a comprehensive public record of human rights violations against Indigenous peoples that the state can no longer deny. In doing so, the commission made visible "how the erosion of self-determination and other political rights has been detrimental to the basic human rights of Indigenous peoples."[13]

Every truth and reconciliation commission must weigh the risks associated with how it decides to interpret and implement its mandate. Canada's TRC, tasked with exposing historical and ongoing injustices perpetrated against Indigenous peoples and guiding the country's first steps towards reconciliation, was no exception. Making recommendations rooted in Indigenous self-determination might trigger a societal backlash that would strengthen, not dismantle systemic racism and inequity.[14] One way to mitigate this risk is by educating the public as to why Indigenous self-determination must be the foundation of authentic reconciliation.[15]

I believe that the TRC commissioners chose to interpret their mandate boldly with a vision for a future where Indigenous peoples and communities flourish on their own terms and in their own ways. My observations on the TRC *Final Report*, calls to action, and the commission's truth-gathering and public education process are viewed through an insider's lens. There was no road map to follow on this journey, and I'm mindful of our many shortcomings and missteps along the way. My aim is to offer some insights into the philosophical and practical underpinnings of the commission's work that highlight the rich potential of working at the crossroads of reconciliation and resurgence.

TRC *Final Report*: Findings and Calls to Action

The TRC *Final Report* calls for the UN Declaration on the Rights of Indigenous Peoples to be the framework for reconciliation in Canada.[16] Implementing the commission's calls to action would decolonize and transform settler colonial systems, institutions, and relationships across all levels and sectors of Canadian society. Such actions are necessary to remedy the significant political and socio-economic inequities that oppress and impoverish Indigenous peoples in their own homelands. Reconciliation is therefore contingent on the land-based resurgence of Indigenous cultures, languages, knowledge systems, oral histories, laws, and governance structures. Indigenous resurgence does not hinge on reconciliation with the settler colonial state but is culturally grounded and community-driven. Implementing the TRC calls to action can support the goals and aspirations of resurgence and provide much-needed practical resources.

The commission's work lays the foundation for a decolonizing paradigm shift in how reconciliation is conceptualized, negotiated, and practised in formal and informal settings. As Tully points out, if the TRC's calls to action are to be implemented successfully, both formal and informal kinds of reconciliation are needed.[17] Although the commission necessarily focuses much of its attention on establishing formal structures of reconciliation, it also highlights the importance of both, observing,

> Reconciliation must become a way of life. It will take many years to repair the damaged trust and relationships in Aboriginal communities and between Aboriginal and non-Aboriginal peoples. Not only does reconciliation require apologies, reparations, the relearning of Canada's national history, and public commemoration, but it also needs real social, political, and economic change. Ongoing public education and dialogue are essential to reconciliation. Governments, churches, educational institutions, and Canadians from all walks of life are responsible for taking action on reconciliation in concrete ways, working collaboratively with Aboriginal peoples. Reconciliation begins with each and every one of us.[18]

The reconciliation volume of the final report was not intended to be the final word on the subject; rather, it serves as a catalyst for ongoing public education, dialogue, and action at national, regional, and local levels.

A common theme runs through the calls to action: Indigenous peoples' rights have been violated, and the state is accountable for remedying this in ways that flow from the fundamental principle of Indigenous self-determination. The commission calls on various levels of government, in partnership with Indigenous peoples, to change laws, policies, and programs to assist Indigenous communities in their efforts to reclaim, revitalize, and regenerate Indigenous ways of life.

Fifty-one of the ninety-four calls to action focus on reconciliation in the context of Indigenous–Crown relations; Indigenous law; apologies; religion and spirituality; education; public memory – dialogue, the arts, and commemoration; and the broader relationship between Indigenous and non-Indigenous citizens as treaty peoples. With regard to latter, the commission observes, "Indigenous peoples have kept the history and ongoing relevance of the Treaties alive in their own oral histories and legal traditions. Without their perspectives on the history of Treaty-making, Canadians know only one side of this country's history ... The history and interpretation of Treaties and the Aboriginal–Crown relationship as told by Indigenous peoples enrich and inform our understanding of why we are all Treaty people."[19]

To signify a new action-oriented commitment to reconciliation, the commission calls on "the Government of Canada, on behalf of all Canadians, to jointly develop with Aboriginal peoples, a Royal Proclamation of Reconciliation to be issued by the Crown."[20]

> The Royal Proclamation of 1763, in conjunction with the Treaty of Niagara of 1764, established the legal and political foundation of Canada and the principles of Treaty-making based on mutual recognition and respect. A royal proclamation is also an important symbol. Issued at the highest level, it sends a message to all citizens about the values and principles that define the country. There is a need for a new proclamation that reaffirms the long-standing, but often disregarded commitments between Canada and Aboriginal peoples. The proclamation would include an official disavowal of the Doctrine of Discovery and commitment to the full implementation of the United Nations Declaration [on the Rights of Indigenous Peoples].[21]

While a royal proclamation in and of itself cannot change a society, it signifies the centrality of nation-to-nation treaty relationships that must be honoured and upheld.

Borrows underscores the central role that treaties play in land-based reconciliation and resurgence. He points out that treaty relationships bind both parties to "the goal of sustainability using ecosystems in ways that preserve Indigenous land-based life. Treaties are also meant to secure healthy, sustainable living for non-Indigenous peoples who subsequently settle on Indigenous lands. Both parties can find environmental benefits flowing from treaty relationships."[22] This is consistent with the commission's findings:

Sustainable reconciliation on the land involves realizing the economic potential of Indigenous communities in a fair, just, and equitable manner that respects their right to self-determination. Economic reconciliation involves working in partnership with Indigenous peoples to ensure that the lands and resources within their territories are developed in culturally respectful ways that fully recognize Treaty and Aboriginal rights and title. Establishing constructive, mutually beneficial relationships and partnerships with Indigenous communities will contribute to their economic growth, improve community health and well-being, and ensure environmental sustainability, which will ultimately benefit Indigenous peoples and all Canadians.[23]

Borrows calls for a resurgence of Indigenous law to inform the process of reconciling our relationship with each other and land, which the TRC also identified as essential to reconciliation. The Commission concludes,

Indigenous peoples' knowledge systems are full of profound teachings, including legal teachings. If used in contemporary circumstances, they can help guide this country into better relationships among all beings inhabiting Turtle Island (North America) ... Ensuring that Indigenous peoples can access and apply their own laws both within their communities and to resolve conflicts and negotiate Treaties and other agreements with the Crown is essential to reconciliation. Without Indigenous law and protocol establishing the common ground on which the parties meet, reconciliation will always be incomplete. At the same time, we recognize that Indigenous forms of reconciliation will not be available to the Canadian state until First Nations, Inuit and Metis peoples decide to offer them, leaving significant power in the hands of Indigenous peoples ... This is as it should be. Indigenous nations are self-determining communities. They have the ability to decide whether they will receive or act on Canada's overtures towards reconciliation.[24]

The TRC calls on the "federal government, in collaboration with Aboriginal organizations to fund the establishment of Indigenous law institutes for the development, use, and understanding of Indigenous laws and access to justice in accordance with the unique cultures of Aboriginal peoples in Canada."[25]

For Asch, historical treaties "represent a possible path to reconciliation [for settler peoples], for, if we are here by agreement, then our settlement is legitimate."[26] He notes that Crown officials were duty-bound to respect the rule of law and uphold the honour of the Crown in the promises they made to Indigenous peoples during Confederation treaty negotiations. Because these treaty promises were subsequently broken, "it is then up to us, the heirs of the men who signed in honour, to return us to that path by addressing the harms inflicted when we disavowed the obligations passed down to us, and honouring the commitments made on behalf of our forebears."[27] Settler peoples must recover and regenerate those values, principles, and practices from our own past in order to achieve just relationships with Indigenous peoples. Asch points out that the majority of non-Indigenous Canadians have come to believe that the treaties are irrelevant today, a "conclusion that ... is reinforced in many ways [by] how we tell the story of Canadian history ... Relations with Indigenous peoples, including treaty-making play a minor role in this account."[28] His observation reinforces the urgent need for continuing public education on this front.

During the TRC's work, it became clear that not only did a significant number of Canadians know nothing about the residential school system, they knew very little about the history of Indigenous peoples' contributions to this country or the importance of treaties.[29] Without this knowledge, our children and youth will be ill-equipped to live together differently in the future.

In the Commission's view, all students – Aboriginal and non-Aboriginal – need to learn that this country's history did not begin with the arrival of Jacques Cartier on the banks of the St Lawrence River. They need to learn about the Indigenous nations the Europeans met, about their rich linguistic and cultural heritage, about what they felt and thought as they dealt with early explorers ... or with the representatives of the Hudson's Bay Company. Canadians need to learn why Indigenous nations negotiated the Treaties and to understand that they negotiated with integrity and in good faith. They need to learn about why Aboriginal leaders and Elders still fight so hard to defend these Treaties, what these agreements represent to them, and why they have been ignored by European settlers or governments. They need to learn about what it means to have inherent rights, what those are for Aboriginal peoples, and what the settler government's political and legal obligations are in those areas where Treaties were never negotiated. They need to learn why so many of these issues are ongoing.[30]

Eleven of the ninety-four calls to action concern education, focusing on equitable education funding for Indigenous students; mandatory

K–12 curriculum on residential schools, treaties, and Indigenous peoples' historical and contemporary contributions to Canada; post-secondary funding to educate teachers on how to integrate Indigenous knowledge and teaching methods into classrooms; and funding to Aboriginal schools to utilize Indigenous knowledge and teaching methods in classrooms. There should be courses in post-secondary professional programs such as law, medicine and nursing, social work, education, and journalism, on the history and legacy of residential schools, the UN Declaration on the Rights of Indigenous Peoples, and treaties and Aboriginal rights. As future professionals, students should receive skills-based training in intercultural competency, conflict resolution, human rights, and anti-racism.[31]

Public Education: Pedagogy and Practices of Reconciliation and Resurgence

The *Final Report* provides insight into how the TRC fulfilled its public education mandate as part of the truth and reconciliation process. Experiential spaces of mutual learning opened up as survivors shared their truths at national events, and others bore witness. These spaces created opportunities for people "to gather the courage to face our troubled history together without minimizing the damage that has been done, even as we learn new decolonizing ways of working together that shift power and perceptions."[32] The pedagogical potential of such spaces should not be underestimated. The *Final Report* notes, "For non-Aboriginal Canadians who came to bear witness to Survivors' life stories, the experience was powerful. One woman said simply, 'By listening to your story, my story can change. By listening to your story, I can change.'"[33]

As its work was underway, the TRC told Canadians not to wait until the final report was issued before taking action on reconciliation.[34] Many Canadians took up this challenge. This was evident, for example, in the many expressions of reconciliation presented to the commission at the TRC's seven national events by federal, provincial, territorial, and municipal governments, and church officials from multiple faiths, post-secondary institutions, non-profit and philanthropic organizations, the corporate sector, and others.[35] Approximately 15,000 students and teachers attended National Event Education Days, and the commission also hosted youth dialogues across the country.[36] Nationally acclaimed artists, some of whom are survivors or intergenerational survivors, explored reconciliation through art, resistance, and cultural politics. Several major art exhibits exploring themes of residential schools, colonization, resistance, and reconciliation ran concurrently with TRC national events.[37] In addition to the commission's own events and activities, commissioners and staff participated in approximately 900 separate reconciliation events held independently by other organizations and groups.[38]

In Tully's view, ethical practices of reconciliation must be informed not only by Western approaches but by Indigenous ecological knowledge systems and treaty-making principles and practices of kinship, shared responsibility, reciprocity, and gift exchange. "Hence ... Indigenous and non-Indigenous people need to join hands and work together, sharing and testing traditional and western knowledge on equal footing if we are going to get at the roots of both the ecological and the social crises and work out conciliatory and sustainable alternatives."[39] The need to join hands together in this way, he says, highlights the "reciprocal educational relationship" between reconciliation with each other and with the land.[40] We learn experientially about "the exercise of shared responsibilities in practices of reconciliation ... by beginning to join together, act together, and learn together in conciliatory and sustainable ways with Indigenous and non-Indigenous people and with the living earth, we begin to *reconnect*."[41] In order to practise joining hands together effectively, there must be opportunities – pedagogical space – for people who have been so profoundly disconnected to meet and engage with one another. The commission's work is a concrete example of what this might look like in practice.

The TRC findings and calls to action underscore that developing pedagogy and practices of reconciliation, particularly Indigenous ways of teaching and learning, is vital. At the TRC's traditional knowledge keepers forum, Blackfoot Elder Reg Crowshoe said, "When we talk about the concept of reconciliation, I think about some of the stories that I've heard in our culture, and stories are important ... We have stories in our culture about our superheroes, how we treat each other, stories about how animals and plants give us authorities and privileges to use plants as healing, but we also have stories about practices. How would we practise reconciliation? How would we practise getting together to talk about reconciliation in an oral perspective? And those practices are so important."[42]

The TRC observes, "Together, Canadians must do more than just *talk* about reconciliation; we must learn how to *practise* reconciliation in our everyday lives – within ourselves and our families, and in our communities, governments, places of worship, schools, and work-places."[43] The national and regional events, community hearings, and other public dialogue forums provided opportunities for Indigenous and settler peoples to practise getting together to talk about reconciliation in ways that Elder Crowshoe and Tully identify. Put another way, "Survivors told us that Canadians must learn about the history and legacy of residential schools in ways that change both minds *and* hearts."[44]

This was done by making space for Indigenous public memory practices of ceremony, testimony, and witnessing in ways that create a counter-narrative to a dominant culture account of national history narrative that has excluded Indigenous peoples as active participants in historical and contemporary life. "Reshaping national history is a public process, one that happens through discussion, sharing, and commemoration. As Canadians gather in public spaces to share their memories, beliefs, and ideas about the past with others, our collective understanding of the present and the future is formed. As citizens, our ideas, worldviews, cultural identities, and values are shaped not only in classrooms and museums or by popular culture but also in the everyday social relationships and patterns of living that become our way of life."[45]

Some observers argue that the TRC truth-gathering process was flawed because it failed to fully incorporate the testimonies of clergy and former staff who taught in the residential schools.[46] Although officials from the settlement agreement churches participated in TRC events, and the TRC conducted oral history interviews with ninety-six former staff, only a few former staff or their family members made public statements.[47] The *Final Report* highlights the challenges of creating safe and respectful space for public dialogue between survivors and former staff who had conflicting memories of the residential schools.

These two seemingly irreconcilable truths are a stark reminder that there are no easy shortcuts to reconciliation. That there were few direct exchanges at TRC events between survivors and former school staff indicates that for many the time for reconciliation had not yet arrived. Indeed, for some, it may never arrive.[48]

Some clergy and former staff who attended the public events may have shared the view of one former staff-person who felt strongly that "this is not the time to try to ask all those former students to sit and listen to the rationale of the former staff because there's just too much emotion there ... and there's too little trust ... So I think really a very important thing is for former staff to hear the stories and be courageous enough just to hear them."[49]

The TRC public events were not intended to achieve a consensus among those in attendance about what happened; indeed, many contradictory views were expressed. Rather it brought Indigenous and non-Indigenous people together to participate in creating a new oral history record. "These conflicting stories, based on different experiences, locations, time periods, and perspectives all feed into a [new] national historical narrative. Developing this narrative through public dialogue can strengthen civic capacity for accountability and thereby do justice to victims not just in the legal sense but also in terms of restoring human dignity, nurturing mutual respect, and supporting healing. As citizens use ceremony and testimony to remember, witness, and commemorate, they learn how to put the principles of accountability into everyday practice. They become active agents in the truth and reconciliation process."[50]

Thus the TRC public events were themselves sites of education, pedagogy, and practice in which "the Commission intentionally made [Indigenous] ceremonies the spiritual and ethical framework of our public education work."[51] Tully notes, "The biggest challenge today is not to design or invent practices of transformative reconciliation" that already exist.[52] Rather than invent a new reconciliation process, the commission made Indigenous approaches to reconciliation central to its work. Tully says that educational institutions have an important role to play in the teaching, learning, and research of practices of reconciliation. There is much more to be learned about the political, cultural, and relational dynamics of Indigenous–settler relations from the reconciliation process itself.

> Research is vital to reconciliation. It provides insights and practical examples of why and how educating Canadians about the diverse concepts, principles, and practices of reconciliation contributes to healing and transformative social change. The benefits of research extend beyond addressing the legacy of residential schools. Research on the reconciliation process can inform how Canadian society can mitigate intercultural conflicts, strengthen civic trust, and build social capacity and practical skills for long-term reconciliation. First Nations, Inuit, and Métis peoples have an especially strong contribution to make to this work. Research partnerships between universities and communities or organizations are fruitful collaborations and can provide the necessary structure to document, analyze, and report research findings on reconciliation for a broader audience.[53]

The TRC calls on the federal government to "through the Social Sciences and Humanities Research Council, and in collaboration with Aboriginal peoples, post-secondary institutions and educators, and the National Centre for Truth and Reconciliation and its partner institutions, to establish a national research program with multi-year funding to advance understanding of reconciliation."[54]

Decolonizing Work of Reconciliation and Resurgence

There is growing consensus among international experts that Indigenous peoples' individual and collective rights must be strengthened by the work of truth commissions. Indigenous peoples should be active participants in all aspects of any quasi-judicial process investigating violations of their rights, "not only as victims (rights bearing and claims making actors) but also as agents of change ... [who are] active participants in the design, implementation, analysis and outreach stages" of its work.[55]

Despite the impacts of colonization, Indigenous people have led in the decolonizing work of reconciliation and resurgence in practical terms. As those who have a sacred responsibility to care for the land and all living things, they have been generous in their willingness to share these teachings with settler peoples. Post-TRC, the words of elders and knowledge keepers continue to guide my own thinking about potential points of convergence between reconciliation and resurgence. At the TRC's traditional knowledge keepers forum held in Winnipeg in June 2014, Anishinaabe Elder Dave Courchene said,

> As people who have gained this recognition to be Knowledge Keepers for our people, we accept that work in the most humble way ... It's going to be the spirit of our ancestors, the spirit that's going to help us to reclaim our rightful place in our homeland ... We've arrived in a time of great change and great opportunity ... We are the true leaders of our homeland and they cannot take that away from us, and they never will because our Creator put us here. This is our homeland and we have a sacred responsibility to teach all those that have come to our homeland how to be proper human beings because we have all been given original instructions on how to be a human being. We have great responsibilities as people to take care of the Earth, to speak on behalf of Mother Earth. That is our responsibility and that's the kind of leadership that we must reflect as a people.[56]

The *Final Report* emphasized that reconciliation is a long-term under-taking and that Indigenous peoples must continue to lead the process:

> Although the Commission has been a catalyst for deepening our national awareness of the meaning and potential of reconciliation, it will take many heads, hands, and hearts, working together, at all levels of society to main-tain the momentum in the years ahead. It will also take sustained political will and concerted material resources ... Canadians have much to gain from listening to the voices, experiences, and wisdom of Survivors, Elders, and Traditional Knowledge Keepers – and much more to learn about rec-onciliation. Aboriginal peoples have an important contribution to make to reconciliation. Their knowledge systems, oral histories, laws, and connec-tions to the land have vitally informed the reconciliation process to date, and are essential to its ongoing progress.[57]

Anishinaabe Elder Mary Deleary told the TRC about the decoloniz-ing work that Indigenous peoples do, and called on settlers to begin their own decolonizing:

> I'm so filled with belief and hope because when I hear your voices at the table, I hear and know that the responsibilities that our ancestors car-ried ... are still being carried ... [E]ven through all of the struggles, even through all of what has been disrupted ... we can still hear the voice of the land. We can hear the care and love for the children. We can hear about our law. We can hear about our stories, our governance, our feasts, [and] our medicines ... We have work to do. That work we are [already] doing as [Aboriginal] peoples. Our relatives who have come from across the water [non-Aboriginal people], you still have work to do on your road ... The land is made up of the dust of our ancestors' bones. And so to reconcile with this land and everything that has happened, there is much work to be done ... in order to create balance.[58]

As Elder Deleary reminds us, the dust of our ancestors' bones – Indigenous and non-Indigenous alike – is now part of the land. Her pro-found observation lies at the heart of reconciliation. Indigenous peoples still hear the strong voices of their ancestors who call on those living today to remember their stories and ceremonies, to care for the land and their families, to regenerate their cultures and languages, and to revive their governance systems, laws, and medicines. She tells us that settler peoples must remember our own history. We must confront the truth of how we acquired and have benefited from the riches of Indigenous peoples' homelands while they have not, how we have dishonoured the treaties, and what we must now do to rectify these injustices.

We too must hear the voices of our ancestors. While some will still whisper the colonial myth of how they had a legal right and moral duty to take the land from Indigenous peoples, others might call on their descendants to remember different stories – of upholding honour, valuing principles of reciprocity and friendship, and standing in solidarity and alliance with Indigenous peoples – the stories of settler peoples who, despite being fully implicated in the colonial project, advocated for and with Indigenous peoples in the struggle over land hold valuable lessons for non-Indigenous people today.[59]

The Gift Is Given, the Responsibility to Reciprocate Is Ours

The TRC collected millions of government and church documents containing the records of residential schools and information about the students who attended them. The commission also gathered 7,000 digitally recorded testimonial statements from survivors, their families, government and church officials, and former residential school staff, and recorded TRC public national events and community hearings. The commission notes, "Of course, previously inaccessible archival documents are critically important to correcting the historical record, but we have given equal weight and greater voice to Indigenous oral-based history, legal traditions, and memory practices in our work and in this final report since these sources represent previously unheard and unrecorded versions of history, knowledge, and wisdom. This has significantly informed our thinking about why repairing and revitalizing individual, family, and community memory are so crucial to the truth and reconciliation process."[60]

The TRC was mandated to establish the National Centre for Truth and Reconciliation (NCTR) (now located at the University of Manitoba) and transfer all of its records and materials to the centre when the commission closed its doors. The NCTR archive is responsible for making these records accessible to survivors and their families, as well as community-based and academic researchers. The private and public testimonies within this collection constitute an invaluable archival collection that will continue to reveal new truths about the residential school system and inform our understanding of reconciliation. As the centre describes its mandate,

A shared vision held by those affected by Indian residential schools was to create a place of learning and dialogue where the truths of their experiences were honoured and kept safe for future generations. They wanted their families, communities and all of Canada to learn from these hard lessons so they would not be repeated. They wanted to share the wisdom of the Elders and Traditional Knowledge Keepers on how to create just and peaceful relationships amongst diverse peoples. They knew that Reconciliation is not only about the past; it is about the future that all Canadians will forge together. This vision is the legacy gift to all of Canada.[61]

The gift has been given; it will now be up to all of us to reciprocate in ways that honour survivors, support the resurgence of Indigenous life-ways, and foster ongoing public education, dialogue, and practices of reconciliation. The need to find sustainable solutions to mitigate global climate change, create green economies, and share wealth and resources more equitably among all living things on earth has never been more urgent. This makes learning how to establish sustainable networks of mutual accountability, solidarity, and reciprocity between Indigenous and settler peoples all the more critical.

NOTES

1 Paulette Regan, *Unsettling the Settler Within: Indian Residential Schools, Truth Telling, and Reconciliation in Canada* (Vancouver: UBC Press, 2010), 18.
2 The TRC was created in 2008 as part of the Indian Residential Schools Settlement Agreement that was negotiated in 2006 to resolve the largest civil class-action lawsuit in Canadian history. The agreement settled the legal claims of former students who had suffered abuses in residential schools run by the federal government in partnership with Protestant and Catholic churches. There were five components to the agreement: an independent assessment process to adjudicate sexual and physical abuse claims and award compensation; monetary reparations awarded as a "common experience payment" based solely on verification of school attendance; a health support program for survivors; a truth and reconciliation commission; and a commemoration program for memorial projects. The Indian Residential Schools Settlement Agreement is available online at http://www.residentialschoolsettlement.ca/settlement.html.
3 *Canada's Residential Schools: Reconciliation, Final Report of the Truth and Reconciliation Commission of Canada* (Winnipeg: Truth and Reconciliation Commission of Canada, 2015), 6:11. Hereafter, *Final Report*.

4 *Final Report*, 6:3.

5 Ibid., 6:11–12.

6 Ibid., 6:12.

7 Ibid., 6:13.

8 For an overview of the settlement agreement, see *Canada's Residential Schools: The History, Part 2, 1939–2000, Final Report of the Truth and Reconciliation Commission of Canada* (Winnipeg: Truth and Reconciliation Commission of Canada, 2015), 1:551–76.

9 International Center for Transitional Justice, *Strengthening Indigenous Rights through Truth Commissions: A Practitioner's Resource* (New York: International Journal for Transitional Justice, 2012), 3–4.

10 For critiques of state-centric approaches to reconciliation, see, for example, Taiaiake Alfred, *Wasase: Indigenous Pathways of Action and Freedom* (Peterborough, ON: Broadview, 2005); Jeff Corntassel and Cindy Holder, "Who's Sorry Now? Government Apologies, Truth Commissions, and Indigenous Self-Determination in Australia, Canada, Guatemala, and Peru," *Human Rights Review* 9, no. 4 (December 2008): 465–89; Glen Sean Coulthard, *Red Skins, White Masks: Rejecting the Colonial Politics of Recognition* (Minneapolis: University of Minnesota Press, 2014).

11 Paige Arthur, "Indigenous Self-Determination and Political Rights: Practical Recommendations for Truth Commissions," in *Indigenous Peoples' Access to Justice, Including Truth and Reconciliation Processes*, ed. Wilton Littlechild and Elsa Stamatopoulour (New York: Institute for the Study of Human Rights, Columbia University, 2014), 227.

12 Deborah J. Yashar, "Indigenous Rights and Truth Commissions: Reflections for Discussion," in *Strengthening Indigenous Rights through Truth Commissions: A Practitioner's Resource* (New York: International Journal for Transitional Justice, 2012), 7.

13 Arthur, "Indigenous Self-Determination and Political Rights," 227.

14 Ibid., 225.

15 Ibid., 223.

16 *Final Report*, 6:25–9.

17 See Tully, this volume, note 1.

18 *Final Report*, 6:20–1.

19 Ibid., 6:34.

20 TRC Call to Action 45. Ibid., 6:230.

21 Ibid., 6:37.

22 See Borrows, this volume.

23 *Final Report*, 6:207–8.

24 Ibid., 6:78.

25 TRC Call to Action 50. Ibid., 6:77–9.

26 Asch, this volume.

27 Ibid.

28 Ibid.

29 *Final Report*, 6:118.

30 Ibid., 6:119.

31 TRC Calls to Action 7–10, 62–3, *Final Report*, 6:224–5, 235.

32 Regan, *Unsettling the Settler Within*, 211.

33 *Final Report*, 6:15.

34 Ibid., 6:10.

35 The TRC received approximately 180 expressions of reconciliation. Truth and Reconciliation Commission of Canada, *Honouring the Truth, Reconciling for the Future: Summary of the Final Report of the Truth and Reconciliation Commission of Canada* (Winnipeg: Truth and Reconciliation Commission of Canada, 2015), 32. See also, *Final Report* 6: 165.

36 *Final Report*, 6: 127–31.

37 Ibid., 6:180–1.

38 *Honouring the Truth, Reconciling for the Future*, 32.

39 Tully, this volume.

40 Ibid.

41 Ibid.

42 TRC, AVS, Reg Crowshoe, statement to the Truth and Reconciliation Commission of Canada, Winnipeg, Manitoba, 26 June 2014, statement number SE049, cited in *Final Report*, 6:13.

43 *Final Report*, 6:17.

44 Ibid., 6:117.

45 Ibid., 6:162.

46 See, for example, Ronald Niezen, *Truth and Indignation: Canada's Truth and Reconciliation Commission on Indian Residential Schools* (Toronto: University of Toronto Press, 2013). On former residential school staff, see *Canada's Residential Schools: The History, Part 1, Origins to 1939. Final Report*, 1:675–738; *Canada's Residential Schools: The History, Part 2, 1939–2000, Final Report*, 1:493–550. On the importance of truth-telling and challenges of hearing testimonies of church members and former staff testimony at TRC public events, see *Final Report*, 6:7–11.

47 *Honouring the Truth, Reconciling for the Future*, 26.

48 *Final Report*, 6:11.

49 Ibid., 6:9.

50 Ibid., 6:166.

51 Ibid., 6:163.

52 Tully, this volume.

53 *Final Report,* 6:126.
54 TRC Call to Action 65, *Final Report,* 6:127.
55 Yashar, "Indigenous Rights and Truth Commissions," 12.
56 TRC, AVS, David Courchene Jr, statement to the Truth and Reconciliation Commission of Canada, Winnipeg, Manitoba, 25 June 2014, statement number SE048, cited in *Final Report,* 6:203.
57 *Final Report,* 6:4.
58 TRC, AVS, Mary Deleary, statement to the Truth and Reconciliation Commission of Canada, Winnipeg, Manitoba, 26 June 2014, statement number SE049, cited in *Final Report,* 6:5.
59 In addition to Asch (this volume), see also Celia Haig-Brown and David A. Nock, eds, *With Good Intentions: Euro-Canadian and Aboriginal Relations in Colonial Canada* (Vancouver: UBC Press, 2006), 7. On the need for more research, see Regan, *Unsettling the Settler Within,* 231–3. On the issue of settler identity and decolonization, see Emma Battell Lowman and Adam J. Barker, *Settler Identity and Colonialism in 21st Century Canada* (Halifax: Fernwood Publishing, 2015).
60 *Final Report,* 6:162.
61 National Centre for Truth and Reconciliation, https://nctr.ca/about-new.php.

7 Reconciliation, Resurgence, and Revitalization: Collaborative Research Protocols with Contemporary First Nations Communities

REGNA DARNELL

I have chosen to retain the markers of oral performance and the context in which a preliminary version of this chapter was first presented. Therefore I begin with the protocols of greeting appropriate for a guest in the University of Victoria's First Peoples House. I am grateful to have been welcomed to the unceded Coast Salish and Strait Salish traditional territory and to their beautiful campus meeting place. I have many old friends in this territory, and each visit establishes new relationships. I bring greetings from my colleagues at Walpole Island, Mississauga, Saugeen, and Marten Falls First Nations and from Six Nations of the Grand River. The immediate occasion of this presentation was an invited response to the lectures of Asch, Borrows, and Tully about the meaning and consequence of reconciliation, delivered at Dalhousie University in 2015 and considered by colleagues speaking from different points in the intercultural discourse at a moment coinciding with the release of the preliminary findings of Canada's Truth and Reconciliation Commission.

On return to my home in southwestern Ontario, I presented a reframed version to an interdisciplinary audience of graduate students in anthropology and the Centre for the Study of Theory and Criticism. To both audiences, therefore, I acknowledged the southwestern Ontario First Nations, whose greetings I had recently carried to Vancouver Island and the contemporary Anishinaabeg, Lenape, and Haudenosaunee stewards of the region in which I live. In the context of the entailed commitment to relationship across territories and community identities, I define my project as the search for a theoretical language of reconciliation that will serve the pragmatic purposes of both Native and non-Native partners in fostering their relationship within the

Canadian nation state. Drawing on relational protocols widely shared by Indigenous knowledge systems, I want to know if my words make sense to friends and colleagues not already steeped in contemporary First Nations discourses. I do not want to speak in one way to academic colleagues, themselves of multiple interdisciplinary persuasions, and in another to Indigenous colleagues deeply embedded in diverse local identities and preoccupations.

As I listened again to the words of Asch, Borrows, and Tully delivered at Dalhousie, my overwhelming impression was that I concurred – and therefore perhaps that I had nothing further to add to the always already interdisciplinary perspectives of political and legal theory. Then again perhaps I do have another way of approaching these issues, coming to them as a linguistic anthropologist, ethnographer, and qualitative researcher, as a student of cross-cultural miscommunication. I was startled by a remarkable convergence across the three speakers, partly because they have been talking to each other for a long time, and partly because they have come to a shared understanding of how we might come to know the ways of others and in turn to share what we have learned.

Many of the terms of this emerging discourse are unfamiliar to a mainstream audience largely restricted to a Judeo-Christian post-Enlightenment European baseline. Words like *beautiful* and *love* and *sincere* are rarely found in academic discourse or in mainstream political and legal rhetoric, but they recur matter-of-factly here and convey a content and commitment that I am unwilling to dismiss as wanton romanticism incompatible with "science." That sustainable futures require sustained discourse should not surprise us. It is written in miniature scale in our ability to talk to each other in the events of our meetings and the entailed commitments of our ongoing relationships; its successful cross-resonance encourages productive dialogue with space for new interlocutors to join. In such a discourse, there would be nothing surprising about the absence of a clear divide between Native and non-Native voices. The divide is formidable but potentially transcendable. Many of the settlers among us, including myself, have spent many years learning to listen, "sitting with" friends and teachers and earning our place by searching for ways to build bridges, to render the consensus emerging among our own conversations intelligible to a wider mainstream audience in dire and urgent need of alternative, complementary ways of knowing and being (a.k.a. epistemologies and ontologies).

To enter into such a conversation "on equal terms" is an uphill battle, fraught with intractable hierarchical relations of power. Michael Asch acknowledges limitations imposed because the Canadian government already has rejected a priori the very possibility of nation-to-nation relationship. It takes two parties to negotiate, and the debilitating power relations are not on the table as subject to revision. In such a negotiation, the party holding less power is necessarily subordinate. Since this is unacceptable in the ostensible parity of nation-to-nation discourse, we are left with the need to find an alternative, non-paralysing route to a just, moral "place to stand," as Michael has long put it.

Jim Tully's argument at first seems to imply that the options for Indigenous communities fall in starkly binary terms: they must either accept the terms offered by the mainstream hegemon, leading to inevitable assimilation, or endure perpetual marginalization. His third option poses dual alternative strategies encouraging cautious optimism. On the one hand, recent legal and political decisions are moving in positive directions, although they have failed to modify the systemic inequities underlying the colonial system. On the other hand, the cumulative effect of everyday practices simultaneously undermines ongoing injustices and models what reconciliation might look like. Change at the public and community levels must integrate institutional macro-politics with individual micro-communicative practices.

I suggest a further alternative possibility, if not in the realm of real-politik, at least in the imaginative realm where histories and stories are constructed and transmitted. For example, Thomas King appropriates the enemy's language and reverses our conventional metaphors, exalting the binaries of Western tropes, only to destabilize them by inverting the values implicit in the stereotypes of their marginalization so that the reflexive reader might be led to rethink the terms of the relationship itself.[1] Violence is not the only mode of challenging the hegemon – humour works too.

The terms posed for our consideration – *reconciliation* and *resurgence* – do not and cannot function independently of one another. I understand *resurgence* as dynamic movement, disturbance of a status quo in need of shaking up, its present direction presenting an imminent danger to life itself. *Reconciliation* seems to me more a question of balance, of trajectory never quite settling into stasis or equilibrium. *Revitalization*, often a third term in our discussions, suggests breathing life into something that has been dormant but retains its form, requiring only the effort to awaken it. Each term begins with "re-," again implying that Indigenous peoples and settlers once lived together in a state of individual and community well-being and that conciliation once was possible, albeit never fully attained or attainable. This language gives us hope that renewed energy will restore a state of collaboration. Can we sing it? Or dance it? Or speak it into existence in our own languages? Or do we delude ourselves by nostalgia for a golden age safely encapsulated in the distant past?

All three speakers present themselves as storytellers. Storytelling, however, is not a monolithic practice of identity-formation. Sometimes it is the storytellers' role to pass on the stories they have heard or have been taught. Other times the storytellers' actions create new stories, expecting that others will tell them in the future. Either way, both the stories we hear and the ones we tell carry a heavy burden of responsibility. Our understanding of what it means to tell stories obliges us to choose to tell a different story, a story of relationship that gives rise to different truths. I follow here Thomas King's Massey Lectures entitled "The Truth about Stories."[2] Stories embed individual experience within an oral tradition of reflecting upon experience and continually bringing it into the present through face-to-face interaction. To inherit or otherwise accept the responsibility for a story or song is to embody it. Traditional speakers across Indian country break into performance when telling stories that have come to them through generations of grandfathers, back to those whose names are no longer known and whose experiential wisdom gained through individual life course has merged into a collective transmitted knowledge. The contemporary speaker becomes the original teller of the story who speaks from personal experience.

I have been thinking about this chain of knowledge-sharing recently in relation to the intergenerational trauma arising from residential school experience. Epigenetic evidence now suggests that the anxiety and depression suffered by traumatized victims is reflected genetically in their descendants. Recent studies of gene expression provide a mechanism for experience-based transmission within direct family lines. Of course, that does not mean that responses of anxiety, stress, and depression are biologically inevitable. It does mean, however, that heredity is a complex matter with triggers that include context, social and natural environment, personal and community experience, and larger historical circumstances. We are not justified in blaming the victim if the victim cannot control most of these variables most of the time. Nonetheless, we can identify and address the underlying conditions, acknowledging that they are wider than the plight of the individual sufferer. That there is a demonstrable biological dimension to such experience underwrites an argument against the conventional binaries – the blacks and whites of mind vs body, or individual vs community – binaries whose starkness precludes healing, understood as well-being rather than absence of disease.

Asch, Tully, and Borrows share a commitment to seeking convergence incorporating difference rather than blanket substitution of one way of life for another. Natives and newcomers are stuck with one another. Each has something to contribute to a potential synthesis of wisdoms, at least insofar as we manage to talk to and listen to our neighbours. Tully, in particular, emphasizes that Western tradition, albeit wildly ethnocentric in its hubris that its "science" is both universal and superior to any "folk" knowledge, lends itself to convergences that resonate productively with Indigenous modes of thought.

For example, emerging theories of complexity foreground nonlinear chains of interdependency. Strange attractors draw like forces in recurrent non-linear but quite real patterns. Fractal patterns operate at multiple scales across the natural and social worlds and call for a less cognitive and anthropogenic mode of responsive agency. Because they must respect intricacies and contingencies of the natural world, the life sciences have become increasingly sensitized to the capacity of natural systems for self-regulation. In the natural world, the evidence available is never complete or bounded in space and time. The physical sciences, in contrast, pose laws without exceptions, perhaps parallel both to the "original instructions" honoured by my Haudenosaunee colleagues and to the responsibilities that Michael exhorts us settlers to share as a result of our problematic presence here. Both modes of knowing are systems: they form non-random patterns, even when the critical variables are too complex to circumscribe. The fluid and contingent may be a more effective way to live in the flux of day-to-day life, but it is equally necessary to have moorings in certainty that are akin to the non-negotiability of (some) physical regularities, such as the intractability of the world/nature. The question for moral philosophy, as for everyday affairs, is to recognize the difference and respond appropriately, to keep the questions in balance and adapt the methodology to the question(s) under consideration.

There are many fine examples of collaboration between Indigenous thinkers and Western science, e.g., the Indigenous Peoples' Network on Climate Change. My own experience over more than two decades of collaborative engagement at Walpole Island First Nation (Bkejwanong, "where the waters divide") downstream from Sarnia, Ontario's, chemical valley has toggled between recording and disseminating within the community the traditional knowledge of a generation of elders who grew up in closer touch with a less damaged land base in their home territory and using the documentary and analytic capabilities of environmental and health sciences to supplement the observations of those who have lived alongside this land for millennia and adapted to its inevitable and ongoing changes. From such a perspective, natural and social relationships are inextricable, reciprocal, and mutually transformative.

Science lacks the time depth taken for granted by traditional ecological knowledge. After all, it is only a few centuries old. Moreover, its models are rarely grounded deeply in time spent on particular land by those who devise them. Many scientific experts never "visit" the land on which they pass judgment based on abstraction from the uniqueness of local contexts. This reductionist methodology masks specific contexts from which "data" arise. Such a position is rarely met with respect locally; Ted Chamberlin has lyrically foregrounded the question, If this is your land, where are your stories?[3] Statistics without interpretation do not underwrite persuasive stories. On the other hand, science can use its knowledge of other cases and contexts to provide guidelines for risk management, clarify priorities for environmental remediation, and facilitate instructive comparison across contrasting cases. Arguments for co-management of water, land, and air resources are based on a community's understanding of its members' experience, both personal and inherited through oral transmission. First Nations communities legitimately seek a seat at the table with provincial and federal governments and industry, as full partners in deciding the fate of the resources that sustain local (and indeed all human) life.

Dr Dean Jacobs, founder and long-term director of the Nin.Da.Waab. Jib Cultural Heritage Centre at Walpole Island First Nation near Wallaceburg, Ontario, has long and effectively represented his community at many such tables and sought to bring the two kinds of knowledge together. A holder of three honorary doctorates, he is trained in and respectful of science within the realms appropriate to science. This respect and the knowledge that underlies it is intelligible to scientists, politicians, and administrators, because the terms of its formulation are familiar. Then Dean guides them in learning how to situate their science in relation to traditional knowledge, with potential convergences mutually strengthening the credibility and accuracy of both modes of understanding. At least in principle, such an approach works towards consensus and hence to successful, mutually respectful negotiation. In practice, sadly, there are glitches, as when a funding application reviewer suggested our research team might want to include community partners as co-authors, apparently assuming that neither Dr Jacobs, a medical doctor, an environmental technologist, nor a nurse manager could possibly be community members, despite clear WIFN affiliation as co-authors.

A series of collaborative projects through the University of Western Ontario's Ecosystem Health team based in the Schulich School of Medicine and Dentistry, regularly co-authored with community research partners, have built upon the long-term commitment of the Walpole Island First Nation to monitoring environmental pollution, particularly in the water, to document the human health effects of that pollution. The community's location downriver from Sarnia's chemical valley renders such commitment more than pressing. Western's core academic team is internally collaborative, which the academy calls interdisciplinary: I am the social scientist, Jack Bend is a toxicologist in the medical school, Charlie Trick is an oceanographer in the Faculty of Science. We are all well established in our professional careers and committed to leaving a legacy of learning how to work together, both inside the academy and beyond it. Gerald McKinley, a medical anthropologist and my colleague in Public Health, leads this team in its transition to a second generation.

I am on less firm ground, however, when I find myself introducing presentations to a community audience about what we have to offer and how our science might intermesh with local modes of knowing. From the point of view of the community members, we are not the experts on their land, and we in fact often have sounded pretty silly. "We at Western have discovered that the environment and human health are closely related," I intone piously, "and we have established an Ecosystem Health research unit to study that connection." Everyone around the table nods sagely, "Ah, you figured that out, did you?" I take the point; I quite deliberately make it ironically. "We are finally catching up with what you have long known." Now perhaps we have something to offer you because *we* understand that we can work together to reinforce what is already known in the community.

Let me give you some examples where collaborative synergy has worked: We know that the overall disease burden for the community far exceeds that of the general Canadian population. Many community members suffer from chronic conditions. But not all of those who are sick suffer from the same ailments. Therefore, they cannot suffer from a single disease calling for a single clinical treatment. On the basis of biomonitoring of hair and blood samples, we demonstrated statistically higher levels of stress among individuals at Walpole Island First Nation than among their neighbours who are not band members. Medical researchers know that stress decreases immunity and renders people more vulnerable, with individual bodies incorporating negative health conditions in variable ways. Stress as a cause of illness cannot therefore be the fault of the victim, a moral flaw, and it cannot be attributed simply to lifestyle choices, as though poverty and addiction result from decisions of the sufferer. So we can reformulate the question of health effects as at least in good part one of defining and ameliorating the causes of stress, especially those that apply widely throughout the community. Two of the most obvious are residential school trauma and fear of environmental contamination. In statistical terms, the causality is multivariate. I will return to the embodiment of traumatic experience.

Environmental contamination is not a simple matter either. Community members agonize over whether to drink the water and eat the fish. Mothers regularly ask us how much fish they should feed their families. Our test results, based on the biomonitoring data, are actually quite reassuring. Testing for over 200 toxic metals and for methyl mercury, we found that levels of contamination were below recommended guidelines for all individuals tested. Methyl mercury is of particular concern for pregnant women, and a few women might choose to limit their fish intake on that ground. Our study of fish consumption by species offered further guidance. However, comparative data do not address the specificity of eating fish at Walpole Island: smaller fish are less contaminated because they are further down the food chain, traditional consumption is intensive seasonally but considerable throughout the year, and portion sizes are larger than among mainstream subjects who in any case consume fish less frequently. Our team is now completing a study of the species of arsenic in our samples, not because arsenic is an active danger to health at Walpole Island, but because arsenic speciation will enable us to identity a water, land, or air source for the trace amounts that appear in our samples. This has enormous implications in directing priorities and strategies for effective remediation.

While teaching "social and cultural determinants of health" and "Aboriginal health" in the fledgling Master of Public Health program at Western, I have been challenged, saddened, and often angered by the closedness of many biomedically and scientifically trained students, and occasionally even colleagues, to Indigenous perspectives. That it is almost always a result of ignorance rather than wilful violence does not make it less hurtful for the few Indigenous students in the classroom. Nor does it encourage me to trust that all public health professionals are trained to be sensitive to the local conditions and concerns of their clients, at either individual or community levels. For example, clinical colleagues often insist that they "fix" people and brush off the community's documentation, in both Anishinaabemowin and English, of fifty-two endangered species in the complex ecosystems at Walpole Island as irrelevant to human health.[4] Even a reference to the well-known image of the canary in the coal mine does not draw them to conclude that plants, small animals, and humans live in the same environment and have shared its resources for millennia in overlapping though non-identical ways. Anishinaabeg wisdom is clear, however, that "all my relations" are not human, and that each contributes to our shared life-world with its own characteristic talents and skills. The further corollary is that humans, because of their capacities to speak and to negotiate of behalf of other living beings, hold a particular responsibility to improve this shared environment. But each of the other relations has its own talents and perspectives that exceed those of the human and must be incorporated in a holistic understanding. Tully calls these "pedagogical relations." Both Borrows and Tully emphasize the capacity to extend our understanding of the organization of systems in nature to that of human social systems: two kinds of knowing but a single commitment to know and to share knowledge. Again, insistence on the binary is destructive to the possibility of meaningful reconciliation.

Both Indigenous and academic partners acknowledge considerable urgency. Complexity theorists tell us that our world stands (ostensibly non-metaphorically) at "the edge of chaos" – for example, with regard to climate change and loss of biodiversity. This state will inevitably catapult us into unpredictable and irreversible non-linear changes. Many Indigenous traditions have a similar understanding. In the Haida version, the world is as sharp as a knife and we are in danger of falling off its edge. Too many would dismiss the latter as a mere metaphor, while granting verisimilitude to the scientific version because it is based on mathematical calculations. The two images, however, reflect similar understandings of how the world works. The symbolic or metaphorical quality helps us to understand the intersection of complex variables outside our direct control. Interestingly, human agency does not figure greatly in causation within complexity or chaos theory, suggesting that the anthropocentricity of Western culture needs dramatic rethinking and encouraging us to remember that "all our relations" make unique contributions to environmental sustainability.

In any case, the thing about metaphors, at least in the Indigenous traditions with which I am familiar, is that they are simultaneously both one thing and another: a butterfly in Tokyo does not cease to be a butterfly when it causes a weather disruption in Topeka, Kansas. Its butterflyness retains the complex local habitat specificity that enabled it to trigger a non-linear (chaotic) reaction through contact. It is a kind of metonymic contagion, uncontrollable. The Haida poet/storyteller also uses his image to show that we cannot control or even identify the "laws" that make the world we live in, because it exceeds the semantic capacity of the butterfly story that is commonly employed to explain the concept of chaos to lay people. But the Haida image of a sharp knife has a further edifying property absent in the butterfly version – it is a tool that can be misused by badly directed human agency. The sharp knife enjoins the hearer to reflect on personal responsibility to keep the world in balance. It enjoins against hubris, including the Faustian curiosity without concern for consequence, which is the very antithesis of responsibility.

Can these two ways of thinking metaphor communicate with one another? To acknowledge our differences and respect the other party's boundaries is an excellent place to start. The parallel canoes of the Haudenosaunee two-row wampum belt emphasize the autonomy of natives and newcomers arising from their treaty relations. But I worry a lot about whether the paddlers talk to each other in an era when treaties too often are disrespected, despite the implication of the metaphor that treaty negotiations entail communication in mutual respect for their differences. In an alternative imagery, an old Cree man once told me a cautionary tale about how people from my culture, when they feel they have a "good" relationship with someone, too quickly presume that the person must agree with them; thus they feel no need to explore the actual views of their interlocutor in further detail. The adjective *good* is redundant in Cree thinking, because it is implicit in the existence of relationship itself. The old man drew two overlapping circles in the dirt with a stick. "That's you," he said. "Now us folks, we do it like this." He drew two more circles whose edges merely abutted at their point of contact. Now they have something to share because they reflect different experiences and standpoints. In the old man's terms, "Why would they talk if there is nothing new to be heard?" To learn to listen is to expect that you will hear something significant. Otherwise, it is point-less, a failed communication.

One awkwardness of my own professional identity comes when I define my field as "cross-cultural miscommunication." I want to approach the question of shared knowledge in relation to the nature of community, responding to Benedict Anderson's idea of an "imagined community" in which citizens of modern nation states do not know, expect to know, or even want to know their fellow citizens; they are, however, prepared to accept that such confreres are much like them-selves.[5] Anderson assumes this to be the basic form of human sociality (a.k.a. relationality). It is the same fallacy of over-generalization identi-fied by the old man with the stick in the dirt.

I suggest that it is more productive to consider community as some-thing arising from the experience of living in small communities con-stituted by personal, face-to-face relations. Larger communities are necessarily constructed by analogy from such relations, taking account of individuality and individual diversity. Larger-scale and more com-plex relations of institutions and codifications of sociality are a second-ary extension of this fundamental human pattern. Small face-to-face communities, moreover, have a tensile strength that comes from their intimate knowledge of the affairs of fellow members and the collec-tive commitment to work things out so that they can continue to live together. Communities certainly splinter, break up, and reconstitute themselves around other relationships in other places. It is in their nature to do so. But the capacity to live together is also the capacity for intimacy and empathy, despite inevitable conflict and the necessity of having mechanisms to resolve it. I do not, of course, believe that we must jettison modernity or even postmodernity in order to live together as our distant forbears did. Even in this global age, we do well to remember that many communities continue to see the world primarily in terms of their relations, however narrowly or broadly the boundar-ies of community are drawn. Is it not possible that our mainstream way has gone too far in the opposite direction and needs to rebalance its pri-orities, to learn from the ground-level local understandings of particu-lar human and natural relationships and practices in their immediate contexts? Reconciliation acknowledges that local communities in their own understanding of themselves constitute the centre of the world. They are not marginalized enclaves within global networks based else-where that they may appear to outsiders.

Let us consider the explanatory capacity of two common metaphors (based primarily on my experience with Anishinaabeg Midewiwin versions), although both are found more widely: "all my relations" and "seven generations in each direction" as the scope of the actor/speaker's responsibility. All one's relations, including the living land itself, are living things within a web of sentience (understood to function in multiple modes appropriate to the variable capacities, interests, and perspectives of different categories of living beings or entities). In a kin-centric cross-species symbiosis, "all my relations" share a habitat, with a geographical specificity that encourages us to explore the symbols of local traditions within a territory or region or a culture area (the latter to be taken as an open-ended and flexible category). We need to think about "the Northwest Coast," for example, as a balanced unit within which multiple features are shared and recombined in a process without a fixed inventory or configuration. I am more comfortable today with "North Pacific Coast" or "Northwestern North America." Trade, migration, and species niches all operate with exchange of complementary, non-identical, and therefore dynamic resources: gift, thanksgiving, and reciprocity in Tully's terms.

"All my relations" can coexist precisely because they are different, each with unique responsibilities. One cannot transplant people or their relations to new territories and expect them to take immediate root. Some relations will necessarily be left behind, and a guide is needed to approach the establishment of new relations in a new place. This is one reason people marry their distant relatives who live in other communities or territories. In cases of natural or human-caused disaster – fire, flood, war, pestilence – there is a place to go where relatives will take you in (and would expect the same from you – though it may be several generations before there is need to call on such responsibility of care; in the meantime, the obligation and its impending reciprocity are passed on from one generation to the next). The Royal Commission on Aboriginal Peoples poignantly documented that Inuit starved when dumped in unfamiliar territory by southern bureaucrats who assumed that one chunk of ice was the same as any other. It is precisely this rootedness, this embeddedness of individuals within landscapes, that facilitates the accumulation of wisdom within a territory over time and insists on maintaining relations of people to land and vice versa.

Spatial relationship shades into temporal over seven generations, quite literally the time depth of direct transmission through oral tradition: My grandfather told me (two generations) what his grandfather told him when he was a little boy (two more) about what he had heard from his grandfather when he too was young (two more). The seventh position, the pivot, is held in temporary stasis at the key standpoint of the contemporary transmitter. The alternate generations are dormant, pending accumulation of experience and the leisure to transmit it, busy in the everyday bustle of making a living, or are yet unborn; they come into more active roles in each pivot position with each shift in the succession of generations. The pivot is always emergent. Past, present, and future cannot be separated. The concurrent processes of continuity and ongoing change shade in and out of one another. This is very different from Western notions of history that pursue an unmediated access to "what really happened" in the past. Like the story of Indigenous–settler relations, this story needs to be retold, and our ongoing relationships across this divide provide us with the tools to retell it in more inclusive ways.

"The Northwest Coast" has disrupted mainstream narratives of settlers, anthropologists, and Western philosophers in productive ways that continue to challenge contemporary legal and political debates. Anthropologist Paul Radin defined the methodology of his discipline as finding the philosophers, the people who like to think about things, in every society and talking to them.[6] And talking some more until a common ground emerges to see the similarities relationally across their different backgrounds, circumstances, and even temperaments. Despite our claims to have moved beyond crude evolutionary models of "civilization," the suspicion still arises in public perception and in some academic and legal myopia that the Northwest Coast cannot be considered civilized because its peoples did not have agriculture until Europeans arrived to introduce them to it. Yet the same peoples had settled villages, monumental architecture, had developed art style, complex hierarchical social and political organization, abundant leisure, and so on. These undeniable facts wipe out the legitimacy of a reified theory of unilineal evolution. Better yet, when we reason without imposing such an arbitrary category, a demystified "agriculture" becomes a continuum rather than a single thing. Horticulture and manipulation of plant and animal species are characteristic of the Anthropocene on the Northwest Coast, in ways best understood through the kinds of relationalities explored above.

The original Delgamuukw decision maintained Indian claims were invalid because they rested on stories (valid only when sung by the properly constituted stewards and heirs in proper regalia worn in authorized public performance) in front of witnesses who could and occasionally did contest inaccurate versions. Outsiders have not easily trusted such sacred stories as genuine, historical, or "true" in the absence of independent and convergent evidence. In 1997, the Supreme Court of Canada, on grounds of natural justice for societies without written records of their distant past, honoured the possibility of evidence from oral tradition but declared it subject to the same standards of reliability and validity that were applied to other forms of evidence. How, then, are we to carry out such an evaluation when confronted with a legal system, especially at the lower court levels, that wants to retain certainty and objectivity regardless of the inevitable distortion entailed? I contend that we must continue to tell our stories and to give good reasons, intelligible to multiple audiences, that they are better stories.

I often wonder how Borrows, Johnny Mack, and other Indigenous lawyers speak to their students, nevermind the courts, about how the languages of Indigenous law and Western law might be calibrated at a philosophical or theoretical level. It seems to me that, although these Indigenous legal scholars are fluently bilingual in both identity and expertise, the languages they use, like their audiences, remain largely separate. One could understand each discourse without having to acknowledge its relevance, never mind commensurability, with the other. From either side the question arises, That's beautiful, elegant, but what has it to do with "the law" as I understand it? I think Asch comes closest to answering it, perhaps because he is neither Indigenous nor a lawyer.[7] We are all treaty people.

I have been thinking for some years on the puzzle of why settlers are so threatened by nomadism, the seasonal exploitation of resources. The model of going in turn to different resources – today these are education, employment, and access to social and medical services – rather than dragging them all home and building a fence around home still manifests itself in the residential choices of First Nations peoples in Edmonton, Alberta and London, Ontario – the two cities where my non-statistical qualitative sample of over two decades each is quite consistent and therefore perhaps persuasive. The home-place remains where one belongs, regardless of where one lives at a given moment. One retains the right to return there, as do one's descendants. All cultures change: both ours and theirs, if we think such a distinction can be made at all. Most contemporary First Nations people eat pizza, many speak only English, and the majority live in cities. However, many of the "urban Indians" go back and forth regularly, maintain ties to their home communities, and expect to return home eventually, or at least that their children or grandchildren might do so. The existence of a home-place is, I believe, a significant force in facilitating the active decision many make to remain Native while living within a larger mainstream society. This is a feasible option only insofar as there remains a home-place.

I believe we must reclaim the label of science for the results of our conversations and the impending synthesis they herald. Rigorous evidence-based investigation of problems with minimal reductionism is possible within qualitative methodologies. But we must carefully choose the stories we tell, as well as their audiences. Relationality, orality, context, history, and geographic specificity are all terms of contextualization that ground us in the particular, so that our generalizations will preserve the beauty and diversity of local experience as well as the human capacity to share that experience across its local variants – perhaps even to take home and adopt some good ideas from elsewhere. Each of us speaks from a standpoint based in personal experience. It is the only ground on which we can presume to speak. When our speaking is combined with that of others, as it is here, there is a building, an evolving possibility of consensus, taking a different form in the mind and experience of each listener. I believe this constitutes "objectivity," though of a kind different from what most of us are accustomed to. The characteristic ethnographic methodology of anthropology relies on first-hand fieldwork through participant-observation, a fluid alternation between engagement with people and their standpoints and a more distanced comparative and analytic framework. We need both, but intensive participation in the worlds we seek to understand is the harder and more urgent challenge. Effective communication must be simultaneously participatory and transformative. Its truths are respectful of multiple subjectivities, including those of "all our relations" and the living land itself.

Hai hai. Meegwetch.

NOTES

1 Thomas King, *Green Grass, Running Water* (Toronto: Harper Perennial, 1993).
2 Thomas King, *The Truth about Stories: A Native Narrative* (Toronto: House of Anansi, 2003).
3 Ted Chamberlin, *If This Is Your Land, Where Are Your Stories? Finding Common Ground* (Toronto: A.A. Knopf, 2003).

4 David White, Christianne Stephens, and Regna Darnell, eds, *E-Niizaanag Wii-ngoshkaag Maampii Bkejwanong (Species at Risk on Walpole Island First Nation)* (Bkejwanong Territory: Nin.Da.Waab.Jib Heritage Centre, 2006).

5 Benedict Anderson, *Imagined Communities: Reflections on the Origin and Spread of Nationalism* (London: Verso, 1983).

6 Paul Radin, *Primitive Man as Philosopher* (1927; New York: Dover, 1957).

7 Michael Asch, *On Being Here to Stay: Treaties and Aboriginal Rights in Canada* (Toronto: University of Toronto Press, 2014).

8 Proceed with Caution: Reflections on Resurgence and Reconciliation

KIERA LADNER

First Words

As I see it, reconciliation is neither a reification nor a binary logic,[1] nor one of mutual exclusivity. That said, it is definitely not about convergence. Colonialism created and enabled a continuous reification of a binary logic of mutual exclusivity. Though some conceptualize decolonization and reconciliation in terms of a mere reframing of this hierarchical binary, or conversely, as a convergence of nations, for me, neither position fully expresses reconciliation in terms that resonate with Indigenous political thought and my understanding of Indigenous political systems and governance traditions. Reconciliation must be understood as and operationalized according to what Sakej Henderson describes as an implicate order of Mi'kmaq consciousness, or what Leanne Simpson terms *Nishnaabewin* or the practices, theories, and ethics that represent a collective Anishinaabe intelligence or world view.[2] Understood in this way, reconciliation, much like governance, is about living the good life (*miyo pimat'siwin*) or living collectively in accordance within an ecological contextuality, or an ethical relationality, like what grounds Nehiyaw (Cree) teachings, practices, ethics, and philosophy.[3] Simply put, it is an ecologically grounded ethical and political philosophy about how we live together in the best way possible or how we live best together.[4] This is always a process of being and becoming, and a recognition of the omnipresence of flux and fluidity. Thus, reconciliation is a process, an action, something that must be continuously created and maintained. It is, as the Royal Commission on Aboriginal Peoples insisted, about finding a way to live together in a mutually agreeable, mutually beneficial manner. In this way, reconciliation begins, not ends, with acknowledging the past and "saying I am sorry." It extends beyond an act of forgiveness. It is an ongoing national project (really, a multinational project in Canada). It is a political project. It is a social project. It is a legal project. It is a historical project. It is a language project. In sum, reconciliation is a process of being and becoming – a project allowing all peoples and all nations to exist, while determining how it is that we live together on these Indigenous lands.

For several decades now, Asch, Borrows, and Tully have been thinking through some of the big questions, considering how all peoples and all nations can live together on these Indigenous lands. Their combined works have helped define and inspire the reconciliation project in Canada and have certainly influenced my work on Indigenous politics, constitutional politics, and Indigenous–settler relations. Thus, it is a great honour to contribute to this project and to have the opportunity to share my thoughts on reconciliation. Nevertheless, it has been a difficult chapter to write, as I find myself in a constant struggle with the notion of reconciliation, as it is predominantly a settler project and one that is typically grounded in denial. Whilst I have struggled with the ignorance and denial that define much of the current settler discourse, I have at the same time been inspired by the words of Borrows, Asch, and Tully – all of whom conceive of reconciliation in dramatically different ways. Yet, at the same time, they articulate a common vision, which is tied to Indigenous lands and the stories that have been told on those lands for centuries. Despite my struggles, and because of their provocations, I have begun to see reconciliation in a different light and as something that has the potential to be truly transformative, mutually beneficial, and mutually agreeable. Moving beyond my misgivings with settler-centred reconciliation, I draw from Nehiyaw philosophy and stories of reconciliation, to inform our understanding of the writings of Borrows, Asch, and Tully. From this vantage, the transformative potential of our law, which is written on the land, is found by recognizing that it must also revitalize its people through the exercise of personal agency.

Proceed with Caution

According to the Supreme Court,

> What s. 35(1) does is provide the constitutional framework through which the fact that aboriginals lived on the land in distinctive societies, with

their own practices, traditions and cultures, is acknowledged and reconciled with the sovereignty of the Crown. The substantive rights which fall
within the provision must be defined in light of this purpose; the aboriginal rights recognized and affirmed by s. 35(1) must be directed towards
the reconciliation of the pre-existence of aboriginal societies with the sovereignty of the Crown.[5]

Ultimately, it is through negotiated settlements, with good faith and
give and take on all sides, reinforced by the judgments of this Court, that
we will achieve what I stated in *Van der Peet, supra,* at para. 31, to be a basic
purpose of s. 35(1) – "the reconciliation of the pre-existence of aboriginal
societies with the sovereignty of the Crown." Let us face it, we are all here
to stay.[6]

True, we are all here to stay, and we must envision a relationship different from what exists at present. But the state's vision, as expressed by
the courts, negates meaningful reconciliation. The court's unwavering
assumption of Crown sovereignty perpetuates the denial of nationhood
for Indigenous nations and the continued assimilation of Indigenous
peoples as mere subjects of the Crown. Though individual adjudicators
may desire otherwise, the endgame for reconciliation is never about
living together as Canadians (viewed either as two founding nations or
as one multicultural nation). Assimilation, shrouded in the language of
reconciliation, is neither mindful of, nor a means to creating, a mutually agreeable, mutually beneficial relationship that allows us to live
together in the best way possible. Meaningful reconciliation is not and
cannot be about convergence. A convergence of nations through a merg-
ing of sovereignties or an attempt to reconcile the past under a new sovereign is still colonialism and a reification of that binary logic of mutual
exclusivity just in a different guise. Convergence necessarily excludes
meaningful reconciliation. Instead, convergence represents the realization of "the fantasy of the master race," to borrow the language of Ward
Churchill. Pierre Elliott Trudeau sought a triumph of colonialism and
envisioned a "just society" that brought Canadians together as equals,
rejecting special status (or at most a limited recognition of "citizens
plus"), thereby denying the significant legacies of our colonial past.[7]
While convergence may represent meaningful reconciliation for some,
if not most Canadians,[8] it is irrefutably a settler solution to the "Indian/
Canadian problem." It is not, nor has it ever been, a mutually agreeable
or acceptable or mutually beneficial vision of the future for Indigenous
nations. To put it nearly as bluntly, but quite not so eloquently, as Dale

Turner has, this "ideal" construction of the future is without consent – the very consent that is required for meaningful reconciliation.[9]

It is impossible for Indigenous people and Canadians to live together in a mutually agreeable and mutually beneficial manner without a transformation of consciousness. I have often heard elders teach that it is impossible to begin again, or to understand the present and to move forward in a good way, without understanding the past. The problem is, many Canadians live comfortably without knowledge of their own history.[10] Few know or understand about our treaties and the relations upon which this country was built. Oft ignored is the violence perpetrated by the church, the state, and others of settler society against Indigenous peoples, their traditions, their cultures, their languages, and their political and legal systems. They are blissfully unaware that "Indian country" is an occupied territory and that Canada sits on stolen lands. They fail to recognize that, just like previous generations, Canadians today continue to benefit individually and collectively from the dispossession and oppression of Indigenous peoples. They simply do not understand. Worse, many are entirely unaware of their communal ignorance, while others consolidate their collective hallucination of reconciliation by deliberately creating a myth to fit their own reality.

Reconciliation without convergence will require acts of remembrance. That is, reconciliation is an impossible, insurmountable task and process without Canadians first coming to terms with those great myths that deny the past, and in so doing continue to deny Indigenous humanity and rights, both in the past and present. Canada needs to reconcile itself with the great historical myths and lies that form the legal and political bedrock of this nation. Thus Canada not only has to confront its past, it must also confront its mythologized exceptionalism. It is a form of mythologized exceptionalism that constructs Canada as the good colonizer, a peaceful nation that did not engage in Indian wars but has instead always dealt justly with Canada's Indigenous peoples.[11] Canada insists that its history is one of peaceful expansion and fair compensation, whilst claiming to be a nation of "peace, order, and good government." This is what differentiates Canada from its American and Australian cousins.

Though Canada may delight in characterizing itself as a nation of "peace, order, and good government," Canadians must recognize that there is nothing peaceful about colonialism, or orderly in using law to effect the near extermination of other human beings, or goodness expressed through the forced assimilation of those who survived.

Colonialism did not bring peace and order to Indigenous communities, and it has not supported good governance (or anything close to it) for Indigenous nations. Canadians need to understand this. Foundational myths must be dismantled and decolonized. Canadians need to acknowledge and reconcile themselves with the true history of these lands. These lands were already occupied by civilized peoples with spirituality, national territories, systems of governance, laws, and science.[12] Peace did not direct the mind of the colonizer, nor guide their colonial intentions, nor ground their relationship with Indigenous peoples. To frame colonialism in Canada in terms that suggest that it was peaceful and righteous is calculated, utterly disingenuous, and historically inaccurate. Disguising genocide by repackaging and re-presenting it in terms of civilization – a project intent on saving Indigenous peoples from their own supposed inhumanity, savagery, and inferiority – is not only unacceptable, it is counterproductive to reconciliation.

Reconciliation can be achieved only by first destabilizing these foundational myths. Without a robust dismantling of history through education and dialogue, the means to meaningful reconciliation will remain elusive, and the grotesque state vision of a renewed relationship based on assimilation will prevail. Reconciliation must begin with the acknowledgment that our shared histories centre on the deliberate and systematic destruction of Indigenous peoples (as nations and individuals). Without this transformation of perspective, attempts to reconcile are an exercise in futility. Perhaps such a conclusion is a bit too cynical and admittedly more cynical than Borrows's vision of hope, or the road map to reconciliation based upon treaties drawn by Asch. Nevertheless, I would suggest that, while their tone is typically far more positive, Borrows, Asch, and Tully would all agree that meaningful reconciliation requires tremendous transformative change. It requires a paradigm shift.

To understand why this is true, one needs only to look at Australia's Decade of Reconciliation. In 1991, the Australian Parliament voted unanimously on legislation to embarked on a ten-year official reconciliation process. This Decade of Reconciliation was intended to address "Aboriginal disadvantage and aspirations in relation to land, housing, law and justice, cultural heritage, education, employment, health, infrastructure, economic development and other relevant matters."[13] More generally, "this process aimed to reconcile Indigenous and non-Indigenous Australians by the conclusion of the formal process at the end of 2000, in time for the centenary of the Commonwealth of Australia in 2001. This process had three broad goals: to educate the wider Australian community about Indigenous issues and reconciliation; to foster a national commitment to address Indigenous socio-economic disadvantage; and to investigate the desirability of developing a document of reconciliation."[14]

Despite the potential of this process, Aboriginal leaders were gravely disappointed, as the government used this process as an exercise in Australian nation-building, refusing to deal with what the state defined as the "politics of symbolism" (i.e., sovereignty and self-determination) and forcing the process to concentrate on the "practical issues" in people's day-to-day lives.[15] In the end, this process failed to achieve Indigenous objectives, for it deliberately avoided issues that questioned colonialism and the legitimacy of Australian rule. Further, it reinforced the existing homogeneity of the nation by offering to reconcile or bring Aboriginals "into the fold," without altering or challenging the constitutional sensibilities and status of the nation. Reconciliation, therefore, attempted to achieve a mutually agreeable political reconciliation[16] by avoiding the primary issues resulting from colonialism, including land rights, sovereignty, and self-determination. Ultimately, it served to "sustain and legitimate existing inequalities between Indigenous and non-Indigenous peoples in Australia."[17]

Australia's attempt at political reconciliation demonstrates many pitfalls in the framing, restriction, and avoidance of the real issues (not to mention the mammoth task of re-educating a settler-nation in its near entirety). This is not to suggest that such processes are devoid of benefit, for this is surely not the case. The Council for Aboriginal Reconciliation and its legacy organization, Reconciliation Australia, have increased settler knowledge about Indigenous people within settler society. Similarly, more recent initiatives such as the National Apology to the Stolen Generation, Closing the Gap policies, and the current constitutional renewal all provide opportunity for dialogue.[18] Nonetheless, neither transformative change nor meaningful reconciliation appears to be on the horizon as the big issues are still being avoided.

As Australia demonstrates, there is most definitely a lack of political will within both settler governments and, more generally, settler society at large, to embark on the kind of transformative politics that is necessary to engage in meaningful reconciliation. I doubt the situation in Canada is very different. That said, I heed the words of Borrows, Tully, and Asch, and I acknowledge their hope and vision. They inspire me to keep walking towards the transformative paradigmatic shift that is required and to honour a fundamentally different understanding of the land and the voices (past, present, and future) that emanate from it.

Lessons from the Land

As Borrows reminds us, the land, the wind, and the waters have lessons to teach – "the law is written on the land" – and many Indigenous nations share this perspective. The stories of old exist on our land, and new stories flow from it every day. Indigenous languages speak of their lands and reflect their relationship to the land. Words capture the manifestations of generations of experience – the *kisikano wapahc'kewin* (observations of the world).[19] The stories express generations of knowledge gathered, created, and shared by people seeking both *miyo wice'tawin* (getting along together or living together with trust and respect) and *wahkohtawin* (kinship or a web of relationships). That is to say, the stories of old tell of the process of living together as a people in a relationship to territory, based upon an understanding of what Henderson refers to as an "implicate order."[20] Collectively, the languages, stories, songs, and ceremonies represent the legal, political, and historical archives of Indigenous peoples over several millennia. They ground the legal and political orders, developed over generations, based upon an understanding of *miyo pimat'sawin*, *kisikano wapahc'kewin*, *miyo wice'tawin*, and *wahkohtawin*. In this way, Indigenous laws and systems of governance express an understanding of the way to live best together as people and in relationship to a territory and all other beings (human and non-human) in a given territory.

Many scholars, including Borrows, Napoleon, Little Bear, Simpson, and Henderson, point to stories, ceremonies, songs, and languages as vital repositories of Indigenous knowledges, philosophies, histories, and ways of being and relating to the world. Stories, songs, ceremonies, and languages provide a foundation for decolonization and the resurgence of Indigenous legal, political, spiritual, and economic traditions. For the purposes of this chapter, the importance of songs, ceremonies, and stories goes far beyond discourses of anti-assimilation, decolonization, and resurgence, as they provide a basis for meaningful, transformative reconciliation. Three stories illustrate this and help connect the work of Borrows, Asch, and Tully to a transformative understanding of reconciliation, one that has grounded my understanding of a Nehiyaw implicate order and an ethical relationality.

The idea of *kanistineaux* (a great flood) is common among Indigenous peoples across the Americas and is found in the stories of Judaism and Christianity, as well as other religious and intellectual traditions.[21] Most of these stories talk of a great turmoil in ancient times that was brought about by an imbalance in the relations between beings (humans and non-humans). Many of our stories teach that the imbalance was caused by broken promises and breaches in the treaties that had been negotiated between the beings that shared a territory. Others speak of this as one of great reckoning and vision, and how peoples responded to the turmoil and flux in order to create something very different. The Niitsitapi (Blackfoot Confederacy) have a story that I remember as "Some Old Man Likes Some Old Woman." It is typically told as part of a larger creation story, such as that relayed by anthropologists Wissler and Duval:

The Making of the Earth

During the flood, Old Man was sitting on the highest mountain with all the beasts. The flood was caused by the above people, because the baby (a fungus) of the woman who married a star was heedlessly torn in pieces by an Indian child. Old Man sent the Otter down to get some earth. For a long time he waited, then the Otter came up dead. Old Man examined its feet, but found nothing on them. Next he sent Beaver down, but after a long time he also came up drowned. Again nothing was found on his feet. He sent Muskrat to dive next. Muskrat also drowned. At length he sent the Duck ... It was drowned, but in its foot it held some earth. Old Man saw it, put it in his hand, feigned putting it on the water three times, and at last dropped it. Then the above-people sent rain, and everything grew on the earth.

Languages Confused on a Mountain

After the flood, Old Man mixed water with different colors. He whistled, and all the people came together. He gave one man a cup of one kind of water, saying, "You will be chief of these people here." To another man he gave differently colored water, and so on. The Blackfoot, Piegan [*sic*] and Blood all received Black water. Then he said to the people, "Talk," and they all talked differently; but those who drank the Black water spoke the same. This happened on the highest mountain in the Montana Reservation ...

The First Marriage

Now in those days, the men and the women did not live together. The men lived in one camp and the women in the other. The men lived in lodges made of skin with the hair on; the women in good lodges. One day Old Man came to the camp of the men, and, when he was there, a woman came over from the camp of the women. She said she had been sent by the chief of the women to invite all the men, because the women were going to pick out husbands.

Now the men began to get ready, and Old Man dressed himself up in his finest clothes: he was always fine looking. Then they started out and, when they came to the women's camp, they all stood up in a row. Now the chief of the women came out to make the first choice. She had on very dirty clothes, and none of the men knew who she was. She went along the line, looked them over, and finally picked out Old Man, because of his appearance. Now Old Man saw many nicely dressed women waiting their turn, and when the chief of the women took him by the hand, he pulled back and broke away. He did this because he thought her a very common woman. When he pulled away, the chief of the women went back to her lodge and instructed the other women not to choose Old Man ...

After a while all the men had been picked out, except Old Man. Now he was very angry; but the chief woman said to him, "After this you are to be a tree, and are to stand just where you are now." Then he became a tree, and he is yet mad, because he is always caving down the bank.[22]

Turmoil did not end with the flood. Stories such as those involving the tricksters remind us that humans are not the most intelligent beings and that they often require many attempts just to get the simplest of things right. Even then, they most often need assistance, as is evidenced by the abundance of stories that tell of humans learning from others about how to live in their territories in the best way possible – in a way that embraced teachings of mutual respect, mutual responsibility, and mutual benefit. The Anishinaabe (like others) have a story of a treaty with the Hoof Clan, encapsulated in this contemporary version by Simpson:

In a time long ago, all the Waawaashkeshiwag, Moozoog, and Adikwag, the deer, the moose, and the caribou, suddenly disappeared from Kina Gchi Nishnaabeg-ogaming.

Well, maybe it wasn't so suddenly. At first, nobody noticed. The relatives of the Hoof Clan had to be very patient. But, after a while, people were starting to notice some changes.

In fall, dagwaagin, hunters, came back with no meat.

When snow blanketed the earth, the people didn't even see a single track in the snow – even for the whole bboon!

By ziigwan, the people were getting worried. No one had seen a deer for nearly a year. No one had seen a moose for nearly a year, and no one could even remember the last time they saw a caribou …

So, those Nishinaabeg decided to do something before everything got all lost. They got up before the sun one morning, lit a sacred fire. They prayed, sang, and offered their semaa.

After a long discussion, where everyone spoke what was in their hearts, the people decided to send their fastest runners out in the four directions to find those hoofed ones.

Those runners ran for four days. Ziigwan was the first to come back. She hadn't seen so much as a tuft of hair. Then Niibin arrived, exhausted, and reported the same. When Dagwaagin came back, he reported that he'd seen no evidence of deer, moose, or caribou either.

Finally, Bboon returned. He was exhausted and said, "When I was in the very north part of our land, I saw one young deer. She explained to me that her relatives had left our territory forever because they felt disrespected."

The people didn't know what to do, so they decided to go and meet with the oldest and wisest people they knew. Those Elders decided to send a delegation of diplomats, spiritual people, and mediators to go and visit the Hoof Clan.

After some negotiation, the people learned that the Hoof Clan had left their territory because the Nishnaabeg were no longer honouring them. They had been wasting their meat and not treating their bodies with the proper reverence. The Hoof Clan had withdrawn from the territory and their relationship with the Nishnaabeg. They had stopped participating.

The diplomats, spiritual people, and mediators just listened. They listened to all the stories the Hoof Clan had to share. They spent several long days of listening, of acknowledging, of discussing, and of negotiating. All the parties thought about what they could give up to restore the relationship. Finally, the Hoof Clan and the Nishnaabeg agreed to honour and respect the lives and beings of the Hoof Clan, in life and in death …

In exchange, the Hoofed Animals would return to our territory so that Nishnaabeg people could feed themselves and their families. They agreed to give up their lives whenever the Nishnaabeg were in need.[23]

Just as we see today, humans did not learn to get along with all other beings after the flood. Turmoil persisted and from time to time devastated relations between both individuals and collectivities (human and non-human). The Haudenosaunee story about the creation of the *Kaienerekowa* or the Great Law of Peace recounts a time of great violence and grief among the Haudenosaunee peoples and how the Peacemaker brought forward a new political and social tradition based upon a philosophy of living together nicely based upon the teachings of peace, power, and righteousness. A very condensed version of this story is recounted below.

> Long ago, the Haudenosaunee Nations were at war with each other. A man called the Peacemaker wanted to spread peace and unity throughout Haudenosaunee territory. While on his journey, the Peacemaker came to the house of an Onondaga leader named Hayo'wetha (hi-an-WEN-ta), more commonly known as Hiawatha. Hayo'wetha believed in the message of peace and wanted the Haudenosaunee people to live in a united way. An evil Onondaga leader called Tadadaho, who hated the message of peace, had killed Hayo'wetha's wife and daughters during the violent times. Tadadaho was feared by all; he was perceived as being so evil that his hair was comprised of writhing snakes, symbolizing his twisted mind. The Peacemaker helped Hayo'wetha mourn his loss and ease his pain. Hayo'wetha then traveled with the Peacemaker to help unite the Haudenosaunee.
>
> The Peacemaker used arrows to demonstrate the strength of unity. First, he took a single arrow and broke it in half. Then he took five arrows and tied them together. This group of five arrows could not be broken. The Peacemaker said, "A single arrow is weak and easily broken. A bundle of arrows tied together cannot be broken. This represents the strength of having a confederacy. It is strong and cannot be broken." The Mohawk, Oneida, Cayuga, Seneca, and Onondaga accepted the message of peace. With the nations joined together, the Peacemaker and Hayo'wetha sought out Tadadaho. As they approached Tadadaho, he resisted their invitation to join them. The Peacemaker promised Tadadaho that if he accepted the message of peace, Onondaga would be the capital of the Grand Council. Tadadaho finally succumbed to the message of peace. It is said that the messengers of peace combed the snakes from his hair. The name Hayo'we:tha means "he who combs," indicating his role in convincing Tadadaho to accept the Great Law of Peace. Joined together, these five nations became known as the Haudenosaunee Confederacy.
>
> When peace had successfully been spread among the five nations, the people gathered together to celebrate. They uprooted a white pine tree

and threw their weapons into the hole. They replanted the tree on top of the weapons and named it the Tree of Peace, which symbolizes the Great Law of Peace that the Haudenosaunee came to live by. The four main roots of the Tree of Peace represent the four directions and the paths of peace that lead to the heart of Haudenosaunee territory, where all who want to follow the Great Law of Peace are welcome. At the top of the Tree of Peace is an eagle, guardian of the Haudenosaunee and messenger to the Creator.

The Peacemaker then asked each nation to select men to be their leaders called *hoyaneh* (plural, *hodiyahnehsonh*). The Peacemaker gave the laws to the Haudenosaunee men, who formed the Grand Council. The Grand Council, made up of fifty hoyaneh, makes decisions following the principles set forth in the Great Law of Peace. When decisions are made or laws passed, all council members must agree on the issue; this is called CONSENSUS.[24]

Understanding These Lessons

All three of these stories speak to reconciliation in a manner that presents transformative change as a requirement for reconciliation, as envisioned at the outset of this chapter. The reconciliation that each speaks of is active and dynamic; it did not simply fall out of the sky, it came as peoples learnt from the turmoil caused by their actions and misdeeds. Simply recognizing that there had been a wrongdoing and apologizing for it did not lead to reconciliation between men and women, or between the Anishinaabe and the hoof clans, or among the peoples who became the Haudenosaunee. The stories all demonstrate that reconciliation is set in motion by humans working to transform their nations and their relations with "other." Human agency is key to effecting reconciliation.

Borrows's work brings an Anishinaabe understanding of law and its relationship to territory: "The law is written on the land." Earth's teachings have been interpreted, retold, and analysed by Indigenous peoples for centuries, taking shape through their relationships with the land and beings in their territories. Earth's teachings, the legal and political traditions that are set out in relationship to territory, and the stories of generations of each peoples, their life in and experiences with a territory, provide a foundation for future Indigenous peoples and for a means towards meaningful reconciliation. What we see at work is the need for more than an intellectual engagement that inspires conversations about resurgence (of law, language, ceremony, and governance) and reconciliation (within and among Indigenous peoples and other beings within our territories). Our stories show that reconciliation requires people to move beyond (the sometimes) exclusionary conversations among word warriors and activists.[25]

Much like Borrows continues to expound, Indigenous law is written on the land. When we pick up those laws, those stories, and that sense of being and becoming, we begin to understand that the land, our relationality, and Indigenous legal traditions based on that land provide strength, vision, and (non-coercive) power. We better understand that this relationship carries responsibility for a broader, more inclusive community. Knowing the law and understanding collective responsibility for territory is insufficient, given the history of British settler societies and the logics of settler-colonialism. Transformation is possible only when people engage collectively and hold steadfast to both territory and law to rebuild their relationships, both within and between nations.

To draw this discussion back to the stories told herein, it is interesting to note that each of these stories speaks to the necessity of human agency in securing transformative change and thus the rebuilding both of nations and of relations between nations. Each draws from the lessons of the land to tell these stories of reconciliation and reminds us that leadership and collective action was needed to overcome the turmoil that characterized the relations between beings (be that men/ women, human/non-human beings or nations). Reconciliation was achieved through a new sense of peace and good governance within a territory as genders, beings, and nations worked to forge a new reality, based upon a shared understanding of *miyo pimat'sawin, kisikano wapahc'kewin, miyo wice'tawin*, and *wahkohtawin*. Further, these collectives of stories (led and inspired by individuals) reveal reconciliation through transformative change. The stories tell of a transformative change brought about as people worked out a new way to live together in the best way possible, grounded in mutual responsibility, mutual benefit, and mutual respect.

For example, the Blackfoot story of reconciliation and renewal told above speaks about a time of great unrest and turmoil, wherein men and women lived apart. As a result of reconciliation, the Blackfoot peoples embodied a new political and legal order, grounded in territory and based upon how the people chose to live together the best way possible. Through this exercise of personal agency, they created a complex, multi-institutional consensus-based system of governance that was devoid of hierarchical and authoritative power and in which both men and women (really all genders) participated within governing processes.[26] Thus, in this case, transformative change meant that a brand new political and legal order was created through the development of *okahn* (the camp circle, which brings together the political, legal, spiritual, and cultural "bodies" of the Blackfoot nations through the gathering of their clans, societies, and bundles), with the explicit intent of living a good life and ensuring good relations among Niitsitapi and with all other beings in the territory. The Blackfoot, rejecting reformative change through reconciliation grounded in binary logics, instead sought a form of reconciliation that completely transformed Blackfoot society, gender constructs, and their political and legal orders as a whole.

Similarly, the story of the Haudenosaunee also tells of a time of great conflict, sorrow, and turmoil within and between the constituent nations. Out of this state of political, social, and economic instability came the Peacemaker's vision of reconciliation and renewal. With great effort, this vision was realized, and a new constitutional order and confederacy of five nations was created through the *Kaienerekowa* (the Great Law of Peace). My understanding is that this constitutional order is fundamentally an attempt to create and maintain that peace and righteousness, premised on the Peacemaker's vision and understanding of the way a people live best together. This new way of living together as individuals and as nations was transformative, as it brought a new political, social, and legal order to the peoples, the clans, the nations, and the confederacy. That is to say, the creation and adoption of the *Kaienerekowa* represents a transformative reconciliation within and between the constituent nations.

In many respects, the transformative change imagined in each of these stories reminds me of Tully's twenty-plus years of thinking through reconciliation. That a parallel exists between Tully and these stories is not surprising, given that he drew his inspiration for *Strange Multiplicity* directly from Indigenous stories of transformative reconciliation and renewal – namely the Great Law of Peace and the stories of Haida Gwaii.[27] In turn, *Strange Multiplicity* has inspired conversations among the intellectual elite, grappling with Tully's vision of and the need to reform Canadian constitutionalism in a manner that is totally inclusive of Canada's national and multicultural diversity. Though it did not seek a new political order and offered largely a reformative vision of reconciliation, Tully's work was transformative in the sense that it radically altered the intellectual conversations in law, constitutional politics, and philosophy – as people confronted Canada's diversity, and issues of legal pluralism, multiculturalism, and federalism. Alongside Tully's new work, which links reconciliation to settler society's need to find a new way to live on Indigenous lands, it is clear that Tully is wrestling with transformative change as he imagines meaningful reconciliation among peoples and between people and territory. As such, Tully's vision is fundamental for achieving the type of transformative change that reconciliation requires. Thus we agree: we cannot even begin to talk about a meaningful reconciliation of nations until the settler nation(s) deals with its mythologized past and acknowledges itself as living on and benefiting from wealth that was acquired through theft and fraud.

As Tully's current work evokes conversations among a global intellectual elite concerning the need to transform settler colonialism, and the need for settler society to engage in a meaningful reconciliation with someone else's territory, Borrows continues to inspire conversations about engaging reconciliation and renewal, within both Indigenous communities and Canada as a whole.[28] Leaving aside Borrows's often discussed vision of reconciliation through a renewal of Canada and of the relationship between Indigenous peoples and their legal orders and Canada and its legal orders, it is important to understand his vision for reconciling communities from within.[29] For years his work has encouraged, influenced, and inspired Indigenous peoples (the intellectual elite, the legal profession, and community leadership, in particular) to pick up stories and traditional teachings and to use them as a foundation for rebuilding and renewing Indigenous nations. He has demonstrated that stories and teachings are vestibules of our law and political orders, containing vital principles, such as the seven grandfathers that can guide the renewal of communities and their institutions (including the Indian Act system of band council government).[30]

Borrows's vision of reconciliation has been concerned largely with renewal and institutional reform. But at its core, his vision is one of transformative potential, or to put it in his terms, emancipatory power. This is because he is engaging a process of reconciliation that could result in transformative change, that asks leaders and communities to work through their traditions as they decide how to govern themselves today. Such a process not only requires a reconciliation of tradition with contemporary realities of settler colonialism, but it also requires communities to engage in reconciliation within, as they (re)create a legal and political order. It is here that I see the transformative power of Borrows's emancipatory vision, as the laws and the stories that are written on the land speak of a different legal, political, and social reality, which is tied to this land and connects a people to the land. Further, these same laws and stories also speak of the human agency necessary to create and sustain the type of transformative change needed. This is evident in the stories retold herein.

Transformative change requires human agency, as we cannot rely simply on the speaking of words and hope that those words inspire conversations and provoke action beyond the usual circles of the intellectual elite. Communities need to be empowered to be the agents of change. Communities need to reimagine themselves and to actively engage in meaningful reconciliation in a way that draws from the past and dreams in the future. Undoubtedly this will be difficult as the colonization of the nation (collectively, institutionally, individually, territorially, and spiritually) is addressed. This process requires individuals and collectives to rethink who they are and to build a new future by addressing core issues such as gender relations, power imbalances, and responsibilities to territory. It requires an understanding of community and kinship that addresses the impact of the state and settler colonialism and its creation of a diaspora of so-called non-status Indians. Communities must address these hard questions and think through how they want to live together in the best way possible. If such processes are to be truly transformative, communities need to collectively engage in the creation of new social, legal, and political orders. This is no small task, but as the stories told herein demonstrate, it can be done.

Similarly, Asch also plants the seed for transformative change in his treaty-based vision of reconciliation. Like so many others, in most instances I see treaties as having already reconciled Indigenous nations with the Canadian nation. Our treaties set forth an understanding of how Indigenous nations and the Queen's people would live together, as separate nations within a shared territory, in a mutually beneficial, mutually agreeable, and mutually respectful manner. The problem, as Asch so clearly states, is that Canada has by and large ignored the treaties and acted as if the legitimacy and authority of Canada is vested in the simple facts of power and population and the myth of superiority. That is to say, it is assumed that "might makes right," justifying the existence of Canada and legitimating its continued colonization and occupation by Canadians. This is the same mindful bliss, ignorance, and settler amnesia that causes me to struggle with the very notion of reconciliation in the contemporary world. Simply put, how does one reconcile with settler peoples who do not know their own history, let alone understand our shared history? Thus, as I stated earlier, reconciliation without convergence will require acts of remembrance.

Asch's work resonates as an act of remembrance and is aimed at educating settler society by unpacking our shared treaty history. He accomplishes this by explaining how to re-examine key tenets of Western Eurocentric thought that reify colonial claims of legitimacy and authority. While his work is not in and of itself a road map for reconciliation based upon the treaties, it does lay a foundation for, and present a vision of, transformative change and thus, meaningful reconciliation between Indigenous nations and the settler state. To achieve this, however, Canadians must not only learn to deal with their mythologized exceptionalism, but they will truly need to grasp what it means to be a treaty person and a member of a treaty nation. True, "treaties offer us the means to reconcile the fact that 'we are all here to stay' with the fact that there were people already here when they first arrived."[31] However, treaties also establish a relationship of *miyo wice'tawin* (getting along together) and *wahkohtawin* (kinship or a web of relationships) between sovereign nations and establish the terms by which they will live together in the territory. Asch recognizes this as he presents his vision for reconciliation based upon the reaffirmation and renewal of a nation-to-nation relationship. He promotes an understanding of Indigenous sovereignties through economic coexistence, which allows for the type of mutual prosperity that was imagined in treaties.

Closing Thoughts

My vision of reconciliation requires a transformation of a magnitude rarely advocated, since it requires much more than a redistribution of power and resources. Both Indigenous nations and the settler state will need to come to terms with what it means to have multiple nations occupying the same space. We will need to find a way to live together, in a mutually respectful, mutually agreeable, and mutually beneficial way on Indigenous lands. We will each need to find a way to govern ourselves in this new reality of *miyo pimat'sawin, miyo wice'tawin,* and *wahkohtawin* while also finding new ways of working and living together without convergence. Figuring this out requires a meaningful reconciliation within each nation as well as between nations. It requires the kind of transformative change that Borrows, Asch, and Tully (among others) have begun to imagine. It also requires the kind of transformative change that was evident in the stories told herein.

NOTES

1 I acknowledge that this conceptualization of colonialism is borrowed, though I am unsure about the source.

2 Sakej Henderson, "Governing the Implicate Order: Self-Government and the Linguistic Development of Aboriginal Communities," in *Les droits linguistiques au Canada: Collusions ou collisions?* ed. S. Léger, 295–301 (Ottawa: Canadian Centre for Linguistic Rights, University of Ottawa, 1995); Leanne Simpson in discussion with the author, 18 March 2016.

3 Dwayne Donald in discussion with the author, 18 March 2016.

4 For a more thorough discussion of how governance can be created as a response to and grounded in an understanding of the way a people lives best together, see Kiera Ladner, "Governing within an Ecological Context: Creating an AlterNative Understanding of Blackfoot Governance," *Studies in Political Economy* 70 (2003): 125.

5 *R v Van der Peet*, [1996] 2 SCR 507 at para 31.

6 *Delgamuukw v British Columbia* [1997] 3 SCR 1010 at para 186.

7 See Ward Churchill, *Fantasies of the Master Race: Literature, Cinema, and the Colonization of American Indians* (San Francisco: City Lights Books, 1998); Pierre Elliott Trudeau, "The Just Society," official statement by the prime minister, 10 June 1968; Government of Canada, Department of Indian Affairs and Northern Development, *The White Paper: Statement of the Government of Canada on Indian Policy* (Ottawa: Queen's Printer, 1969); Alan Cairns, *Citizens Plus: Aboriginal Peoples and the Canadian State* (Vancouver: UBC Press, 2000).

8 See Mordecai Richler, *Oh Canada! Oh Quebec!: Requiem for a Divided Country* (Toronto: Penguin Books, 1992); Tom Flanagan, *First Nations, Second Thoughts?* (Montreal and Kingston: McGill-Queen's University Press, 2000).

9 See Dale Turner, *This Is Not a Peace Pipe: Towards a Critical Indigenous Philosophy* (Toronto: University of Toronto Press, 2006); Dale Turner, "Aboriginal Relations in Canada: The Importance of Political Reconciliation," Equity Matters, blog, 2011, http://www.ideas-idees.ca/blog/aboriginal-relations-canada-importance-political-reconciliation.

10 Truth and Reconciliation Commission of Canada, *Honouring the Truth, Reconciling for the Future: Summary of the Final Report of the Truth and Reconciliation Commission of Canada* (Winnipeg: Truth and Reconciliation Commission of Canada, 2015); *Report of the Royal Commission on Aboriginal Peoples* (Ottawa: Indian and Northern Affairs Canada, 1996); Government of Ontario, *Report of the Ipperwash Inquiry* (Toronto: Government of Ontario, 2007).

11 I use "Canada's" Indigenous peoples here to denote that sense of ownership and subjugation.

12 See Vine Deloria Jr, *God Is Red: A Native View of Religion* (Vancouver: Fulcrum Publishing, 1994); Ladner, "Governing within an Ecological Context"; Vine Deloria Jr, *Red Earth, White Lies: Native Americans and the Myth of Scientific Fact* (Vancouver: Fulcrum Publishing, 1995).

13 Kiera Ladner, "Take 35: Reconciling Constitutional Orders," in *First Nations, First Thoughts: The Impact of Indigenous Thought in Canada,* ed. Annis May Timpsons (Vancouver: UBC Press, 2009), 286–7.

14 Andrew Gunstone, *Unfinished Business: The Australian Formal Reconciliation Process* (Melbourne: Australian Scholarly Publishing, 2007), 89, 290.

15 See Damien Short, "Reconciliation, Assimilation, and the Indigenous Peoples of Australia," *International Political Science Review* 24 (2003): 491.

16 According to de Gruchy, political reconciliation "refers to projects such as the process of national reconciliation in South Africa, the overcoming of sectretarianism in Northern Ireland, or the achievement of sustainable peace in the Middle East." John W. de Gruchy, *Reconciliation: Restoring Justice* (Minneapolis: Fortress, 2002), 26.

17 Martha Augoustinos, Amanda LeCouteur, and A. John Soyland, "Self-sufficient Arguments in Political Rhetoric: Constructing Reconciliation and Apologizing to the Stolen Generations," *Discourse & Society* 13, no. 1 (2002): 105.

18 See Megan Davis and George Williams, *Everything You Need to Know about the Referendum to Recognise the Indigenous Australians* (Sydney: University of New South Wales Press, 2015); Prime Minister Rudd, "Apology to Australia's Indigenous Peoples," 13 February 2008, https://www.australia.gov.au/about-australia/our-country/our-people/apology-to-australias-indigenous-peoples; Council of Australian Governments, *National Indigenous Reform Agreement (Closing the Gap)* (Canberra: Council of Australian Governments, 2008). http://www.federalfinancialrelations.gov.au/content/npa/health/_archive/indigenous-reform/national-agreement_sept_12.pdf.

19 See Henderson, "Governing the Implicate Order."

20 Ibid.

21 See Deloria Jr, *God Is Red;* and indeed amongst many Indigenous peoples globally.

22 Clark Wissler and D.C. Duvall, *Mythology of the Blackfoot Indians* (Lincoln: University of Nebraska Press, 1995), 19–23. I use this version of the story because it already appears in print.

23 Leanne Simpson, *The Gift Is in the Making: Anishinaabeg Stories* (Winnipeg: Highwater, 2013), 9–11.

24 National Museum of the American Indian, "Haudenosaunee Guide for Educators" (New York: Smithsonian Institution, 2009), 2–3, http://nmai.si.edu/sites/1/files/pdf/education/HaudenosauneeGuide.pdf.
25 See Turner, *This Is Not a Peace Pipe.*
26 See Ladner, "Governing within an Ecological Context"; Kiera Ladner, "When Buffalo Speak: Creating an Alternative Understanding of Traditional Blackfoot Governance" (PhD diss., Carleton University, 2001).
27 See James Tully, *Strange Multiplicity: Constitutionalism in an Age of Diversity* (Cambridge: Cambridge University Press, 1995).
28 See John Borrows, *Recovering Canada: The Resurgence of Indigenous Law* (Toronto: University of Toronto Press, 2002).
29 See John Borrows, *Drawing Out Law: A Spirit's Guide* (Toronto: University of Toronto Press, 2010).
30 See John Borrows, "Seven Generations, Seven Teachings: Ending the Indian Act" (Vancouver, National Centre for First Nations Governance, 2008), http://fngovernance.org/resources_docs/7_Generations_7_Teachings.pdf.
31 Michael Asch, *On Being Here to Stay: Treaties and Aboriginal Rights in Canada* (Toronto: University of Toronto Press, 2014), 152.

9 Learning from the Earth, Learning from Each Other: Ethnoecology, Responsibility, and Reciprocity

NANCY J. TURNER AND PAMELA SPALDING

Introduction

Hishuk ish ts'awalk, or "everything is one," embodies the Nuu-Chah-Nulth sacredness and respect for all life forms and their approach to resource stewardship.[1]

The Nuu-chah-nulth epigraph is just one of countless messages in hundreds of Indigenous languages that reflect people's relationships with their homelands and with the other species of the planet. This phrase, explained and elaborated by Atleo,[2] became the motto of the eighteen-member Scientific Panel for Sustainable Forest Practices in Clayoquot Sound, of which Dr Atleo was co-chair, along with wildlife ecologist Fred Bunnell. The work of the Scientific Panel,[3] although focused on only one region of Nuu-chah-nulth territory along the central west coast of Vancouver Island, with its beginnings over twenty years ago, stands as a potential model for ways in which Indigenous and non-Indigenous people can come together with respect to address a mutual goal of reducing our human impact on the earth, together reconnecting with landscapes in which we are embedded, and finding more sustainable ways to harvest and use forest resources.

In the initial chapters of this volume, the challenges we face are set out clearly. We presently have a tremendous opportunity for reconciliation between non-Indigenous peoples and Indigenous peoples in Canada, after over a century of relationships of domination, discrimination, and assumptions of superiority by the (mostly) Euro-Canadian settlers. As Justice Murray Sinclair emphasized, "Reconciliation is about forging and maintaining respectful relationships. There are no shortcuts."[4]

Furthermore, this reconciliation cannot be achieved without reconciling our way of life with the earth itself – with all of the earth's life-forms and entities on which we completely depend. As Tully writes, "The unsustainable and crisis-ridden relationship between Indigenous and non-Indigenous people that we are trying to reconcile has its deepest roots in the unsustainable and crisis-ridden relationship between human beings and the living earth."[5]

Borrows[6] points out that, even in the present day, over thirty years after the repatriation of the Canadian Constitution and nearly twenty years after the Royal Commission Report on Aboriginal Peoples,[7] "Aboriginal peoples' lives are drastically shorter than other Canadians and marked by more suffering as measured by considerably higher rates of poverty, injury, and incarceration, and significantly lower levels of education, income, and health." Asch describes how treaties between First Peoples and newcomer governments, created and signed on many occasions, have not been properly adhered to in spirit, let alone in practice, by government officials and their successors.[8] Since these treaties in general relate to upholding First Peoples' rights to use their lands and resources (even if in somewhat limited ways), failure to uphold their stated commitments has resulted in losses of First Nations' food and other resources, losses of their ability to maintain and sustain these resources, and, ultimately, a marked decrease in their capacity to pass on their important cultural knowledge, practices, and underlying belief systems to younger generations. This knowledge is key to Indigenous peoples' ability to maintain their identity and to thrive within their traditional territories and beyond. It is perhaps even more important to stress because suppression of intergenerational knowledge transmission is less recognized than some other impacts.[9] Furthermore, intergenerational learning is critical to reversing the unsustainable relationship with the living earth noted by Tully and so prevalent in the world's mainstream societies.

Clearly, if we in dominant Canadian society are to reconcile ourselves with Indigenous peoples, we need to live up to the treaties that have been signed by our governments, as well as follow through on the policies that were established at the time of the initial contact between First Nations and the settler governments. We are obligated to support Indigenous peoples' rights (including title) and to ensure that, as Canada's First Peoples, they are able to thrive, to maintain their own languages and cultural distinctiveness, to benefit from the resources of their own territories, and to achieve their cultural responsibilities to "maintain, nurture and preserve" their lands and resources for the future.[10] We need to go even further, if we want true reconciliation. We all need to strive to understand and learn from Indigenous peoples, so that we can broaden our perspectives and embrace, in a respectful way, their teachings and approaches. This may allow us to develop more conciliatory and sustainable lifestyles and reduce our destructive behaviours towards the earth and the other species on which we all rely. We all need to become "caretakers for the generations to come."[11]

Ethnoecology includes not only the study of practical factual knowledge (e.g., about plants and animals that can be used as sources of food, materials, or medicines, where they are found and how they can be harvested and prepared), but also of people's attitudes, world views, and values as they pertain to the environment. It also examines modes of communicating and transmitting traditional ecological knowledge, as well as the cultural institutions that facilitate and perpetuate this knowledge and its applications. One role of ethnoecology is to document peoples' varying perspectives of species, places, and natural processes and to determine how these different points of view determine our actions, practices, and relationships to the lands and waters around us. Ethnoecological knowledge is useful in informing past land and resource use (when used in concert with archeological and historical data) and also with charting the changes to and adaptive practices in land use over time. Specifically when we just focus on humans' use and relationships to plants – captured in the study of ethnobotany – we acquire many insights into changing relationships to cultural landscapes and key places for Indigenous groups. All humans use plants for food, and as materials and medicines. As such, knowledge of and relationships to plants and their habitats serve as an ideal medium through which to conduct cross-cultural and historical analyses of human-environment interactions.

The varied faces and textures of colonialism, and the relationships between Indigenous and non-Indigenous populations of Canada, are reflected in aspects of ethnoecological and ethnobotanical research. At the centre of some of the most serious conflicts are the ways in which resources are used, and associated clashes of values, within the lands and waters of Indigenous peoples' traditional homelands. These deep conflicts are embedded within fundamentally different world views between European settlers and First Nations peoples of cultural norms regarding individual and communal "ownership" of lands and resources.[12] In this chapter, we apply the lens of ethnoecology to facilitate understanding of Indigenous and colonial relationships with place and outline some of the potential insights that this research can provide. First, we explore at some length how the First Nations' relationships with plants and associated landscapes were severed by the impact of newcomer settler groups. We then discuss mechanisms through which reconciliation has been and can be achieved, in part, through resurgence efforts, and we examine more closely examples of resurgence stemming from collaborative ethnoecological research.

Indigenous peoples' ecological knowledge systems, known collectively as traditional ecological knowledge, incorporate an entire "cumulative body of knowledge, practice and belief, evolving by adaptive processes and handed down through generations by cultural transmission."[13] It is important to recognize that every cultural group has its own body of ethnoecological knowledge, and, furthermore, that much of this knowledge is specialized and held by different individuals and groups within a given community. For example, men and women often hold different types of knowledge, and those who specialize in certain areas – such as weather forecasting, fishing, canoe building, or medicine – will have very specific knowledge, acquired through training and guided experience. Leaders and "chiefs" are usually recognized and trained from a very early age to be able to take on the roles prescribed for them through inheritance or other selection processes.

One of the main goals of ethnoecology is to understand how humans can live sustainably within our environments, to learn about what models we can follow, and how we can maintain and enhance our relationships with other species and our own cultural diversity. Practices and knowledge relating to traditional land and resource management – sustaining and enhancing resource productivity over time – may serve as an effective window, both into changes in Indigenous societies, their lands, and resources, and into the potential for restoration of lands and management systems in contemporary society. In fact, Thornton, Deur, and Kitka Sr suggest that "the *cultivation of relationships* [emphasis added], rather than the management of resources, becomes the critical matrix for sustainability behaviour."[14] Thus, sustaining respectful relationships is seen to be a key to reconciliation both between settler and Indigenous groups, and between humans and our environments.

First Nations of western Canada, as of many parts of North America, have commonly been referred to as "hunter-gatherers." This term, however, does not do justice to the complex and productive systems people developed for sustaining the resources on which they have relied for thousands of years.[15] These systems include strategies and techniques for food production and for harvesting materials and medicines, most tightly aligned with natural processes, such as periodic burning of particular landscapes, pruning berry bushes, tilling soils, and selective harvesting. They also incorporate effective social systems of regulation and, over time, incorporate complex belief systems, in which strategies for maintaining and enhancing the species and resources on which they depend become encoded in stories, taboos, ceremonies, art, and ethics within a given culture. Overall, traditional management approaches have maintained and enhanced ecological and biological diversity in First Nations' territories. As active managers of their resources, Indigenous peoples of western Canada, at the very least, should be recognized as "complex cultivators" and astute managers of their landscapes and resource species. These practices involve indigenous plants that are largely unknown to most Canadians. For over a century, by characterizing the land outside of the minority urban lands in British Columbia as either "uncultivated waste lands" to be developed, or "pristine wilderness" to be protected, the governing society effectively scrubbed out the potential for acknowledging, sustaining, and restoring First Nations' relationships and proprietorship of plants and habitats in this region.

Seeing without Understanding

In Two Places particularly, we saw several Acres of Clover growing with a Luxuriance and Compactness more *resembling the close Sward of a well-managed Lea than the Produce of an uncultivated Waste.*[16]

For example, when Chief Factor James Douglas (later Governor Sir James Douglas, KCB) arrived on southern Vancouver Island in 1841, to evaluate the area we now call Victoria as a potential site for a Hudson's Bay Company fort, he, like others before him, was struck by the bountiful landscape of the place they called "Camosack" and vicinity, with extensive patches of indigenous clover (*Trifolium wormskioldii*). In fact, he named the point where he first landed Clover Point, because "a large area of ground here was found covered with a species of red clover, growing most luxuriantly."[17] Seeing the parklike garry oak (*Quercus garryana*) woodlands interspersed with sweeping meadows of blue camas (*Camassia* spp.) and other spring-flowering plants, he called this area a "perfect Eden," and he assumed it was naturally abundant.[18] Douglas later extolled, "The grouth [*sic*] of indigenous vegetation is more luxuriant than in any other place I have seen in America, indicating a rich productive soil. Though the survey I made was rather laborious, not being so light and active of foot as in my younger days, I was nevertheless delighted in ranging over fields knee deep in clover, tall grasses and ferns reaching above our heads, at these unequivocal proofs of fertility."[19]

Douglas's initial observations and comprehension of the landscape of southern Vancouver Island demonstrates how the lack of recognition of Indigenous people's cultivation and management of the oak savannahs and other habitats led to a cumulative and complex impact on the health and autonomy of Indigenous communities, still felt today. Such colonial attitudes explain a resultant pattern of behaviour that undermined Indigenous peoples' life-ways, identity, food security, and overall health and well-being. In referring to this area as "an uncultivated Waste," Douglas overlooked the fact that the entire area was an anthropogenic landscape, created and maintained by the local Songhees and other Straits Salish peoples through periodic burning and intensive digging and "cultivating" of the camas, whose bulbs were a staple carbohydrate food. These people had occupied villages all around the waterfront, sustaining their camas fields, berry patches, wetlands, clam beds, and other productive features of the landscape and seascape, for countless generations, probably two and a half thousand years or longer. Douglas's enthusiasm over the clover, ferns, and prairies he observed was for the potential productivity of the soil and anticipated conversion of the land into English-style farms and settlements. The subtle but significant Indigenous management practices of the area, involving the use of fire, weeding and clearing, pruning, selective harvesting, seeding-while-harvesting, soil aeration, replanting of bulbs and root fragments, and even transplanting from one area to another were simply unrecognized.[20]

The *British Columbian* reflected the prevailing mood of the time: "According to the strict rule of international law territory occupied by a barbarous or wholly uncivilized people may be rightfully appropriated by a civilized or Christian nation."[21] "Improving the land" was the overriding theme, repeated in settlers' journals and letters, and in official documents from the time of the first established settlements to the present day. These settlers, like those who were starting to occupy other areas of the globe, from New Zealand and Australia to Africa, held an expansionist perspective that pervaded the Western world. The newcomers' strong Eurocentric beliefs were reflected in the works of philosophers like John Locke and Swiss jurist Emmerich de Vattel, who maintained that unless land is settled and cultivated (in the style of the agriculturalists of Europe), or used as pasture for domesticated animals, it was not truly occupied. In turn, by this logic, the Indigenous peoples could neither morally nor legally possess or own such lands.[22] The narrow definition of settlement and cultivation ultimately resulted in tremendous changes wrought on lands and indigenous species and ecosystems around the globe.[23]

The savannahs and prairie lands where many Indigenous plant foods were produced were the exact habitats where the settlers wished to grow their own crops and graze domesticated animals. Soon key Indigenous food production areas were destroyed; the extensive and productive clam beds in Victoria's inner harbour were filled in,[24] the salmon streams and vast wetlands in the vicinity of Clover Point and Ross Bay were blocked and drained; and pigs, cattle, and other livestock were set to graze on the rich camas prairies throughout the region.[25] Douglas made an attempt to acquire these lands from First Nations through the "Douglas treaties." It is clear, however, that the same cross-cultural communication breakdown continued into the Douglas treaty process, where the treaties were negotiated primarily with the interests of the settlers in mind and without the informed consent of the First Nations involved. Soon most of the "unoccupied" lands where First Peoples were free to hunt, according to the treaties, were claimed by the newcomers for their own use, and First Nations' resource use was increasingly constrained. This pattern of takeover continued throughout the province, except that, unlike Douglas, the second wave of colonial administrators made no attempt at treaty making, and the narrow yardstick of European-style cultivation was rigidly applied on what lands could be acquired for the incoming settlers, as reflected in the words of Joseph Trutch, chief commissioner of Lands and Works: "I am satisfied from my own observation that the claims of Indians over tracts of land, on which they assume to exercise ownership, but of *which they make no real use*, operate very materially to prevent *settlement and cultivation*" (emphasis added).[26]

An extension of this assumption of unused wilderness, ready for takeover and cultivation, was that the lands and resources acquired by the new colony were limitless and could be harvested up until their products were no longer desirable as commodities in world economic markets. This attitude is well-exemplified in the wasteful and destructive fishing practices of the late 1800s into the 1970s by the cannery and fishing fleet owners.[27] Pacheedaht Chief Charlie Jones (*Queesto*) recalled a Fraser River sockeye run in 1902, where the waste fish were piled up to four feet (1.3 m) high, and he observed, "That is how Europeans handled things."[28] Another prevailing bias, still widely held today, is that Indigenous populations were so small before contact that their resource harvesting simply did not adversely damage the ecosystems within this region.[29] In fact, before the disease epidemics that swept through the region in the 1700s and 1800s, First Peoples were much more numerous than commonly assumed.[30] Yet, despite these numbers, and although they had the technologies, in the form of weirs and traps, to eliminate the immense salmon runs in the hundreds of streams and rivers all along the coast in a single season, the First Peoples maintained the salmon, using them and other resources sustainably.[31] The settler groups, on the other hand, began major forms of habitat modification and over-harvesting of fish stocks and other resources in commercial ventures that have degraded and depleted almost all indigenous species of the region's lands and waters.

This is only one example of many where early settler behaviour, largely ignoring Indigenous peoples' complex cultivation, resource management, and land ownership, was rooted in a set of values that settlers were unwilling to challenge in the face of evidence to the contrary. As settler governments became more entrenched, these values that emphasized European agriculture and classified the region's lands and resources as wild, unencumbered, and limitless, underscored all new legislation, regulations, and policies.

Ignorance Institutionalized in Colonial laws

While diseases (most notably smallpox, influenza, measles, and tuberculosis) had catastrophic impact on Indigenous populations, it was the imposed laws and policies of settler governments that undermined First Nations' complex cultivation and permanently alienated them from many of their key resources. The imposition of Crown legal tenures on First Nations lands in BC restricted Indigenous people from using their traditional land base, and associated resources, such as camas and other root vegetables, giant cedar trees and other forest resources, berries, salmon, waterfowl, and game.[32] It is instructive to examine this pattern of institutionalized alienation from the perspective of one key food source throughout Indigenous communities in BC: berries of many different types, picked in immense quantities and dried for winter use as well as immediate consumption.[33]

Production of species such as huckleberries and blueberries (*Vaccinium* spp.), trailing blackberries (*Rubus ursinus*), blackcaps (*R. leucodermis*), and strawberries (*Fragaria vesca, F. virginiana*) was actively managed by Indigenous peoples through regular burning and practices such as pruning, coppicing, and fertilizing. Individual leaders sometimes owned and maintained productive berry patches. By the early 1900s, however, forestry and other government regulations first discouraged and finally banned landscape burning altogether, even though the purpose of this Indigenous practice was known by then to officials.[34] Many Indigenous elders have attributed the decline in the abundance of berry production to this moratorium on burning.[35] Mount Currie Lil'wat Elders Alec Peters and Margaret Lester commented, "It's real hard to get berries now. We have to sneak them. They won't [even] let us in to where they're logging."[36]

Large-scale commercial logging of forested lands throughout British Columbia is managed through a complex system of legislation, policies, leases, and licences. In large measure these have alienated First Nations from a supply of many significant plant species and limited their participation in the management of the same. Heavy logging mimics, to some extent, previous Aboriginal landscape burning practices, and logged-over areas have often served as sources of edible berries and other resources for First Nations during the past century or so. Clear-cut logging followed by slash burning produces clearings and open canopy required for optimum berry production. Nlaka'pamux Elder Annie York once observed, however, that although the berries "do come after logging but it's not the right kind; it's not as good."[37] Further, the intense heating and drying of the soil following clear-cutting, and other policies and practices of logging in British Columbia such as spraying pesticides, intensive slash burning, and introduction of aggressive invasive species have decreased the overall production of this key Indigenous food source for First Nations.[38]

Urbanization is another cause of loss and deterioration of berry resources. Musqueam and Squamish elders of the Vancouver area and Songhees plant specialists from Victoria have noted significant depletion in many plant species, including blueberries on the lower mainland and wild strawberries and berries in general in the Victoria area. One account from around 1860 noted, "The forest [near Fort Victoria] is as full of wild strawberries as possible, and it abounds with other fruit bearing shrubs: last summer the officers of the 'Grappler' made enough preserves from the wild berries to last them all through the winter."[39] Today, other than introduced Himalayan blackberries (*Rubus armeniacus*), it would be very difficult to find enough wild berries around Victoria to fill a cup, let alone to gather a winter's supply. In the "natural" areas of the region, Douglas-fir forests are gradually replacing garry oak savannahs and open prairies, and many of the species associated with the latter, including other culturally important species like wild caraway, or yampah (*Perideridia gairdneri*), are also in decline.[40]

More recently, in the 1990s the provincial government, in what was largely seen as a progressive move, legislated a series of new parks and protected areas throughout British Columbia. Unfortunately, these parklands were established in areas where First Nations' traditional villages and gathering areas were situated (e.g., Brooks Peninsula Provincial Park), without the expressed consent of First Nations, while also banning any plant harvesting or plant cultivation within park boundaries. Clearly, in examining just one group of plant resources that were significant to First Nations, we can see how land and resource laws and policies directly affected those relationships to a land-based economy so integral to cultural regeneration.

Cascading Impacts of Laws and Regulations

In the previous section, we highlighted some of the direct impacts to plant resources and cultivation by reviewing one resource type, berries. Many other laws and policies affected Indigenous peoples' relationships with plants and key landscapes in an increasingly destructive manner. Indirect impacts from federal legislation came about through several revisions to the Indian Act to establish the Indian band governance structures, impose Indian residential schools, and ban the potlatch as a key cultural institution.[41] One of the sad legacies of residential schools was reducing First Nations children's access to their family's seasonal rounds, traditional teachers, and outdoor "classrooms," which profoundly affected the intergenerational transfer of knowledge required to cultivate, manage, harvest, process, and store (using traditional technology) berries and other traditional resources. General repression of Indigenous cultural identity, including suppression of ceremonial and social management of resources through the potlatch ban and imposition of new community governance structures to replace hereditary leadership systems, has been equally damaging. The potlatch is an overarching name for a varied and multifaceted institution of Northwest Coast peoples.[42] An under-recognized function of the potlatch is its role in regulating resource use, production, and dissemination. In other words, the potlatch embodied a political institution that oversaw and directed people's land use and occupancy, and their proprietorship over lands and resources. It reinforced historical rights and responsibilities, in ceremonial re-enactment of land and resource renewal, and ensured that surplus resources were redistributed.[43] Early Christian religious leaders and colonial government officials, however, considered potlatches as destructive, degrading, and "evil," and in 1884 the Canadian federal government banned potlatching. Anyone hosting or attending a potlatch was subject to severe punishment, confiscation of all potlatch goods, and imprisonment. Villages were burned, leaders and elders were imprisoned, children were apprehended and put up for adoption, all in retribution for potlatching during the period of prohibition.[44]

The effects of the potlatch ban were far-reaching. Some impacts on food-related traditions are reflected in an excerpt from a letter dated 6 April 1919 requesting that the potlatch be legalized because of its immense importance to people's culture and well-being:

> We all know that things are changing. In the old days the only things that counted were such things as food dried fish, roots, berries and things of that nature. A chief in those days would get possession of all these things and would pass them on to those who had not got any and in many instances would call another tribe and help them out too. We wish to continue this custom. In the old days when feasts were given, those who remained at home were remembered and those who attended would carry stuff home for their wives and children. This is all about our feasts, and we want to have the same thing today.[45]

It wasn't until 1952 that the potlatch ban was repealed, following an appeal by the Native Brotherhood of British Columbia.[46] By this time, very few people still held detailed knowledge and understanding of the potlatch as a governance system; the associated teachings and protocols regarding resource use and harvesting had been notably disrupted. Some of them conveyed "deep" teachings, like the sacred cedarbark ceremony[47] and the *Atlágimma* "Spirits of the Forest" dance – proprietary dances performed only under the protocols and requirements of the hereditary leaders and their families who own them.[48] The cedarbark ceremony teaches respect and reverence towards the cedar tree, in turn reflecting traditional management systems for cedar, in which canoe trees are carefully selected and cedarbark and cedar planks are harvested carefully from standing, living trees – as reflected today in the thousands of culturally modified cedar trees up and down the coast. Many of these very old trees are still living, after having been partially harvested but, intentionally, kept alive because they are recognized as spiritual and sentient beings who are our relatives.[49] The *Atlágimma* dance similarly teaches the interconnectedness of all entities and processes of forest ecosystems, and about not overharvesting or abusing the resources people depend on. Fortunately, key individuals, such as Clan Chief Adam Dick (Kwaxsistalla), preserved the memory of these ceremonies that link to Indigenous resource management practices and values. Nonetheless, the loss of cultural knowledge and practice wrought by the potlatch ban, linked to so many other imposed laws and regulations, has been immense.[50]

During the period after European settlement right up until the present day, First Nations continued to be heavily involved in fishing and shellfish harvesting, and to a lesser but significant degree in forestry and hunting (as they transitioned into the commercial fisheries, forestry, and guide/outfitting).[51] The knowledge of plant cultivation and management, once held by everyone to a greater or lesser degree, became increasingly specialized within First Nations communities over time. On the one hand, it is remarkable how much plant knowledge is retained, and how ongoing (often unofficial) harvesting of plants off reserve on public lands continued up until the late twentieth century and continues to be a tremendous symbol of cultural resilience and tenacity. On the other hand, the knowledge of plants, their uses and roles in First Nations' food systems, technologies, economies, land and resource rights, cosmologies, and world views has been held by fewer and fewer cultural specialists within First Nations, although this situation is changing.

Four Phases of Cumulative Effects on Human–Plant Relationships

Indeed, one can see a pattern of at least four phases marking the loss of botanical and environmental knowledge among First Nations in British Columbia. From the 1770s until the mid-1800s, there was active trading between Europeans and Americans and First Peoples; despite terrible epidemics and the introduction of firearms and alcoholic beverages, First Nations for the most part maintained their traditional use and management systems for plants and other resources, and the knowledge continued to be passed down through the generations. From the 1850s until the 1920s, many Indigenous people remained highly fluent in plant use and knowledge. Epidemics continued to cause profound losses to families and communities, and alienation from specific harvesting areas due to settlers and colonial governance occurred at increasing rates, particularly due to the establishment of reserves. This, in addition to the initial banning of the potlatch, forced First Nations' political and economic institutions underground, in many cases to be practised in secret. Although residential schools were in existence, many Indigenous families at first were able to avoid their attendance and live and teach according to their own cultural norms. Men and women began to work in both the traditional and cash economies, continuing many of their original practices in a "moditional" lifestyle.[52]

The period from the 1920s to the 1970s brought about a much more pervasive era of change, with settler culture affecting First Nations' connections to lands and resources in major ways. Mandatory residential schooling was introduced in 1920, and, at the same time, the potlatch ban was enforced more strongly. A greater dependency on the cash economy through seasonal participation in commercial fisheries, canneries, and other industrial enterprises took its toll, and overall, plant cultivation and management practices were undercut by decreased access to traditional lands and conversion of these lands to European-style farming and livestock rearing. Nevertheless, even with a highly reduced participation in traditional plant management, the knowledge and use of plants and environments remained widespread, with many people continuing to rely largely on their traditional foods. Some children were hidden by their parents and grandparents so they would not be taken away to school, and some children participated in a modified seasonal round with elders in the summers, where they continued to be taught traditional knowledge of plants and environments by grandparents, often in their own language. These children worked alongside their grandparents and extended family members, often gathering culturally significant plants (such as cascara bark, and basket-making materials, such as cedar roots, birch bark, and cherry bark) that were useful for participation in the moditional economy.

By the 1970s, marking the beginning of the fourth phase, however, the cumulative impacts of children being alienated from their own knowledge systems, people's limited access to their traditional territories, and the increasingly strident development and environmental policies that ignored Indigenous uses and needs resulted in highly reduced participation in traditional plant management. This era, however, coincided with an Indigenous political and cultural resurgence, the beginning of litigation, and a renewed push to document the old ways before this knowledge passed, along with its cultural specialists.

The application of Indigenous knowledge as evidence in Aboriginal rights and title cases has opened up many interesting opportunities and challenges for many academic researchers, particularly in examining the role played by previous academics in creating and perpetuating colonial attitudes and policies. In particular, as the Delgamuukw[53] and Tsilhqot'in[54] trials reveal, it has been very challenging to argue the legitimacy of presenting Indigenous knowledge systems as evidence within the Commonwealth legal framework. This debate has highlighted academics' roles in perpetuating colonial attitudes and values.

Colonialism is often characterized as the practice of explorers, government administrators, and businessmen. Researchers in the social sciences, in particular anthropology, have examined extensively their own role in inspiring or perpetuating colonial attitudes and policies.[55] Yet other academic areas have supported and promoted colonial values and interests in British Columbia for over a century.[56] The relationship between settlers, the laws they created, and those who have studied British Columbia and provided data to the resulting governments is complex but significant. Provincial legislation and policy are not created in a vacuum but are based on research – and the research agenda, theory, methods, and applications for lands and resource data are set in academia. The predominant tools for understanding flora and fauna of British Columbia are based in the paradigms and knowledge set of Western science. For the better part of the last century, throughout North America, land and resource research has been conducted as though human impact were largely confined to urban/suburban areas – and the remainder of the province were a form of untouched wilderness to be studied or exploited or protected for current and future generations. As Indigenous plant and resource management systems are not understood by most citizens – i.e., the landscape has no past – these are not included in either current management or decision-making activities such as timber harvesting, mining, or protected area designation.

Ethnoecology, the study of the ecological knowledge systems of a group of people, is closely tied to land use issues and to the ways in which people care for and sustain their lands and resources, including other life forms. It also covers the attitudes and relationships people maintain with their environments, how they have developed over time, and how concepts and entities in the natural world are classified and named.[57] Ethnoecology has strong roots in social anthropology and it also closely parallels the science of ecology. Ethnoecology is more holistic than ecology, however, because it embraces human social, cultural, and political aspects of ecosystems. It acknowledges that virtually every ecosystem and land base on earth has been modified and manipulated by humans at some time in the past hundred thousand years.[58] Ethnoecology's close ties to social anthropology, which celebrates different ways of knowing and organizing human knowledge, beliefs, and practices, has helped to reveal the cultural landscapes that cover what was once characterized as wilderness by conservation ecologists. As such, the naive notion of a "pristine wilderness" untouched by humans is a myth, and persistence with this world view only gives an incomplete picture of the biosphere in which we are all embedded. Ethnoecology now weaves together conservation ecology, human ecology, social anthropology, archeology, environmental history, human nutrition and medicine, political ecology, environmental economics, and cultural geography, among other disciplines. The colonial view of natural landscapes untouched by humans is persistent, however. Not only has it underwritten political decisions, but it has also heavily affected scientific research on species and the environment, which in turn has been presented as factual evidence in the courts through which to justify the alienation of Indigenous lands and resources.

Discussion

In the previous sections, we highlighted colonial attitudes and policies that affected Indigenous peoples' traditional environmental knowledge and resource management systems. European newcomers were generally blind to Indigenous resource use and management practices and, as a consequence, developed laws and regulations that effectively destroyed Indigenous peoples' abilities to maintain their full traditional knowledge and management systems. Further, the underlying principles and practices of scientific and academic thought reinforced the policies and laws of settler government – the cumulative effects of these being to sever the ties of reciprocity between First Nations and their lands and resources.

Newcomers' obliviousness to Indigenous peoples' reliance on their entire territories, and to their complex resource management systems – from maintenance of camas prairies to salmon stewardship, to keeping giant cedars living while still using parts of them – was, and to some extent still is, a reflection of a broader assumption of European superiority, not only in food production systems, but in religion and belief systems, language, governance structures, and economies.[59] It was therefore not only the land use policies and alienation of Indigenous peoples from their own territories and resources through the reserve system, but also the enforcement of the potlatch ban, language suppression, prohibitions against voting in elections, and numerous other laws and regulations that favoured newcomers at the expense of the Indigenous peoples.[60] Indigenous communities were forced to follow policy directives through an Indian agent and to replace their traditional leadership institutions with the British system of elected chief and council, just at a time when populations were decimated by smallpox and other epidemics. Their participation in the wage economy, it can be argued, was at least in part a voluntary adaptation measure, but full participation was constrained through imposed laws and regulations, such as the banning of Indigenous fishing technologies.[61] The agricultural imperative – large-scale introduced crops and livestock rearing – was pervasive and is reflected both in the wording of the Douglas treaties – in which people were allowed to retain their "enclosed fields" – and in many other documents from the colonial era, where the "progress" people were making in farming was discussed and assessed.[62]

The loss of native prairies, grasslands, waterways and estuarine lands to agriculture, industrial use, and settlement was particularly difficult.[63] For example, the camas and clover prairies of southeastern Vancouver Island discussed earlier are today smothered with introduced grasses, English ivy, Scotch broom, and Himalayan blackberry. Not having been cultivated or harvested for generations now, many are diminished in size from overcrowding and competition. As well as the introduced species, native shrubs such as snowberry and wild rose, and native trees such as Douglas-fir, have taken over many of the original prairie lands, no longer cleared by landscape burning. Most of the remaining camas populations and other indigenous food species exist in privately held lands or in parks, where any harvesting is generally prohibited.

Forcing children to attend residential schools was perhaps one of the most devastating settler actions, resulting in the suppression of Indigenous environmental knowledge systems and practices around resource management and stewardship. Many children at these schools died, and those who survived often lost an appreciation of their own foods, languages, and cultural traditions, as the practices and world views of the dominant society were inculcated. Residential schools caused lasting harm to the health and well-being of their students and inflicted untold harm on their parents and grandparents, who were deprived of their children, often forcibly, and were unable to fulfil their responsibilities to teach them in their own life-ways. The result has been generations of grieving[64] for people who, through no fault of their own, lost much of the knowledge and skills of their ancestors in Indigenous food production.[65]

All of these different measures and agencies have profoundly affected peoples' cultural knowledge and ability to use and manage their traditional resources and ecosystems.[66] At the same time, the environmental effects of industrial development – roads, railroads, mining, urbanization, commercial forestry and fishing, agricultural development, overgrazing, and road and powerline construction – and the pollution, introduced species, land alienation, and other impacts accompanying them – have imposed immense harm on Indigenous peoples' ability to use and manage their lands sustainably.

Renewal and Revitalization

Despite the immense obstacles – loss of knowledge, habitats, species and productivity, loss of sacred lands and sacred songs and ceremonies, impacts of invasive species and of climate change – there is considerable potential for ethnoecological restoration. Indigenous peoples' food systems, Indigenous languages, and traditional resource management methods can be renewed and revitalized, and with them the health and well-being of both Indigenous peoples and their lands are rejuvenated.[67] Modern treaty-making, through the BC treaty process, has established provisions for "plant gathering areas" off treaty settlement lands, although how these will function as a vehicle through which First Nations can re-establish their connections to species and landscapes is as ill-defined as "enclosed fields" are in the historic Douglas treaties. The more that all Canadians are informed about the sustainability of Indigenous management systems, such as "clam gardens," "camas prairies," "root gardens," and "berry gardens" – all part of a "keeping it living" philosophy,[68] the more there is reciprocal learning and reconnecting with respect for true reconciliation.[69]

Canadians from every sector of contemporary society need to find ways to transform loss into rediscovery and reconciliation between Indigenous peoples and the rest of Canada. Effective mechanisms for doing this might include formally acknowledging both the recent and ancient history of Indigenous groups, bringing this understanding into all levels of curriculum and supporting the many cultural resurgence efforts of Indigenous Canadians. A recent and highly effective example of cultural resurgence is in the re-establishment of reef net fishing by Tsawout cultural specialist Nick Claxton. In his doctoral project, Claxton drew upon many sources of information on reef net fishing technology to re-initiate the practice at an ancient fishing site of the Tsawout First Nation off the coast of Pender Island, BC.[70] He used this project to engage his community in relearning these fishing methods. For example, working with his uncle and other knowledgeable family members, he taught Tsawout schoolchildren how to help him construct first a model and then a full-sized reef net from willow bark, cedar bark, and stinging nettle fibre. He is now working to apply this technology towards more sustainable commercial fishing practices in the region. During Claxton's public lectures on this project (e.g., on Pender Island, November 2015), he captured the imagination of many non-Indigenous groups, from university students, to local historical societies and church groups seeking reconciliation. These groups, in turn, are eager to support future resurgence of Tsawout reef net fishing by offering facilities, food, and other support as the fishing activities expand and are repeated.

Ethnobotany and ethnoecology, while by no means the only venue for reconciliation, can provide a useful bridge over which to establish cultural resurgence. Past examples of this include re-establishing the practice of traditional pit-cooking as a teaching tool.[71] The Gitga'at Plant Project at Hartley Bay involved Indigenous students undertaking research on culturally important plants as part of their school curriculum, including interviewing elders in their community about these plants and their uses, which was ultimately published in a handbook for use by future classes.[72] A restoration plan for culturally significant indigenous plants was developed in collaboration with the Sellemah (Joan Morris) and other members of the Songhees First Nation for Tl'ches (Chatham Island) near Victoria, as a way of reducing the impact of introduced species, which were dominating plant life in this fragile ecosystem.[73] The Nature Conservancy of Canada's Garry Oak Reserve, near Duncan, BC, has been the locus of several research projects into better understanding camas cultivation, harvesting, and management.[74] This research, supported by Cowichan First Nations, has contributed to a better understanding of the development and maintenance of the unique garry oak landscapes of southeastern Vancouver Island that had been cultivated by these First Nations over thousands of years. These projects were initiated through collaborations between Indigenous and non-Indigenous people, resulting in supportive environments whereby everyone can develop a deeper understanding of anthropogenic landscapes, significant plants and their habitats, and First Nations' history. Filling these knowledge gaps provides long overdue opportunities for many citizens to participate in reconciliation between Indigenous and settler communities.

Ethnobotanical and ethnoecological research can also assist in the formal process of resurgence and reconciliation that is now being contemplated by federal and provincial governments. Ideally, these local examples of cultural resurgence activities can also be brought to government-to-government relationships through treaty negotiations and land-use planning. Bringing traditional ecological knowledge of Indigenous cultural specialists from communities to classrooms, and to planning and negotiation tables as a means of discussing past, present, and future use of plants and their habitats helps to situate these complex problems of use and ownership in real places.[75] Establishing this understanding of the relationships with the tangible world helps to prepare negotiators and discussants on both sides for considering not only the importance of Indigenous food, materials, and medicines for people's well-being, but also the intangible aspects such as kin relations and world views.

Finally, we cannot stress enough the importance of the involvement of many players on the road to reconciliation. Too often, the governments of Canada and British Columbia expect First Nations to prove their rights to lands and resources. Governments need to better recognize their *own* responsibilities to understand the significance of First Nations landscapes and to recognize ongoing requirements for lands and resources in terms of people's identity, health, and well-being. This is everyone's story; all parties have a responsibility to share in understanding and expressing it. If these issues are still largely left to be resolved through the court system, if government officials aren't required to assume responsibility for understanding this history, the uneven and discriminatory circumstances will simply be perpetuated. In order to move away from receiving, repeatedly, all direction from the courts about recognizing the rights of Indigenous peoples to use and manage their own homelands, towards true reconciliation, we must all cease placing the burden solely on First Nations to prove their occupancy of this land that we now share.

Conclusions

Plant use and cultivation of species and habitats are a significant practice of BC First Nations that has been downplayed and often overlooked since the time of the first European settlers. Their convenient
oversight allowed for the development of laws, regulations, and policies that alienated First Nations from the plants and cultural landscapes
that they used and managed for thousands of years. The cumulative
effect of policies and laws governing every aspect of First Nations
individuals and communities undermined these key relationships by
removing access to the resources as well as to the sites of teaching and
learning about their importance and how to use them. As seen from the
examples cited above, the newcomers' impacts on First Nations' homelands, resources, and cultures have been relentless and cumulative.[76]
As noted by Fisher, "Gradually, the ecological balance that the Indian
way of life was based on was being eroded ... When the Indians lost
their land, it was not only their means of subsistence that was removed.
They were also deprived of a major part of their social and spiritual
identity."[77] It is our contention that unless this profound oversight can
be corrected, reconciliation with present-day First Nations communities will be incomplete.

Reconciliation between First Nations and the dominant settler culture will occur over time and on many fronts. Because of settlers'
enduring misunderstanding of Indigenous plant use and cultivation, First Nations' complex relationships with plants and landscapes
throughout their traditional territories have been largely ignored. This
oversight must be redressed, not only as a moral imperative to allow
First Nations communities to reconnect with their ancient knowledge
systems and the landscapes in which they have arisen, but as a vehicle
for teaching the larger community of British Columbians about the rich
history of the anthropogenic landscapes of this region, and about Indigenous peoples' sustainability and ecological resilience over time.

Reconciliation demands a much higher standard than concluding
land and economic deals or improving overall relations. In his concluding remarks to the Tsilhqot'in case, trial Judge Vickers said, "Reconciliation is a process. It is in the interests of all Canadians that we begin to
engage in this process at the earliest possible date so that an honourable
settlement with Tsilhqot'in people can be achieved."[78]

Reconciliation involves acknowledgment of the past and ensuring
that First Nations have a seat at the planning table to navigate the

future. Everybody at that table needs to have some understanding of the historic relationship between First Nations, their landscapes, and specific species within those landscapes. Everyone in these negotiations has a responsibility to learn about traditional ecological knowledge and to be open to understanding how it is expressed in the present and its potential to be articulated in the future. First Nations are seeking more than revenue sharing and economic benefits (although these will continue to be a significant component of negotiated solutions). True reconciliation requires seeking commonality – with all parties negotiating in an informed environment where understanding and innovation can occur.[79] Aboriginal title has finally been proven in court. It will be proven again. It's time to move beyond waiting for legal decisions to decide progress and to reconcile through negotiation and sharing common understandings.[80]

NOTES

1 Clayoquot Scientific Panel, *First Nations' Perspectives on Forest Practices in Clayoquot Sound, Report 3* (with appendices) (Victoria: Scientific Panel for Sustainable Forest Practices in Clayoquot Sound, 1995), vii.
2 Richard E. Atleo (Chief Umeek), *Tsawalk: A Nuu-chah-nulth Worldview* (Vancouver: UBC Press, 2004); Atleo, *Principles of Tsawalk: An Indigenous Approach to Global Crisis* (Vancouver: UBC Press, 2011).
3 Clayoquot Scientific Panel, *First Nations' Perspectives*; Clayoquot Scientific Panel, *A Vision and Its Context: Global Context for Forest Practices in Clayoquot Sound, Report 4* (Victoria: Scientific Panel for Sustainable Forest Practices in Clayoquot Sound, Cortex Consulting, 1995); Clayoquot Scientific Panel, *Sustainable Ecosystem Management in Clayoquot Sound, Report 5* (Victoria: Scientific Panel for Sustainable Forest Practices in Clayoquot Sound, Cortex Consulting, 1995).
4 Murray Sinclair and TRC members, *Final Report, TRC* (Winnipeg: Truth and Reconciliation Commission of Canada, 2015).
5 Tully, this volume.
6 Borrows, this volume.
7 Royal Commission, *Report on Aboriginal Peoples* (Ottawa: Indian and Northern Affairs Canada, 1996).
8 Asch, this volume.
9 N.J. Turner, R. Brooks, C. Gregory, L. Failing, and T. Satterfield, "From Invisibility to Transparency: Identifying the Implications (of Invisible

Losses to First Nations communities)," *Ecology and Society* 13, no. 2 (2008): 7.

10 Robert Davidson, cited by Tully, this volume.

11 Robin Wall Kimmerer, *Braiding Sweetgrass: Indigenous Wisdom, Scientific Knowledge and the Teachings of Plants* (Minneapolis: Milkweed Editions, 2015).

12 C. Harris, "How Did Colonialism Dispossess? Comments from an Edge of Empire," *Annals of the Association of American Geographers* 94 (2004): 165.

13 Fikret Berkes, *Sacred Ecology: Traditional Ecological Knowledge and Resource Management,* 3rd ed. (Philadelphia: Taylor and Francis, 2012).

14 Thomas Thornton, Douglas Deur, and Herman Kitka Sr, "Cultivation of Salmon and Other Marine Resources on the Northwest Coast of North America," *Human Ecology* 43 (2015): 191.

15 Nancy J. Turner and Fikret Berkes. "Coming to Understanding: Developing Conservation through Incremental Learning," in "Developing Resource Management and Conservation," special issue, *Human Ecology* 34, no. 4 (2006): 495; Nancy J. Turner, Douglas Deur, and Dana Lepofsky, "Plant Management Systems of British Columbia's First Peoples," in "Ethnobotany in British Columbia: Plants and People in a Changing World," *BC Studies* 179 (2013): 107.

16 James Douglas, Douglas's report, Fort Vancouver, 12 July 1842, quoted in E.O.S. Scholefield, *British Columbia: From the Earliest Times to the Present,* vols 1–2 (Vancouver: S.J. Clarke, 1914). Emphasis added.

17 J.T. Walbran, *British Columbia Coast Names, 1592–1906, to Which Are Added a Few Names in Adjacent United States Territory; Their Origin and History* (1909; Vancouver: Vancouver Public Library and J.J. Douglas, 1971), 96.

18 John S. Lutz, "Eden: Aboriginal Land Use and European Settlement" (paper presented to the 1995 Meeting of the Canadian Historical Association, Université de Québec à Montréal, Montreal, 1995).

19 James Douglas, quoted in G.P. Glazebrook, ed., *The Hargrave Correspondence 1821–1843* (Toronto: Champlain Society, 1938).

20 Turner, Deur, and Lepofsky, "Plant Management Systems"; Nancy J. Turner, *Ancient Pathways, Ancestral Knowledge: Ethnobotany and Ecological Wisdom of Indigenous Peoples of Northwestern North America,* McGill-Queen's Native and Northern Series number 74, 2 vols (Montreal and Kingston: McGill-Queen's University Press, 2014).

21 *British Columbian,* 1 June 1869.

22 Michael Asch, *On Being Here to Stay: Treaties and Aboriginal Rights in Canada* (Toronto: University of Toronto Press, 2014); Robin Fisher, *Contact & Conflict: Indian–European Relations in British Columbia, 1774–1890,* 2nd ed. (Vancouver: University of British Columbia Press, 1992), 104.

23 Jared Diamond, *Collapse: How Societies Choose to Fail or Succeed* (New York: Viking, 2005); Alfred W. Crosby, *Ecological Imperialism: The Biological Expansion of Europe, 900–1900* (Cambridge: Cambridge University Press, 1986).

24 Walbran, *British Columbia Coast Names*, 96.

25 Nancy J. Turner and Katherine L. Turner, "'Where Our Women Used to Get the Food': Cumulative Effects and Loss of Ethnobotanical Knowledge and Practice," *Botany* 86, no. 1 (2008): 103; Wayne P. Suttles, "The Economic Life of the Coast Salish of Haro and Rosario Straits" (PhD diss., University of Washington, 1951); Brenda R. Beckwith, "The Queen Root of This Clime: Ethnoecological Investigations of Blue Camas (*Camassia quamash, C. leichtlinii;* Liliaceae) Landscapes on Southern Vancouver Island, British Columbia" (PhD diss., University of Victoria, 2004).

26 Joseph Trutch to colonial Secretary, 20 September 1865, in British Columbia, *Papers Connected with the Indian Land Question, 1850–1875* (Victoria: Government Printer, 1875), 30. Reprinted 1987 as *Indian Land Question, 1850–1875*, 1877.

27 John S. Lutz, *Makuk: A New History of Aboriginal-White Relations* (Vancouver: UBC Press, 2008); Turner, Deur, and Lepofsky, "Plant Management Systems."

28 *Ottawa Citizen*, 5 September 1987.

29 Douglas Deur and Nancy J. Turner, eds, *"Keeping It Living": Traditions of Plant Use and Cultivation on the Northwest Coast of North America* (Seattle: University of Washington Press, 2005).

30 Robert T. Boyd, *The Coming of the Spirit of Pestilence: Introduced Infectious Diseases and Population Decline among Northwest Coast Indians, 1774–1874* (Vancouver: UBC Press, 1999).

31 E.N. Anderson, *Ecologies of the Heart: Emotion, Belief and the Environment* (New York: Oxford University Press, 1996).

32 Cole R. Harris, *The Resettlement of British Columbia: Essays on Colonialism and Geographical Change* (Vancouver: UBC Press, 1998); Nancy J. Turner, "'Time to Burn': Traditional Use of Fire to Enhance Resource Production by Aboriginal Peoples in British Columbia," in *Indians, Fire, and the Land in the Pacific Northwest*, ed. Robert T. Boyd, 185–218 (Corvallis: Oregon State University Press, 1999); Turner, *The Earth's Blanket: Traditional Teachings for Sustainable Living* (Vancouver: Douglas & McIntyre, 2005).

33 Nancy J. Turner, *Food Plants of Coastal First Peoples* (Vancouver: UBC Press, 1995).

34 Robert T. Boyd, ed., *Indians, Fire and the Land in the Pacific Northwest* (Corvallis: Oregon State University Press, 1999), 27; Turner, *Ancient Pathways*, 214.

35 Turner, "'Time to Burn.'"
36 Personal comment to Nancy Turner, 1987.
37 Cited in Turner, "'Time to Burn,'" 192.
38 Boyd, *Indians, Fire and the Land*; Baptiste Ritchie, quoted in Turner, "'Time to Burn.'"
39 Cited in Allan Pritchard, "Letters of a Victorian Naval Officer: Edmund Verney in British Columbia, 1862–65," *BC Studies* 86 (1990): 32–3.
40 Ze'ev Gedalof, Marlow Pellatt, and Dan J. Smith, "From Prairie to Forest: Three Centuries of Environmental Change at Rocky Point, Vancouver Island, British Columbia," *Northwest Science* 80, no. 1 (2006): 34.
41 D. Sewid-Smith (My-yah-nelth), *Prosecution or Persecution* (Cape Mudge: Nu-yum-balees Society, 1979).
42 Atleo, *Tsawalk*; Kim Recalma-Clutesi, dir. *Ancient Sea Gardens: Mystery of the Pacific Northwest*. Documentary (Aquaculture Pictures, Toronto, 2005); Recalma-Clutesi, dir. *Smoke from His Fire*. Documentary (Winnipeg: Aboriginal Peoples Television Network, 2007).
43 Wayne P. Suttles, ed., *Coast Salish Essays* (Vancouver: Talonbooks, 1987); Ronald L. Trosper, *Resilience, Reciprocity and Ecological Economics: Northwest Coast Sustainability* (London: Routledge, 2009).
44 Sewid-Smith (My-yah-nelth), *Prosecution or Persecution*.
45 Namgis (Nimpkish) chiefs, Alert Bay, to deputy superintendent general of Indian affairs, Ottawa: "An Appeal by the Indians of Vancouver Island," *Journal of American Folklore* 36, no. 141 (1923): 295. See also Christopher Bracken, *The Potlatch Papers: A Colonial Case History* (Chicago: University of Chicago Press, 1997), 221.
46 See Douglas Cole and Ira Chaikin, *An Iron Hand upon the People: The Law against the Potlatch on the Northwest Coast* (Vancouver: Douglas & McIntyre, 1990).
47 Daisy Sewid-Smith (Mayanilth) and Adam Dick (Kwaxsistalla), interviewed by Nancy J. Turner, "The Sacred Cedar Tree of the Kwakwaka"wakw People," in *Stars Above, Earth Below: Native Americans and Nature*, ed. M. Bol, 189–209 (Pittsburgh: Carnegie Museum of Natural History, 1998); Turner and Berkes. "Coming to Understanding."
48 Turner, *Ancient Pathways*.
49 Deur and Turner, *"Keeping It Living"*; Kimmerer, *Braiding Sweetgrass*; Turner, Deur, and Lepofsky, "Plant Management Systems."
50 Turner et al., "From Invisibility to Transparency"; Sewid-Smith, *Prosecution or Persecution*.
51 Lutz, *Makuk*.
52 Ibid.

53 R. Daly, *Our Box Was Full: An Ethnography for the Delgamuukw Plaintiffs* (Vancouver: UBC Press, 2013).

54 *Tsilhqot'in Nation v British Columbia*, 2007 BCSC 1700.

55 Edward Said, *Orientalism* (New York: Vintage, 1994); James Clifford, *Returns: Becoming Indigenous in the 21st Century* (Cambridge, MA: Harvard University Press, 2013); James Clifford and George E. Marcus, *Writing Culture: The Poetics and Politics of Ethnography: A School of American Research Advanced Seminar* (Berkeley: University of California Press, 1986).

56 Bruce Braun, *The Intemperate Rainforest: Nature, Culture, and Power on Canada's West Coast* (Minneapolis: University of Minnesota Press, 2002).

57 Berkes, *Sacred Ecology*; Virginia D. Nazarea, ed., *Ethnoecology: Situated Knowledge/Located Lives* (Tuscon: University of Arizona Press, 1999); Nancy J. Turner, Marianne B. Ignace, and Ronald E. Ignace, "Traditional Ecological Knowledge and Wisdom of Aboriginal Peoples in British Columbia," *Ecological Applications* 10, no. 10 (2000): 181; Thomas Thornton and Douglas Deur, "Introduction to the Special Section on Marine Cultivation among Indigenous Peoples of the Northwest Coast," *Human Ecology* 43 (2015): 187.

58 W. Balée, *Cultural Forests of the Amazon: A Historical Ecology of People and Their Landscapes* (Tuscaloosa: University of Alabama Press, 2013); Trosper, *Resilience, Reciprocity and Ecological Economics*.

59 Rosemary E. Ommer and Nancy J. Turner, "Informal Rural Economies in History," *Labour/Le Travail: Journal of Canadian Labour Studies* 53 (2004): 127.

60 Harris, "How Did Colonialism Dispossess?"

61 Nicholas Xemtoltw Claxton, "To Fish as Formerly: A Resurgent Journey Back to the Saanich Reef Net Fishery" (PhD diss., University of Victoria, 2015); Douglas C. Harris, *Fish, Law, and Colonialism: The Legal Capture of Salmon in British Columbia* (Toronto: University of Toronto Press, 2001); Lutz, *Makuk*.

62 British Columbia, *Papers Connected with the Indian Land Question*.

63 Douglas Deur, Nancy J. Turner, Adam Dick (Kwaxsistalla), Daisy Sewid-Smith (Mayanilth), and Kim Recalma-Clutesi (Oqwilowgwa), "Subsistence and Resistance on the British Columbia Coast: Kingcome Village's Estuarine Gardens as Contested Space," in "Ethnobotany in British Columbia: Plants and People in a Changing World," special issue, *BC Studies* 179 (2013): 13.

64 Sinclair, *Final Report*.

65 Turner and Turner, "'Where Our Women Used to Get the Food.'"

66 Ommer and Turner, "Informal Rural Economies in History"; Turner, *Ancient Pathways*; Turner et al., "From Invisibility to Transparency."

67 Harriet V. Kuhnlein, Bill Erasmus, and Dina Spigelski, eds, *Indigenous Peoples' Food Systems: The Many Dimensions of Culture, Diversity, and Environment for Nutrition and Health* (Montreal: Centre for Indigenous Peoples' Nutrition and Environment, 2009); Harriet V. Kuhnlein, Bill Erasmus, Dina Spigelski, and Barbara Burlingame, eds, *Indigenous Peoples' Food Systems for Health: Interventions for Health Promotion and Policy* (Montreal: Centre for Indigenous Peoples' Nutrition and Environmen, 2013); Thiago Gomes, "Restoring Tl'chés: An Ethnoecological Restoration Study in Chatham Islands, British Columbia, Canada" (MA thesis, University of Victoria, 2012); Joseph Leigh, "Finding Our Roots: Ethnoecological Restoration of *Lhásem* (*Fritillaria camschatcensis* (L.) Ker-Gawl), an Iconic Plant Food in the Squamish River Estuary, British Columbia" (MSc thesis, University of Victoria, 2012); René Senos, Frank Lake, Nancy J. Turner, and Dennis Martinez, "Traditional Ecological Knowledge and Restoration Practice in the Pacific Northwest," in *Encyclopedia for Restoration of Pacific Northwest Ecosystems*, ed. Dean Apostol, 393–426 (Washington: Island, 2006); Judith C. Thompson (Edōsdi), "'*Hede Kehe*" Hotzi' *Kahidi* – Our Ancestors Are in Us': Strengthening Our Voices through Language Revitalization from a Tahltan Worldview" (PhD diss., University of Victoria, 2012); Turner and Turner, "'Where Our Women Used to Get the Food.'"
68 Deur and Turner, *"Keeping It Living."*
69 Kimmerer, *Braiding Sweetgrass.*
70 Claxton, "To Fish as Formerly."
71 Turner, *Ancient Pathways.*
72 Nancy J. Turner and Judith C. Thompson (Edōsdi), eds, *Plants of the Gitga'at People: "Nwana"a lax Yuup* (Hartley Bay: Gitga'at Nation, 2006).
73 A. Cuerrier, N.J. Turner, T. Gomes, A. Garibaldi, and A. Downing, "Cultural Keystone Places: Conservation and Restoration in Cultural Landscapes," *Journal of Ethnobiology* 35, no. 3 (2015): 427.
74 Katherine Y. Proctor, "Renewing Central Coast Salish Camas (*Camassia leichtlinii* (Baker) Wats., *C. quamash* (Pursh) Greene; Liliaceae) Traditions through Access to Protected Areas: An Ethnoecological Inquiry" (MSc thesis, University of Victoria, 2013).
75 Nancy Turner and Pamela R. Spalding, "'We Might Go Back to This': Drawing on the Past to Meet the Future in Northwestern North American Indigenous Communities," *Ecology and Society* 18, no. 4 (2013): 29.
76 Turner, *Ancient Pathways*; Turner et al., "From Invisibility to Transparency."
77 Fisher, *Contact & Conflict.*
78 *Tsilhqot'in Nation v British Columbia*, 2014 SCC 44, [2014] 2 SCR 256.

79 James Tully, *Public Philosophy in a New Key: Democracy and Civic Freedom* (Cambridge: Cambridge University Press, 2008), 1:223–88.
80 The authors are grateful to countless Indigenous botanical experts and knowledge holders of British Columbia and beyond who have shared their knowledge and insights with us over many years. In particular, we acknowledge Dr Richard Atleo (Umeek), and thanks to Drs Tully, Borrows, and Asch for their leadership and for inviting our participation in this volume. We also thank Dr Eric Peterson and Christina Munck of the Tula Foundation – Hakai Institute for supporting our work, as well as the P.E. Trudeau Foundation and the Social Sciences and Humanities Research Council of Canada.

10 Indigenous and Crown Sovereignty in Canada

KENT MCNEIL[*]

Sovereignty is fundamental to any discussion of European colonization and Indigenous rights in North America. It figures prominently in the work of Asch, Borrows, and Tully[1] and yet tends to be ignored – or, more likely, deliberately avoided – when Canadian courts address issues of Indigenous rights. The probable reason is not difficult to identify: as courts are one of the three branches of government in the Canadian state, their own authority depends on acceptance of Crown sovereignty over the territory and people of Canada, and so they take it for granted. Nonetheless, acceptance of the reality of Crown sovereignty does not necessarily mean that it is legal or legitimate – those are separate issues.[2] Legitimacy is more a matter of moral and political philosophy than law, whereas legality can be determined only in the context of a specific legal system.[3] In this chapter, I will examine the matter of sovereignty from these different perspectives and question the legality and legitimacy of the Crown's acquisition of factual sovereignty in Canada.

The Distinction between Factual and Legal Sovereignty

Peter Russell has recounted that, at a meeting with Dene leaders on his first visit to the Northwest Territories in 1974, the discussion was opened by a Dene woman asking, "Professor Russell, I have two questions for you: What is sovereignty? And how did the Queen get it over us?"[4] Here is how he described his response many years later: "For the

* A version of this chapter, entitled "La relativité de la souveraineté *de jure* au Canada, 1600–2018," has been published in the *Ottawa Law Review / Revue de Droit d'Ottawa* 49:2 (2018): 305.

first question, I had a nice, pat answer based on Bodin, Hobbes, and my understanding of European international law. But I stumbled over the second. The truth of the matter is that I didn't have a clue how Queen Victoria and her Canadian henchmen had 'got sovereignty' over the Dene."[5]

Peter has since told me that, when he got back to the University of Toronto, he asked his colleagues in political science how they thought the Queen got sovereignty, and they didn't know either. But as he learned more about the history of Canadian colonization of Dene territory, he writes that he "came to know that the right answer to the Dene woman's second question was – in a word – 'trickery.' Or, to use the more ironic concept I learned from an Australian Aboriginal friend, it was 'the white man's legal magic' that did the trick."[6]

The concept of "legal magic" suggests that sovereignty is a matter of law. Of course it is, but it is also a matter of fact.[7] Distinguishing between the two can assist, not only in understanding how the Crown got sovereignty over Canada, but also in conceptualizing the pre-existing sovereignty of the Indigenous peoples in North America.

Legal or de jure sovereignty is really a European concept that was formulated as unified nation states emerged from what one author has called the "parcellized sovereignty" of the medieval period.[8] The concept, as described by political theorists such as Jean Bodin,[9] envisaged separate political entities that are theoretically equal to one another and supreme within their territorial limits. The nation state model developed as the monarchies in France, England, and elsewhere in Europe rejected the universalist claims of the Pope and Holy Roman Emperor and asserted their complete independence.[10] This model, which emerged over centuries of political struggle, is commonly regarded as having received general European acceptance at the end of the Thirty Years' War with the signing of the Peace of Westphalia in 1648.[11] The nation state model established the framework for the European law of nations (later, international law) and through colonialism was spread around the world.[12] Though weakened in recent times by globalization, it continues to be the dominant feature of international relations.[13]

Factual or de facto sovereignty does not depend on European legal concepts. Instead, it involves the intention and capacity of a people to have control over and be responsible for a territory. Leroy Little Bear refers to de facto sovereignty as "the operational notion of sovereignty," which he describes as "basically the notion of self-determination. As a society occupying this particular territory, we as a group make our own decisions. We make decisions without interference from anyone else. To a large extent, sovereignty really has to do with being able to make up your own mind."[14]

Viewed from this operational perspective, on the historical facts it is evident that the Indigenous peoples of North America were sovereign at the time of European colonization. There was no need for them to fit into the conception of sovereignty that came to be based on the nation state model. That conception was developed to meet the social and political needs of a certain place and time, namely Europe as it emerged from the Middle Ages. The Indigenous peoples played no part in the development of that conception or in formulating the resulting international law principle that sovereignty is vested in nation states.

Unlike de facto sovereignty, which is an empirical matter, de jure sovereignty depends on the application of a particular body of law. In Europe, the domestic law of each nation state governs legal rights internally, whereas relations between nation states are governed by international law, formerly the law of nations.[15] Likewise in North America, Indigenous peoples had their own bodies of domestic law, as well as law governing their relations with one another, which I will refer to as Indigenous inter-nation law.[16] In order to determine whether a particular people has de facto sovereignty in a certain territory, one needs to examine the evidence of actual control and exercise of authority within the territory. But to determine whether they have de jure sovereignty, one first must decide which body of law to use in resolving this question. In other words, there is an initial choice of law question to be answered,[17] which can depend on who is asking the question and for what purpose, as well as on the legitimacy of the application of one body of law rather than another in that specific context.

The answer to who has de jure sovereignty may well vary, depending on which body of law is applied. Moreover, the answer to this question may not correspond with de facto sovereignty. This can be illustrated by the modern example of Rhodesia during the fifteen-year period after Ian Smith's government issued its Unilateral Declaration of Independence (UDI) in 1965, during which time his racist government clearly exercised de facto sovereignty.[18] Internally, after an initial period of hesitation, Rhodesian judges accepted this reality and acknowledged the legality of the Smith regime.[19] Externally, the international community refused to recognize the independence of Rhodesia, and so its de facto sovereignty did not give it de jure sovereignty in international law.[20] Likewise, British courts decided that the UDI was illegal, and so sovereignty was denied in English law.[21] So de facto sovereignty resulted in de jure sovereignty in domestic Rhodesian law, but not in international or English law, illustrating the relativity of de jure sovereignty.

As mentioned earlier, there can be no doubt that Indigenous peoples had de facto sovereignty in North America prior to European colonization. As the domestic law of the colonizing European nation states would not have applied until they acquired de facto sovereignty, those bodies of law would be irrelevant for the purpose of determining pre-existing Indigenous de jure sovereignty. Although the early European law of nations may have acknowledged the sovereignty of the Indigenous peoples, by the nineteenth century that body of law had been transformed by legal positivism into international law, an exclusive legal system in which only nation states that were acknowledged as such by European nation states were admitted. Indigenous peoples were outside this system, and so their pre-existing sovereignty was no longer acknowledged.[22] European nation states operating within this exclusive system therefore denied de jure sovereignty to them. But why, one must ask, should international law apply at all in this context when Indigenous peoples had no part in creating it, were denied legal personality within it, and were outside its geographical scope? Surely it would be more appropriate to assess the de jure sovereignty of these peoples within their own bodies of law, both domestic and inter-nation.

Turning to European acquisition of sovereignty in North America, this issue also has to be examined from the perspectives of de facto and de jure sovereignty. De facto sovereignty depends, of course, on actual presence in and control of a territory, involving, among other things, the exercise of authority. In the context of European colonization, assessment of such acquisition requires empirical investigation into the historical facts in specific geographical areas. On the other hand, we have seen that determination of de jure sovereignty has to start with identifying which bodies of law are relevant, and then assessing the validity of European claims within each of them. In the context of European colonization of North America, I think the relevant legal systems would be the law of nations/international law, the domestic law of the colonizing nation state, Indigenous inter-nation law, and Indigenous domestic law. In certain situations and periods where interactions between Indigenous peoples and Europeans resulted in inter-societal law governing their relationship, this body of law would also be relevant.[23] It is very likely that, in a given territory, a colonizing nation state could have had de jure sovereignty in one or more of these legal systems, but not in others. A choice of law issue therefore arises, the resolution of which involves a question of legitimacy: which of the relevant legal systems should be favoured to decide this issue of de jure sovereignty?

De Jure Sovereignty: A Matter of Choice of Law[24]

Our starting point should be acknowledgment that the Indigenous peoples of North America had not only de facto sovereignty but also de jure sovereignty within their own systems of law, both domestic and inter-nation, at the time of European colonization.[25] One would therefore think that it would have been impossible for European nation states to acquire de jure sovereignty over them and their territories by original means such as discovery, symbolic acts of possession, or settlement. These means of acquisition of European sovereignty would have required a denial of the de jure sovereignty of the Indigenous peoples, which no doubt would have been inconsistent with their systems of law, both domestic and inter-nation.[26] Instead, acquisition by the derivative modes of conquest or cession by treaty would have been required. And yet, internally and in their dealings with one another, the European nation states acted as though they could acquire sovereignty in North America by original means.[27] They did so by resorting to the legal fiction that the continent, though peopled by numerous Indigenous peoples, was *terra nullius* insofar as de jure sovereignty was concerned.[28] Evidence of this can be found in French assertions of sovereignty by symbolic acts of possession in the St Lawrence and Great Lakes regions and the Mississippi Valley, and in English charters purporting to grant huge expanses of territory to individuals and companies.[29] While it is not my intention to assess the effect of these acts and charters in French and English domestic law, they were obviously thought to have legal significance,[30] for otherwise what was their point? But clearly they could not have had any impact in Indigenous law.[31]

European claims to sovereignty vis-à-vis one another were supposedly governed by the law of nations. Leaving aside Spanish claims to the south and west, effective European colonization in eastern North America began in the first decade of the seventeenth century with French settlements in Acadia and La Nouvelle France, and the English settlement in Virginia. The extent of French and English de facto sovereignty would have been limited to the areas actually controlled by the settlers. But did France and England acquire de jure sovereignty over much larger areas by discovery, symbolic acts of possession, and royal charters, as they asserted? Whatever the effect of these measures in French and English domestic law, they would have been effective only to confer de jure sovereignty vis-à-vis other European nation states if the law of nations so provided.

Historians and international jurists have delved into this matter extensively and generally concluded that there were no set rules before the nineteenth century on what was necessary for European nation states to acquire de jure sovereignty over areas of the world populated by Indigenous peoples.[32] Nation states naturally tried to rely on methods that supported their own claims: Spain and Portugal thus favoured discovery and papal grants, whereas France relied more on symbolic acts and England on settlement pursuant to royal charters.[33] With the ascension of legal positivism in the nineteenth century, effective occupation came to be accepted as the only valid mode of acquiring sovereignty in international law over territories that were not already subject to a sovereign acknowledged as such by the nation states having legal personality in that body of law.[34] In the first half of the twentieth century, international tribunals accepted this standard and applied it at least as far back as the sixteenth century.[35] Then in 1975 the International Court of Justice in its advisory opinion in the *Western Sahara Case* decided that territories occupied by nomadic peoples with a social and political organization, such as those in that part of North Africa, were not *terra nullius* and so sovereignty over them could not be acquired by European occupation.[36] This decision threw into question the effective occupation standard previously thought by jurists to apply to such territories.[37]

The uncertainty regarding this aspect of the European law of nations was not acknowledged by the Supreme Court of the United States when the matter came before it in 1823 in *Johnson v M'Intosh*.[38] In this landmark case, Chief Justice Marshall regarded the matter as having been settled by agreement among the colonizing European nation states who were all eager to acquire as much territory as they could in North America. In these circumstances, he said, "it was necessary, in order to avoid conflicting settlements, and consequent war with each other, to establish a principle, which all should acknowledge as the law by which the right of acquisition, which they all asserted, should be regulated as between themselves. This principle was, that discovery gave title to the government by whose subjects, or by whose authority, it was made, against all other European governments, which title might be consummated by possession."[39]

Apparently Marshall CJ's main source for this conclusion about the existence of such an agreement and the resulting principle of the law of nations, which became known as the doctrine of discovery,[40] was a book by George Chalmers, entitled *Political Annals of the Present United Colonies from their Settlement to the Peace of 1763*, published in 1780.[41] In it, Chalmers had written in regard to the European "discovery" of North America, "It soon became a law among the European nations, that the counties which each should explore shall be deemed the absolute property of the discoverer, from which all others shall be entirely excluded."[42]

Marshall CJ accepted Chalmers's assessment in volume 1 of his *Life of George Washington*,[43] published in 1804, and from there incorporated it, as Lindsay Robertson has demonstrated, into his judgment in *Johnson v M'Intosh*.[44] Unfortunately, Chalmers's opinion was not supported by the authorities he cited,[45] and, as revealed by subsequent research, was simply wrong.[46] But as a result of *Johnson v M'Intosh*, his erroneous assessment of the European law of nations became part of American law.[47]

Chief Justice Marshall modified his views when he returned to the doctrine of discovery in 1832 in *Worcester v Georgia*.[48] In *Johnson v M'Intosh*, he appears to have regarded the de jure sovereignty conferred by discovery as having the effect of diminishing the pre-existing sovereignty of the Indigenous peoples. Referring to the Indian nations, he concluded that "their rights to complete sovereignty, as independent nations, were necessarily diminished, and their power to dispose of the soil at their own will, to whomsoever they pleased, was denied by the original fundamental principle, that discovery gave exclusive title to those who made it."[49] In *Worcester v Georgia*, he realized that discovery alone could not diminish the rights of the Indigenous peoples because, as a principle of the European law of nations, the doctrine of discovery could apply only among those nations that had agreed to it. Discovery, he wrote, "was an exclusive principle which shut out the right of competition among those who had agreed to it; not one which could annul the previous rights of those who had not agreed to it. It regulated the right given by discovery among the European discoverers, but could not affect the rights of those already in possession, either as aboriginal occupants, or as occupants by virtue of a discovery made before the memory of man."[50]

Marshall CJ thus understood the relativity of de jure sovereignty: a principle of the law of nations could result in one European nation state acquiring sovereignty vis-à-vis other European nation states but could not confer sovereignty vis-à-vis Indigenous peoples who were not subject to that body of law. Those peoples had "previous rights," which must have been sourced in their own legal systems[51] and which, as decided by Marshall CJ in *Johnson v M'Intosh*, included "rights to complete sovereignty, as independent nations."[52] For those rights to be diminished, the colonizing European nation state had to acquire sovereignty vis-à-vis the Indigenous people in question (which at that point would be de facto and presumably de jure sovereignty in the law of nations and the domestic law of colonizing nation state), either by conquering or entering into a treaty with them.[53]

Although Chief Justice Marshall's insight into the relativity of de jure sovereignty and his resulting reformulation of the doctrine of discovery in *Worcester v Georgia* did not have a lasting impact in American law,[54] it does help us appreciate how de jure sovereignty depends on choice of law. The question then comes down to deciding which body of law should apply in any particular context, which as mentioned earlier, is a matter of legitimacy. But before offering some thoughts on this question, let us examine what the Supreme Court of Canada has said about Indigenous and Crown sovereignty.

The Supreme Court Prevaricates[55]

Canadian courts have always tended to take Crown sovereignty for granted.[56] As mentioned above, since Crown sovereignty is the basis for their own authority, to deny the one would be to give up the other. The usual way for courts to avoid this conundrum is to treat the issue of sovereignty as non-justiciable by resorting to the act of state doctrine. That doctrine places certain matters beyond the jurisdiction of domestic courts by classifying them as executive acts in relation to foreign affairs that are within the prerogative power of the Crown.[57] Acquisition of sovereignty is regarded as coming within the scope of the act of state doctrine, and so the courts usually defer to the executive branch whenever the issue of Crown sovereignty is raised.[58] The Australian High Court has relied upon the act of state doctrine explicitly to avoid questioning the Crown's acquisition of sovereignty there.[59] However, resort to the act of state doctrine is just a way of sidestepping the issue – it leaves the matters of legality and legitimacy undetermined. Moreover, in Canada at least, the issues of how and when the Crown acquired sovereignty have been treated as justiciable, in part because the existence of Aboriginal title depends on proof of exclusive occupation of land by Indigenous peoples at that time.[60]

As to how and when Crown sovereignty was acquired, Canada has usually been divided into the parts the British Crown acquired derivatively from France by conquest and cession,[61] and the rest of the country where sovereignty was supposedly acquired by the original modes of discovery and settlement.[62] Regarding French Canada, this simply pushes the matter back in time: how and when did the king of France acquire sovereignty?[63] Again, we have to distinguish between de jure and de facto sovereignty, as France claimed sovereignty over much larger areas than it actually occupied and controlled.[64] As discussed above, its claims to de jure sovereignty would have to be assessed relative to specific bodies of law – while they may have been valid in French domestic law, they would not necessarily have been valid in the law of nations and certainly would not have been valid in Indigenous law, absent conquest or a cession of sovereignty by the Indigenous peoples concerned. And when the French in North America were conquered by British forces and the French king ceded territory to the British, presumably only territory over which the French had de jure sovereignty in the law of nations would have been included, as this is the law that would have governed treaty relations between France and Great Britain.[65]

Turning our attention to the so-called settled areas of Canada, judges have assumed that the British Crown was able to acquire de jure sovereignty there by original means, though the precise method of acquisition – whether discovery, settlement, or mere assertion – has never been entirely clear.[66] The best-known illustration of this, relating to lands in British Columbia, is the statement by Dickson CJ and La Forest J, for a unanimous court in *R v Sparrow*, that "there was from the outset never any doubt that sovereignty and legislative power, and indeed the underlying title, to such lands vested in the Crown."[67] As the authority cited for this was *Johnson v M'Intosh*,[68] one can assume that the Court accepted Marshall CJ's formulation of the doctrine of discovery in that case, without taking into account his acknowledgment of the relativity of de jure sovereignty in *Worcester v Georgia*.[69] Then in *Delgamuukw v British Columbia*,[70] the Supreme Court accepted 1846 as the year of Crown assertion, and apparently acquisition, of de jure sovereignty, though discovery had occurred much earlier in British Columbia.[71] The significance of 1846 is that Britain and the United States then settled their rival claims to the Pacific Northwest by signing the Washington (Oregon Boundary) Treaty that extended the international boundary along the forty-ninth parallel from the Rocky Mountains to the sea.

However, while this treaty amounted to a recognition of British de jure sovereignty north of that line that would be binding on the United States and have significance in international law, it is not at all clear how it could give the Crown sovereignty over the Wet'suwet'en and Gitksan territories that were involved in the *Delgamuukw* case, given that they lie hundreds of kilometres further north in an area where the Crown's presence and jurisdiction were virtually non-existent at the time.

A significant shift in the Supreme Court's approach to the issue of sovereignty occurred in 2004, when Chief Justice McLachlin handed down her unanimous judgments in *Haida Nation v British Columbia*[72] and *Taku River Tlingit First Nation v British Columbia*.[73] For the first time, the Court acknowledged "pre-existing Aboriginal sovereignty"[74] and referred to Crown sovereignty as "de facto."[75] The promise of section 35 of the Constitution Act, 1982,[76] McLachlin CJ said, "is realized and sovereignty claims reconciled through the process of honourable negotiation," leading to treaties that "serve to reconcile pre-existing Aboriginal sovereignty with assumed Crown sovereignty."[77] From this, it appears that Crown sovereignty, though de facto, may not be legitimate until made de jure through the treaty process.[78]

However, in her more recent unanimous judgment in *Tsilhqot'in Nation v British Columbia*,[79] Chief Justice McLachlin apparently accepted 1846 – the year of the Oregon Boundary Treaty – as the commencement of Crown sovereignty in British Columbia, as Lamer CJ had done in *Delgamuukw*.[80] As the British did not then exercise the control and jurisdiction necessary for de facto sovereignty in Tsilhqot'in territory, the Crown's sovereignty at the time could only have been de jure.[81] The Court therefore appears to have accepted that de jure sovereignty could be acquired by assertion, combined with recognition thereof by another nation state in the international community.[82] But if so, how can this be reconciled with the Court's acknowledgment of pre-existing Aboriginal sovereignty in *Haida Nation*? If Aboriginal sovereignty is to be taken seriously, surely the Crown's de jure sovereignty, even in international law,[83] would depend on treaties with the Indigenous peoples of British Columbia that, as McLachlin CJ stated in *Haida Nation*, would "serve to reconcile pre-existing Aboriginal sovereignty with assumed Crown sovereignty."[84]

Conclusion: Legality and Legitimacy

Given Canada's effective occupation and jurisdictional control of most if not all of the territory included in Canada on contemporary maps, the Crown's de facto sovereignty needs to be acknowledged as a reality. However, this does not mean it is legitimate, or even legal. As we have seen, any assessment of legality has to start with a choice of law: which legal system is to be used to determine de jure sovereignty? The answer depends, in turn, on the normative question of legitimacy: which system should be used? The answer to the second question can depend on the context in which the question is asked. If asked in the context of a border dispute between Canada and the United States, international law should no doubt be relied upon, but this does not mean that this is the appropriate body of law to apply in the context of Canada's sovereignty claims vis-à-vis the Indigenous peoples. It is important to keep in mind that de jure sovereignty is relative.

Regarding the choice of law question, the relevant legal systems we have identified are the domestic law of the Canadian nation state, international law, Indigenous domestic law, Indigenous inter-nation law, and inter-societal law. Canadian courts acknowledge the Crown's de facto sovereignty over Canada, but as apparently suggested by Chief Justice McLachlin in *Haida Nation* and *Taku River*, it is not necessarily legal, even in Canadian domestic law. Her apparent reluctance to rule on the legality of Crown sovereignty is consistent with the act of state doctrine, which excludes the issue of de jure sovereignty from the jurisdiction of domestic courts. Looking beyond domestic law, Crown sovereignty appears to be taken for granted internationally, given Canada's membership in the United Nations and the general acknowledgment of this sovereignty by the international community.[85] However, although the means by which the Crown acquired sovereignty has never, to my knowledge, been determined by an international tribunal, the advisory opinion of the International Court of Justice in the *Western Sahara Case* has cast doubt on whether the Crown could have acquired de jure sovereignty by an original mode such as occupation or settlement, especially in the nineteenth century in British Columbia.[86]

Assessment of the legality of Crown sovereignty in Indigenous domestic law would have to be done in the context of specific Indigenous legal systems. Without attempting to examine this aspect of any particular body of Indigenous law, I think it highly unlikely that any such body of law would permit acquisition of sovereignty by a European nation state by unilateral taking, which is what acquisition by occupation or settlement really amounts to. As conquest of Indigenous peoples did not occur in Canada,[87] this leaves cession as the sole possibility. Whether this occurred in any particular context would depend on the existence of a treaty between the Indigenous people in question and the Crown, by which the Indigenous party agreed to give up its sovereignty. In most instances, agreement to this effect appears to have been absent: Indigenous peoples generally assert that, rather than involving a transfer of sovereignty to the Crown, their treaties created a nation-to-nation relationship whereby the sovereignty of each party was acknowledged, and lands and jurisdiction were shared.[88]

Indigenous inter-nation legal systems governed the relationships among Indigenous nations themselves. As the European nation states were not subject to these bodies of law, it would be inappropriate to rely on them to assess European claims to sovereignty, just as it is inappropriate to use the European law of nations to determine Indigenous sovereignty. However, the inter-societal law that developed in certain contexts out of interactions between the Indigenous peoples and Europeans would no doubt have drawn from Indigenous inter-nation law, as well as from the law of nations with which the European nation states were familiar. Thus, in the negotiation of the historical treaties from the seventeenth to nineteenth centuries, one can identify protocols and other elements from both Indigenous and European legal traditions.[89]

To conclude, even if the Crown has de jure sovereignty over Canada in Canadian domestic and international law (which, as we have seen, is not entirely clear), the application of these bodies of law to assess Crown acquisition of sovereignty vis-à-vis the Indigenous peoples lacks legitimacy, because they had no role in creating these legal systems, did not consent to their application in this context, and were entirely outside their scope. So, for instance, while American acknowledgment of Crown sovereignty north of the forty-ninth parallel by the 1846 Oregon Boundary Treaty undoubtedly had international law significance for the parties, it could not have given the Crown de jure sovereignty over the Gitksan, Wet'suwet'en, Tsilhqot'in, and other Indigenous peoples in what is now British Columbia. Unless valid in Indigenous domestic or inter-nation law (which defies logic), Crown sovereignty thus remains illegitimate until consented to by Indigenous peoples in treaties that respect the inter-societal nature of these agreements and the continuing sovereignty of these peoples.[90] This could well be what Chief Justice McLachlin had in mind when she said in *Haida Nation* that "sovereignty claims [are] reconciled through the process of honourable negotiation," leading to "treaties [that] serve to reconcile pre-existing Aboriginal sovereignty with assumed Crown sovereignty."[91] The treaties, in turn, would be sources of inter-societal law that would govern the ongoing relationship between the parties and the sharing of territory and sovereignty, as discussed by Asch in chapter 1.[92] By pursuing this course, Canada could set an example for decolonization in so-called settler states where Indigenous peoples have become what Vine Deloria and Clifford Lytle have termed "nations within" the nation states that now encompass them.[93]

NOTES

1 For instance, see James Tully, *Strange Multiplicity: Constitutionalism in an Age of Diversity* (Cambridge: Cambridge University Press, 1995), esp. 66–82, 192–5; John Borrows, "Sovereignty's Alchemy: An Analysis of *Delgamuukw v. British Columbia*," *Osgoode Hall Law Journal* 37 (1999): 537; Michael Asch, "First Nations and the Derivation of Canada's Underlying Title: Comparing Perspectives on Legal Ideology," in *Aboriginal Rights and Self-Government: The Canadian and Mexican Experience in North American Perspective*, ed. Curtis Cook and Juan D. Lindau (Montreal and Kingston: McGill-Queen's University Press, 2000), 148.

2 See Mark D. Walters, "The Morality of Aboriginal Law," *Queen's Law Journal* 31 (2006): 470; Burke A. Hendrix, *Ownership, Authority, and Self-Determination: Moral Principles and Indigenous Rights Claims* (University Park: Pennsylvania State University Press, 2008).

3 See Kent McNeil, "Indigenous Nations and the Legal Relativity of European Claims to Territorial Sovereignty in North America," in *Philosophy and Aboriginal Rights: Critical Dialogues*, ed. Sandra Tomsons and Lorraine Mayer (Don Mills, ON: Oxford University Press, 2013), 242.

4 Peter H. Russell, "Doing Aboriginal Politics," *Canadian Political Science Association Bulletin* 30, no. 2 (2001): 7.

5 Ibid., 8.

6 Ibid. Similarly, John Borrows has referred to this magic as "sovereignty's alchemy": Borrows, "Sovereignty's Alchemy."

7 See Michael Ross Fowler and Julie Marie Bunck, *Law, Power, and the Sovereign State: The Evolution and Application of the Concept of Sovereignty* (University Park: Pennsylvania State University Press, 1995), esp. 6–8.

8 Perry Anderson, *Lineages of the Absolutist State* (London: Verso, 2013), 25. See also J.H. Burns, *Lordship, Kingship, and Empire: The Idea of Monarchy, 1400–1525* (Oxford: Clarendon, 1992).

9 Jean Bodin, *The Six Bookes of a Commonweale*, trans. Richard Knolles, ed. Kenneth Douglas McRae (1576, trans. 1606; Cambridge: Harvard University Press, 1962).

10 See Sidney Painter, *The Rise of the Feudal Monarchies* (Ithaca, NY: Cornell University Press, 1951); Joseph R. Strayer, *On the Medieval Origins of the Modern State* (Princeton: Princeton University Press, 1970).

11 See Leo Gross, "The Peace of Westphalia, 1648–1948," *American Journal of International Law* 42 (1948): 20.

12 See Antony Anghie, *Imperialism, Sovereignty, and the Making of International Law* (Cambridge: Cambridge University Press, 2005).

13 See Fowler and Bunck, *Law, Power, and the Sovereign State*; Spyridon Flogaitis, *The Evolution of Law and the State in Europe: Seven Lessons* (Oxford: Hart Publishing, 2014); Stephen Tierney, ed., *Nationalism and Globalisation* (Oxford: Hart Publishing, 2015).

14 Leroy Little Bear, "An Elder Explains Indigenous Philosophy and Indigenous Sovereignty," in Tomsons and Mayer, *Philosophy and Aboriginal Rights,* 6 at 7.

15 Of course this has been modified in recent times by the creation of the European Union, but it was nonetheless the case in the period of European colonization of North America. See Konrad Schiemann, "Europe and the Loss of Sovereignty," *International and Comparative Law Quarterly* 56 (2007): 475.

16 See Robert A. Williams Jr, *Linking Arms Together: American Indian Treaty Visions of Law and Peace, 1600–1800* (New York: Oxford University Press, 1997); James (Sa'ke'j) Youngblood Henderson, *Treaty Rights in the Constitution of Canada* (Toronto: Carswell, 2007); John Borrows, *Canada's Indigenous Constitution* (Toronto: University of Toronto Press, 2010).

17 All too often this question is not even addressed, as it is wrongly assumed that international law is the only relevant body of law: e.g., see *Tsilhqot'in Nation v British Columbia*, [2008] 1 CNLR 112 at paras 591–602 [*Tsilhqot'in Nation* BCSC].

18 See D.J. Devine, "The Status of Rhodesia in International Law," *Acta Juridica* 1 (1973): 78–9; Isaak I. Dore, "Recognition of Rhodesia and Traditional International Law: Some Conceptual Problems," *Vanderbilt Journal of Transnational Law* 13 (1980): 33–8.

19 See *Madzimbamuto v Lardner-Burke NO*, 1968 (2) SALR 284 and 457 (RAD); *Dhlamini and Others v Carter NO*, 1968 (2) SALR 445 and 464 (RAD); *Dhlamini and Another v Carter NO*, 1968 (2) SALR 467 (RAD); *R v Ndhlovu*, 1968 (4) SALR 515 (RSA).

20 See Dore, "Recognition of Rhodesia"; John Dugard, *Recognition and the United Nations* (Cambridge: Grotius Publications, 1987), 90–8.

21 See *Madzimbamuto v Lardner-Burke and Another*, [1968] 3 All ER 561 (PC); *Adams v Adams*, [1970] 3 All ER 572 (PDA).

22 See Michel Morin, *L'Usurpation de la souveraineté autochtone: Le cas des peuples de la Nouvelle-France et des colonies anglaises de l'Amérique du Nord* (Montreal: Boréal, 1997).

23 See Brain Slattery, "Aboriginal Sovereignty and Imperial Claims," *Osgoode Hall Law Journal* 29 (1991), esp. 701–3; Walters, "Morality of Aboriginal Law"; Janna Promislow, "I Smooth'd Him Up with Fair Words: Intersocietal Law, from Fur Trade to Treaty" (PhD diss., York University, 2012).

24 This part draws on the more detailed discussion in McNeil, "Indigenous Nations."

25 As I do not claim expertise in any of these systems of law, I am relying on the authority of Indigenous academics such as John Borrows and Sa'ke'j Henderson. I am also aware that the European concept of sovereignty, involving exclusive authority over and control of a specific territory, may not fit well with Indigenous world views, political organizations, and legal systems. However, as Leroy Little Bear and other Indigenous leaders and scholars have made clear, Indigenous peoples have their own ways of conceptualizing political authority that, while not the same as the European notion of sovereignty, nonetheless entail responsibility for and control over territory, and govern their relationships with one another and with the natural/spiritual world. For instance, see Taiaiake Alfred, *Peace, Power, Righteousness: An Indigenous Manifesto* (Toronto: Oxford University Press, 1999), esp. 54–69; Taiaiake Alfred, "Sovereignty," in *Sovereignty Matters: Locations of Contestation and Possibility in Indigenous Struggles for Self-Determination*, ed. Joanne Baker (Lincoln: University of Nebraska Press, 2005), 33; John Bird, Lorraine Land, and Murray MacAdam, eds, *Nation-to-Nation: Aboriginal Sovereignty and the Future of Canada*, new ed. (Toronto: Irwin Publishing, 2002); Dale Turner, *This Is Not a Peace Pipe: Towards a Critical Indigenous Philosophy* (Toronto: University of Toronto Press, 2006), esp. 66–70; Tomsons and Mayer, *Philosophy and Aboriginal Rights*, part III.

26 It is inconceivable that any body of law would countenance original acquisition of sovereignty over the territory where that law applied, because that would necessarily entail denial of the sovereign authority that gave rise to that body of law in the first place.

27 Inconsistently, European nation states, particularly England (later Britain), entered into treaties of peace, alliance, and commerce with Indigenous nations: see Williams, *Linking Arms Together*; Henderson, *Treaty Rights*; *R v Sioui* [1990] 1 SCR 1025 at 1052–3; *R v Marshall [No. 1]*, [1999] 3 SCR 456.

28 See Patrick Macklem, *Indigenous Difference and the Constitution of Canada* (Toronto: University of Toronto Press, 2001), 113–15; Michael Asch, "From *Terra Nullius* to Affirmation: Reconciling Aboriginal Rights with the Canadian Constitution," *Canadian Journal of Law and Society* 17, no. 2 (2002): 23.

29 See John Anthony Caruso, *The Mississippi Valley Frontier: The Age of French Exploration and Settlement* (Indianapolis: Bobbs-Merrill, 1966); Brian Slattery, *French Claims in North America, 1500–1559* (Saskatoon: University of Saskatchewan Native Law Centre, 1980); Slattery, "Paper Empires: The Legal Dimensions of French and English Ventures in North America," in *Despotic Dominion: Property Rights in British Settler Societies*, ed. John McLaren, A.R. Buck, and Nancy E. Wright (Vancouver: UBC Press, 2005), 50.

30 See John Thomas Juricek, "English Claims in North America to 1660: A Study in Legal and Constitutional History" (PhD diss., University of Chicago, 1970); Patricia Seed, *Ceremonies of Possession in European Conquest of the New World, 1492–1640* (Cambridge: Cambridge University Press, 1995).

31 Regarding English charters, this was acknowledged by Marshall CJ in *Worcester v Georgia*, 31 US (6 Pet) 515 (1832) at 546, where he stated, "These grants asserted a title against Europeans only, and were considered as blank paper so far as the rights of the natives were concerned."

32 In addition to the works cited in notes 29–30 above, see L. Oppenheim, *International Law: A Treatise* (London: Longmans, Green, 1905), 1:265; M.F. Lindley, *The Acquisition and Government of Backward Territory in International Law* (London: Longmans, Green, 1926); Julius Goebel Jr, *The Struggle for the Falkland Islands: A Study in Legal and Diplomatic History* (1927; Port Washington: Kennikat, 1971), 47–119; Friedrich August Freiherr von der Heydte, "Discovery, Symbolic Annexation and Virtual Effectiveness in International Law," *American Journal of International Law* 29 (1935): 448.

33 See Juricek, *English Claims*; Slattery, "Paper Empires"; Seed, *Ceremonies of Possession*; Morin, *L'Usurpation de la souveraineté autochtone*.

34 For instance, see Travers Twiss, *The Law of Nations Considered as Independent Political Communities* (Oxford: Clarendon, 1884), 196–211; Oppenheim, *International Law*, 1:275–80; T.L. Lawrence, *The Principles of International Law*, 4th ed. (London: Macmillan, 1911), 148–61; William Edward Hall, *A Treatise on International Law*, 8th ed., ed. A. Pearce Higgins (Oxford: Clarendon, 1924) 139–40; Lindley, *Acquisition and Government of Backward Territory*, 139–51; Heydte, "Discovery, Symbolic Annexation and Virtual Effectiveness"; James Crawford, *Brownlie's Principles of Public International Law*, 8th ed. (Oxford: Clarendon, 2012), 220–9.

35 *Island of Palmas Case*, (1928) 2 RIAA 829; *Legal Status of Eastern Greenland Case* (1933), 2 PCIJ, Series A/B, No 43; *Minquiers and Ecrehos Case*, 1953 ICJR 47.

36 *Western Sahara* 1975 ICJR 12.

37 Significantly, the period to which the court applied its ruling was the 1880s, when most jurists thought effective occupation was sufficient: see works cited in note 34 above.

38 *Johnson v M'Intosh* 21 US (8 Wheat) 543.

39 Ibid., 573.

40 For recent critical assessment, see Robert J. Miller, Jacinta Ruru, Larissa Behrendt, and Tracey Lindberg, *Discovering Indigenous Lands: The Doctrine of Discovery in the English Colonies* (Oxford: Oxford University Press, 2010).

41 George Chalmers, *Political Annals of the Present United Colonies from Their Settlement to the Peace of 1763* (1780; New York: Burt Franklin, 1968).

42 Ibid., 6.

43 John Marshall, *The Life of George Washington, Commander in Chief of the American Forces, during the War Which Established the Independence of His Country, and First President of the United States*, vol. 1 (Philadelphia: Wayne, 1804).

44 Although Chalmers's book was not expressly mentioned by Marshall CJ in his judgment, it was cited in argument by counsel (middle of 2nd para just before Marshall's judgment) and had been relied upon by him in *The Life of George Washington*, ibid., vol. 1, which he then used in writing his judgment; see Lindsay G. Robertson, "John Marshall as Colonial Historian: Reconsidering the Origins of the Doctrine of Discovery," *Journal of Law and Politics* 13 (1997): 759.

45 For more detailed discussion, see Kent McNeil, "The Doctrine of Discovery Reconsidered: Reflecting on Robert J. Miller, Jacinta Ruru, Larissa Behrendt, and Tracey Lindberg, *Discovering Indigenous Lands: The Doctrine of Discovery in the English Colonies* and Felix Hoehn, *Reconciling Sovereignties: Aboriginal Nations and Canada*," *Osgoode Hall Law Journal* 53 (1916): 699.

46 See works cited in notes 32–4 above.

47 See Lindsay G. Robertson, *Conquest by Law: How the Discovery of America Dispossessed Indigenous Peoples of Their Lands* (New York: Oxford University Press, 2005), esp. 103. For relatively recent affirmation of the doctrine of discovery as formulated in *Johnson v M'Intosh*, see *County of Oneida, New York v Oneida Indian Nation of New York State*, 470 US 226 at 434 (1985), referred to in *City of Sherrill v Oneida Indian Nation of New York*, 544 US 197 (2005) at 203 n1.

48 *Worcester v Georgia.*

49 Ibid., 574; see also 603.
50 Ibid., 544. This conclusion is consistent with the international law rule that agreements are generally binding only on the parties thereto: see *Direct United States Cable Company v Anglo-American Telegraph Company* (1877), 2 App Cas 394 at 421 (PC); *Clipperton Island Case* (1932), 26 AJIL 390 at 394; Lord [Arnold Duncan] McNair, *The Law of Treaties* (Oxford: Clarendon, 1961), 309–21; Malcolm N. Shaw, *International Law*, 7th ed. (Cambridge: Cambridge University Press, 2014), 672–4.
51 Marshall CJ acknowledged the existence of these Indigenous legal systems in both *Johnson v M'Intosh*, at 593, and *Worcester v Georgia* at 542–3. However, in the latter case at 559 he also suggested a natural law source for prior Indigenous rights: "Indian nations had always been considered as distinct, independent political communities, retaining their *original natural rights*, as the undisputed possessors of the soil, from time immemorial" (emphasis added).
52 *Worcester v Georgia* at 574; see also 603.
53 In *Johnson v M'Intosh* at 587–91, Marshall CJ relied more on conquest, whereas in *Worcester v Georgia* at 547–56, he emphasized treaties. In *United States v Santa Fe Pacific Railroad Co*, 314 US 339 (1941) at 347, the Supreme Court noted that, after their incorporation into the United States, Indian lands could still be taken by conquest or treaty.
54 See Robertson, *Conquest by Law*, 138–42.
55 This part draws on the more detailed discussion in McNeil, "Discovery Reconsidered."
56 See Walters, "Morality of Aboriginal Law," esp. 509–13.
57 See W. Harrison Moore, *Act of State in English Law* (London: John Murray, 1906).
58 See *Duff Development Co v Government of Kelantan*, [1924] AC 797 (HL); *R v Kent Justices*, [1967] 1 All ER 560 (QB) at 564–5; *Adams v Adams* at 583, 585; Kenneth Roberts-Wray, *Commonwealth and Colonial Law* (London: Stevens & Sons, 1966), 116.
59 See *Coe v Commonwealth of Australia* (1979), 53 ALJR 403; *Mabo v Queensland* (1992), 175 CLR 1 at 31–2 (Brennan J), 78–9 (Deane and Gaudron JJ); *State of Western Australia v Commonwealth* (1995), 128 ALR 1 at 12.
60 At trial in *Tsilhqot'in Nation* BCSC, para. 585–602, the Crown in right of Canada argued for several different dates for Crown assertion of sovereignty, but Justice Vickers came to his own conclusion on the evidence, deciding on 1846, which date the Supreme Court did not question on appeal: see *Tsilhqot'in Nation v British Columbia*, [2014] 2 SCR 257 [*Tsilhqot'in Nation* SCC].

61 E.g., see *R v Marshall; R v Bernard*, [2005] 2 SCR 220 at para 71, where the court proceeded on the basis that Britain acquired mainland Nova Scotia in 1713 (the year of the Treaty of Utrecht with France), northern New Brunswick in 1759 (the year the British defeated the French at Quebec), and Cape Breton Island in 1763 (the year France transferred its remaining colonies in what is now Canada to Britain by the Treaty of Paris).

62 For more detailed discussion, see Kent McNeil, *Common Law Aboriginal Title* (Oxford: Clarendon, 1989), 267–90.

63 In *St Catharines Milling and Lumber Company v R* (1887), 13 SCR 577 at 643–44, aff'd (1888), 14 App Cas 46 (PC), Taschereau J, in his concurring judgment, relied expressly on discovery as the basis for French sovereignty in La Nouvelle France, and in *R v Syliboy* Patterson J explained French sovereignty in Acadia in the same way. Compare *R v Côté*, [1996] 3 SCR 139 at paras 42–9, where Lamer CJ was more ambivalent.

64 See the works cited in note 29. In his unanimous decision in *Sioui*, note 27 at para 65, Lamer J (as he then was) referred to "France's *de facto* control in Canada" prior to the British victory on the Plains of Abraham in 1759 and the capitulation of Montreal in 1760.

65 In *Sioui*, ibid., at para 66, Lamer J stated that "Great Britain's *de jure* control of Canada took the form of the Treaty of Paris of February 10, 1763."

66 See, however, *R v Adams*, [1996] 3 SCR 101 at para 32, where Lamer CJ stated, "Under the British law governing colonization, the Crown assumed ownership of newly discovered territories subject to an underlying interest of indigenous peoples in the occupation and use of such territories."

67 *R v Sparrow*, [1990] 1 SCR 1075 at 1103. For critical commentary, see Michael Asch and Patrick Macklem, "Aboriginal Rights and Canadian Sovereignty: An Essay on *R. v. Sparrow*," *Alberta Law Review* 29 (1991): 498.

68 See note 38. Likewise, in *Guerin v R*, [1984] 2 SCR 335 at 377–8, Dickson J (as he then was) cited this American decision and apparently accepted the doctrine of discovery.

69 See note 31. See text at notes 38–53.

70 [1997] 3 SCR 1010 at para 145.

71 See *Tsilhqot'in Nation BCSC*, at paras 585–602.

72 [2004] 3 SCR 511 [*Haida Nation*].

73 [2004] 3 SCR 550 [*Taku River*].

74 *Haida Nation*, at para 20.

75 *Taku River*, at para 42. See also *Haida Nation*, at para 32; *Manitoba Metis Federation Inc v Canada (AG)*, [2013] 1 SCR 623 at para 66. For insightful discussion and analysis, see Felix Hoehn, *Reconciling Sovereignties: Aboriginal Nations and Canada* (Saskatoon: University of Saskatchewan Native Law Centre, 2012).

76 Schedule B to the *Canada Act 1982* (UK), 1982, c 11. Section 35(1) provides, "The existing aboriginal and treaty rights of the aboriginal peoples of Canada are hereby recognized and affirmed."

77 *Haida Nation*, at para 20.

78 See Walters, "Morality of Aboriginal Law," 513–17; Michael Asch, *On Being Here to Stay: Treaties and Aboriginal Rights in Canada* (Toronto: University of Toronto Press, 2014), 32–3; Joshua Nichols, "A Reconciliation without Recollection? *Chief Mountain* and the Sources of Sovereignty," *UBC Law Review* 48 (2015): 535–6.

79 *Tsilhqot'in Nation SCC*, esp. paras 50, 60.

80 Although the chief justices used the term *assertion* rather than *acquisition* of sovereignty, they must have regarded 1846 as the year sovereignty was *acquired*, because that was when the Crown got its underlying title to Aboriginal title lands (see *Delgamuukw* at para 145), presumably as a result of the common law doctrine of tenures that could not have applied prior to Crown sovereignty. See McNeil, *Common Law Aboriginal Title*, esp. 79–84, 241–3.

81 Compare *Tsilhqot'in Nation* BCSC at para 602, where Vickers J concluded, "By 1846 there was a *de facto* British presence in the area. The Treaty of Oregon is a treaty with another nation settling a boundary dispute and providing international recognition of sovereignty to the land and territory north of the 49th parallel. The assertion of sovereignty, recognized by another nation, is clear at this point in our history." However, with all due respect, his detailed factual findings relative to the history of the region fail to show the effective occupation necessary for the Crown to have acquired sovereignty in international law. His reliance on 1846 and his reference to the Oregon Boundary Treaty reveal that he too regarded that bilateral international agreement as giving the Crown de jure sovereignty over Tsilhqot'in territory.

82 Although McLachlin CJ acknowledged in *Tsilhqot'in Nation* at para 69, that the "doctrine of *terra nullius* (that no one owned the land prior to European assertion of sovereignty) never applied in Canada," her bracketed definition of the term reveals that she had property rights, not sovereignty, in mind. See John Borrows, "The Durability of *Terra Nullius: Tsilhqot'in Nation v. British Columbia*," *UBC Law Review* 48 (2015): 701.

83 See the *Western Sahara Case*.

84 *Haida Nation* at para 20.

85 There are, however, areas in the Arctic where Canada's claims are disputed by some nation states.

86 In this context, a question arises over whether the decision in the *Western Sahara Case*, which related to North Africa in the 1880s, can be applied

retroactively in other parts of the world where colonization took place earlier. The intertemporal doctrine provides that legality has to be determined by the international law of the time, not by subsequent developments: see *Island of Palmas Case*, at 831; T.O. Elias, "The Doctrine of Intertemporal Law," *American Journal of International Law* 74 (1980): 285; Shaw, *International Law*, 366–7. So the validity of Crown assertions of sovereignty would probably have to be assessed on the basis of the international law at the time the assertion took place in the specific area of Canada in question. Given the lingering uncertainty in international law prior to the *Western Sahara Case* over the means by which de jure sovereignty could be acquired over territories inhabited by Indigenous peoples, determining the international validity of Crown assertions of sovereignty in the past could prove to be an illusive task. An international tribunal might try to avoid the problem by relying on prescription (peaceful exercise of de facto sovereignty over a long period of time), but that is by no means certain either, as the application of the prescription doctrine apparently depends on acquiescence by the previous sovereign: e.g., see D.H.N. Johnson, "Acquisitive Prescription in International Law," *British Yearbook of International Law* 27 (1950): 332; R.Y. Jennings, *The Acquisition of Territory in International Law* (Manchester: Manchester University Press, 1963), 20–8; Yehuda Z. Blum, *Historic Titles in International Law* (The Hague: Martinus Nijhoff, 1997), 6–37; Crawford, *Brownlie's Principles*, 229–35; Shaw, *International Law*, 364–6; Asch, *On Being Here to Stay*, 38–41.

87 This was judicially confirmed in *Haida Nation* at para 25.

88 E.g., see Sharon Venne, "Understanding Treaty 6: An Indigenous Perspective," in *Aboriginal and Treaty Rights in Canada: Essays on Law, Equality, and Respect for Difference*, ed. Michael Asch (Vancouver: UBC Press, 1997), 173; Harold Cardinal and Walter Hildebrandt, *Treaty Elders of Saskatchewan: Our Dream Is That Our Peoples Will One Day Be Clearly Recognized as Nations* (Calgary: University of Calgary Press, 2000); Bird, Land, and MacAdam, *Nation-to-Nation*; Asch, *On Being Here to Stay*. For comprehensive treatment of the treaty relations between Indigenous peoples and the Crown in Canada, see Henderson, *Treaty Rights*.

89 See John Borrows, "Wampum at Niagara: The Royal Proclamation, Canadian Legal History, and Self-Government," in Asch, *Aboriginal and Treaty Rights*, 155; Williams, *Linking Arms Together*; Henderson, *Treaty Rights*; John J. Borrows and Leonard I. Rotman, *Aboriginal Legal Issues: Cases, Materials & Commentary*, 4th ed. (Markham, ON: LexisNexis Canada, 2012), 12–18.

90 See Venne, "Understanding Treaty Six," 206–7; Asch, "From *Terra Nullius* to Affirmation," 34–8; Asch, *On Being Here to Stay*.
91 *Haida Nation* at para. 20.
92 In his concurring judgment in *Mitchell v Canada (MNR)*, [2001] 1 SCR 911, Binnie J, along with Major J, envisaged the possibility for a sharing of sovereignty in Canada. Referring to the 1996 *Report of the Royal Commission on Aboriginal Peoples*, he observed at para 135, "What is significant is that the Royal Commission itself sees aboriginal peoples as full participants with non-aboriginal peoples in a shared Canadian sovereignty. Aboriginal peoples do not stand in opposition to, nor are they subjugated by, Canadian sovereignty. They are part of it."
93 Vine Deloria Jr and Clifford Lytle, *The Nations Within: The Past and Future of American Indian Sovereignty* (New York: Pantheon Books, 1984).

11 Treaty Ecologies: With Persons, Peoples, Animals, and the Land

BRIAN NOBLE

In this chapter I will be expanding on the vital contributions of Borrows, Asch, and Tully, starting with a focal story and history shared with me by Piikani and Ktunaxa peoples. The story – about following black-tail deer – was shared by these Indigenous friends purposefully: that is to help me understand their people's land-responsive, inter-political practices – an integrated set of conjoined actions I call "treaty ecologies."

With this doubled term, *treaty ecologies*, I am referring *not* to what passes as hegemonic statist discourse of treaties that, against the grain of negotiated reciprocity, all too often play out as asymmetrical, colonizing instruments in their own right. Rather, I am referring to a mode of living well together with other peoples, animals, and non-humans (visible and non-visible), and with the lands, air, and waters. It is, as Marcel Mauss would call it in his "Essai sur le don," a "system of total prestations" that takes in persons and peoples, the earth, and all its inhabitants.[1]

This Piikani, Ktunaxa story has also animated my understanding of how reconciling action at the level of everyday, reciprocal *living-with* the world – as Borrows and Tully have discussed reconciliation – will also animate and fuel the resurgence of decolonial, liveable political relations between settler and Indigenous peoples, this at the level of reciprocal *living-together* as peoples. This latter aspect of treaty praxis resonates with what Asch has posited as critical to honourable resolution of settler-presence in Indigenous territories.

Michi Saagig Nishnaabeg thinker, writer, and decolonial activist Leanne Betasamosake Simpson has pointed to her people's practices, which also fit closely to the idea of treaty ecologies that I am positing, and I will bring her work to the fore towards the conclusion of the chapter. It is there that I imagine kinds of actions that could come together – an alliance of transformative resurgence – by and between committed Indigenous and settler peoples, to actualize all that treaty ecologies promise.

In stages, the initial section of this chapter draws out the treaty-ecological praxis of *living-with-and-together* conveyed in the Following Deer and Treaty 7 stories that follow. Then, I outline how I see doubled aspects of *coloniality* in capitalist circuits in order to present what confounds such reciprocal treaty ecologies and inter-peoples relations, and also to foreground the grip this continues to have in settler-modern conditions of life. This will then stage discussions of dovetailing *modes of resurgence* from Borrows, Tully, and Asch, drawing on each scholar's presentations to better think about the Piikani and Ktunaxa accounts – and vice versa. Finally I take up Simpson's accounts of learning treaty through intimacy of care as humans and with animals, as starting between mother and nursing baby, reaching out to her people's relations with animal collectives, arriving at inter-peoples (eco-social) treaties, much of this in the same key as the Following Deer story.

First, the stories.

Following Deer, Living, and Learning Treaty Praxis

Two stories convey more of what I am getting at – one an oral and transmitted account of inter-political, transactional relations of Piikani people with Ktunaxa (Kootenay) people to the west, and a second about the 1877 treaty between the Canadian Crown and the Blackfoot people, including the Piikani, understood by the Blackfoot as a land-sharing treaty.[2] Living and practising in a treaty-way is the first aspect – or register – of activated treaty ecologies.

The first story brings us to how a reciprocal practice of following deer (and arguably many other collectives of animals, beings, persons where strong ceremonial relations exist) for these peoples, is key to these possibilities. The initial story of following blacktail deer came to me in 2004, in the course of my work partnering with Piikani Blackfoot people on museum repatriation and authority regarding cultural material and knowledges.[3] Eventually echoed and affirmed to me by Ktunaxa elders in the fall of 2005, it is a story of practised treaty relations between peoples where their territories come together – a political and territorial authority accord between the Piikani and the Ktunaxa peoples, which is at the same time an accord between persons, and between persons and animals, and indeed with all the earth. Such accords are the second aspect – or register – of active treaty ecologies.

Some years back, I asked Piikani friend and ceremonialist Reg Crowshoe how the Piikani understood the extent and borderlands of their territory, in the time before settler people brought their maps and their property-imposing practices into Piikani lands. Interestingly enough I was told stories not of delineated borders, or borders defended (typical of the Hobbesian state), but of transaction and ceremonial relations between persons (human, animal, earth-borne) as the basis for mediating and sanctioning a shared zone between lands that counted as their territory and that of other peoples. It was a tale of the continuity of intimate and political relations.

Reg described how things were done by relational encounter and everyday negotiation, between the Piikani and other peoples where their territories met and overlapped. He discussed the Cree to the north of Piikani territory, especially along the North Saskatchewan river, with whom the Piikani have had difficult relations at times. Then, to give an example of good relations, he turned his story to the Ktunaxa, and the lands where Piikani territory met Ktunaxa territory in the front ranges of the Rocky Mountains around what is now called Crowsnest Pass, and in particular he described the personal, inter-species relations between the Ktunaxa and blacktail deer.[4]

As told to me, the defining situation took place one day some 200 years ago. A Ktunaxa hunting party was tracking a group of these deer over the Rocky Mountain passes, bringing them into the hunting lands of the Piikani, and the borderlands of their peoples' two territories. The deer were moving, as deer do, through mountain valleys where there was good browsing food. The Ktunaxa party followed them, as hunters do. *This way of hunting was responsive, attentive, moving with the animals, and full of respect. In effect the deer drew them there, and they felt obliged to follow.* But these usual practices were amplified, as the Ktunaxa had a special obligation in the blacktail deer ceremony, a practice that aided in hunting such deer.[5] The gift of the blacktail deer was more than its flesh to become food for the Ktunaxa; it was also the powerful spirit in this medicine. Respect also meant following the medicine, as the hunting and the medicine worked together.

The story continued, however, with a surprise turn that the Ktunaxa had not necessarily anticipated – an encounter with a Piikani hunting party moving through these same valleys. The Piikani knew this was their own hunting territory and that the Ktunaxa were transgressing.

Put on the spot, the Ktunaxa had to answer about their hunting, which would soon elicit their ceremonial obligation to follow the deer.

In short order, a lodge or tipi was set up for the two groups to meet and sort matters out, following ceremonial protocol. The Ktunaxa said the hunting was good, and they followed the deer here, because of their mutual obligations with the deer. Acknowledging fully that they were now in Piikani hunting territory, the Ktunaxa went about setting right these relations with the Piikani. They proposed to transfer to the Piikani certain of the rights to the powerful medicine ceremony, the Blacktail Deer Dance, the very ceremony that animated the conditions of their following the deer. A ceremony was undertaken, the transfer of rights was made, and the Ktunaxa and Piikani to this day understand they both will follow and hunt these deer in what we might now see as this border territory of sharing the land, not merely sharing as peoples but sharing between peoples and all the natural beings in this border area.

In retrospect, I now understand this story as the recounting of a formal, protocol-rich exchange of medicine and promises to allow free movement in the area. The two peoples agreed to share in the area, living with the land and its diverse living inhabitants, and so to live together as peoples there as well. This was a praxis of treaty, animated by an ecology of sharing in the land and its fruits, of exchange, reciprocity, mutual obligation, extended relations through ceremonial-material encounter among persons, animal-persons, animal collectives, and peoples' collectives – a cooperation of Ktunaxa, Piikani, and blacktail deer.

The endurance of this treaty praxis and its attendant ecologies is reiterated when the Piikani speak of the ongoing strength of their political relations with the Ktunaxa, ever reinforced by the ongoing efficacy of the blacktail deer medicine ceremony as practised by both the Ktunaxa and the Piikani. The hunting remains good if the ceremony is honoured, the spiritual relations with all the powers in the Blacktail Deer Dance properly reciprocated, nurtured, and so secured.

The *living-together relations* between peoples (through the transaction of the ceremony between peoples for the right to hunt in an area) are reinforced by their *living-with relations*, the carrying out of the ceremony, following and apprehending of the deer, recognizing the hunting efficacy in so doing, while extending and honouring *all their relations* with both animals and peoples at the same time.[6]

Witnessed to me, through this story out of lived history, is a clear expression of how the political-territorial authority and autonomy of these two peoples has been respected and secured, in the same moment that their inter-political relational networks are put into action. Their alliance, their treaty, their resolution of conflict by acknowledging the co-presence of the blacktail deer and its ceremony establishes and assembles their *autonomous collectives*, as well as their *conjoined collectivities*.

Put in another, perhaps more helpful way, it was through the necessary action of *living-with co-presences* (meaning the relations among intimates in persons and animal-persons) that the Piikani and Ktunaxa were able to intensify and adjust their *living-together* co-presences (the relations between polities within their territories), so that they could eventually share their territories by sharing and exchanging rights to ceremony and access to hunting lands.

This stands, in my new understanding, as a non-colonial, reciprocity-activated, inter-political relation, where multiple co-present, cooperating, and co-witnessing beings can live together respectfully without any of them problematically subordinated to others. All retain their distinction and difference, by sharing a common territory in their borderlands, by honouring and respecting one another, by living freely in difference in common worlds, where they renew their relations frequently and necessarily.[7]

In terms of my larger proposition, I also call attention to the way the relations of treaty obligation and treaty reciprocity operate at these two continuous, entwined registers – the register of the interpersonal and the register of the inter-political. But here there is a seamless continuity from the interpersonal to the inter-political. I will return to this "double-register" matter throughout, including specific thinking about how treaty praxis has been undermined by the sequestered double-register of practices associated with coloniality.

Now I will return to the possibility of the Piikani living-together, inter-politically, with the collective of newly settling people who were represented by the Crown in right of Canada, with whom the Piikani formed a treaty in 1877, at a place called Blackfoot Crossing.[8]

In the events surrounding the signing of that treaty, many of the conditions allowing for *a living-with to living-together move* were, arguably, put into play, co-enacted by all the parties involved. At the core of this were committed hunting relations with bison, a mainstay of the Blackfoot people, with whom they also had many powerful ceremonial relations, and that indeed continue to this day in their tipi ceremonies, the Natooas Sundance ceremony, and more. The Crown promised to help protect the bison populations and the Blackfoot hunting areas within the territory as railroad development and settlement would proceed. Notwithstanding modernist, biopolitical readings that there were cultural misunderstandings in the making of numbered treaties of which Treaty 7 was one – a matter on which Asch has cogently disabused us – I have been compelled to consider the relations in terms of the enactments that took place on the treaty field and also relayed to me by Reg Crowshoe.

Notably, the commissioners who came to Blackfoot Crossing undertook an exchanges of promises, bound ceremonially in the lived practice of smoking ceremonial pipes together; in the exchange of signatures on a page inscribed with the transaction; in an exchange of gifts (see Tully on the vital importance of reciprocity); in the cash ("treaty annuities") handed over to all the Blackfoot present and treaty medals to leaders; in hearing and acknowledging the willingness of the Blackfoot to share their land with settler folks; in promising provisions and protections for the Blackfoot for all time; in agreeing to be as brothers (see Asch); and in promising to act together mutually upon the honour of the Crown (the Queen is mentioned explicitly) and the honour of the Creator (the source of life) in perpetuity.[9] As remarked upon by elders and reiterated by Hugh Dempsey recently, "It's the spirit of the treaty that was signed as a bond of trust between the natives and government."[10]

The often-cited words of Crowfoot, who was speaking chief at Blackfoot Crossing, refer to the extent and the limits of that exchange: "As a present we will give you anything you can take with you, but we cannot give you the land,"[11] the understanding being that the fruits of the land were plenty, but the land in its ecological totality was, to use the language of property, inalienable.[12]

These combined living-with transactions multiply, assemble together, and move into a living-together transaction involving all the political collectives participating in this inter-political action, producing the bond of trust, upon sharable territory. Here again were the double, entwined registers of praxis constituting treaty ecology. Rather than the legalist-normative document named "treaty" – and although a document was produced – my attention has been drawn to the relational network imploding and radiating in a living-with array of exchanges at the moment of affirming a living-together relation. As with the Ktunaxa-Piikani living-together transactions, this is what I have been referring to as "treaty praxis" or more pointedly as "treaty ecology." This is an instance of inter-political or inter-collective relational ecologies at play, very much analogous to the Blacktail Deer Dance exchange and its treaty ecology. It is one way to recognize how political collectivities, which might assume different "worlds" and have different means of apprehending them, can be in relation with others but without subsuming those others. Rather they interact reciprocally and equitably by honouring the source of authority informing the other, including all the seen and unseen agents that are active.[13]

This practice of mutual honouring is precisely what I have witnessed in my relations with Piikani people, some 100, 200 years after these acts of treaty ecology exchange took place. It has reached me after all these years that the Piikani always and already approached me as treaty persons and treaty people do when meeting those with whom they are in a treaty relation. The doubly personal *and* political principle is to welcome folks, including Euro-Canadians and other folks from elsewhere, into their territory in a relation of sharing the land – as they did with the Ktunaxa in the mountain valleys and with the Crown at Blackfoot Crossing. They were comporting me in the present century as a "treaty person" from the collective with whom they had in 1877 entered into treaty – an enduring and consummate political ecology of relations in the living land, their territories. And I believe they engaged me this way because, within the limits of my living-with capacity, I had honoured the material, intangible, agent-ful transactions *as well as the obligations* that flow from having entered into those transactions (i.e., not from any kind of categorical imperative, Kantian or otherwise). I found myself deeply entangled in their (actually *our*) fully political, relational, mutual anthropology and ecology – the demand placed upon me to act in the most respectful manner within the territories that their people had so generously shared in perpetuity with my settler forbears, as they are now shared with me.

On the latter, and now borrowing from Isabelle Stengers, this conjoined and responsive treaty of all things, and/or of many collectives, is the alternative to the modernist praxis of coloniality. It offers an alternative *ethos* that takes place at the same time within an alternative *oikos* – the habitus and locale we share.[14] It is this resurgence of "living together" by the expanded action of "living with" that gives shape to decoloniality, conformed as a seamless "system of total prestations." To put this into higher relief, I now turn to this contrasting counter-ethos and anti-ecology, coloniality.

Coloniality and the Decolonial Answer in Treaty Ecologies

Recently, while attending the funeral of Secwepemc leader and activist Arthur Manuel, I was sitting with Elder Mike Arnoose discussing how Art worked tirelessly and caringly to protect the land and waters, for the next generations, in the face of continual oppressions by the Canadian state. Elder Arnoose offered a simple observation: "The red man gives, and the white man takes."

Treaty ecologies are about giving and not taking, so what are we to make of the ways treaties have been taken up by Canada?

For many, the word *treaty* has been debased, becoming a problem word in the context of Canadian/Indigenous political discourse. In short it has been colonized. It is often seen as a form of betrayal, a trick to put in place a contract assuring certainty and finality in relations,[15] tit-for-tat exchange, instead of a relation of mutual obligations, promises, rights, and responsibilities – the latter being an ecology, much in the sense of symbiosis, as Tully discusses matters. It is a contract that often takes away, with finality, instead of proposing and acting on reciprocal relations in perpetuity.

For some time now, I have been considering the conditions that confound the realization of living-with-and-together relations. The story of relations expressed in the Following Deer story stands as peaceful non-colonizing counteraction to the practices that have come to characterize settler–Indigenous relations under Euro-Canadian settlement, individualist-focused common law, Westphalian confederation, and expansive capitalism, where the expectation is that the dominance of the settler polity and its proprietary ambitions must and will prevail. The Ktunaxa-Piikani relations keep people, animals, worlds, and the complex among them all at play, responsively and symmetrically. It is an etho-ecology of peace in relations. It is also a stay against forces of expanding "accumulation by dispossession."[16]

What is going on in this ceremonial-political exchange is very different from the norm of action in deeply entrenched liberal settler–Indigenous political, social, cultural, and economic life. I refer to this latter norm of action as "coloniality," echoing aspects of what Latin American decolonial scholars have called the "coloniality of power." Coloniality constrains and trains freedom to conform to a particular power arrangement, through two entwined aspects, both of which stand in diametric opposition to the entwined aspects of treaty praxes. Rather than flow (or system) of total prestations, coloniality is a dispositif, more about hardening boundaries around people, land, and things, creating separation rather than advancing reciprocity in relations.

I have written elsewhere on the first of these two aspects of coloniality, tracing how it operates, in the initial register, as a mode of encounter:

> Coloniality is premised on the modern opposition of the relation between a self and an other. In these terms, coloniality can be thought of as the tendency of a "'self'" in an encounter to impose boundary coordinates – such as those of territory, knowledges, categories, normative practices – on the domains of land, knowledge, ways of life of an other who has had prior, principal relations with those lands, etc. Importantly, coloniality as encounter makes an additional move to rationalize the dominant presence of this self within those coordinates and to make the presence of the other subordinate to it – often as a tactic for dispossession. As encounter, coloniality extends to many sub-forms of colonialism – that is, we can speak variously of settler colonialism, geopolitical colonialism, administrative colonialism, cultural colonialism, colonial property, scientific colonialism, colonial law, the colonization of consciousness, etc. All are premised on the dominating–subordinating relation of self over other.[17]

However, coloniality is enacted not just through *encounter* as above, but in the encompassing register as the ongoing milieu or apparatus – a dispositif or "set-up" – as I further noted:

> The second dimension of coloniality is how it operates as an apparatus of modernity, a workaday containment field for defining, constraining, and incorporating persons as well as delimited populations and polities. In this sense, coloniality can be thought of as a corollary of Foucaultian governmentality (the conduct of conduct), imposing an effective ontology of territory, ownership, knowledge, rule, and much more. Crucial here, is the way that coloniality as apparatus is the embracing milieu for coloniality as encounter, where it appears to sustain the other and maintain a dialogue between the self and the other, while always ensuring by whatever flexible means, that the other remains other, partially welcomed into the arrangement, but necessarily in a subordinate position, subjugated, inscribed as other by self, thereby securing the power position of self.[18]

By now, what I hope is evident is how coloniality, with its inherent asymmetries, is the mirror opposite of the double register of treaty praxis embraced by the Piikani in their relations. Coloniality as encounter opposes and corrodes living-with relations. Coloniality as milieu displaces and occludes living-together relations.

Having placed these two approaches in high relief, the work of deco-lonial resurgence becomes quite clear. Coloniality is what resurgent treaty ecologies refuse and dissolve by enacting reciprocal living-with / living-together relations. From where I stand, it is also what the think-ing and practice of Borrows, Asch, and Tully work to dissolve.

Three Voices: Resurgent Reciprocity and "Responsibility for Shared Futures"

Having laid out what the Piikani have taught me about enacting treaty ecologies and setting that against what in settler-capitalist circuits con-founds such enactments of treaty ecologies, I now turn to the potent coming-together in the life-project work, thought, and propositions of Borrows, Asch, and Tully.

As noted in their introduction, in 2012 to 2014 I had the honour of hosting the Dalhousie University McKay Lectures, inviting our three colleagues to come and share their knowledge and experience about "reconciliation." Each moved well beyond the meaning of the term and practice emerging in the context of the then in-progress Truth and Reconciliation Commission, and in directions very different from the doctrine of reconciliation in Canadian Aboriginal law.[19] In very literal ways, all three have turned dominant ideas of reconciliation on their heads.

The focus of the lectures was "responsibility for shared futures." Whereas we gathered knowing quite well the histories of colonizing forces that figured in the disintegration of good relations, in these lec-tures the aim was to consider *who it is,* including ourselves, that bear responsibility to reconcile relations out of the colonial mess. From there, we could explore how precisely we all might respond. With that, the aim would finally be to imagine and "look toward particular kinds of liveable futures."[20] Ultimately, as I witnessed it, the focus of Borrows, Asch, and Tully was as much on the profoundly needed *resurgence* of over-shadowed modes of praxes.

I start with Borrows, whose approach echoes and gives further guid-ance on what I have called "living-with" relations, reciprocity between intimates, both human and non-human. Then I turn to Asch, who guides us back through what he calls the "linking principle" to what are "living-together" relations, or reciprocity between polities, treaty.

And finally, I take up Tully's propositions for resurgence of ecologically conciliated praxes as the means and ends in moving past vicious unsustainable relations, to virtuous sustainable relations in expanding networks of relations. It is in the convergence of all three modes of resurgence that the potency of the Following Deer story and decolonial treaty ecologies are recapitulated. I also argue that the interleaved result offers a more original, transformative, and liberating mode of reconciliation than has been articulated pragmatically to this day. From here, I seek how each of our three colleagues moves towards a relinking and making-continuous of living-with relations and living-together relations.

Borrows: Physical-Intimate Resurgence of Reciprocal Living-With

Borrows calls for the resurgence of the Anishinaabe practice of *Akinoomaagewin* – the physical, always-responsive philosophy with the active living, dying, transforming world of things, beings, and relations. The emphasis I take from Borrows is upon *living-with relations*, and this accords with the story of Following Deer and its lesson of the ever-present, responsive reciprocity of human exchanges with animals.

This kind of ecological praxis speaks to the fulsome, felt connection between persons and other persons, and between persons directly engaging and responding to forces of the land and water and weather and creatures, but as well with the intangible, also-felt forces of emotion, spirit, nostalgia, memory, pain, story, ancestors, and relations. In this discussion Borrows's continuous renewal of *Akinoomaagewin* relations will be considered against what the Piikani shared with me in the story of Following Deer and the human exchanges with animals. The emphasis is, as such, on *living-with relations*, a mode of lived reconciliation that attends to intimate relations and embodied, physical philosophy.

Borrows tells us how *Akinoomaagewin* "is derived from observation and practice; learning in this way does not stem from identifying first principles and deducing conclusions from abstract propositions. The word *gikinawaabiwin* communicates this same point. Anishinaabe physical philosophy is inductive and derives conclusions from experience, observation, and discussion."[21]

Taking this one step further, he writes how terms like *Akinoomaagewin* – the lessons we learn from pointing to and taking directions from the Earth – encourage Anishinaabe people "to draw analogies from our surroundings and carefully apply or distinguish them in our daily lives. The Earth is a profound resource for legal reasoning. *Akinoomaage* suggests a physical philosophy that requires attentiveness to place-based context in making decisions: parallel situations are correlated, dissimilar situations are distinguished."

Among these parallel situations from land-based engagement come principles including a responsive obligation to live well with the world. Following deer, reconciling relations with others through reciprocity and exchange of ceremony, would be just such a responsiveness to obligation, a demand placed on living respectfully with animals and other humans. Borrows also points out how this is always an emergent process, not a prescriptive or totalizing one – it comes from embodied and lived practice, often characterized by impermanence and continual transformation of conditions and encounters. His attention to passing of seasons, to the arrival and dissipation of rain, to death and smoke, all of these gesture to a living-with responsiveness, a reciprocity-with the world and with whatever beings and persons one encounters.

These forces, conditions, and powers in the world are also a source for thinking – winter and the withering of plants, later moving to thaw in spring, to warmth and new growth. All of this takes attention, hesitation, patience, care, the lingering on events and relations to find adequate meaning. A potent Ojibwe word he calls forth is *nuh*, to pay attention – very similar to the "unh" I have heard from Blackfoot speakers, as an acknowledgment that one is paying attention, agreeing with others, with the world.

Although these may be reckoned by some as psychological, cognitive, and sensory details, they are also core to what I have come to understand as the necessary disposition for relations among intimates, about being intimate with the world of things, beings, events, forces, and conditions. Borrows calls our attention to listening to the subtle sounds of a stream, the change of sound along its course, the change of sound as it enters a lake. "Nuh," pay attention, be intimate-with, live-with the land, with the food, the water "as a friend." As philosopher and colleague, Isabelle Stengers remarked in our conversations together, this disposition is one open to always seeing "where it will take us."[22] For Borrows, this is an act of freedom, or freedom-with the world, a world that is at once kind and giving, ugly and harsh, brilliant and dark – earth teachings, "the lessons we learn from pointing to and taking directions from the Earth."[23]

Asch: Treaty Resurgence through Reciprocal Living-Together

Asch seeks to guide us to the next move, emphasizing what I refer to as *living-together relations*. In his text on the Confederation treaties, Asch speaks to the exchange made between First Peoples who entered into treaty, an exchange of sharing the land allowing settlement, for protection of the Crown. He points to the enormous political validation that was conferred on Canada when Indigenous peoples entered into land-sharing treaties, such that "to violate the promises we made to bring Confederation into being is to violate the authority we have to build a home on these lands."[24] Asch then expresses his confidence that the Canadian government will seek eventually to properly honour its promises.

In his 2014 book *On Being Here to Stay* Asch embraces praxis of treaty founded on what he calls the *linking principle* between political societies. In effect he is pointing to a shifting of registers from relations between intimates, to the relations between the collective of "citizen"-members of the two political societies, together. Asch writes of how this linking principle, which may be referred to in "Western" terms, "is so secure that it alone is sufficient to bind us together permanently."[25] Asch recounts a text where Kiotseaeton, Mohawk chief of the Six Nations, speaks to the power of the bond, where such a link binds persons so tightly that "even if the lightning were to fall upon us, it could not separate us; for, if it cuts off the arm that holds you to us, we will at once seize each other by the other arm."[26]

Asch goes on to show how this is the bond offered by many Indigenous peoples through treaty to allow settler peoples to stay – but with a caveat, that this is also a bond of respect for the land. His cautionary note: "Saying that the linking principle has the power to bind us to this land is one thing. Believing it to be possible is another," especially where "the idea that sovereignty over a territory takes precedence is so fundamental in our thinking."[27] I will truncate Asch's argument, rich and intricate as it is, and cut to its chase. Surrendering and being subsumed to a common authority has become a requisite of Hobbesian and Westphalian sovereignty, in line with the dispositif of coloniality I have described. This is the idea that peoples, however diverse, must be universalized and contained, made same, in a bounded territory – a country. Returning to the linking principle, and to Elder Harold Johnson, however, Asch contours it as a praxis that would make Indigenous peoples and settler peoples as kin to one another, retaining their own differences, their own community of kin, yet related collectively, where "each of us is now a member of both families and shares a responsibility to sustain them both."[28]

This stages the possibility of a potent nation-to-nation relationship, what I call inter-peoples relationships. And here Asch is guiding us through the Hobbesian model, to the possibility of reciprocal relations between polities, caring in common to sustain the land and our relations upon it. In his chapter, he speaks to the arrangement that was struck in the Confederation treaties: "We would live together, sharing the land, and they would be protected from our excesses by the fact that they would have a direct relationship with the Queen (through the governor-general)."[29]

Asch soon comes to his call for a "paradigm shift": those who adopt and enact the linking principle and so enter into this form of reciprocal, inter-peoples relation, also take upon themselves a new responsiveness to sustain relations, returning again and again to the principle, so as to renew it, responsively, and in perpetuity.

From here, continuously responsive living-with relations are transposed into inter-political action. Asch's nuanced discussion, through marriage exchange and inter-kin relations, generates an image for him, one that helps him to better comprehend, from Cree, "the word *Witaskewin*," meaning "living together on the land."[30] He continues to describe this mode of sharing as in the Oxford Dictionary definition: "to participate in ... to perform, enjoy, or suffer in common with others"[31] – what we might call a practice of shared belonging, wholly alternative to belonging through property (as featured in coloniality).

Finally, Asch takes us back to his experience with Dene people, who referred so potently to the treaty relationship, as a practice of "building a house together." With that, he calls forth the obligation, demand, and responsibility to caring relations for those political collectives (settler or Indigenous) who would enter Indigenous peoples' lands and wish to stay honourably with the consent of Indigenous peoples:

> The families we are joining have been building houses here for a long, long time. As a result, as Leanne Simpson points out, they have already developed protocols through links they have established with others, including "animal nations," which provide a way of ensuring that human beings live in balance with the natural world, their family, their clan, their

nation, and beyond. As new participants, then, it is our responsibility to take particular care in contributing to building lest we inadvertently damage the houses already here, for, whether or not we claim sovereignty, we have much to learn from Indigenous peoples about how to live on these lands, despite our predisposition to believe the opposite.[32]

In my reading this is a mode of conjoined, fully reciprocal *living-with and living-together*, but approached by Asch from the other direction, so to speak – that is, from the direction of concern for inter-*peoples* relations. Borrows, on the other hand, leads us along the path of inter*personal* relations, between intimates. But at the end, the two modes, the two ethoses are seamless, continuous, if at present working at different *registers* (a provisional term I offer again to describe erstwhile separated domains of practice, more typical under coloniality). Once adopted, however, and activated robustly together, there is promise to arrive at the seamless system of complex, sharing reciprocities. This hearkens again the *system of total prestations* that Mauss sought to describe in his consideration of peoples whose economies were based upon gift, reciprocity, and sharing, rather than upon alienability of all things, including land and ideas, rather than a political ethos bent relentlessly on the bounding out of people against people, people against the rest of the living world. Following Tully, this offers the displacement of vicious cycles by virtuous cycles, of which he writes so eloquently.

Treaty ecologies, at the end, can be understood as the antidote, the counter-spell to the dispositif of coloniality, the means of its undoing. Recall that Asch's concern is decidedly focused on settler polities, hence his call for a paradigm shift. To bring this home once more, the Piikani-Ktunaxa story lives out much of the paradigm that Asch proposes, rooted as it is in the ceremonial obligation to follow the blacktail deer, and moving on inter-political and inter-legal obligations in harmony with that. Through the shared ceremony – as mode of accord and treaty ecology – they practised intimate-political reciprocity between them that would be returned to again and again, so renewing and sustaining their relations continually. And, presumably, the ecological-ceremonial linking principle will be sustained, the accord or "treaty" continuing indefinitely.

It is Tully who offers a potential force that could empower the paradigm shift that Asch calls for – the force of facing worldwide ecological crisis, if not yet catastrophe.

Tully: Gaia Resurgence and Conciliated Beings

I turn now to Tully's call for *virtuous cycles* of gift-gratitude-reciprocity in eco-social-political relations and the necessary relinking of treaties between peoples, to treaties with all things – coming closer to a fully reintegrated living-with / living-together ethos. What Tully points to is a thoroughgoing philosophy of responsive engagement with the living, animate, and inanimate earth, at a moment of planetary ecological necessity.

Tully's position is like that of Asch, and myself – that settler-citizens need to make a decisive, transformative move that will enable reconciliation. You cannot reconcile a relationship if only one of the parties in the colonial relationship is ready to work towards reconciliation. Tully is clear on what is needed, which he refers to as a double reconciliation – between Indigenous peoples and newcomers or settlers, and then between peoples together and the earth. Tully's position, as with my own – and that of the Piikani and Ktunaxa – is a deeply ecological one. He is also emphatic about the necessity of activating the constituents of this ecology, writing, "We can't do one without the other," or we will ultimately fail.

The source to energize this double reconciliation, for Tully, is the demand of our ecological situation – the earth in crisis due to a failing relation with the earth – and the solution is sourced in the earth as well, where a renewed relation will install renewed and sustainable virtual relations with the land and with other people. The ethos, familiar in much Indigenous ceremonialism and land relations, is one based in the triple action of gifting, showing gratitude, and reciprocating the gift given. Here we come back to Mauss's proposition of *"le don"* (the gift), and the call for what amounts to his system of total prestations, a robust ecology of sharing and gifting relations. Tully sees this as a fundamental ethos of inter-dependence: "This is a basic mode of being-in-the-lifeworld with other living beings; a reciprocal and interactive relationship of ongoing sensuous attunement, disturbance, and re-attunement by means of our pre-reflective, embodied, and reflective senses, perception and cognition."[33]

And he is clear about how this mode of being must displace the "disembedded" lives we lead through property and capitalism. Now calling forth treaty, Tully describes this condition to be displaced: "We have been shaped and formed by an alienated relationship to the living earth and each other in the modern period. It is as if we are negotiating treaty relationships with one another and not realizing that we are also walking on this living earth, breathing its clean air, and receiving all the gifts it provides to keep us alive. As deep ecologists say, we independent and autonomous moderns overlook our interdependent 'ecological footprint' and 'ecological self.'"[34]

He demonstrates how this "alienated view of our social and ecological relationships and responsibilities is self-defeating" but notes how intensely challenging it is to free ourselves of its grip. Here he lays out the modern dispositif, approaching what I have referred to as "coloniality," as encounter activated within a consumption-oriented milieu: "We are ourselves located within the self-destructive relationships: subject to them and their legitimating ideologies, governed and swept along by them in our everyday producing and consuming activities."[35] He adds, we "are conscripts of the vicious system whether we accept or critique the scripts that legitimate it ('domination without consent')."[36]

Tully also accepts that alienation and disconnection are not absolutely given but rather so deeply embedded in the milieu of practice as to seem intractable. Countering this, he speaks to how human action, if sufficiently prompted by necessity, can prevail. Drawing on Polanyi, he points to how the earth-bound demands (what Isabelle Stengers refers to as "Gaia's intrusion"[37]), witnessed in planetary destruction, would push us collectively to a "new synthesis," a symbiosis where we would "realize that when we are citizens of social systems, such as states, corporations and markets, we are also Gaia citizens of the ecosystems in which these social systems are embedded and on which they depend."[38]

Here, the milieu of capital – states, corporations, and markets – is itself situated in a more encompassing organic, ecological milieu (an earth oikos), which those forces of capital constantly disturb, to the detriment of all. Finally, he speaks to how, through a complex series of virtuous cycles taking off as a consequence of responding to the ecological, economic demand, there will be a rising synergy of perturbations: "As the small, local, symbiotically coordinated webs of steps and practices of reconciliation grow, they first reach tipping points and bring about transformations of vicious relationships locally. These small changes have significant ripple effects, especially on the younger generations who see and hear about them. If these continue to multiply and accumulate here, there, and everywhere, they have the potential gradually to reach a point where the global vicious system as a whole is transformed into an assemblage of virtuous ones."[39]

When I read this, I conjure a rising multitude, concerned for living well with the earth – an expanding and expansive ecology of human persons and more-than-human persons in expanding living-with relations, coalescing into an extensive assemblage and relational network.

Moving registers again, Asch's discussion on Confederation treaties gives further inter-political expression to Tully's deeply persuasive propositions and observations on the transformations necessary and expanding in our common ecological milieu. That is, Asch brings more specific attention to the *living-together* register of action. This is captured in his statement where members of the Settler polity and of the Indigenous polities would become as "'brothers to each other' and 'children' of the Queen," and therefore Indigenous polities would not fall under the Crown, or vice versa.[40] In other words, each would retain its own collectivity, difference, and jurisdiction – but conjoined by the linking principle, in reciprocal, responsive, mutually protective perpetuity. Thus, a practice of reciprocity and mutual care would be operating more resolutely at the register of encounters and in the register of the milieu that conditions how peoples live with the world and others.

This doubled move – the earth conciliating *living-with* action put forward by Tully and Borrows, and the inter-peoples treaty action put forward by Asch – would realize the fuller continuity of *living-with-and-together* relations. With all of these moving together, we can begin to imagine the fully decolonial response to the conditions of coloniality, and the refusal of its vicious-cycle political economic ethos, which Tully describes as "a 'super-predatory' system. It depends on, and is nested within, the informal social and ecological relationships that sustain life on earth. Yet, at the same time, it preys on them in an extractive, linear and non-reciprocal way."[41]

In contradistinction to such a "super-predatory" system, for all three of Borrows, Asch, and Tully, resolution turns on advancing a responsive-reciprocal and perpetual-sustainable relation with each other. We can discern two directions of transformation: from the personal to the political, and from the political to the personal. Tully and Borrows orient us more to the former, Asch to the latter – but action in both directions would likely accelerate and intensify the transformations imagined, pressing and disturbing and disintegrating the hegemony of a colonizing relation of self and other, and of the colonizing milieu.

What might the contours of such action look like? Two are clear from the Piikani-Ktunaxa treaty ecology of Following Deer, and this is mirrored in what I have gleaned from Borrows, Asch, and Tully:

first, honouring relations with all persons, including animals and all of the other-than-human beings of the world (relation of intimates); and second, honouring the relations between collectives, the inter-peoples treaties of sharing in land (relation of polities).

For further instruction, I will turn to Simpson and her parallel insights in the scaling up *from living with to living together* relations, a full-blown treaty ecology, as the Nishaabeg have lived it. Simpson's insights reiterate and bring added nuance and variation to those in the Following Deer story, including how the intimacy of human-human, animal-human relations become core practices and models of how to live, breathe, and act in treaty with the earth and with others.

Learning Treaty Ecologies through Animal and Human Intimacy

Marilyn Strathern once wrote of how the "gift relation" is enacted differently among different Melanesian and Polynesian peoples – there is a Maori gift, a Fijian gift, a Trobriand gift, etc.[42] Likewise the Following Deer story of treaty ecology is but one of a diverse array of Indigenous peoples' treaty ecologies. Michi Saagig Nishnaabeg thinker, writer, and decolonial activist Leanne Simpson offers an exquisite counter case, from her own people's stories, histories, and relations.

As previously noted, Asch highlighted Simpson's point that there were "diplomatic agreements between human and animal nations."[43] He quotes her directly:

> In many instances, clan leaders negotiated particular agreements with animal nations or clans to promote *Bimaadiziwin* and balance with the region. In Mississauga territory, for example, the people of the fish clans, who are the intellectuals of the nation, met with the fish nations twice a year for thousands of years at *Mnjikanming*, the small narrows between Lake Simcoe and Lake Couchiching. The fish nations and the fish clans gathered to talk, to tend to their treaty relationships, and to renew life just as the *Gizhe-mnido* (Creator) had instructed them. These were important gatherings because the fish nations sustained the Nishnaabeg Nation during times when other sources of food were scarce. Fish were a staple in our traditional foodway. Our relationship with the fish nations meant that we had to be accountable for how we used this "resource." Nishnaabeg people only fished at particular times of the year in certain locations. They only took as much as they needed and never wasted. They shared with other members of their families and communities, and they performed

the appropriate ceremonies and rituals before beginning. To do otherwise would be to ignore their responsibilities to the fish nations and to jeopardize the health and wellness of the people.[44]

Asch was highlighting how treaties between Nishnaabeg people and others coming into their territories operated by "application of principles they have applied more generally";[45] in this instance between Nishnaabeg clans through their ceremonial, ecological, indeed *political*, obligations with animal nations, the fish nations.

This relation accords with the *living-together* mode to which I have been pointing. Yet it is crucial to note that Simpson also drew her treaty principles from *living-with* modes. In her poignant decolonial accounts of treaty relationships, she builds on both the writing of Borrows and on teachings from her many Nishnaabeg elders.[46] Simpson starts with breastfeeding as a treaty praxis – that is, the practice of breastfeeding her own children, a most intimate relation of love, and more, a "meeting of hearts." She writes how she learned from Elder Edna Manitowabi that "breastfeeding is the very first treaty ... Where our children learn about treaties, the relationships they encode and how to maintain a good treaty relationship."[47]

Simpson's writing captures through embodied action what I have also been trying to identify with the framing of living-with-and-together relations:

Nursing is ultimately about a relationship. Treaties are ultimately about a relationship. One is a relationship about sharing between a mother and a child and the other a relationship based on sharing between two sovereign nations. Breastfeeding benefits both mother and the child in terms of health and in terms of their relationship to each other. And treaties must benefit both sovereign nations to be successful.[48]

Simpson then moves to treaties with animals and other non-humans, including the treaties with the fish nations that Asch quotes: "A long time ago our clan leaders negotiated particular agreements with animal nations or clans to promote *mino bimaadiziwin* and balance with the region."[49]

Recounting Borrows, she follows with another story on the demand to carry out Nishnaabeg ceremonies honouring treaty relations with animals, lest they lose the animals altogether, along with the lifeways that sustain them economically. Simpson's accounts continually situate these relations of care and exchange, what Tully observed

as practices of gift-gratitude-reciprocity, always in Nishnaabeg territory, the place where people's and animals' lives are lived out: treaty
ecologies.

In due course, Simpson points us to how the deep mutuality of care
practised in animal-human treaty relations is meant to be mirrored by
treaties between peoples, as it has been for the Nishnaabeg in their
"nation-to-nation" relations. She writes of how such relations arise and
thrive in places and languages of living land connection, which come
together in the collective sense in the practice of nation, as a pragmatic
gathering of hearts. She draws this poignantly from common "heart"
rootings of Nishnaabeg words, including *oodena*, meaning "where the
hearts gather," or the word for strawberries – *odeminon*, "heart berries" –
articulated further in the word for nation, *odaenauh*, leading her to
express the idea and praxis of Nishnaabeg "nation as an interconnected
web of hearts."[50]

What we may take from Simpson's thought and practice, then, is
that the body-personal merges with the body-politic in an ecology of
co-extensive mutual care, of treaty being that between two polities
wedded by mutual responsiveness, care, and nourishment in constant
renewal – one gathering of hearts caring together, joining another gath-
erings of hearts, taking care of each other, care multiplying care. This is
treaty ecology, a personal-political ecology of love.

Of course, this echoes the Following Deer story, providing yet another
layer of relations, where a shared intimate understanding of the obligation to honour and do ceremony with one's child, with animals, with
the animate world, is also an animating force for relations between
peoples and in matters of territorial relations and sharing. Everything
is in motion: bodies of humans, animals, and peoples responding to
the mutuality of obligations to the living world, ancestors, the rights
of territorial connection, the rightful residents of the territory, ceremonial commitments, keeping peace, sharing in hunting and survival, the
greater possibility of sharing together on the land, and sustaining all
relations in an ongoing way.

Resurgent Decolonial Etho-ecologies

In her book *In Catastrophic Times*, which takes up the challenge of
planet-wide climate and ecological disruption, Isabelle Stengers
speaks of how "the intrusion of Gaia ... now has the power to question us all."[51] There is neither a technical answer of carbon targets
and systems, nor a master peace plan to address the moment. There

is only the demand it places upon the entire arrangement, and upon all who inhabit it – deer, hunters, montane forested passes, states bent on staying with ever-better economic conditions – to respond, or not to respond. As Stengers points out, the intrusion of Gaia "imposes a question without being interested in the response," even while we are witness to the rising effect of a "considerable number of living species who will be swept away with unprecedented speed by the change in their milieu on the horizon."[52] Meanwhile, Indigenous peoples and settler-state citizens ally together to protect waters and lands and fellow forms of life from the ravages of extractive industries. Meanwhile, Indigenous peoples continue to respond in the intimate, responsive ways, in pleasure and pain, certainty and doubt that Borrows conveys to us. Meanwhile, the multiplicity of conciliated beings, if anything, rise to the imperative to conciliate more in the face of relation-disrupting effects of property encroachment, climate change, and the vicious-destructive march of capitalist exploitation, as Tully conveys to us. And meanwhile, rising numbers of settler citizens struggle in hope to embrace their treaty obligations as Michael Asch conveys to us, challenging state-crafters who otherwise err in deploying treaty as instrument of acquiescence, certainty, and control, leaving Indigenous peoples to be subordinated to the state polity, rather than entering into a fulsome relation of polities.

There is hope of resurgence in these assembled movements, and it appears that ecological demand may well be the strongest force compelling action, as Tully has argued.

The pragmatic universe of practices offered to us by Piikani and Ktunaxa peoples in their relations, from the elders and ceremonialists I have been honoured to learn with, and from the Nishnaabeg as elaborated by Simpson, thrive by a seamless continuity of the intimate and the political. They are non-colonial by virtue of being honourable, responsive, reciprocal, ecological, intimate-political – many people in Indigenous land-sensitive societies are familiar with this way of living; settler-modern peoples less so, yet increasingly many yearn to be.

That yearning may be key, propelled by the growing ecological necessity and catastrophe, and from that, a care for what awaits future generations. Our challenge – the challenge I take from Asch, Tully, and Borrows considered together – and from Stengers – is putting what we know through the intimacy of care and reciprocal obligation into practice in *both* our personal and our political relations. "Reconciliation" then becomes what is realized through a resurgence of inter-peoples relations, animated by living-with-and-together praxes, through resurgent ecologies of love in lands shared honourably among peoples, always with abiding care for future generations who will be able to live well together on a healing, healthy planet.

Ultimately, as with my colleagues in this volume, what I have taken from my relations with Indigenous peoples, under conditions of an embattled earth, under conditions of ongoing colonial refusal, is that everyone, settler and Indigenous peoples alike, is faced with the demand for a resurgence of reciprocity. That is the first order. If *reciprocity of honour in relations* is living well and in action, a viable praxis of reconciliation follows – as we continue to refuse coloniality. Simpson has also asserted this refusal, in calling for "culturally inherent resurgence" that "challenges settler colonial dissections of our territories and our bodies" – a recurring form of cultural violence performed in ongoing coloniality.[53]

Treaty ecologies promise sustainable political etho-ecologies, as well as a potent alternative to and counter-force against coloniality. The decolonizing effects of treaty ecologies will have transformative purchase as they gradually overcome the problem of coloniality – its pernicious form of encounter, its pernicious milieu facilitating such forms of encounter as power-over, all of which are also being interrogated, critiqued, and refused. Borrowing Tully's terms, the virtuous cycles of treaty ecologies, when put into play, hold promise to displace the vicious cycles of coloniality, which are already aligned with modern, capitalist-property power.

Mills, in this volume, gestures to a much-needed *intentionality* to act in a treaty way and to draw upon the force that action can generate:

> Once we see the other's rootedness, we see that we can have a good relationship, no matter the degree of difference in our norms ... We recognize that through our mutual rootedness we're always already in relationship, and we choose to strengthen that relationship and thereby to honour one another. This now intentional relationship strengthens our capacity to share our gifts with one another so that all have their needs met ... in the treaty relationship.[54]

To move from the challenge of good relations to outcomes requires of us all a critical vigilance and a refusal of coloniality, coupled to a *resurgence* of shared, active peace-making, followed by shared active peace-sustaining. Resurgence of relational reciprocity has to be actively practised, and *it has to be actively practised together* interpersonally and inter-politically. This came home to me again recently from Mi'kmaq activist-scholar Sherry Pictou, when she conveyed the treaty praxes of the paired "Mi'kmaw concepts of *Ankukamkewe* (meaning: making relations) and *Ankukamkewel* (meaning:making more than one set of relations)," again echoing the simultaneous possibility of bringing interpersonal and inter-political relations together.[55]

Resurgent reciprocity offers a mode of reconciliation that does not depend on recognition politics, or on power-over, but only on power-with, to use Hannah Arendt's terms. It is a flight from and a refusal of the oppressive. The anti-ecologies of coloniality are dissolved by enacting the pro-ecologies of treaty, by way of reciprocal, caring fulfilment of obligation to others, all the way down.

A pragmatist's *will to care* is called for now. Such intimate willing care empowers us to think and to act together in our respective natural-political assemblages. This, in turn, can strongly enable us to peacefully and respectfully co-generate a world of treaty ecologies in which we may, in every sense, enjoy living-with and living-together for generations to come.

NOTES

1 Mauss's classic formulation describes such a system as multiplex and thorough-going, taking in law, exchange and circulation, obligation, material culture expression, enspirited being, political arrangements, and more, forming into an intricate and pervasive array of socio-material workings animating and moving in and beyond institutions. See Marcel Mauss, *The Gift: Forms and Functions of Exchange in Archaic Societies*, trans. Ian Gunnison (1923; New York: Norton Library, 1967), 3–4.

2 Treaty 7, still in force today, included the Canadian Crown, the three Blackfoot First Nations (Piikani, Kainai, Siksika), as well as the Stoney's (Nakoda) and the Sarcee (Tsu'tinna), and took in the entire area south of the Red Deer River to the current borders with the United States, British Columbia, and Saskatchewan. See W. Hildebrandt, D.F. Rider, and S. Carter, *The True Spirit and Original Intent of Treaty 7*, vol. 14 (Montreal: McGill-Queen's University Press, 1996).

3 B. Noble and R. Crowshoe, "Poomaksin – Skinnipiikani – Nitsiitapii Law, Transfers, and Making Relatives: Practices and Principles for Cultural

Protection, Repatriation, Redress, and Heritage Law Making with Canada," in *First Nations Cultural Heritage and Law*. Vol. 1, *Case Studies, Voices, Perspectives*, ed. C. Bell and V. Napoleon (Vancouver: UBC Press, 2008), 258–311.

4 Settler communities and ecologists in the Ktunaxa territories have noted a regional variant of the mule deer, which has an all-black tail, and it is often reckoned as a subspecies of the mule deer. See Emily Latch, Dawn Reding, James Heffelfinger, Carlos Alcalá-Galván, and Olin Rhodes, "Range-Wide Analysis of Genetic Structure in a Widespread, Highly Mobile Species *(Odocoileus hemionus)* Reveals the Importance of Historical Biogeography," *Molecular Ecology* 23, no. 13 (2014): 3171–90. See also Matthew Cronin, "Mitochondrial and Nuclear Genetic Relationships of Deer *(Odocoileus* spp.) in western North America," *Canadian Journal of Zoology* 65, no. 5 (1991): 1270–9.

5 The ceremony is referred to by David Duvall in C. Wissler and D.C. Duvall, *Mythology of the Blackfoot Indians* (New York: Trustees of the American Museum of Natural History, 1909), 2:147–9.

6 Blackfoot people may speak about their sometimes mistrust of the Plains Cree folks to the north and tell of warring relations and bad medicine. In similar accounts where Cree were encountered in Piikani territory, and where transactions of ceremonies, bundles, and medicines took place, it seems that, over time, some of those ceremonies have proven not to have efficacy, or they may have even been associated with further problems, exacerbating the inter-political relations rather than resolving them. Here, I would argue, the living-with relations have failed the living-together relations. These exchanges gone awry rather result in conflict, the absence of peace – necessitating constant vigilance, amid efforts to attain peace, to achieve symmetrical reciprocity of relations. That is to say that poor relations are not irreconcilable. Rather, by enacting more robust reciprocal medicine relations, good relations are always there to be restored. Asch provided an analysis of conflict and peaceful relations through exchange, especially kin exchange, following propositions from Lévi-Strauss. He quotes this crucial text from Lévi-Strauss: "There is a link, a continuity, between hostile relations and the provision of reciprocal prestations. Exchanges are peacefully resolved wars, and wars are the result of unsuccessful transactions. This feature is clearly witnessed to by the fact that the transition from war to peace, or at least from hostility to cordiality, is accomplished by the intermediary of ritual gestures, a veritable 'reconciliation inspection.'" M. Asch, "Levi-Strauss and the Political: The Elementary Structures of Kinship and the Resolution of Relations between

Indigenous Peoples and Settler States," *Journal of the Royal Anthropological Institute* 11, no. 3 (2005): 436. See also C. Lévi-Strauss, *The Elementary Structures of Kinship*, trans. J. Harle Bell, J.R. von Sturmer, and R. Needham (1949; Boston: Beacon, 1969).

7 I have elsewhere summarized such First Peoples' political ethos expressly where "one pays respect by *recognizing*, humbling oneself, and acting upon the source of power and authority of the other not simply in the moment but also in the perpetual unfolding of relations." B. Noble, "Owning as Belonging / Owning as Property: The Crisis of Power and Respect in First Nations Heritage Transactions with Canada," in Bell and Napoleon, *First Nations Cultural Heritage*, 469. On the relation between power, territorial relations, and political authority of Indigenous peoples, see H.A. Feit, "Hunting and the Quest for Power: The James Bay Cree and Whitemen in the 20th Century," in *Native Peoples: The Canadian Experience*, ed. R. Morrison and C. Wilson, 181–223 (Toronto: McCelland & Stewart, 1995).

8 Hildebrandt, Rider, and Carter, *True Spirit and Original Intent of Treaty 7*, 241.

9 See J. Thunder, "Voices from Our Past: Crowfoot Valued Land More Than Gov't Money," *Windspeaker* 5, no. 9 (1987): 35.

10 Doug Hintz, "Calgary Author Dispels Myths about Historic Treaty 7," *Calgary Herald*, 25 October 2015.

11 "Our land is more valuable than your money. It will last forever. It will not perish as long as the sun shines and the water flows, and through all the years it will give life to men and animals, and therefore we cannot sell the land. It was put there by the Great Spirit and we cannot sell it because it does not really belong to us. You can count your money and burn it with a nod of a buffalo's head, but only the Great Spirit can count the grains of sand and the blades of grass on these plains. As a present we will give you anything you can take with you, but we cannot give you the land." Thunder, "Voices from Our Past," 35.

12 Also see the discussion of intent of sharing versus alienating among Interior Salish peoples, in E. Feltes, "Research as Guesthood: The Memorial to Sir Wilfrid Laurier and Resolving Indigenous–Settler Relations in British Columbia," *Anthropologica* 57, no. 2 (2015): 469–80.

13 Blackfoot "shadow" practices associated with embodied and material relations are discussed in B. Noble and R. Crowshoe, "Niitooii – 'The Same That Is Real': Parallel Practice, Museums, and the Repatriation of Piikani Customary Authority," *Anthropologica* 44, no. 1 (2002): 113–30. Also see the discussion of intent of sharing versus alienating among Interior Salish peoples, in Feltes, "Research as Guesthood."

14 Isabelle Stengers refers to *oikos* of any being in relation to its ethos as "the habitat of that being and the way in which that habitat satisfies or opposes the demands associated with the ethos." I. Stengers, "The Cosmopolitical Proposal," in *Making Things Public: Atmospheres of Democracy*, ed. B. Latour and P. Weibel (Cambridge: MIT Press, 2005), 998.

15 See Carole Blackburn's discussion of the BC treaty process, which shows how "certainty" becomes the means by which the Crown advances its own territorial powers over First Nations engaged in this process. C. Blackburn, "Searching for Guarantees in the Midst of Uncertainty: Negotiating Aboriginal Rights and Title in British Columbia," *American Anthropologist* 107, no. 4 (2005): 586–96.

16 See Coulthard's arguments on primitive accumulation in relation to this. Glen Sean Coulthard, *Red Skin White Masks: Rejecting the Colonial Politics of Recognition* (Minneapolis: University of Minnesota Press, 2014).

17 B. Noble, "Tripped up by Coloniality: Anthropologists as Instruments or Agents in Indigenous–Settler Political Relations?," *Anthropologica* 57, no. 2 (2015): 429–30.

18 Ibid., 430.

19 Constance MacIntosh, "The Reconciliation Doctrine in Chief Justice McLachlin's Court: From a 'Final Legal Remedy' to a 'Just and Lasting Process,'" in *Public Law at the McLachlin Court: The First Decade*, ed. David Wright and Adam Dodek, 201–34 (Toronto: Irwin Law, 2011).

20 The quoted phrases in this paragraph are taken directly from the final accepted proposal submission for the McKay Lecture series, 2011–12.

21 J. Borrows, *Freedom and Indigenous Constitutionalism* (Toronto: University of Toronto Press, 2016).

22 These shared points from Stengers came while she visited my home university, Dalhousie, in March 2012, supported by the SSHRC-funded Situating Science Knowledge Cluster. Indeed the series of several seminars, shared conversations, workshops, and lectures were gathered together under the umbrella title, "To See Where It Takes Us."

23 Borrows, *Freedom and Indigenous Constitutionalism.*

24 Asch, this volume.

25 Michael Asch, *On Being Here to Stay: Treaties and Aboriginal Rights in Canada* (Toronto: University of Toronto Press, 2014), 118.

26 Full quote is in a draft of chapter 7, "Treaties and Sharing," prepared for Asch, *On Being Here to Stay.*

27 Asch, *On Being Here to Stay.*

28 Ibid., 125.

29 Asch, this volume.

30 Asch, *On Being Here to Stay* at 114.
31 From M. Asch's original McKay Lecture, "Back to the Future," 4 October 2012. Transcript provided by M. Asch.
32 Asch, *On Being Here to Stay*, 132.
33 Tully, this volume.
34 Ibid.
35 Ibid.
36 Ibid.
37 I. Stengers, *In Catastrophic Times: Resisting the Coming Barbarism* (London: Open Humanities, 2015), 43.
38 Tully, this volume.
39 Ibid.
40 Asch, *On Being Here to Stay*, 90.
41 Tully, this volume.
42 M. Strathern, "A Community of Critics? Thoughts on New Knowledge," *Journal of the Royal Anthropological Institute* 12, no. 1 (2006): 191–209.
43 L. Simpson, "Looking after Gdoo-naaganinaa: Precolonial Nishnaabeg Diplomatic and Treaty Relationships," *Wicazo Sa Review* 23, no. 2 (2008): 33.
44 Asch, *On Being Here to Stay*, 117–18, quoting Simpson, "Looking after Gdoo-naaganinaa." Also see L. Simpson, *Dancing on Our Turtle's Back: Stories of Nishnaabeg Re-Creation, Resurgence, and a New Emergence* (Winnipeg: Arbeiter Ring, 2011), 109–10.
45 Asch, *On Being Here to Stay*, 118.
46 She discusses Borrows on Nishnaabeg relations, drawing on his volume: J. Borrows, *Recovering Canada: The Resurgence of Indigenous Law* (Toronto: University of Toronto Press, 2002), 16–20.
47 Simpson, *Dancing on Our Turtle's Back*, 106.
48 Ibid.
49 Ibid., 109.
50 Ibid., 94.
51 Stengers, *In Catastrophic Times*, 11.
52 Ibid., 47.
53 L. Simpson, "Land as Pedagogy: Nishnaabeg Intelligence and Rebellious Transformation," *Decolonization: Indigeneity, Education & Society* 3, no. 3 (2014): 23.
54 Mills, this volume.
55 S. Pictou, "Decolonizing Mi'kmaw Memory of Treaty: L'sitkuk's Learning with Allies in Struggle for Food and Lifeways" (PhD diss., Dalhousie University, 2017), 40, 159.

Contributors

Michael Asch

Michael Asch is professor (limited term) in the Department of Anthropology and adjunct professor in political science at the University of Victoria, and professor emeritus of anthropology at the University of Alberta. His publications include *Home and Native Land: Aboriginal Rights and the Constitution* (1984), *Aboriginal and Treaty Rights in Canada: Essays on Law, Equality and Respect for Difference* (1997), and *On Being Here to Stay: Treaties and Aboriginal Rights in Canada* (2014). Dr Asch served as an expert witness at the Mackenzie Valley Pipeline Inquiry. He was senior research associate for anthropology at the Royal Commission on Aboriginal Peoples, and research director of the Dene/Metis Mapping Project for the Dene Nation. Dr Asch received the 2001 Weaver-Tremblay Award for distinguished service to Canadian applied anthropology by the Association for Applied Anthropology in Canada, and in 2002 was elected a fellow of the Royal Society of Canada. His book *On Being Here to Stay* received the 2015 Canada Prize for the Social Sciences (English) from the Federation for the Humanities and Social Sciences.

John Borrows

John Borrows is the Canada Research Chair in Indigenous Law at the University of Victoria. His publications include *Recovering Canada: The Resurgence of Indigenous Law* (Donald Smiley Award for the best book in Canadian political science, 2002), *Canada's Indigenous Constitution* (Canadian Law and Society Best Book Award 2011), *Drawing Out Law: A Spirit's Guide* (2010), *Freedom and Indigenous Constitutionalism*

(2016 Donald Smiley Award), *The Right Relationship* (with Michael Coyle, ed.), all from the University of Toronto Press. John is Anishinaabe/Ojibway and a member of the Chippewa of the Nawash First Nation in Ontario, Canada.

Regna Darnell

Regna Darnell is Distinguished University Professor of Anthropology and First Nations Studies at the University of Western Ontario, with cross-appointments to Theory and Criticism, Ecosystem Health, and Public Health. Her books include *Franz Boas as Public Intellectual: Theory, Ethnography, Activism* (ed. with Michelle Hamilton, Robert Hancock, and Joshua Smith); *Edward Sapir: Linguist, Anthropologist, Humanist; And Along Came Boas; Theorizing the Americanist Tradition* (ed. with Lisa [Phillips] Valentine*); Invisible Genealogies* and *Historicizing Canadian Anthropology* (ed. with Julia Harrison). She is general editor of the Franz Boas Documentary Edition, editor of *Critical Studies in History of Anthropology* and *Histories of Anthropology Annual.* She has developed models for collaborative research in partnership with Plains Cree in northern Alberta, Anishinaabeg in southern Ontario, and Kwakwaka'wakw and mainland communities in BC.

Kiera Ladner

Kiera Ladner is Canada Research Chair in Indigenous Politics and Governance and an associate professor in the Department of Political Studies at the University of Manitoba. Her research focuses on self-determination, treaty constitutionalism, rights and responsibilities within multiple contexts (Indigenous and settler – in Canada, Australia, and New Zealand), Indigenous political thought, federalism, and gender diversity. In 2010 she edited a collection on Oka @ 20 with Leanne Simpson entitled *This is an Honour Song: Twenty Years since the Blockades* (Arbeiter Ring) and is writing a book on Indigenous constitutions and constitutional politics tentatively entitled *This Is Not a New Book*. Kiera's projects include the Indigenous Leadership Initiative; the comparative Indigenous constitutional politics project, which examines constitutional renewal, Indigenous constitutional visions, and Indigenous rights debates in Canada, Australia, and New Zealand; and a project with Dr Shawna Ferris (Women's and Gender Studies) on a community-centred digital archives project, which is compiling three archives: the Sex Work Database, the Missing and Murdered Indigenous Women Database, and the Post-Apology Indian Residential School Database.

Kent McNeil

Kent McNeil is a distinguished research professor (emeritus) at Osgoode Hall Law School in Toronto, where he has taught since 1987. He is the author of numerous works on the rights of Indigenous peoples, including two books: *Common Law Aboriginal Title* (1989) and *Emerging Justice? Essays on Indigenous Rights in Canada and Australia* (2001). He has also co-edited a collection, *Indigenous Peoples and the Law: Comparative and Critical Perspectives* (2009). His work focuses on Indigenous land rights and governance authority.

Aaron Mills

Aaron Mills is a doctoral candidate at the University of Victoria working on Anishinaabe constitutionalism. He is an Anishinaabe from Couchiching First Nation, Treaty #3 Territory, and from North Bay, Robinson-Huron Treaty Territory. He belongs to the Bear Clan. Aaron is a Vanier Canada scholar, a Trudeau Foundation scholar, and the 2016 SSHRC Talent Award winner.

Brian Noble

Brian Noble is associate professor in Dalhousie's Department of Sociology and Social Anthropology. He has worked with Canadian First Nations for the last two decades, addressing matters ranging from Indigenous knowledges and intellectual/cultural property rights, relations with the Canadian state, and international regimes of law. His anthropological research addresses the socio-political conditions allowing for reconciliation of political relations between First Nations and Canada, the rise of Indigenous law, and the processes animating recognition of Indigenous land, resource, and knowledge rights in global arenas. He has worked with Piikani Blackfoot, Shushwap, Kwakwka'awakw, Mi'kmaq, and Cree communities. He also works in the anthropology of science and techniques.

Paulette Regan

Dr Paulette Regan worked for the Truth and Reconciliation Commission of Canada as the senior researcher and lead writer for the Reconciliation volume of the TRC Final Report and speaks frequently about the TRC's work at conferences, public dialogues, and intercultural competency workshops. As a scholar/practitioner, she brings a decolonizing perspective and applied experience to the theory, ethics, and practice of reconciliation processes, focusing on the contested politics, affective and pedagogical dimensions of public memory, social responsibility, and national history in Indigenous–settler contexts. Paulette provides expertise and practical advice to public commissions, inquiries, and research centres in Canada and abroad. She is the author of *Unsettling the Settler Within: Indian Residential Schools, Truth Telling and Reconciliation in Canada* (UBC Press, 2010). The book was short-listed for the 2012 Canada Prize by the Canadian Federation for the Humanities and Social Sciences and is widely used by educators across the country.

Pamela Spalding

Pamela Spalding is a doctoral candidate in the School of Environmental Studies at the University of Victoria. She has extensive experience in analysing the challenges in using traditional ecological knowledge (TEK) when applied to issues within government, land use planning, and Aboriginal rights. Through her professional and academic experience, she has explored ethical and methodological problems associated with representation, authority, and use of TEK when it is removed from its cultural context. She has engaged widely with First Nations' communities in British Columbia, as well as with consultants, academics, and community workers on First Nations' traditional use studies and land use and treaty negotiations.

Gina Starblanket

Gina Starblanket is assistant professor of political science at the University of Calgary. She is of Cree/Saulteaux and French/German ancestry and is a member of the Star Blanket Cree Nation. Gina's scholarship is centred in Indigenous political theory and takes up questions of treaty implementation, gender, decolonization, resurgence, and relationality. Her dissertation research involves a critical analysis of the contemporary politics of treaty implementation, with a specific focus on Treaty 4.

Heidi Kiiwetinepinesiik Stark

Heidi Kiiwetinepinesiik Stark (Turtle Mountain Ojibwe) is an associate professor of political science at the University of Victoria. She is the Director of the Centre for Indigenous Research and Community-Led Engagement (CIRCLE) and the Director of the Graduate Certificate in Indigenous Nationhood. She has a PhD in American studies from the University of Minnesota. Her research interests include Indigenous law and treaty practices, Aboriginal and Treaty rights, and Indigenous politics in the United States and Canada. She is the co-editor of *Centering Anishinaabeg Studies: Understanding the World through Stories*, with Jill Doerfler and Niigaanwewidam Sinclair, and is the co-author of *American Indian Politics and the American Political System* (3rd and 4th editions) with Dr David E. Wilkins. She has published articles in journals such as *Theory and Event, American Indian Quarterly, American Indian Culture and Research Journal*, and *Michigan State University Law Review*.

James Tully

James Tully is professor emeritus at University of Victoria. He has taught at McGill University, University of Toronto, and University of Victoria in political and legal theory, relations between Indigenous and non-Indigenous peoples, and ways of civic engagement. His publications include *Strange Multiplicity: Constitutionalism in an Age of Diversity* (1995), *Public Philosophy in a New Key* (2 volumes, 2008), and responses to dialogue partners in Tully et al., *On Global Citizenship: James Tully in Dialogue* (2014), R. Nichols and J. Singh, eds, *Freedom and Democracy in an Imperial Age: Dialogues with James Tully* (2014), and D. Karmis and J. Maclure, eds, *Civic Freedom in an Age of Diversity: The Public Philosophy of James Tully* (forthcoming).

Nancy J. Turner

Nancy J. Turner is an ethnobotanist and ethnoecologist whose research focuses on traditional knowledge systems and traditional land and resource management systems of Indigenous peoples of western Canada. She is a 2015 Pierre Elliott Trudeau Fellow and professor emerita with the School of Environmental Studies, University of Victoria. She has worked with First Nations elders and cultural specialists in northwestern North America for over forty-five years, helping to document, retain, and promote their traditional knowledge of plants and environments, including Indigenous foods, materials, and traditional medicines.

Index

www.ingramcontent.com/pod-product-compliance
Lightning Source LLC
Chambersburg PA
CBHW030234030426
42336CB00009B/98